The New Testament

A Literary History

The New Testament

A Literary History

Gerd Theissen

Translated by
Linda M. Maloney

Fortress Press
Minneapolis

THE NEW TESTAMENT
A Literary History

Cover image: Frescoes in the Monastery of St. Theodora in Thessaloniki, Greece, Copyright Portokalis, 2010. Used under license from Shutterstock.com
Cover design: Tory Herman
Book design: The HK Scriptorium, Inc.

Library of Congress Cataloging-in-Publication Data

Theissen, Gerd.
The New Testament : a literary history / Gerd Theissen ; translated by Linda M. Maloney.
p. cm.
Includes bibliographical references.
ISBN 978-0-8006-9785-3 (alk. paper)
1. Bible. N.T.—History. 2. Bible. N.T.—Canon. 3. Bible. N.T.—Criticism, interpretation, etc. 4. Christian literature, Early—History and criticism. I. Title.
BS2315.T44 2011
225—dc23
2011021848

The paper used in this publication meets the minimum requirements of American National Standard for Information Sciences—Permanence of Paper for Printed Library Materials, ANSI Z329.48-1984.

Manufactured in the U.S.A.

15 14 13 12 1 2 3 4 5 6 7 8 9 10 11

Dedicated to the Theological Faculty
of the Károli Gáspár University, Budapest,
in gratitude for the honorary doctorate
granted to me

Contents

Part Three

The Authority of the Independent Forms: The Functional Phase

Part Four

The New Testament on Its Way to Becoming a Religious World Literature: The Canonical Phase

List of Tables and Figures

Preface

This outline of a literary history of the New Testament is based on a lecture given before the Philosophical-Historical Class of the Heidelberg Academy of Sciences on 27 November 2004. It is a subject rooted in Heidelberg's traditions. The Heidelberg New Testament scholar Martin Dibelius wrote one of the first basic proposals for a "history of early Christian literature" (1926), and his student Philipp Vielhauer developed his ideas in an extensive "history of early Christian literature" (1975); as his assistant, I was present at the origins of this work. Both scholars emphasized the isolation of early Christian literature from its Hellenistic context. A counter-current running against this view began in the 1970s. Thus, my colleague Klaus Berger was able to point out a great many "Hellenistic genres in the New Testament" (1984). The Heidelberg professor of Classical Philology Albrecht Dihle treated early Christian literature in his 1989 work "Die griechische und lateinische Literatur der Kaiserzeit" as a part of ancient literature. The present proposal continues all these lines. Since I began to study theology and German literature I have had the dream of a literary history that would make it possible, through the use of literary-critical methods, to understand the origins of the New Testament as the beginnings of one of the most important collections of texts in the literature of world religion. The presentation concentrates on the development of the formal language of the New Testament in four phases, intending thereby to make visible its connection to its environment and to the overall history of early Christianity. The preparation of this book was made possible by a study year at the Alt. Kolleg, Heidelberg 2005–2006, which allowed time for a thorough revision of the first draft. I thank all those who made that research year possible for me. I am grateful to Corina Cloutier and Kristina Wagner for their assistance in reading the proofs, and to Dr. Bernhard Mutschler for a critical reading of the whole manuscript and many valuable suggestions.

I dedicate this book to the theological faculty of the Reformed Károly Gáspár University in Budapest, who bestowed an honorary doctorate on me in October 2005. Thirteen years ago, with a series of lectures in Budapest on "Gospel Writing and Church Politics," I began my thoughts on a literary history of the gospels. Some of the ideas then presented in Budapest have been carried out in this book with regard to the entire New Testament.

Introduction

The Problem of a Literary History of the New Testament

The New Testament contains twenty-seven writings from a small religious subculture in the Roman empire of the first two centuries. All the writings originated between about 50 and 130 C.E. They constitute a segment of an extensive body of early Christian writing, of which about ninety documents have survived, either entire or as fragments.[1] The early Christian writings outside the canon are summarized under the rubric of "New Testament Apocrypha."[2] Since the seventeenth century one group of "orthodox" writings among these has been singled out as "the Apostolic Fathers" because their authors supposedly lived in apostolic times; in fact, they originated in the post-apostolic period (ca. 90–150 C.E.).[3] On the other hand, many apocryphal writings were considered more or less "heretical." Most of these are documents related to Gnosis, a radical redemptive piety that from the beginning of the second century C.E. onward offered a profound reinterpretation of early Christian faith.

The idea of a canon, attested since about the year 180, and its acknowledgment in the next two centuries constituted the end of early Christian scriptures, in which we may count all the writings that formally continue the literary history of the New Testament and in their content draw on the same complex of convictions and traditions as the New Testament writings. With the acknowledgment of the idea of canon there arose a theology characterized less and less by a creative continuation of New Testament content and forms in new documents, and more and more by interpretation of the New Testament and the adoption of forms and motifs from the general literature of antiquity. Patristic literature replaced early Christian literature. We can illustrate the literary-critical transformation in terms of two developments between 100 and 180 C.E. The first is very revealing of the attitude of early Christianity toward itself and its traditions: the (second) conclusion to the

Gospel of John, at the end of the first century, points to an indefinite number of possible gospels: "There are many other things that Jesus did . . . if they were all to be written, I suppose the whole world could not contain the books that would be written" (John 21:25). In contrast, Irenaeus asserted around 180 that there was a fourfold gospel, corresponding to the four wind directions and the four figures around the divine throne (*Haer*. 3.11.7-9). For him there were necessarily four gospels and no more. The idea of a closed canon is present; all that seems to remain open is the actual extent of the epistolary literature. A second development is indicative of Christianity's relationship to its environment: at the beginning of the second century Tacitus, Suetonius, and Pliny[4] all agreed that Christianity was an enormous superstition. On the other hand, in about 176/180 C.E. the Platonic philosopher Celsus published a polemical writing against the Christians, his "True Discourse" (*alēthēs logos*). In it he took Christianity seriously as a philosophy, even as he rejected it as a novelty and a deviation from ancient truth.[5]

"Literature" comes from *littera* (letters). A nominal definition of the word could describe every written and printed text as literature. But receipts, forms, and lists—that is, texts without connected sentences—are not literature, despite their written form. The great national epics and many small forms such as fairy tales, legends, sagas, jokes, and anecdotes were originally handed on orally and yet were undoubtedly literature, even in their oral form. The Bible, too, stems from streams of oral tradition and remained embedded in them: biblical writings were disseminated orally, by being read publicly at worship. Thus a usable definition of literature for our purposes would be: *Literature is constituted by coherent oral and written texts that, by their nature and intention, are public.* However, their public nature is evident only when the writing and the general nature of the addressees are viewed in combination. What precedes is literature in the process of origination. Paul's letters were only subsequently literature, when they were published with the claim that they were directed not only to their addressees in Corinth or Rome but to all Christians. Originally they were correspondence, that is, occasional texts, but their content pointed far beyond the situation of their origin. Therefore, a complete definition of literature would be: *Literature consists of coherent oral and written texts that are intended to be public and are not exhausted by the immediate purpose for which they are used.* Contracts, edicts, and collections of laws are accordingly not literature—unless they have a sense beyond their use value, as do, for example, the laws in the Old Testament.

But many kinds of texts, including religious literature and poetry, have a value beyond their immediate use.[6] Therefore we must ask further: what is special about religious literature? It is not purposeless, like poetry. On the contrary, the New Testament texts were shaped by their social use. They are intended to influence people, to win them to faith, and to encourage them to action. But they, too, have an indirect value of their own beyond those purposes: they are intended to make transcendence accessible and thus point toward an absolute intrinsic value that gives them a literary quality. The relationship to this intrinsic value explodes the use value of the texts. In classical aesthetics, religious texts therefore belong not to the beautiful, but rather to the exalted, in which the content can explode the form. The Greek Bible, the LXX, was first quoted in the first century C.E. in a pagan text "On the Sublime": "Similarly, the legislator of the Jews, no ordinary man, having formed and expressed a worthy conception of the might of the Godhead, writes at the very beginning of his Laws, 'God said'—what? 'Let there be light, and there was light; let there be land, and there was land'" (9.9).[7] The sublime consists in the experience of what, because of its superior power, strength, and perfection, exceeds our power of comprehension. It works through repulsion and attraction, as *mysterium tremendum et fascinosum*.[8] Religious texts thus, precisely through their relationship to transcendence, have an aesthetic quality. In addition, they share four qualities with poetic texts: by their nature they are poetic, pictorial, fictional, and form-giving.

Poetical quality consists in the fact that texts, in the form in which they present themselves to the senses (through rhyme, assonance, alliteration, and parallelisms) are self-referential. In the New Testament there are many texts with such a self-referential poetic quality: hymns, beatitudes, doxologies, the Our Father. One aspect of literary criticism of the New Testament is bringing its poetic qualities to the fore. Of course, poetic quality (in the narrower sense) is not what is decisive.

More important is the *imagery* of New Testament texts. Poetry expresses in concrete events and images something that far surpasses what is immediately signified. The same is true of the New Testament. In it, all forms of discourse in images, in metaphors, allegories, similitudes, parables, example stories, illustrative sayings, symbols, and myths point beyond the realm that furnishes the imagery to the realm of God. The Bible is full of the language of religious imagery.

For the first Christians these images were unassailable realities. They were not being poetic when they spoke of heaven and the underworld, of devils and demons, of the Son of God and of angels. It is only the modern mind that has to deliberate with itself about what it regards as poetry and what as reality. Only in the poetic texts of the New Testament, such as similitudes and parables, is there a common understanding between ancient authors and modern readers about the *fictional character* of these texts.

Literary criticism of the New Testament is not theological criticism. The texts have effect not only by *what* they say theologically, but also *in the way* they say it. The formal language of the New Testament literature gives them a solid location in interpersonal communication and in religious communication between human beings and God. This *formal language* is the primary object of a literary-critical history of the New Testament. Its content cannot be separated from it. Only where there is plausible agreement between statements of content and particular forms has a literary critique achieved its goal.

A brief glance at this formal language will give us a preliminary overview. In the New Testament we find two basic forms and three subforms: gospels and letters are the two basic forms, multiply attested. There are four gospels and twenty-one letters. In contrast, the three subforms, the Acts of the Apostles, Revelation, and the letter to the Hebrews, which has been given a ramshackle letter frame,[9] appear in only one example each. Even in the ancient church the collection of these writings had begun to be transformed into a diachronic arrangement.[10]

Among the gospels a distinction was made between the older, Synoptic Gospels and the later Gospel of John as the "spiritual gospel." The gospels were arranged in their supposed chronological order, which they have since maintained in the canon: the Gospel of Matthew was regarded as the oldest gospel because it supposedly came from an apostle and eyewitness. With it, the New Testament begins. It is followed by the Gospel of Mark as something written by an interpreter of Peter. In third place was the Gospel of Luke, as the witness of a companion of Paul. The gospel writing was completed by the latest gospel, that of John, attributed to a beloved disciple of Jesus who had grown very old.

Among the letters, two collections were distinguished: the letters of Paul and the catholic letters. Paul's letters were addressed to concrete communities and persons, while the letters of the other apostles and the brother of the Lord were directed to all Christians. The latter were therefore called "general" (or "catholic") letters.[11] The collection of Pauline letters is always placed before the catholic letters. Within the individual letter collections, the ordering is by length, beginning with the longest letter, Romans.[12]

The three individual examples of genres are positioned within the New Testament in interesting fashion: Acts does not follow the Gospel of Luke, although it regards itself as that gospel's continuation. In the manuscript tradition it was seen as the introduction to the catholic letters, so that the "deeds of the apostles" (*praxeis apostolōn*) are followed by their "words" in the form of letters. The letter to the Hebrews appears in three different places in the manuscripts: either at the beginning of the collection of Pauline letters, after Romans, or in the middle, after the congregational letters, or at the very end of the Pauline collection.[13] The Apocalypse of John (Revelation), as a prophecy of the future, has its fixed place at the end of the New Testament, but this separates it from the other Johannine writings. A general overview can make clear the resulting structure of the New Testament:

Table 1: The Structure of the New Testament in the Ancient Church Tradition

Gospels		**Letters**	
(a) Synoptic Gospels		(a) Pauline Letters	
Matthew		Romans	
Mark		[Hebrews]	
Luke		1–2 Corinthians	
		Galatians	
		Ephesians	
		Philippians	
		Colossians	
		1–2 Thessalonians	
		[Hebrews]	
		1–2 Timothy	
		Titus	
		Philemon	
		[Hebrews]	
(b) Gospel of John	Acts of the Apostles	(b) Catholic Letters	Revelation
The spiritual gospel	= Introduction to the catholic letters	James	= third part of the *Corpus Iohanneum*
		1–2 Peter	
		1–3 John	
		Jude	

Modern historical criticism made further distinctions possible. It organized the gospels in a new way: The Gospel of Mark was recognized as the oldest gospel. Alongside (and probably before) it was the so-called Sayings Source, a common source for Matthew and Luke. These two old sources were followed by the two long Synoptic Gospels, Matthew and Luke, whose origins were dated between 80 and 100 C.E. The Gospel of John, with its new interpretation of the figure of Christ, somewhat akin to Gnosis, was considered the latest gospel. An analogy to its reinterpretation of the Jesus tradition was found in the *Gospel of Thomas,* discovered in 1945, since in that gospel also the Jesus tradition was revised in a gnosticizing direction.

Modern criticism also distinguished among genuine and non-genuine Pauline letters. By general consensus there are seven genuine letters: 1 Thessalonians, Galatians, 1 and 2 Corinthians, Philippians, Philemon, and Romans. There is agreement about their relative sequence only with regard to 1 Thessalonians, 1 and 2 Corinthians, and Romans, since 1 Thessalonians is certainly the oldest Pauline letter (written ca. 50/51), and Romans is clearly Paul's "testament," that is, a Pauline letter containing Paul's last will, independently of whether the letters to the Philippians and Philemon preceded or followed it. All other Pauline letters are regarded as non-genuine or "deutero-Pauline": it is true that Colossians and 2 Thessalonians are occasionally defended as genuine even by very critical exegetes, but increasingly they are regarded as non-genuine even by conservative scholars. There is consensus on the non-genuine character of all the other letters: Ephesians, 1 and 2 Timothy, Titus, and Hebrews.

Regarding the catholic letters, only a minority of exegetes assume that the names of the authors are accurate. There is, however, agreement that all the letters are dependent on Paul in terms of their form. Without him the letter would not have become the second basic form of early Christian literature. Acts is seen as the second part of the twofold Lukan work, while Hebrews and Revelation represent independent theological initiatives. The modern exegete's picture of the New Testament looks something like Table 2.

With such distinctions between an older and a newer layer we have the beginnings of a literary history of the New Testament. Its task is (1) to organize the writings that are placed alongside one another atemporally in the canon in an order of historical development, (2) to locate their formal language within the history of ancient literature, and (3) to interpret these forms as the expression of the social dynamics of early Christian groups. In all three cases it is necessary to understand the special character of this literature. Nowadays the so-called "introductions to the New Testament" contain textbook knowledge about author, origins, and time of composition of the individual New Testament books—with a few recognized alternatives that are subject to discussion. For a comprehensive literary history that distinguishes phases and follows lines of development, on the other hand, there is no established body of knowledge. There are even many skeptical voices that, because of the fragmentary character of our tradition, doubt that such a coherent literary history is possible.[14] It is right to say that we have only fragments of an early Christian literature. We know scarcely anything about the lives of its authors. A biographically oriented description is impossible. The datings are uncertain. Likewise difficult are attempts to distinguish phases of development. To date there has not been a single attempt in that direction. The same is true of localizations. We do not know what writings belong together regionally. But the fragmentary

Table 2: The Origins of the New Testament from a Critical Viewpoint

Jesus Tradition		*Epistolary Literature*	
THE OLDEST SOURCES		GENUINE PAULINE LETTERS	
Sayings Source (Q) Gospel of Mark		1 Thessalonians Galatians 1–2 Corinthians Philippians Philemon Romans	
THE GREAT SYNOPTICS		DEUTEROPAULINE LETTERS	
Matthew		Colossians Ephesians 2 Thessalonians 1–2 Timothy Titus	
Luke +	Acts of the Apostles	Hebrews	
GOSPELS CLOSER TO GNOSIS		CATHOLIC LETTERS	
Gospel of John +		1–3 John	Revelation
[*Gospel of Thomas*]		James 1–2 Peter Jude	

character of our body of writing should not deter us. "Literature is the fragment of fragments; the least of what happened and was said has been written down, and of what was written, the least part has remained."[15] If literature is fundamentally a fragment, the fragmentary character of early Christian literature should not prevent us from considering it from a literary-critical point of view, especially since there are good predecessors and preliminary works leading to a literary history of the New Testament. Four phases of this work can be distinguished.

Efforts to produce a literary history of the New Testament began in the eighteenth century with Johann Gottfried Herder (1744–1803).[16] He was the first to recognize that there had been an oral prehistory of the gospels and letters. The New Testament writings contain the oral proclamation of the apostles. Orality was characteristic of their message: "A law is written; a message of good news is proclaimed."[17] Their preaching was composed of brief pericopes: "The common gospel arose out of individual bits, narratives, parables, sayings, pericopes."[18] This in turn is explained by the fact that this is popular literature: "It attests to the truth of the Gospel that it is made up of such parts: for people such as most of the apostles were can more easily remember a saying, a parable, an apophthegm that struck them than the connected speeches in which John later depicted his friend."[19] The New Testament was a literature not of the learned, but of simple people. It arose within Judaism, which was part of the "childhood of the human race" and as yet was unaware of any foreign literature, but rather, in its ancient holy books, "dwelt as in the sanctuary of all wisdom."[20] Herder saw clearly the relative isolation of this literature in contrast to the remainder of ancient literature and its relationship to Jewish literature. For him, the Old and New Testaments were the poesy of an immature humanity, which must be understood historically. He thus founded a historical-aesthetic approach to the Bible that is able to value it positively and is free of dogmatic premises.[21] It is true that one must pose the critical question: Can the Bible really be understood as the expression of a naïve, childish mentality, and are eighteenth-century categories adequate to an aesthetic appreciation of it as poetry? The song of the Suffering Servant speaks about a mysterious figure: ". . . he had no form or majesty that we should look at him, nothing in his appearance that we should desire him" (Isa 53:2). Whether the Servant is the people of Israel or an individual figure—in any case, the aesthetic of the beautiful and the naïve is inadequate here!

A new phase of literary-critical study of the New Testament began in the nineteenth century with Franz Overbeck.[22] For him, literary-historical criticism was the history of literary forms.[23] His thesis was that of the two basic forms of the New Testament, the gospel is an original creation of early Christianity, while the letter, as a practical text, is not real literature. He called both forms "primitive literature" (i.e., literature that is seen as still in its formative phase). Such literature, for him, displayed two characteristics: On the one hand it was creative in producing something entirely new, such as the gospel form, which he regarded as a historically underivable genre that originated in the soil of early Christianity. On the other hand "primitive literature" was not yet independent of its author, with whom in this formative period the addressees could interact, as in the case of the letters of Paul. The author could not yet be separated from his writing. Hence primitive literature was still part of the prehistory of literature proper, its influence dependent on the existence of its author. For Franz Overbeck, isolation was also characteristic of early Christian literature. In its origins it was totally unconnected to the greater literary world of the time, and its influence was likewise not in sequence with anything in the history of the church. The real history of Christian literature, according to Overbeck, began with patristic literature, that is, the Apologists and the Church Fathers, when Christianity adopted the forms of secular literature. Until that time it had kept its literary forms separate from the world.[24] To understand Overbeck's concept of a primeval literature one must realize that for him the New Testament "primitive literature" is part of the "primitive history" of Christianity, a history without any continuation in the world because it was shaped by an eschatological anticipation of the imminent end and was not conceived as being the beginning of a long history in this world. Thus, the origin of early Christian literature was paradoxical: why should people who expected an immediate end to the world produce writings, since the whole world, with its writings and its books, would soon be gone?

The third phase of literary-historical criticism was shaped by the so-called form criticism of the twentieth century, in the work of Rudolf Bultmann, Martin Dibelius, and Karl Ludwig Schmidt.[25] They affirmed in principle Overbeck's postulated underivability of the gospel form, but focused on a historical and sociological derivation of the very singularity of the New Testament writings. Their explanation was that here groups who were unfamiliar with literature had taken up the pen.[26] Comparable forms were popular books, unpretentious literature in little tracts and brief writings.[27] No wonder that these texts did not make use of an elevated literary language! The "Sitz im Leben" of this literature was the lower class. The transition from the people's oral tradition to written literature explained their uniqueness and "underivability," and above all why they were so strongly marked by conventions and recurring typical motifs. Thus, in essence these writings were collective creations, not the expressions of individual talent. The evangelists were first reduced by form criticism to redactors, collectors, and tradents; only in a second stage, so-called redaction criticism, were they rediscovered as authors and theologians with their own literary and theological intentions. This explanation, too, stumbled across a paradox: if early Christianity came from non-literary classes, why did it produce such a rich literature? Why did people take up the pen if they were not at all "programmed" to produce literature?[28]

At present people are moving a step further, seeing that early Christian literature is not unique because of its non-literary background, but rather is part of a separate literary culture, that of Jewish-Hellenistic *koinē* literature.[29] With the Septuagint (LXX), the Greek translation of the Old Testament, Judaism had created a literature for itself in the Greek language, using not the elevated form of Greek, but the everyday form, the so-called *koinē*. In doing so it departed from non-Jewish ancient literature. Within the sphere of influence of this special Jewish literature there arose, in turn, another special literature, that of early Christianity. The narrative style of the evangelists—episodic, with few authorial narrative interventions, but containing many dialogues in which persons within the narrative comment on what is happening—has a model, for example, in the Septuagint. As with the other proposals, we encounter a paradox here: if the Septuagint (or the Hebrew Bible in the Aramaic-speaking Jewish Christianity of Palestine) was the Bible of the first Christians and had such great significance that it shaped their language and style—why were they not content with that Bible? Why did they create a new group of writings that later, as the "New Testament," augmented the Old? And why are so many non-Jewish, Hellenistic influences evident in the formal language of the New Testament?[30]

Thus, the origin of the New Testament is associated with three paradoxes: people who expected the end of the world created a literature for the ages, as if the world would last a long time. People from non-literary classes took up the pen and created a literature that remains alive today. People who were at home with their Bible created a new Bible with a formal language that was not derived from their familiar "Bible." These paradoxes make it appear almost "miraculous" that there was any early Christian literature at all. But all three paradoxes may be resolved.

The thesis about the imminent expectation of the end as a factor impeding literary creation is false. Jewish apocalyptic writing is full of imminent expectations and yet attests to a flourishing literary production. The author of the book of Daniel was convinced that the end of the world would happen 1,290 days after the desecration of the sanctuary in the year 167 B.C.E. (Dan 12:11). While work on the book of Daniel was still in progress the expected time passed, and he had to offer a new reckoning. He extended the deadline by forty-five days and called those blessed who endured and attained 1,335 days! (Dan 12:12). His expectation of the imminent end did not prevent him from writing a book that was quite extensive in contemporary terms. He wrote for a group, for eschatologically motivated groups need scriptures with which they can legitimate their expectations, maintain the unity of the group, and secure themselves against doubt. Since they lived in a culture in which writings possessed religious authority, they would scarcely have done without this way of maintaining group cohesion. Some authors may even have dreamed of being able to study scrolls even more intensively in the new world that was about to break in![31]

It is also possible to understand why people from a non-literary lower class became active producers of literature. Writing presumes a high degree of self-confidence. What a person experiences, suffers, dreams, or hopes must appear so valuable to her or him that she or he communicates it in writing. That was precisely the case with the first Christians. The awareness of standing on the threshold of a new world gave them a high sense of their own personal worth. What had happened to their founding figure was as important to them as the story of a king or philosopher whose biography might be written. Equally important to them was the history of their little group. It was worthwhile to report on it in the Acts of the Apostles in a way that otherwise only the history of whole nations deserved. In their own self-understanding, they were not members of the unimportant sub-classes, but the elite of the new world: the elect, the saints, those who had been called.

Does having a Bible prevent the production of a new Bible? The letter of *Barnabas* attests to the possibility, at a much later time, of grounding Christian faith solely in an allegorical interpretation of the Old Testament. It is possible that the first Christians might have been content with the Jewish sacred scriptures if they had remained part of Judaism. But they pushed very quickly beyond the bounds of Judaism and attracted non-Jews to their beliefs. Thus, it is no accident that their first writings came out of the Gentile mission, where Paul had to solve and give answers to a very different set of problems. Paul wrote long texts without reference to the Jewish Bible—for example, 1 Thessalonians, Philippians, Philemon.

That an early Christian literature was created is thus not as paradoxical as it seems at first glance. What is much more in need of explanation is *how* it was formed and shaped. We found a number of explanations proposed by form criticism for its unique literary character: as the poesy of an immature humanity it attests to its naïve origins; as a primitive literature it is an original creation of early Christianity; as minor literature it is the product of lower literary classes; and as a *koinē* literature it is an outgrowth of the Septuagint and Hellenistic Judaism. All four suggestions contain some truth, but they all ignore not only the paradoxes we have mentioned, but problems that make a new proposal worthwhile.

Johann Gottfried Herder was correct: the Bible is a piece of literature, human poesy, that must be read altogether, in historical terms, as a human testimony. But is it really the product of a naïve and immature creative power? The aesthetics of the Bible can only be understood against the background of the history of the sufferings of the people Israel. It is not an aesthetic of beauty and harmony, but of hideousness and failure. The simple "people" who exercised their creativity here do not fit into any popular idyll; they were an oppressed nation of little people. The New Testament must thus be read, with Herder, in a historical-aesthetic light, but as the expression of a broken aesthetics. A modern aesthetics that knows how to deal with the absurd, the broken, and the fragmentary is better suited to these writings than a classical aesthetics.[32]

Some of the New Testament writings may be primitive or primeval literature in Franz Overbeck's sense, but by no means all of them. Of the twenty-seven documents, at least ten are pseudepigraphic writings that imitate genuine documents. In such counterfeits the real author hides behind a different name and withdraws from interaction with his or her readers. The author is not creative, but imitative. Using both of Overbeck's criteria, therefore, one must clearly distinguish these pseudepigraphic writings from a "primitive literature." We must ask: did the primitive literature end with the pseudepigraphic writings in the first century C.E., and not with the transition to patristic writings in the second century? Or must we not distinguish at least two phases within the history of early Christian literature, a first phase of "primitive literature," and a second, imitative phase of pseudepigraphic literature?[33] And in that case do we encounter further phases—for example, when early Christian authors disengaged from the great charismatic authorities and models and created writings according to their own formal laws, as in the case of the Acts of the Apostles or the letter to the Hebrews?

The early Christian writings were certainly minor literature. The form critics correctly perceived that. This characteristic in particular distinguishes this literature from the biblical writings of the Jews, whose center was the Law that exists for the whole people. According to tradition, kings were involved: a Jewish king with regard to Deuteronomy, a Persian with Ezra's law, a Ptolemy with the origins of the Septuagint, even though it was no king, but God who was regarded as the origin of the Law. The New Testament, in contrast, was the literature of a small group. No king gave it a public character. No nation sought to use it as a rule for the whole of life. Thus we must ask: how did people from small groups decide to commit to paper these ideas with their universal claims? What role did they assume in doing so? Were they really part of a literary underclass? Did they not necessarily have a certain competency in literary writing—in the midst of a population of which perhaps ten to thirty percent were able to read and write at all, and in which literary types within that ten to thirty percent were themselves a vanishing minority?[34] Nevertheless, the form critics were right on one point: what is special about the New Testament may be that, while authors with literary competency and from relatively educated classes were writing, they were deliberately creating a literature for non-literary lower classes. One unique feature of early Christian literature may have been that it crossed class boundaries.

The early Christian writings would be unthinkable without the Jewish *koinē* literature in the wake of the Septuagint. Nevertheless, the two basic

New Testament forms, gospel and letter, have fewer models in the Septuagint than in Greek and Roman literature. There was no writing in the Judaism of the time that was so thoroughly concentrated on a single person as are the gospels,[35] but there were many biographical texts in non-Jewish antiquity. There was no letter collection in Judaism (in the Septuagint) that could have served Paul as a model for his letters, but there were many collections of letters in the Greco-Roman world. Although the New Testament is part of Jewish-Hellenistic *koinē* literature, its basic forms were inspired by the non-Jewish world. Hence the question: Is the reason for the special nature of the New Testament that in its formal language (just as in its content) it crosses cultural boundaries? Klaus Berger and David Aune have quite rightly and consistently located the formal language of the New Testament within Hellenistic literature.[36]

In response to these four questions, the present book will sketch the fundamental outlines of a literary-critical history of the New Testament. In the process, the contradictions we have addressed will be resolved. Early Christian literature does not consist exclusively either of creative primitive literature or of literature dependent on traditions; it is bound neither to non-literary lower classes nor to literary upper classes in its Jewish or its non-Jewish shape. What is characteristic of it, rather, is that it crosses boundaries. This can best be shown by describing its origins and development. Four phases may be discerned, and we will describe them first in a few words. Each will then be discussed at greater length.

The history of the New Testament literature began with Jesus and Paul. These two charismatics, through their work and in very different ways, brought the two fundamental forms of the New Testament—gospels and letters—into existence. In this first phase the *authority of persons* was dominant. Only in this early stage can one, in my opinion, speak of "primeval literature" in Overbeck's sense, for gospel and community letter are new creations by early Christianity, even though they took inspiration from their environment.

In the second phase this literature was continued by means of a *fictive self-interpretation* of Paul in the non-genuine Pauline letters and a fictive self-interpretation of Jesus in additional gospels. This was no longer "primeval literature," but imitative traditional literature. It presumes the authority of the writings and forms created in the first phase and bases itself on the authority of the tradition created by the two great charismatics, Jesus and Paul. It hides behind these charismatics. It is pseudepigraphic or deuteronomic (that is, it makes use of someone else's name).

In a third phase, genres were created from *functional* standpoints. That is: texts now gained their authority not only from being traced to known charismatics, but also through the material demands of particular genres. To the authority of persons and traditions was added the authority of form. The Acts of the Apostles is a historical work intended to meet the material criteria of historical writing. The Apocalypse is revelatory literature that contains within itself its own authority. The letter to the Hebrews is a discourse fulfilling rhetorical demands for a good disposition and elegance of language. Of these new forms only the Acts of the Apostles, the letter to the Hebrews, and the Apocalypse were received into the canon. Other functional genres such as "dialogue with the Exalted One" or pure "collections of sayings" are part of the (apocryphal) early Christian literature outside the New Testament.

The final phase was the *construction of the canon*. It looms at different points as a potential compromise, but was hastened in response to the catalyst of an alternative canon proposed by Marcion in the second century C.E. Marcion's canon, consisting of *one* gospel and *one* apostle, is not the positive model for the new canon but its negative model: against it, the plurality of gospels and of authors of letters and the duality of Old and New Testament became the consensus position. Marcion had only one gospel, only one apostle, and only the one New Testament. In rejecting him, the remaining Christians found it easier to come together. The canon is the expression of a religious community of the church type, which tolerates internal plurality and at the same time distinguishes itself from groups (such as the Marcionites) standing in too much tension with the world. Through the construction of the canon, the New Testament writings became a religious world literature.

The division of phases suggested is ultimately supported by the fact that the "apocryphal" early Christian literature can be understood as the posterior effect of the forms and motifs of these four phases. We will therefore attempt in a final chapter to interpret the New Testament apocrypha as the expression of new charismatic beginnings, the continuation of pseudepigraphic literature, but above all an expression of the tendency to establish functional genres. Since what we present here is only a sketch for a literary-critical history of the New Testament, the relatively brief treatment of the extracanonical writings is justifiable. But even if we concentrate on the New Testament, the literary history of the whole of early Christianity constitutes the necessary background.

The program for a literary-critical history of the New Testament presented here thus consists of two fundamental ideas: first, the suggestion that charismatic, pseudepigraphic, functional, and canonical phases should be distinguished within it; second, the proposal that this four-phase development reflects the social dynamics of early Christianity and that a variety of structures of authority follow one another and overlap: the authority of the person, of tradition, of form, and of community. Writings with characteristics of the first phase thus coexist with writings from subsequent phases, and the various writings overlap chronologically. This is especially true of the transitional period from New Testament to patristic literature, during which forms from all four phases existed simultaneously. These four phases will now be described in fuller detail.

PART ONE

The Twofold Beginnings of a History of Early Christian Literature

A. The Charismatic Beginnings of Gospel Literature in Jesus

One may speak of literature in the strict sense only when a text (1) exists in written form and (2) is addressed to a general audience. In this regard the two basic forms of the New Testament moved in different directions. The Jesus tradition existed in oral form at first, but it was addressed to the whole people of Israel. It was used in the mission to Israel and thus was not initially directed to all people. It became literature when it was written down and extended to all peoples in the 60s/70s C.E. Paul's letters, by contrast, existed in written form from the beginning. They were addressed to individual Gentile communities. It is true that the letter to the Romans came close to being a public document, but it was only the posthumous collection of all Paul's letters that gave them a common addressee, as private letters often become public literature when they are collected for publication. This also took place in the 60s/70s. Those years saw the universalizing of the audience for the traditions of Paul and Jesus, and in the case of Jesus the writing down of the traditions as well. Thereby these texts became literature for the first time. Our question is now: Were comparable factors at work in the gospels as in the letters that caused them to become literature? Can the prehistory of the gospels and the letters of Paul properly be assigned to one and the same phase? Further, why were the letters fifteen years earlier (with the letter to the Romans) in becoming written literature than the gospels? Why, within the same literary-historical phase, was there a temporal delay for the gospels?

1 The Oral Prehistory of Early Christian Literature with the Historical Jesus

The Beginning of the History of Early Christian Literature

Jesus is said once to have written something—but he wrote in sand, in which the traces vanish (John 8:8). We have retained not a single line from him. He taught in synagogues and undertook the reading of scripture in worship (Luke 4:16-21). Such traditions would not have arisen if he had not been able to read and write. Nevertheless, he did not commit his message to writing. The reason is that he lived in a culture of oral communication. We must first ask: How did this differ from written communication? Can we detect anything at all of the oral prehistory of the tradition behind the written texts before us, to say nothing of reconstructing it? One relevant conclusion of form criticism is that in the case of oral tradition what is primarily visible is its formal language.[1] We may be uncertain whether Jesus spoke certain *words*, but that he used particular forms is undisputed: he taught as a prophet, a wisdom teacher, a teacher of the Law, and a storyteller. The storyteller is known especially from his similitudes; his are the first such to be attested in Jewish literature. The stories about him must be strictly distinguished from his words, for these are texts that were not shaped by Jesus. They include the apophthegms that appear in Jewish tradition for the first time in the Jesus traditions: short, polished statements with narrative frames; in addition, there are the miracle stories, which have many parallels in Jewish and non-Jewish antiquity; and finally, there is also the passion story.

Jesus was not the only person who left no writings. His "teacher," John the Baptizer, did not write any books either. Jesus used the oral culture of communication much more deliberately for his purposes than did the Baptizer; the latter let people come to him, but Jesus went out as a wandering teacher to the people and brought his message into their world. He strengthened his effectiveness by sending disciples out into the villages with his message. They asserted a public claim within Israel, but the groups they addressed remained limited to Jews.[2] His disciples do not appear to have left any writings, either, although secondarily a number of writings were attributed to them; however, the Gospel of Matthew was certainly not written by the apostle Matthew, the Gospel of John is not by the apostle John, and the letters of Peter are not by Peter. What is true of all these figures is that they lived in an oral culture. Oral communication was the sole means of mass communication among ordinary people. Other "media" were controlled by the powerful. They made coins that passed through many hands; these were used by the rulers to spread political messages. Public inscriptions were also erected by those who had money and power, and these were read by many people. They were not the people's medium. The only medium everyone could use was oral report, the news spread from mouth to mouth. There is much in favor of the supposition that Jesus organized and used this medium of communication in a new and effective form.

About twenty to thirty years of oral communication elapsed before his tradition was written down—first in the Sayings Source (between 40 and 65 C.E.), then in the Gospel of Mark shortly after 70 C.E. Even after it was written, the oral transmission of his words continued alongside it. The writings in turn affected the oral tradition, for in antiquity writings were primarily read out loud. Often the primary and secondary oral traditions merged.

It is true that skeptics ask: Was there ever really such an oral tradition before the gospels? Can we be sure that it was not some gifted writer who composed the Jesus tradition, as Walter Schmithals thinks?[3] We cannot, of course, look behind the written texts. We can only draw conclusions. "Constructive conclusions" permit us to make a few direct statements about the oral tradition: Jesus directed his disciples to proclaim his message orally. He did not say: "Whoever reads you, reads me!" but "Whoever listens to you listens to me!" (Luke 10:16). The commission in Matthew 28:19-20 makes oral preaching by itinerant teachers an obligation. The Acts of the Apostles depicts the oral dissemination of this preaching but makes no mention of a written medium—with the exception of the letter containing the apostolic decree (Acts 15:23-29). The Lukan prologue speaks clearly of eyewitnesses whose tradition was only secondarily written down. Even Papias, at the beginning of the second century C.E., gives preference to the "living and enduring voice," that is, oral tradition, over what is written (Eusebius, *Hist. eccl.* 3.39.4). Added to these constructive conclusions based on direct statements about oral tradition are "analytical conclusions" based on the form of these texts: the memorable form of the tradition points to an oral origin. It consists of brief pericopes shaped mnemonically for oral tradition by parallelisms, alliteration, and antitheses. The factual variability of the tradition can be better explained by oral variants than by conscious scribal activity. Even the words of Jesus handed on in the apostolic fathers do not always indicate written sources. Here, too, the oral tradition has not died out.[4] Finally, we can make some comparisons. Charismatic movements also prefer oral traditions: this was true for John the Baptizer, and also for the Montanist prophecy![5]

But we must also ask: During the years of oral tradition, was the Jesus tradition changed so much as to become unrecognizable, so that the memory of Jesus was overlain by other factors? In fact, the degree to which the Jesus traditions had pre-Easter origins, or whether they were radically reshaped by the post-Easter faith, as well as whether they were subject to some control or were able to develop freely and without restraint are matters of dispute among scholars. This question is mainly discussed within the framework of Jesus research, but it is also important for a literary history of the New Testament: the issue here is whether the formative phase of the gospel tradition began with Jesus or only after his death.

Beginnings of Oral Tradition with the Historical Jesus?

Classic form criticism regarded faith in the cross and resurrection as the crucial formative factor in the Jesus tradition: in particular instances it is traceable to the historical Jesus, but it has been so thoroughly reworked through the faith of the first Christians and their needs that the burden of proof of a historically accurate memory of Jesus rests with the advocates of the historicity of the Jesus traditions. The tradition is said not to have been subject to any formal controls (for example, by appointed "teachers"). Recurring situations in which the tradition was used, the *Sitz im Leben,* are supposed to have given it a certain stability, but since this *Sitz im Leben* was radically changed in the transition from Palestinian to "Hellenistic" early Christianity, there was not much continuity! To summarize, one can formulate the form-critical view as follows: Post-Easter shaping and little social control of the Jesus tradition are reasons for a broad historical skepticism. Early post-Easter Christianity is the formative phase of the gospel traditions.

The Scandinavian view of tradition (Birger Gerhardsson), in contrast, was oriented to contemporary analogies in Judaism: as a rabbi, it says, Jesus taught his disciples, his "pupils," to learn and memorize his words. Thus the tradition was shaped by its pre-Easter origins and was "tended" after Easter as normative tradition. It is much more reliable than form criticism supposed. Samuel Byrskog[6] expanded this concept: according to him, in antiquity it was the eyewitnesses and their oral history that were conclusive. They were sought out so that one might appeal to them. To summarize this in a formula: here we assume a pre-Easter shaping and strict control of the Jesus tradition. The result is a high degree of trust in the historicity of the tradition. Jesus' teaching activity is the crucial formative phase of the gospel tradition.

The new concept of tradition (James D. G. Dunn)[7] begins with the study of oral literature in antiquity. Homer's epics are interpreted in light of Serbo-Croatian heroic hymns.[8] Observations on oral tradition in the contemporary Mediterranean world show that oral tradition is independent of any "original version"; its handing on is not the reproduction of a model, but a new creation based on a wealth of existing formulae, themes, and structures. Every version is an original.[9] The handing on is not arbitrary, but is influenced by the hearers, whose social control of the tradition is all the more rigorous the more important it is for the identity of the society. It is more strict with regard to brief, pointed sayings than for stories with narrative development.[10] The beginnings of the tradition are seen to lie with Jesus before Easter: the group of disciples was the first *Sitz im Leben* for the tradition (Heinz Schürmann).[11] In my opinion, this new view of tradition is only a refinement of classic form criticism. If we reduce it to a formula, it says that the pre-Easter beginnings and informal social control by listeners make it likely that we can critically evaluate the tradition for knowledge of the historical Jesus. Both the historical Jesus *and* post-Easter early Christianity are parts of the formative phase of the gospel tradition.

In my view, the "new" understanding of tradition comes closest to the truth. Negatively, we can say that at certain points the tradition was not, as one might expect, shaped by the needs of the post-Easter communities. What we know of the social needs of the early Christian communities has often left little trace in the Synoptic traditions. For example, every social group has to define who belongs to it and who does not belong. There was a quarrel over this in the early Christianity of the 40s: Was male circumcision a necessary criterion for acceptance, or not (Gal 2:1-21; Acts 15:1-29)? This dispute left no traces in the Synoptic tradition. Nowhere do we find any saying of Jesus for or against circumcision. Only the *Gospel of Thomas* contains a corresponding saying of Jesus (*Gos. Thom.* 53). The legitimation of authority structures is just as important. In the first generation we already hear about "presbyters" (Acts 11:30 and elsewhere), or "*episkopoi* and *diakonoi*" (Phil 1:1). But nowhere do we find any saying of Jesus to back this up. Can the influence of the *Sitz im Leben* really have been so thorough, if elementary social needs did not shape the tradition?

However, we can also trace the beginnings of the tradition back to the historical Jesus in a positive sense. During his life there naturally arose situations that caused Jesus' disciples to learn the basic features of his preaching and be able to hand them on independently.

a. Jesus was an itinerant teacher, traveling with his disciples from place to place. He offered the same message everywhere. There was no need to say something different each time. Rather, he would have repeated his words often, with the variations typical of oral tradition. So there is no need to suppose some kind of orderly schooling to explain the repetitions. The existence of an itinerant teacher outside the routine of daily life created quite enough opportunity for repetition!
b. Jesus lived with his disciples in close community. Their common itinerant existence had to draw them together. Communities develop rules and rituals. So he would have taught his disciples the "Our Father" as a community prayer. Now and again a new disciple would have been added to the group. Each time the newcomer was instructed in what was expected of a disciple.
c. Jesus sent his disciples on itinerant missions. They had to repeat his message in many different places! They must have brought a few orally composed texts with them, and committed them to memory through repetition. Three or four villages would have sufficed. One might object: Doesn't the mission discourse and the peace greeting by the disciples point to a time when the shadow of war lay across the land—that is, a time after Jesus (Paul Hoffmann)?[12] Favoring the historicity of the mission is that the disciples did not preach the parousia of the returning *Kyrios*, but *metanoia* (Mark 6:12). They promised the coming of the reign of God (Luke 10:9). They did not baptize, but preached and healed. They didn't even demand "belief"! All that points to the time before Easter. The Jesus tradition was probably shaped not so much in an orderly schooling process as in a "mission campaign" organized by Jesus himself.

Jesus may have had a model for his itinerant existence: Judas Galilaios.[13] Josephus calls him a "Sophist" (*B.J.* 2.118,[14] 433). He came from Gamala in Gaulanitis, and while teaching in Galilee he was called "the Golanite" (*Ant.*

18.4); later, when he was agitating against the taxation census in Judea after 6 B.C.E., he was called "the Galilean."[15] These two appellations suggest mobility. If he called on the people to refuse the tax, he had to carry his message to the villages. An analogy makes this likely: Shortly before the outbreak of the Jewish War, the Jewish aristocracy tried to save the peace by a final effort: "the members of the council dispersed to the various villages and levied the tribute" (*B.J.* 2.405). Wouldn't the opponents of the tribute likewise have gone into the villages? How else were they to influence the people?

Jesus, too, wanted to reach the whole people with his message. If a previous generation had already engaged in an oral campaign against taxation, he had to distinguish himself from them, since the call to refuse taxation was a call for rebellion. It is therefore no accident that in the mission discourse Jesus seems twice to distance himself from other itinerant preachers:

First, he orders his messengers to enter houses with a peace greeting (Q^{Lk} 10:5). The magical power of this greeting is supposed to spread and rest on the household or, if the messengers are rejected, be withdrawn. In the Lukan version the peace depends on whether a "peaceful person" is in the house (Luke 10:6). In the Matthean version the disciples are supposed to find out who is worthy before they enter a house (Matt 10:11). By means of their peace greeting, Jesus' disciples distinguish themselves from Judas Galilaios's campaign. Refusal of taxation was a declaration of war. The pericope on the tribute (Mark 12:13-17) attests that Jesus really did have to separate himself from Judas Galilaios. Thus, a comparable distinction in the mission discourse is also possible.

We may mention a second move: Jesus' messengers are not to go around, like Cynic itinerant philosophers, with staff and bag. That makes sense only if itinerant preachers who called themselves Cynics were a familiar sight. We ought to consider that a man could walk around with a beard, bag, and walking staff without being a Cynic. All that was really necessary was bringing an unconventional message. Judas Galilaios and his adherents brought such a message. Josephus presents them as a fourth Jewish philosophy (*Ant.* 18.23). He equates the Essenes with the Pythagoreans (*Ant.* 15.371), the Pharisees with the Stoics (*Vita* 12), the Sadducees indirectly with the Epicureans.[16] As a fourth philosophy there remained only the Cynics,[17] since Cynicism was nothing but a radicalized Stoic philosophy.[18] It is therefore quite possible that Judas Galilaios might have pretended outwardly that his "philosophy" was Cynicism. He came from a city that was not too distant from Gadara, where Cynic traditions are attested over a number of centuries.[19] But the Cynic shell would have been superficial. The formal language of Hellenistic culture would only have served, here as so often in the Middle East, to give additional lustre to native content.

Three Tradents of the Jesus Tradition after Easter

The origins of the Jesus tradition can thus be seen in Jesus' teaching and itinerant existence. Their transmission was relatively secure, inasmuch as the disciples continued their itinerant life after Easter and—inspired by the Easter experience—persevered in the mission. Itinerant charismatics retained important parts of the tradition of Jesus' words. They were able to represent Jesus' radical ethos in believable fashion, that ethos of homelessness, distance from family, critique of possessions, and nonviolence, for all of which I coined the concept of "itinerant radicalism." The Sayings Source Q (see below; p. 32) emphasizes their homelessness: "but the Son of Man has nowhere to lay his head" (Luke 9:58). Critical of family are the words "whoever comes to me and does not hate father and mother, wife and children, brothers and sisters, yes, and even life itself, cannot be my disciple" (Luke 14:26). One should let the dead bury one's father (Luke 9:60-61); war within families is regarded as unavoidable (Luke 12:51-53). In such circles one could criticize the rich and live like the birds of heaven (Luke 6:20-49; 12:22-34). Since Jesus himself was an itinerant preacher, the early Christian itinerant charismatics constitute a certain guarantee that his words were retained for us in his spirit. They were the real agents of the new movement, and we can demonstrate their presence in Syria-Palestine for a considerable time.

Besides the itinerant charismatics, there were locally settled groups of sympathizers, including the most important, the local community of Jerusalem—existing as "home harbors" for many itinerant charismatics, but also as the place of Jesus' last days. Probably memories of Jesus' passion were handed on in that community. As a rule the Jesus tradition consisted of small, complete units, but in the passion story we have a coherent narrative made up of many units, either a short account of arrest, trial, condemnation, and crucifixion like the one beginning in Mark 14:43, or a longer account beginning in Mark 14:1 with the decision of the Sanhedrin to arrest Jesus. The Synoptic Gospels, in any case, agree remarkably well with the Gospel of John in the passion story. All the gospels may be dependent on a common passion narrative, retained in its oldest form in the Gospel of Mark. Favoring the great age of this passion story are the "indicators of familiarity" in Mark—that is, references in the text that presume familiarity with persons and places mentioned there. Two examples: during the arrest, two persons remain anonymous. A follower of Jesus wounds a member of the arresting group with his sword (Mark 14:47), while another escapes naked after being seized (Mark 14:51-52). In both cases the anonymity may be for protection: as long as members of the arresting body were alive it was not opportune to reveal the names of the two followers of Jesus who defended themselves during the arrest. We can thus assume that the passion story was shaped in Jerusalem in the 40s/50s.

A second tradition that is not made up simply of short pericopes points to southern Palestine: the "Synoptic apocalypse" in Mark 13, which revises an older tradition. In the middle of this text, people in Judea are addressed directly: "but when you see the desolating sacrilege set up where it ought not to be (let the reader understand), then those in Judea must flee to the mountains!" (Mark 13:14). Mark probably adopted here a prophecy from the Caligula crisis in the years 39/40. At that time a statue of the emperor was made in Phoenicia; it was intended to be brought by Roman soldiers and set up in the temple by force. That was the "desolating sacrilege." As soon as it was installed in the temple, where it should not stand, the final eschatological crisis and the end of the world would occur. This prophecy stems from the years 39/40. It was probably handed down in Jerusalem, which was most affected by the Caligula crisis.

In any case, itinerant charismatics were not the only bearers of the Jesus traditions. His localized followers also talked about him. In addition, there were traditions about Jesus that were generally current among the people: the miracle stories. It is often said in the gospels that word about Jesus' miracles had spread throughout the whole country (e.g., Mark 1:28). These notes about the spread of the news presume that at a very early time people told about Jesus' healings and exorcisms, even where people had little interest in the rest of his teaching. We have at least one attestation of this: in the *Testimonium Flavianum* Jesus is called a "wonder-worker" (*paradoxōn ergōn poiētēs*) (*Ant.* 18.63-64). Josephus had heard about his miraculous deeds. He would have valued Jesus just as he did the exorcist Eleazar, whose exorcisms in the presence of Vespasian and his officers he recounts, filled with pride at the power of the Jewish king Solomon:

> The manner of the cure was this:—He put a ring that had a root of one of those sorts mentioned by Solomon to the nostrils of the demoniac, after which he drew out the demon through his nostrils; and when the man fell down immediately, he abjured him to return into him no more, making still mention of Solomon. (*Ant.* 8.46-48)

Thus, after Jesus' death his traditions were handed down in three social contexts: among disciples, in communities, and by the general public. We should not imagine these disciples', community, and popular traditions as separate. What was handed down among the people was also told among Jesus' followers. What was told among Jesus' localized followers was also known to the itinerant charismatics. These last handed on the core of his teaching. Their tradition was set down in the Sayings Source, while the community and popular traditions were recorded a generation later in the Gospel of Mark. But what forms and genres made up this Jesus tradition with its threefold *Sitz im Leben*?

The Formal Language of Jesus' Proclamation

Genres are institutionalized forms of communication. They link the production and reception of texts by means of preprogrammed models and motifs and thus create the formal conditions for understanding, that is, the general expectations and pre-understandings that make comprehension possible. The use of existing genres is part of a general social exchange. In speaking as in other things we are confronted with pre-programmed role expectations. They determine what speech utterances are expected of us and how they are interpreted. The same was true for Jesus. He was experienced by his contemporaries in two, perhaps three roles:

a. He was a *prophet*. It is true that he is nowhere addressed as "prophet," but his appearance created the presumption that he was a prophet (Mark 6:15; 8:26; Matt 21:11; Luke 7:16; 24:19).
b. He was a *teacher*. There is ample attestation of his being addressed as "teacher." Matthew suppresses it because in his eyes it was too trivial for Jesus' role. In Matthew's Gospel it is only Judas who addresses Jesus as "teacher." But here, too, he is "the teacher" pure and simple (Matt 23:8-10).
c. As prophet and teacher, he entered into discussion with *scribes*. He took positions on Torah and interpreted it. He made an impression because he taught, differently from the scribes, "with authority." But that did not mean he was perceived in the role of a scribe.

The genres in which Jesus' words were transmitted correspond exactly to these roles. These are primarily prophetic and wisdom forms. Rules and legal prescriptions, such as are characteristic of rabbis learned in the law, are only weakly attested. Jesus did not formulate any *halakah*, any binding interpretations of the law—except for his teaching about divorce (Mark 10:11-12 *parr.*). His interpretation of the law in the antitheses has wisdom features: he formulates commandments regarding anger and sexuality that are not subject to legal regulation through sanctions. He offers ethical principles instead of legal norms. Hence the roles of prophet and teacher are generally adequate to describe his activity. Very seldom does he appear in the role of a scribal Torah teacher, a role that, after all, was not fundamentally different from that of a sage.

Both as prophet and as teacher, Jesus was a gifted teller of similitudes. To the extent that similitudes speak of the reign of God, they are part of the prophetic role. To the extent they are obvious, they are aspects of wisdom. And yet Jesus' similitudes have no models in the prophetic and wisdom literature of Judaism. Jesus differs from later rabbinic tellers of similitudes also in the fact that his similitudes did not interpret Torah. They rest within themselves.

Jesus' double role as wisdom teacher and prophet is directly addressed in one saying—the twofold word about the Queen of the South and Jonah: "The Queen of the South will rise at the judgment with the people of this generation and condemn them, because she came from the ends of the earth to listen to the wisdom of Solomon, and see, something greater than Solomon is here! The people of Nineveh will rise up at the judgment with this generation and condemn it, because they repented at the proclamation of Jonah, and see, something greater than Jonah is here!" (Q^{Lk} 11:31-32). This double role constitutes a unity: as teacher, Jesus fascinated his audience and taught them with authority. As prophet, he was rejected—not only in his hometown, but also in Jerusalem and among his people. His teaching was the basis of his charisma, his prophetic role was his stigma. Charisma and stigma go together. Attempts to separate the role of the sage, who spoke paradoxical wisdom sayings like a Cynic itinerant teacher, from the role of the prophet who proclaimed the inbreaking of the reign of God are inappropriate.[20]

In every genre we find three forms in the tradition as we now have it:

1. Forms primarily containing an appeal (in the second person singular or plural),
2. Forms consisting of statements in the third person, and
3. Forms containing a statement of Jesus about himself (often in the first person singular).

Jesus probably used most of the forms listed below. They are part of his formal language, even if not every example of a form handed down to us need be genuine. Most disputed are the "self-statements." It is most often suspected, in their case, that they have been colored or shaped by a post-Easter view of the person of Jesus, since they make fundamental statements about his significance and mission: the words about Jesus' having come are often seen as post-Easter retrospective views of his mission, the *sophia* sayings as expressions of an early Christology according to which Jesus was a messenger of Wisdom. The allegories in which there may be a self-reference are usually regarded, because of the very fact that they are allegories, as early Christian creations. Only the antitheses formulated in the first person are nearly always recognized as authentic forms of speech used by Jesus (see Table 3).

Table 3: The Formal Language of Jesus' Sayings

	Appellative statements (often 2d person)	**Objective statements (2d and 3d person)**	**Self-statements (1st person)**
Prophet	Macarisms and judgment sayings: preaching of salvation and judgment	*Basileia* sayings and crisis sayings: preaching of salvation and judgment	Mission sayings: Jesus' having come for salvation and judgment
Wisdom teacher	Warnings (2d person) (a) singular (b) plural	Proverbs (3d person) (a) general statements (b) statements about roles (c) images	*Sophia* sayings: Jesus as messenger and speaker of wisdom
Teacher of the Law	Rules for disciples: discipleship sayings, rules for mission	Legal sayings	Antitheses: Jesus as critical interpreter of the Law
Teller of similitudes and parables	Parables: advocacy for unusual behavior	Similitudes: argumentation by means of typical events	Allegories: coded self-statements

We will select, by way of example, some forms from this language: similitudes, sayings (word traditions), and miracle stories (narrative tradition).

Similitudes cannot be understood as a continuation of Jewish literature. The few Old Testament precursors contain anthropomorphically portrayed plants or animals.[21] They are more fables than similitudes. But with Jesus there is no trace of anthropomorphic stylizing! It is deliberately omitted. So in the similitude of the fig tree Jesus works with traditional fable material in which a fig tree itself spoke. But he retains a human spokesperson who speaks as the fig tree's representative (Luke 13:6-9).[22] We can see a similar development in the similitude of the wicked tenants (Mark 12:1-12): Isaiah's song of the vineyard (Isa 5:1-7) underlies it; there the vineyard is addressed directly, like a human partner. In Jesus' similitude, in contrast, it is not the vineyard but its tenants who are God's conversation partners. Where we find animals and plants in Jesus' similitudes they are not anthropomorphized. They do not speak and they have no feelings—even when they clearly represent human beings, as in the case of the lost sheep or the seed on the fourfold field. For us, Jesus is the first to introduce the similitude form in Judaism. But he was probably not the first person who told similitudes, since the rabbis also told them and represent a narrative tradition that probably goes back to New Testament times. Most nearly comparable is the fable literature of antiquity, to the extent that it does without anthropomorphized plants and animals. If we ask, then, about the movement from the few Old Testament fables to the development of New Testament and rabbinic similitudes, we will (with David Flusser) have to take into account the long influence of Hellenism in Palestine.[23]

Jesus' sayings belong partly to the wisdom, partly to the prophetic tradition. They often appear in the tradition with a narrative frame attributing them to a situation and a particular author. Thus we encounter for the first time in Jewish literature (not with Jesus himself, but in the Jesus tradition) apophthegms, that is, sayings attributed to a particular person in a particular situation. The only models for these were in pagan literature.[24] Here, then, we are dealing with the (narrative) embedding of the form of the saying, coming from Judaism, in the communication form of the apophthegm, something new to Judaism.

This borrowing from general, including non-Jewish forms of communication is clearest in the miracle stories. The topics of the New Testament miracle narratives can be found in many non-Jewish texts. The miracle stories themselves contain indications of their "intercultural" character. A Gentile woman from Syrophoenicia has heard about Jesus' miracles and therefore comes to Jesus to beg healing for her sick child. It is simply assumed as a matter of course that even in Jesus' lifetime Gentiles were talking about his miracles (Mark 7:24-30). When the tongue of a deaf-mute is loosed, Jesus does forbid him to tell of it, but the more he forbids it, the more people talk about it (Mark 7:36), as if the real miracle did not consist in the freeing of the tongue of a deaf-mute, but rather in the fact that the tongues of the eyewitnesses to the miracle were loosed and they became proclaimers who spread everywhere the story of what they had seen.

In the first generation after Jesus, then, Jesus traditions were circulating among three groups: as the traditions of the disciples, the communities, and the people in general. There Jesus appeared in the role of a prophet and sage. The prophetic and wisdom formal language he used also shaped the continuing history of the tradition of Jesus' words. This we can see in the Sayings Source.

2 The Sayings Source Q

The First Written Form of the Jesus Tradition

The Sayings Source is the first written form of the Jesus tradition. It was discovered in the process of work on the "Synoptic question" (i.e., the question of the relationships among Matthew, Mark, and Luke, the three Synoptic Gospels). In the nineteenth century the opinion that the kinship of the Synoptic Gospels was explained by mutual use became accepted. Until today, the "two-source theory" is accepted: that is, the proposition that Matthew and Luke used two sources, Mark and the Sayings Source, plus special material (Matthew^{S} and Luke^{S}), in oral or written form. This source theory is, as a rule, represented thus:

Figure 1: The Two-Source Theory

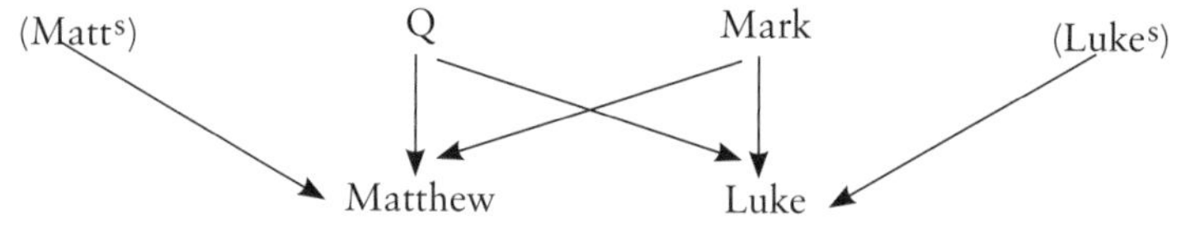

The "double tradition" in Matthew and Luke can best be explained if they have a common source ("Q," for *Quelle*, "source"). Since most of the material transmitted twice is made up of Jesus' words, the source is called the "Sayings Source." A statistical argument favors its existence: where Matthew and Luke reproduce the source we have retained, the Gospel of Mark, their word agreement is 56 percent. Where they reproduce the no-longer-extant source Q, it is 71 percent. If with 56 percent agreement we have to conclude to an undoubtedly existing source (Mark), how much more can we postulate, on the basis of a 71 percent agreement, the no-longer-extant source Q! Its existence is confirmed by occasional overlaps between Mark and Q material. Sometimes the gospels contain doublets, that is, the same tradition twice—once according to Mark, another time according to Q. So, for example, Luke's Gospel tells of the sending of twelve disciples, according to Mark, in Luke 9:1-6, and a second sending of seventy disciples, according to Q, in Luke 10:1-12; there is a first eschatological discourse by Jesus from Q in Luke 17:22-37, and a second from Mark in Luke 21:5-36.[1]

It is possible that the early Christian witness of Bishop Papias of Hierapolis (either ca. 115 or 140 C.E.) attests to both of these ancient sources. Eusebius, writing his church history in the fourth century C.E., quotes from Papias's work:

> Mark became Peter's interpreter and wrote down accurately, but not in order, all that he remembered of the things said and done by the Lord. For he had not heard the Lord or been one of his followers, but later, as I said, a follower of Peter. Peter used to teach as the occasion demanded, without giving systematic arrangement to the Lord's sayings, so that Mark did not err in writing down some things just as he recalled them. For he had one overriding purpose: to omit nothing that he had heard and to make no false statements in his account. (Eusebius, *Hist. eccl.* 3.39.14-15)

> Matthew compiled the sayings in the Hebrew language, and each interpreted them as best he could. (Eusebius, *Hist. eccl.* 3.39.16)[2]

What Papias recorded here was a tradition he had already received. That would explain why Eusebius found notes from him on only two gospels, even though Papias may have been familiar with the Gospel of John as well, something that, however, is uncertain. If one reads the two notes objectively one must think of the Gospel of Mark as a depiction of Jesus' words and deeds (as is the case with Mark), and of the writing attributed to Matthew as a collection of sayings. It is possible that Papias had in mind the two oldest gospel sources: he attributed the collection of sayings to Matthew either because he confused it with the Gospel of Matthew or because the sayings collection he possessed was thought to be the work of the apostle Matthew. What Papias describes could be a variant of the Sayings Source. Of course, one must ask whether it could have been known in Asia Minor around the turn of the century. That is possible. In 1 Tim 5:18 a proverbial saying is cited as "scripture" (together with Deut 25:4): "The laborer deserves to be paid." This corresponds to the logion in Q^{Lk} 10:7. The Pastorals certainly belong to Asia Minor—probably to Ephesus, which was not far from Hierapolis, where

Papias was bishop. The author of the Gospel of Matthew used this sayings collection as a source. Possibly for that reason his gospel was attributed to a "Matthew" and the toll collector "Levi" in the Gospel of Mark became "Matthew" in the Gospel of Matthew (Mark 2:14; Matt 9:9): a toll collector was the most likely of the otherwise uneducated disciples (Acts 4:13) to be able to write down Jesus' words. This also makes it understandable that the Sayings Source has not survived: if two writings were in circulation, both attributed to a "Matthew," and one of them (the Gospel of Matthew) contained the whole of the other (Q), the more complete writing would always prevail. What is important for us is that we find an indication of a "collection of sayings" very early in Christianity. The reconstruction of that source is not easy. We can never be certain whether there was more in it than what Matthew and Luke have in common (against Mark). It is also always difficult to assert that something was *not* in Q. It is easier to say positively what *was* in it. It seems that Luke has preserved the sequence of the sayings in Q better than Matthew, which is why Q is quoted according to Luke (in what follows, for example, "Q^{Lk} 10:7" refers to the Q logion preserved in Luke 10:7).

The Structure of Q

The Sayings Source Q begins in chronological order with the preaching of John the Baptizer (Q^{Lk} 3:2-4) and (probably) Jesus' baptism, with his "appointment" as Son of God, since in the temptation of Jesus that follows (Q^{Lk} 4:1-13) he is addressed as "Son of God" when he refuses to kneel before the Satan in order to obtain sovereignty over the world. He shows himself to be a model Jew who knows that no one is to be worshiped but God alone. Jesus refuses other miracles for show that would demonstrate his majesty, for no one may test God by demanding miracles. Because Jesus passes the test, he can teach persuasively.

1. This introduction to the Sayings Source is followed by a programmatic discourse (Q^{Lk} 6:20-49) that Matthew shaped into the Sermon on the Mount. It begins with beatitudes for the poor, the hungry, and the sorrowing. Its central demands are love of enemies (Q^{Lk} 6:27-28) and the prohibition against judging one another (Q^{Lk} 6:37, 38). At the end it is emphasized that only someone who acts according to these words has built on rock (Q^{Lk} 6:47-49).
2. After this, Jesus' effect on various contemporaries is depicted: the Gentile centurion from Capernaum acknowledges him

(Q^{Lk} 7:1-10). His appearance after the programmatic discourse underscores the power of Jesus' words. The Baptizer takes a wait-and-see attitude toward him (Q^{Lk} 7:18-23), but "this generation" rejects Jesus and the Baptizer, even though both are messengers of Wisdom (Q^{Lk} 7:31-35).

3. In a third section Jesus calls his disciples to follow him (Q^{Lk} 9:57-62), sends them on mission (Q^{Lk} 10:1-16), and offers them a special relationship to God (Q^{Lk} 10:21-24): God's revelation of his "Son" is for them, and they in turn may address God as Father (Q^{Lk} 11:2-4). In the discipleship sayings and the mission discourse the itinerant charismatics are visible as the tradents of the material collected in Q.
4. The expulsion of a demon (Q^{Lk} 11:14-15) introduces a section in which Jesus argues with opponents. He rejects the accusation that he is in league with Satan (Q^{Lk} 11:17-26) and attacks the Pharisees and those learned in the Law in a series of "woes" (Q^{Lk} 11:39-52). Punishment will fall on "this generation" because they have rejected Wisdom and her messengers.
5. The fifth section is about "the life of disciples in light of the end" (Q^{Lk} 12:2-59). It begins with sayings against fear of human beings and of public confession of Jesus (Q^{Lk} 12:8-9). An admonition not to worry shows that the bearers of this tradition worried no more about the source of their livelihood than the birds (Q^{Lk} 12:22-31). Their eccentric way of life was only possible because the end of the world was near. A series of further traditions in Q deals with this last age. This fifth section has very little unity of theme—a typical sign of a collection of pericopes. The redactor at first had a lot of material to choose from and was therefore able to shape the beginning very carefully, but at the end he had only a number of scraps that had to be incorporated. (In the Sermon on the Mount also, the third major section beginning with Matt 6:19 is less systematically composed than the first two parts.)

The conclusion is a little "apocalypse" on the end of the world (Q^{Lk} 17:22-35). It warns against false expectations of a messiah and announces the appearance of the "Son of Man," who will break unexpectedly into a time of peace. It may be that Q ended with the saying about the twelve tribes of Israel: in the new world the disciples will rule the renewed people of God (Q^{Lk} 22:28-30).

The Time of Q's Origins

In my view, the Jewish War is a *terminus ad quem*: since the Son of Man—differently from Mark 13—is supposed to enter a peaceful world (Q^{Lk} 17:23-37), Q must have been created before the Jewish War. The destruction of the temple is not yet presumed. This, of course, is not undisputed, because in Q^{Lk} 13:34-35 God announces that he will abandon the temple:

> Jerusalem, Jerusalem, the city that kills the prophets and stones those who are sent to it! How often have I desired to gather your children together as a hen gathers her brood under her wings, and you were not willing! See, your house will be left in ruins (NRSV: is left to you). And I tell you, you will not see me until the time comes when you say, "Blessed is the one who comes in the name of the Lord."

Tacitus (*Hist.* V.13.1) and Josephus (*B.J.* 6.299-30) report, from the time before the destruction, that there was a voice announcing the departure of the deity. Probably the comparable prophecy in Q also came from before the beginning of the war. The question is only: how long before? The fear that the divine presence would withdraw from the temple was always acute when the temple was criticized and its destruction was expected—thus since Jesus' prophecy about the temple, but at the latest since the woe invoked over the city and the temple by the prophet of doom Jesus, son of Ananias (62 C.E.). The prediction that the divine presence would come again corresponds to Rom 11:26: the redeemer will come from Zion. Unbelieving Israel will have another chance, in direct confrontation with the Exalted One!

A *terminus a quo* is the attempt by the emperor Gaius Caligula in the year 39/40 to transform the temple into a sanctuary of the imperial cult, since the Caligula crisis is worked into the temptation story.[3] Three motifs favor this: (1) Gaius wanted to have himself worshiped in the Jerusalem temple, as does the devil in the temptation story. (2) In Rome he demanded that he be worshiped with *proskynesis*, just as the devil demands that Jesus bow down to him. (3) Gaius had the power to bestow lands—as, for example, he gave Galilee and Judea to his friend Agrippa I. The temptation story rejects miracles for show that were supposed to authenticate Jesus. We know that after 35 C.E. there appeared increasing numbers of "signs prophets" who led their followers to the place of a promised miracle. They tried to authenticate themselves through showy miracles. Theudas (after 44 C.E.) promised that the waters of the Jordan would part, as at the occupation of the Land (*Ant.* 20.97-99; Acts 5:36). Under Felix (52–59 C.E.) there appeared an Egyptian who promised to repeat the miracle at Jericho on the walls of Jerusalem (*Ant.* 20.169-72; Acts 21:38). At the same time pseudo-prophets led their followers into the desert and promised miracles there (*Ant.* 20.167-68). Is it an accident that the two miracles for show in the temptation story were supposed to take place in Jerusalem and in the desert—where the signs prophets also expected miracles? This would also fit well with the rejection of any sign other than the sign of Jonah (Q^{Lk} 11:16-30). In that case, experiences from the 40s and 50s would have been reworked in the temptation story.

In my opinion, Q originated between 40 and 65 C.E.—probably in Palestine or Syria, but not far from Palestine. Individual traditions indicate a Galilean perspective; these mention little places like Chorazin, Bethsaida, and Capernaum (Q^{Lk} 10:13-15). But that need not be the perspective of the entire writing. Its localization in Galilee is not impossible, but much less certain than many think. If the words of itinerant preachers were recorded in Q, we could locate it anywhere throughout the area in which the itinerant preachers were working.

The Tradition-Critical and Theological Location of Q

The Sayings Source contains traditions from itinerant radicalism, thus representing an early Jewish Christianity. Within Jewish Christianity it was close to the moderate wing of the mission to Israel, which did not conduct a mission to the Gentiles but accepted it at the Apostolic Council. Paul's letters are a document of the Gentile mission; Q is a document of the mission to Israel.

Q collects traditions from itinerant charismatics (and translates them into Greek). These itinerant preachers could plausibly represent Jesus' radical ethos of homelessness (Q^{Lk} 9:58), distance from family (Q^{Lk} 9:60-61; 12:51-53; 14:26), critique of possessions and nonviolence (Q^{Lk} 6:20-42; 12:22-34). The Sayings Source itself need not have been written by an itinerant charismatic. It is more probable that a Christian in a local community wrote down the traditions of itinerant charismatics and translated them into Greek in order to retain them for the Christian communities and secure their dissemination independently of the itinerant charismatics—much as Papias, the bishop of Hierapolis in Asia Minor at the beginning of the second century, collected Jesus traditions from itinerant preachers. He writes:

> Unlike most, I did not delight in those who say much but in those who teach the truth; not in those who recite the commandments of others but in those who repeated the commandments given by the

> Lord. And whenever anyone came who had been a follower of the elders, I asked about their words: what Andrew or Peter had said, or Philip or Thomas or James or John or Matthew or any other of the Lord's disciples, and what Aristion and the presbyter John, disciples of the Lord, were still saying. For I did not think that information from books would help me as much as the word of a living, surviving voice. (Eusebius, *Hist. eccl.* 3.39.3-4)[4]

This is the model by which we should understand the origins of Q: a locally resident Christian writes down traditions about Jesus because he treasures them above all else. The stream of oral tradition continued, of course, even after it was thus first committed to writing. Perhaps Q was meant to serve as a little handbook for missionaries, perhaps even as a document intended to win Christians to the role of itinerant charismatics, since the mission discourse begins with a petition to God to send workers into his harvest: "the harvest is plentiful, but the laborers are few; therefore ask the Lord of the harvest to send out laborers into his harvest" (Q^{Lk} 10:2). The call to discipleship is not only heard before the mission discourse (Q^{Lk} 9:57-62), but is encountered again in discipleship sayings toward the end (Q^{Lk} 14:26-27, 33). The similitude of the talents at the conclusion is an appeal to risk something in this life (Q^{Lk} 19:11-27)!

Q is deeply rooted in Judaism. It is a document of Jewish Christianity. There are no statements critical of the law (sabbath conflicts, fundamental abrogations of the category of external purity, direct critique of the temple). Even the Israelites who rejected Jesus' message still have a chance. Jesus appeals to the Jerusalemites who have killed the prophets and stoned the messengers sent to them in the name of Wisdom: "you will not see me until the time comes when you say, 'Blessed is the one who comes in the name of the Lord'" (Q^{Lk} 13:35; this interpretation is disputed, however). Paul is aware of the comparable hope that at the Lord's return all Israel will be saved (Rom 11:26). This ties these two witnesses to the first generation.

In Q, Jesus is the messenger of Wisdom. He was the latest of a sequence of prophets and messengers of Wisdom to die a martyr's death for his cause (Q^{Lk} 11:49-51). But he is nevertheless more than a prophet and teacher of wisdom. How does the Sayings Source express that "more"?

a. Jesus is the Son of Man. He does not merely teach what God demands. He himself, as judge, will demand an accounting (as the parable of the talents at the end of Q shows).
b. Jesus is above all the Son of God. The title of Messiah is absent (just as in the *Gospel of Thomas*). But the titles "Son of God"

> and "the Son" stem from messianic tradition. Already in Q, Jesus as the Son stands alongside God and is the exclusive revealer: "All things have been handed over to me by my Father; and no one knows who the Son is except the Father, or who the Father is except the Son and anyone to whom the Son chooses to reveal him." (Q^{Lk} 10:22)

Is this a repudiation of monotheism? No! For Jews at that time it was imaginable that there were divine figures besides God, such as Wisdom (Proverbs 8), the Logos (Philo), and the Son of Man (Daniel 7). What was, however, unthinkable was that a human being could lay claim independently to being such a divine figure. This the Sayings Source excludes. It tells, in the temptation story, how Jesus had rejected any worship of another being besides God. Only after Jesus has withstood the test of his monotheism are statements made about him that set him alongside God.

Ultimately, the Sayings Source is a document of the mission to Israel. It courts Israel intensely. The saying about the Twelve who will judge Israel is not aimed at Israel's condemnation, for the assembly of the twelve tribes it presupposes is a saving event. The judgment by the Twelve corresponds to the Messiah's "judging" in *Pss. Sol.* 17:26—and that, too, is a ruling that saves.[5] But the proclamation of the messenger Jesus brings Israel to a crisis that began with the Baptizer. Jesus' message is no harsher than his preaching. It is an appeal to Israel, despite its rejection. Often, it is true, the polemic against "this generation" has been seen as a radical criticism of Israel, interpreted as a reaction to the failure of the preaching in Israel. Israel, it is said, has no further chance. But many traditions in Q speak against this: within this "capricious" generation there are children of Wisdom who accept Jesus and the Baptizer (Q^{Lk} 7:31-35). Not all are lost. Q announces judgment on individual cities in Israel, which makes sense only if other cities have a chance at the judgment (Q^{Lk} 10:13-15). Judgment is to pass right through individual houses and families. Thus individuals may be saved (Q^{Lk} 17:34-35). In addition, the message of judgment is no more severe than that of John the Baptizer. The latter was a given for Jesus and is not a secondary reflection on failure. Had the Sayings Source left no chance at all for the people Israel, the Jesus of the Sayings Source would be one of those scribes who close the door of the reign of God against people, but precisely those scribes are harshly criticized (Q^{Lk} 11:52). The Gentile mission is not actively pursued in Q, but Gentiles are set up as positive models: the centurion at Capernaum (Q^{Lk} 7:1-10), the inhabitants of Tyre and Sidon (Q^{Lk} 10:13-14), and the Queen of the South as well as the Ninevites in the North (Q^{Lk} 11:31-32). All these are supposed to "irritate" Israel into believing. We find a comparable idea, as far as the subject is concerned, in Romans 11. According to Paul the converted Gentiles ought to "irritate" the unconverted Jews into belief. This attitude to the Gentiles allows us to conclude that here we have a moderate Jewish Christianity that accepts the Gentile mission. Thus, we have in Q a witness to that Jewish-Christian branch of early Christianity that accepted the Gentile mission at the Apostolic Council, while feeling itself obligated to the mission to Israel. Their primary representative is Peter. One could, of course, object that his name is not found in the Sayings Source. But no disciple is mentioned by name there. Only at the end do we encounter the "Twelve," but the Twelve are clearly related to the twelve tribes of Israel. And there can be no doubt that Peter was the leading disciple among the group of the Twelve.

The Genre of Q: A Prophetic Book and More?

A crucial question for any literary-historical critique is: What kind of genre is revealed in Q? Two proposals have been made in the course of research: Q is either regarded as a wisdom writing (James Robinson) or a prophetic work (Migaku Sato). Sometimes it is seen as a *corpus permixtum* made up of various genres (Marco Frenschkowski).[6] The overall frame undoubtedly resembles that of a prophetic book. Only in the prophetic books does the prophet appear as clearly in his individuality as does Jesus in Q. In the wisdom books the sage is often concealed behind the great wise man Solomon or remains a bland figure like Jesus Sirach.

The individual profile of the prophet appears in narratives. The narrative portions of Q are the temptation story, that of the centurion of Capernaum, and the exorcism at the beginning of the Beelzebub discourse. There is no narrative of the death of Jesus. These narrative sections are indicative: we know of no wisdom books with narrative introduction (cf. Proverbs, Sirach, Pseudo-Phocylides), but we do have prophetic books with narrative texts such as the call of Isaiah (Isa 6:1-8) or Amos's conflict in Bethel (Amos 7:10-17). And yet, in the prophetic books as in Q, there is no account of the death of the prophet. In prophetic books the narratives legitimate the prophet through his calling and describe his conflicts.

The prophetic character of Q is further evident in Jesus' words: these can be contextualized much better as common wisdom sayings. They are addressed to the generation before the end and speak of places like Chorazin, Bethsaida, Capernaum, and Jerusalem. They specify the opponents as Pharisees and teachers of the law. The contrast with the Baptizer lends Jesus a distinctive profile: unlike the Baptizer, he is a glutton and a drunkard. Wisdom traditions, unlike these, have a tendency to decontextualization! They name no individual persons and names. The *framing texts* of Q are also prophetic: the Sayings Source begins with the Baptizer's preaching of judgment and the promise of the one who is to come (Q^{Lk} 3:7-12). It ends with sayings about the coming of the Son of Man, the similitude of the talents about judgment, and the saying about the Twelve judging Israel (Q^{Lk} 22:28, 30). Within this frame we find a great many wisdom sayings. The programmatic discourse (Q^{Lk} 6:20-49) contains, for example, the saying about love of enemies, the golden rule, the warning not to judge, the sayings about the blind leading the blind, the speck and the log, the tree and its fruits. Q is therefore a prophetic writing containing wisdom sayings. That is: the authentic formal language of Jesus' sayings has led here to an initial written genre. For Jesus' formal language was that of a prophet and wisdom teacher. Almost all the forms of his preaching are found also in Q, with the exception of the antitheses. From a form-critical point of view we can observe a surprising degree of continuity between Jesus' formal language and that of the Sayings Source (Table 4):

Table 4: Jesus' Formal Language in the Sayings Source

	Appellative Sayings	**Material Sayings**	**Personal Sayings**
Prophet	Macarisms (6:20-23) and woes (11:39-52) as sayings about salvation and judgment	*Basileia* and crisis sayings (17:23ff.) as sayings about salvation and judgment	Mission sayings about having come for judgment (12:51-53) and salvation (7:34)
Wisdom Teacher	Warnings in the second person: (a) singular (17:3-4) (b) plural (12:4-5)	Proverbs in the third person (many examples)	*Sophia* sayings: Jesus as the messenger of Wisdom
Teacher of the Law	Rules for disciples: discipleship sayings, rules for mission	Legal sayings: divorce (16:18)	No antitheses, but a statement of divine law: "Everyone who acknowledges *me* . . . (12:8-9)
Teller of Similitudes	Parables: the banquet, the talents	Similitudes: building a house, children, servant, mustard seed, leaven, lost sheep (drachma)	Allegorical equation: in the Last Supper similitude, in the lost sheep

There are two objections to classifying Q as a prophetic book: there is no call narrative, and Jesus in Q is more than a prophet.

On the first point we should say that if there is a narrative of the baptism of Jesus, that would be a kind of call narrative. In any case, the temptation story, which follows immediately, has a legitimizing function. It is a qualifying test. Jesus proves himself to be a model monotheist. He is legitimized much more emphatically than all the prophets, namely, in a threefold fashion: through another prophet, through the voice of God at his baptism, in case the Baptizer story was part of Q, and through the overcoming of Satan. If the temptation on the mountain represents a contrast story comparing Jesus to Caligula, Jesus' claim would be a concealed statement of opposition to political power.

To the second objection we may say that Jesus, in Q, is in fact much more than a prophet, but according to Q the Baptizer was also more than a prophet (Q^{Lk} 7:26). In Q, Jesus even calls blessed all the eyewitnesses who see what prophets and kings desired to see and did not see. Even they are superior to the prophets (Q^{Lk} 10:23). But above all, Jesus must be more than a prophet. This "more" explains all the features that go beyond a prophetic book. No prophet announced his own coming at the end of the ages, but Jesus speaks of the coming of the Son of Man and means himself. No prophet said that the fate of humanity rested with him. Q ends with a little apocalypse, with apocalyptic sayings about the coming of the Son of Man. But Q is not an apocalypse, for no previous (pseudonymous) authority testifies to the truth of the prophecy, but rather Jesus himself. He appears as a prophet, but he is more than that, for he is the fulfillment of all prophecy.

It is likewise impossible to separate wisdom and prophetic layers in Q.[7] The two forms are linked. In the double saying about Jonah and the Queen of the South, Jesus is seen as both a prophet and a wisdom teacher (Q^{Lk} 11:31-32). The *Sophia* sayings combine the idea of Jesus as messenger of Wisdom with the deuteronomistic tradition according to which the prophets were rejected and killed. This combination of wisdom and prophetic traditions is not attested before the *Sophia* sayings (and before Q).

Thus, the first written version of Jesus' preaching relied on a familiar genre from the Old Testament, but developed it further. Just as Jesus was more than a prophet, Q is more than a prophetic book. And yet, Q could have been placed at the end of the Old Testament canon as an additional prophetic book. Its form expresses the claim to be a continuation and conclusion of Old Testament revelation! But it was *this* very writing, its formal shape resting on the Old Testament, that did not survive as an independent document. What in Q points beyond a prophetic writing could, in fact, be better shaped within a different framing genre.[8]

3 The Gospel of Mark

The Second Written Form of the Jesus Tradition

The Gospel of Mark is the second written form of the oral Jesus tradition. While the Sayings Source was based on the formal language of Jesus' words, in the Gospel of Mark the formal language of narrative tradition furnishes the shape: Mark's Gospel relates two cycles of apophthegms, a Galilean cycle at the beginning (2:1–3:6) and a Jerusalem cycle at the end (12:13-44), while miracle stories run throughout the whole gospel. But primarily, this is a passion narrative with an extended introduction. It projects a more exciting image of Jesus than does Q, demanding a much greater power of literary and theological integration, for the image of Jesus in various genres shaped from the perspective of a third party was necessarily more heterogeneous than in the sayings tradition whose formal language goes back to Jesus himself. In the traditions reworked by Mark, Jesus appears as a miracle worker, a teacher who made gripping points, and simultaneously a failed royal pretender. While Q put into writing the traditions of the disciples as itinerant charismatics, Mark includes congregational and popular traditions alongside some of those of the disciples. Here we see much more of the perspective of the local communities and the people as a whole. But there are overlaps between the two streams of tradition, as is evident from the more than twenty logia common to Q and Mark.

The Structure of Mark's Gospel

The Gospel of Mark is artfully structured. It consists of individual pericopes, each of which makes its own point. Through their arrangement into a gospel they acquire a "surplus of meaning": in the framework of the story of Jesus they point to the mystery of Jesus' person, which is revealed only in the entirety of the story. The individual narratives are therefore, on the one hand, superficially structured into a plausible chronological and geographical order, but at the same time they are interpreted by a christologically motivated ordering. A geographical and a christological outline overlie each other:

Geographical order: The first part of Mark's Gospel centers on Galilee, the second part on Jerusalem. Jesus travels from Galilee to Jerusalem in 10:1-52. But fundamentally he has been on the way to Jerusalem since the first passion prediction in Mark 8:31.

1.	1–4	Jesus' activity in Galilee
2.	4–8:30	Jesus' activity beyond Galilee. His journey to the Gentiles
		Peter's messianic confession: 8:29
1.	8:31—10:52	Jesus' journey to Jerusalem
2.	11–13	Jesus' activity in Jerusalem
3.	14–16	Jesus' suffering in Jerusalem.

Christological order: The heavens are opened three times in Mark's Gospel. God's voice and messenger speak to the human world and reveal successively who Jesus is. They always link to human expectations, surpassing and correcting them. Human beings suspect who Jesus is, but his true nature is known only through a self-revelation of God—perhaps in a deliberate three-step process from adoption at his baptism (1:11) to presentation at the transfiguration (9:7) and his reception into the world of God through his resurrection, proclaimed by an angel (16:6). These three "epiphanies" structure Mark's Gospel. At the center are Peter's confession (8:29) and the transfiguration. Previously Jesus works in Galilee and its neighborhood; afterward he begins his journey to Jerusalem and suffering. Previously his disciples do not understand his majesty; afterward they do not comprehend the humiliation of his suffering. Previously the mystery of the reign of God has been given only to the disciples in parables. But at the end his opponents understand that the parable of the wicked tenants is aimed at them (12:1-12). Peter's confession of Jesus as Messiah is the turning point.

Before we present the subtle fabric of the Gospel of Mark through a brief summary of its contents, we need to illustrate these mutually dependent and overlapping divisions in a table. The three epiphany-scenes will be particularly emphasized as the fundamental structure of Mark's Gospel (Table 5):

Table 5: The Structure of Mark's Gospel

1:1-13: Beginning of the gospel: the Baptizer announces the *Stronger One*	His affirmation by the voice from heaven as "*Son of God*" at his baptism (1:9-11)
1:14–4:34: Jesus' activity in Galilee	His personal secret: only demons recognize Jesus' dignity (1:24, 34; 3:11; 5:7) The disciples' understanding: the disciples, despite the miracles, do not understand Jesus' majesty (4:39ff.; 6:52; 8:14ff.)
4:35–8:26: Jesus' journey to the Gentiles	The secret of the miracles: despite Jesus' forbidding it, the miracles are told (1:44-45; 5:18ff.; 7:36-37) Jesus' secret teachings: he instructs the disciples in the open (4:10-20) and "in the house" (7:17ff.)
8:27–9:10: Center of the gospel: Peter's confession of Jesus *Messiah* and the call to discipleship in suffering	Confirmation of Jesus as "*Son of God*" by the voice from heaven (9:7)
9:11–10:52: Jesus' journey to Jerusalem	The personal secret: people also recognize Jesus' dignity (Peter, 8:29; centurion, 15:39)
11:1–13:37: Jesus' teaching in Jerusalem	The disciples' understanding: the disciples do not understand Jesus' humility (8:32; 9:32; 14:39ff.)
14:1–15:47: Jesus' suffering in Jerusalem	Jesus' secret teachings: Jesus teaches in the house (9:28-29, 33ff.; 10:10ff.) and in the open (13:3ff.)
15:38–16:8: Conclusion of the gospel: the centurion's confession of the dead *Son of God* (15:39)	The angel's message about his *resurrection* (16:6)

The introduction to Mark's Gospel: Jesus is legitimized through words of scripture (Exod 23:20; Mal 3:1-3 + Isa 40:3), the Baptizer's prophecy, and the voice from heaven. The voice from heaven and the bestowal of the Spirit are depicted as subjective experiences of Jesus. The reader is privileged; he or she knows that Jesus is the Son of God not through birth but through adoption. Yet it will be a long time before the people in Mark's Gospel understand that. For a long period only demons recognize who Jesus is (Mark 1:24; 1:34; 3:11), while the disciples do not understand him (4:41; 6:52; 8:21-28). Therefore, Jesus forbids the demons to talk about him, but tries to get his disciples to understand him—for a long time without success. The beginning of the Gospel of Mark has parallels to the beginning of Q; both start with the Baptizer, and not with Jesus' birth.

Jesus' activities in Galilee (1:14–4:34): At the beginning we hear of Jesus' success (1:14-45) in calling disciples and in healing. The flood of sick people forces Jesus to shift to other places. This is followed by a counterpoint: the description of a growing enmity (2:1–3:6) in a cycle of confrontational dialogues with increasing accusations of blasphemy (2:1ff.) culminating in the decision to kill Jesus (3:6). The result is a separation between followers and outsiders (3:7–4:34): the followers are gathered through the attraction of the crowds and the calling of the Twelve. But opponents come from Jerusalem and accuse him of alliance with the devil. In contrast to these, his group of followers, as *familia dei*, desire to do the will of God. Only the disciples, as insiders, receive an explanation of the similitudes.

Jesus' journey to the Gentiles (4:35–8:26): Jesus' travels beyond Galilee are a symbol of the journey to the Gentiles, and are full of obstacles. This is signified by the three crossings of the sea that organize this section: stilling of the storm, walking on the sea, and crossing while discussing the leaven. When crossing the sea, Jesus is alone with his disciples. The theme is their lack of understanding, which steadily intensifies, as shown by three sayings about their failure to understand: In 4:40, after the stilling of the storm, Jesus asks: "Have you still no faith?" After his walking on the sea the narrator asserts in 6:52: ". . . they did not understand about the loaves, but their hearts were hardened." In the discourse about the leaven in 8:14-21 Jesus reproaches them for their blindness in face of *both* bread miracles!

The sections between these crossings of the sea are shaped by two contrasts: of *King Herod* with Jesus (5:21–6:44)—his banquet with dancing, intrigue, and the murder of the Baptizer has its opposite image in Jesus' feeding miracle. Jesus, in contrast to Herod, is the good shepherd who has compassion on the people. Afterward the *Pharisees* are contrasted with him (7:1–8:13): they insist on excluding the Gentiles by means of purity laws. By alleviating these, Jesus opens the way to the Gentiles: he heals the daughter of the Syrophoenician woman and (in Gentile territory?) heals a deaf-mute and performs a second bread miracle.

After a symbolic healing of a blind person, hinting that the eyes of the disciples have to be opened by a miracle, Peter recognizes Jesus as Messiah but rejects his path to suffering (8:27-33). Jesus calls him, together with the disciples and the people, to follow the cross. On the mountain Peter and the sons of Zebedee see the transfiguration of Jesus in glory, with Moses and

Elijah. Peter, who wants to build three booths for these three figures thus giving them equal status, still does not understand his unique dignity: Jesus is the only Son of God to whom they are to listen as their authority and beside whom Moses and Elijah fade into obscurity (9:7). The vision on the mountain is not to be made known until the resurrection of the Son of Man (9:9)—an indication that aspects of an Easter vision have been reworked in this episode. Jesus' exaltation on the mountain is deliberately contrasted with the powerlessness of the disciples at the mountain's foot: they cannot heal the epileptic boy.

Jesus' journey to Jerusalem (8:31-32; 9:11–10:52): From the time of his first passion prediction, Jesus has been on the way to Jerusalem. This path is organized by prophecies of suffering:

1. The first passion prediction (8:31) teaches the necessity of suffering.
2. The second passion prediction (9:11-12) parallels the fate of Elijah (= the Baptizer) with that of Jesus. Both will be killed. But this corresponds to scripture.
3. The third passion prediction (9:31) emphasizes the paradox: The Son of Man will be given into the hands of human beings, but he will rise again.
4. The fourth passion prediction (10:32-33) makes Jesus' suffering concrete, attributing it to Jewish and Gentile authorities. The "human beings" of 9:31 are distinguished socially.
5. The fifth passion prediction (10:45) gives the passion, "as a ransom for many," a soteriological meaning. This interpretation will be repeated anew at the Last Supper.

The sections between the passion predictions take community problems as their theme: in the transfiguration, Jesus is legitimized as teacher: "Listen to him!" (9:7). Since the transfiguration is an anticipation of Easter, the teaching that follows is aimed at the post-Easter community and deals with its problems, beginning and ending with the problem of cooperation in the community and in the middle that of the family in the household. Cooperation is a problem in every community: the disciples' dispute over rank is criticized, and the demand to overcome oneself (by abandonment of hand, foot, and eye) is emphasized in harsh sayings. Everything is to be at the service of peace in the community! (9:33-50). Problems in the household include marriage, children, property, and the renunciation of possessions. Besides locally resident Christians, who are married, we glimpse here a different manner of life: disciples leave their wives, reject children, give up their possessions (10:1-31). Finally, cooperation in the community is thematized again in closing. Martyrdom is the only place of honor Jesus has to bestow. The rule of service in the community is that the first should be prepared to become last (10:35-45).

Jesus' teaching in Jerusalem (11:1—13:37): Jesus provokes his opponents by two symbolic actions. His entry into Jerusalem provokes the political, his cleansing of the temple the priestly power-brokers. He justifies his actions with his discourse on authority and his parable of the vinedressers. Jesus teaches openly in the temple and out of public sight on the Mount of Olives. In the temple he engages in controversy dialogues with his opponents (about authority, taxes, and the resurrection). With regard to the twofold love commandment he even achieves agreement with a sympathetic scribe. At the end is his teaching for the people who are sympathetic to him: on the son of David and the Messiah, the woe against the scribes, the example of the poor widow (12:35-44). On the Mount of Olives he teaches the "Synoptic apocalypse" exclusively for his disciples and prepares them for the time after his death. It will be a time of suffering for them, too (13:1-37).

Jesus' suffering in Jerusalem (14:1—16:8): The passion narrative is divided into a farewell portion in which Jesus is alone with his followers and a judicial section in which he is arrested and executed. His isolation increases: first Jesus is betrayed by a disciple, then three of his disciples fall asleep in Gethsemane, and finally they all flee. Stories about women bring some light into this darkness: a woman anoints Jesus and others follow him to the cross. Beneath the cross a Gentile centurion acknowledges him: "Truly this man was God's Son!" (15:39). An angel corrects this statement by proclaiming the Easter message at the tomb: the one who died *was* not God's Son. "He *is* risen" (16:6). God is victorious over death. Only after Easter can the disciples publicly proclaim Jesus as the Son of God.

Time and Place of Mark's Gospel

Mark's Gospel was written shortly after 70 C.E. Jesus predicts the destruction of the temple in Mark 13:1-2 just as it had occurred: only the "buildings" of the temple (*hieron* in 13:1) will be destroyed; the temple platform still remained. The temple building would not be rebuilt. Before the Sanhedrin, in contrast, Jesus is accused of a quite different version of this prediction as "false witness": that he would destroy the temple (*naos* in the singular!) and rebuild it in three days (14:58). In Mark's Gospel *naos* always means the inner sanctuary in contrast to the whole temple complex (*hieron*).[1] Thus this prediction applies only to the central sanctuary. It is, in fact, false: not Jesus, but the Romans destroyed the temple, and not only the sanctuary itself but all the buildings on the temple platform. A new temple would never be built. The reader still has 13:1-2 in his or her ears. There Jesus has correctly predicted that all the "great buildings" (in the plural!), but not the whole sanctuary with its platform, would be destroyed. The formulation in the passive leaves open who will destroy the temple, so that it could also be the Romans. Nothing is said about a rebuilding. Jesus' words in 13:2 thus correspond precisely to the reality, while the supposed false statement in 14:58 contradicts it. If we (like the Markan evangelist) regard 13:1-2 as a correction of 14:58, it would be a correction that adapts Jesus' saying to the actual events. In that case, however, the temple has already been destroyed. Some exegetes believe nevertheless, with good arguments, that Mark wrote shortly before 70 C.E., because in Mark 13:1-2 Jesus does predict the destruction of the temple, but in answering the disciples' question about when that would happen he nowhere refers clearly to the destruction of the temple (13:3-37).

The Markan evangelist wrote in Syria. It is true that ancient church tradition says that he wrote in Rome and identifies the author with the "John Mark" from Jerusalem who in 1 Peter 5:13 is associated with Rome (= Babylon). But the information about Palestine is too erroneous on one point to have come from a Jerusalemite. Gerasa, according to Mark 5:1-20, lies on the lake of Genesareth, while in fact it was about fifty-five kilometers south of it. However, the author could not have been living too far from Palestine, for he is still familiar with oral Jesus traditions such as were more likely to be circulating in the neighborhood of Palestine than in distant Rome. He anchors Jesus in a rural world that is also his own, for the lake of Genesareth, for him, is a "sea," not a "lake" as it is for the more worldly wise Luke. A Jerusalemite who had reached Rome would not have spoken in Rome of a Galilean "sea." Also against a Roman location is that he equates the smallest coin of the Roman Empire, the quadrans, with two still smaller coins (Mark 12:42). This was true only of the Herodian coinage in the East, while in Rome the quadrans itself was considered the smallest coin (Plutarch, *Cicero* 99.5). The evangelist is thus familiar with the Herodian coinage, which circulated only in the East, but does not orient himself to Roman usage. Since in Syria also the quadrans was known as the smallest coin (Matt 5:26), it could very well have served to explain the Herodian coinage to a Syrian readership. He promises the disciples persecution by governors and kings (Mark 13:9). But those existed only in the provinces, with Roman client kings located primarily in the East. He also shares traditions of Syrian Christianity before and during the time of Paul: the concept of the "gospel" (*euangelion*), the Last Supper tradition, and the genre of the vice list (Mark 7:21-23), all of them traditions and forms that are also found in Paul as existing tradition and that Paul would have adopted from his Syrian home communities (for example, in Damascus and Antioch).

Ancient church tradition saw Mark as the interpreter of Peter, writing down from memory his traditions about Jesus. It refers to Papias (beginning of the second century C.E.), who supposedly received this information in turn (Eusebius, *Hist. eccl.* 3.39.15). Those who choose to believe this tradition[2] can point out that in Mark's Gospel Peter does in fact play a central role. He is the first disciple mentioned, and the last (Mark 1:16; 16:7), and he appears at crucial points: his confession of Jesus as the Messiah, the transfiguration, and the passion narrative. But this is a fragmented Peter tradition: Peter's mother-in-law is healed, but where is Peter's wife, who after Easter traveled through the world with him (1 Cor 9:5)? The transfiguration on the mountain could be the vestige of Peter's Easter vision (Mark 9:2-13). But it has become a preliminary revelation during the life of Jesus in which Peter lacks a correct understanding. Nowhere is the first Easter appearance credited to Peter, not even in Mark 16:7, where all the disciples (together with the women?) are promised an encounter with the Risen One in Galilee. The kernel of truth in the Papias tradition could consist in the fact that the Gospel of Mark belongs to a stream of tradition that goes back to Peter. Some things may recall attitudes in Peter's circle: the mission to Israel is primary, but the Gentile mission is recognized (Mark 7:27; cf. Gal 2:1-10). The food regulations are invalid, but that is to be taught (and practiced?) only in secret (Mark 7:14-23; cf. Gal 2:11-14). The message of salvation is called "gospel": in Galatians 2:7 the "gospel" for the uncircumcised is also assigned to Peter and in 1 Corinthians 15:1, 11 the "gospel" is a message common to Paul and the other apostles, including Peter. At the center of this gospel, according to 1 Corinthians 15:3-11, is the crucifixion and resurrection of the Messiah. That is the goal to which the whole of Mark's Gospel is also directed. Now, there were Peter traditions in many places. He was certainly much better known in Syria than in the West. It is demonstrable that he had followers in Antioch and Corinth (1 Cor 1:12). The fact that the Markan evangelist has been made his interpreter could be a conclusion drawn from the Gospel of Mark itself: this evangelist often uses Aramaic words and expressions and sometimes explains them (Mark 3:17; 5:41; 7:11, 34; 10:46; 14:36; 15:22; 15:34). This conclusion was perhaps supported by the fact that Mark's Gospel circulated very early as a "gospel *according to* Mark," for that unusual superscription is attested in antiquity only for translations. According to the Papias tradition, the Gospel of Matthew must have had a different superscription, because it was indeed considered a translation, but Matthew was the author who was translated and *not* the translator. Papias writes that others translated it as each was able. Hence there may be a kernel of truth in the Papias tradition. Even the name "Mark" could be accurate. If the name had been invented later, the Gospel of Mark would have been attributed to an apostle. When Papias says critically that Mark did not present the traditions in their correct order, that conclusion could have been drawn from Mark's Gospel itself: for example, Mark presumes the arrest of the Baptizer already in Mark 1:14, but only tells of it in retrospect in Mark 6:14-29. There is no Easter appearance, but instead he presents, by way of anticipation, such an appearance (in the transfiguration) in the midst of Jesus' life (Mark 9:2-10). He says nothing at the beginning of his gospel about Jesus' birth and hometown, but in Mark 6:1-5 he simply presumes a hometown for Jesus without explicitly identifying it with Nazareth. Finally, the Gospel of Mark reports a mission of the disciples (Mark 6:7-13) before they have recognized Jesus as the Messiah. A Christian reader might have regarded that as "illogical." Thus the Papias tradition need not necessarily have had our Gospel of Matthew or Gospel of John in view for comparison when it attributes a bad ordering of the traditions to the Gospel of Mark. On the whole, one cannot take the Papias tradition literally in all respects. Too much is uncertain. Thus the superscription "*according to* Mark" could also have originated secondarily on the basis of the tradition that the Gospel of Mark was a representation of Peter's recollections produced by a translator.

In terms of its theological-historical location, the Gospel of Mark may be located within Gentile Christianity. This gospel culminates in the recognition of Jesus as "Son of God" by a Gentile centurion (15:39). The evangelist now and then explains Jewish customs for Gentile readers (7:3-4). But his gospel also reveals considerable affinity to Judaism, a monotheistic sensibility that was lost on Gentile Christians. Mark knows that the worship of a human being as Son of God is a problem. A comparison between Jesus in Mark's Gospel and Agrippa I in Acts is revealing. Agrippa accepts being reverenced as God and is punished by death (Acts 12:19-23). Jesus, in contrast, refuses to be divinized by human beings. He suppresses the demonic voices that call him "Son of God" (Mark 3:11-12). His exaltation and revelation belong to God alone. Mark also expresses this positively. In 12:29 Jesus utters Israel's monotheistic confession of God as Lord alone. A scribe agrees: "he is one, and besides him there is no other" (12:32). But in Mark's own time Christians were already worshiping Jesus as "Lord" together with God. Therefore Mark immediately quotes Psalm 110:1: "The Lord (= God) said to my Lord (= Jesus), 'Sit at my right hand . . .'" (12:36). Beside the one God the only one who can be "Lord" is the one whom God has exalted, and that is what happens in the raising of the Crucified One. The traditional interpretation of the "messianic secret" is thus correct: in Mark's Gospel the worship of Jesus as Son of God, which was originally tied to his resurrection, was projected back into the life of Jesus. Jesus was the Son of God, but during his lifetime he was so only secretly.[3] Jesus and his followers had to wait for God's decisive action in order to be able to acknowledge him as Son of God. They thus averted the suspicion that Jesus attributed divine status to himself of his own accord. That would have been blasphemy (2:6-7; 14:64).

Just as in terms of the history of theology the Gospel of Mark stood on the boundary between Jews and Gentiles, so in terms of social history it stands on the border between itinerant charismatics and local congregations. It primarily collects the traditions that had always penetrated as far as the local communities and the people, but at the same time it works with the traditions of the itinerant charismatics in such a way that it makes them more easily accessible to all Christians.

Narrative traditions extended quite soon beyond Jesus' followers: narratively framed apophthegms, passion narrative, miracle stories. The external perspectives they contain were more heterogeneous than the image yielded by the Sayings Source. It was the service of the Gospel of Mark to have combined these heterogeneous traditions. Miracle stories and the passion narrative are here tied together by the motif of the secret. The picture in the miracle stories is, for this gospel, not the whole of the revelation about Jesus. The whole picture emerges only when one follows Jesus on the way to the cross and Easter. The apophthegms are integrated as Mark uses them to depict conflicts between Jesus and his opponents and so creates an arc of tension that points toward the passion. After the first cycle of controversy dialogues, his opponents plan his execution (Mark 3:6). After the second, he is crucified.

But Mark also integrates the traditions of the itinerant charismatic group into his gospel and makes them accessible to his communities. He expands the concept of "discipleship" in such a way that it applies also to local communities. The toll collector Levi is a disciple (2:13-17). He invites Jesus into his house and holds a banquet there. Levi is not in the list of the twelve disciples who are always to be with Jesus (3:13-19). Mark thus indicates that Levi remained in his house. He is to be a figure of identification for members of the local communities who did not share Jesus' itinerant existence. When, at his banquet, many "follow" his invitation, "followership/discipleship" becomes participation in dinners that were part of the life of every local community. A further expansion of the concept of discipleship is found at the center and at the end of the gospel: here discipleship is defined as readiness to suffer (8:34-35) and care for others (15:41). This was true both of itinerant charismatics and of local communities.

Jesus' disciples are joined by suffering: after the first passion prediction he challenges the disciples: "If any want to become my followers, let them deny themselves and take up their cross and follow me" (8:34). Mark addresses Christians who are being persecuted (13:9-13). Their identity will at some point be unavoidably recognized, just as Jesus' identity was recognized. At some point they will stand before judges and have to confess themselves Christians, just as Jesus confessed his messianic status before his judges (14:61-62). When at the beginning the Son of God wants to remain in secret he gives his followers a good conscience if they do not unnecessarily push themselves into the public sphere and provoke conflicts.

It may be that the Gospel of Mark also contains a critique of other concepts of what it means to be Christian: the disciples, in following Jesus, reveal themselves as blind and lacking understanding. They understand neither Jesus' majesty (6:52) nor his humility (8:32-33; 10:32); they comprehend neither the miracle stories nor the passion story—that is, both groups of texts that are suppressed or absent in the Sayings Source. It could be that in the incomprehending disciples there is a critique of the type of itinerant charismatics who are behind Q.[4] That is not certain. In any case, the uncomprehending disciples provide a foil for the true understanding of Jesus to which Mark wants to lead the readers.

Genre: A Biography with a Public Claim

The model for the gospel was the ancient biography.[5] But we also recognize that it was written by and for people who were familiar with prophetic books. Its content is a prophetic message: the "gospel," whose story the Gospel of Mark intends to trace back to its "beginning." This message is prophetic: it announces the coming of the reign of God (Mark 1:14-15). The message is more important than the prophet; hence his biography begins with his call. However, that this follows the pattern of an ancient biography is evident from the fact that the traditions are organized in a plausible chronological and geographical framework, and that his death is interpreted in terms of the conflicts in his life. All that is lacking in the prophetic books. The "life story" of a prophet is here told in the form of a biography. Two objections may be raised against this thesis of a prophetic tradition restructured in terms of ancient biography: (1) there is no birth story, as would be proper to a biography, and (2) the Gospel of Mark consists entirely of individual pericopes.

The beginning, with the appearance of the Baptizer and the baptism of the protagonist, is in fact unusual for a biography. But this is a special biography about the life and activity of the Son of God. For Mark, Jesus first became Son of God when he was baptized. Since Mark has information about Jesus' origins and family (6:1-6) and could easily have begun with them, his beginning with the appearance of the Baptizer and Jesus' baptism resulted from a deliberate decision. He is writing for Christians, for whom their own real lives only began at baptism. Therefore, with this audience, he can count on a sympathetic reception of his "incomplete" biography. Just as their true lives had begun at baptism, so they let Jesus' life begin with his baptism. If they knew the Old Testament prophetic books they would have taken no offense at this abbreviated portrayal. Mark 1:1 begins with the expression "beginning of the gospel (*archē tou euangeliou*) of Jesus Christ [the Son of God]." At the beginning of the book of the prophet Hosea, with which in the LXX the prophetic books began, the sayings were introduced with a related formula: "beginning of the words of the LORD (*archē logou kyriou*) to Hosea" (Hos 1:2). Then follows a commission from God containing a narrative: Hosea is to marry a prostitute. The readers and hearers of Mark's Gospel were familiar with such prophetic writings, which began with the word of God coming to a human being, nothing being said about the prophet's previous history. In addition, in the biographies of pagan antiquity the accent was always on the public actions of the person, not his or her beginnings and youthful development.

The second objection to regarding Mark's Gospel as a biography is founded on the character of this gospel as a collection. It seems like an awkward assemblage of individual traditions. Such collections of sayings, mixed with a few narratives, are certainly familiar to us from the prophetic books. But Mark's Gospel is more: it is a little work of art that skillfully arranges traditional stories one after another and, by means of motifs in the individual stories, creates an overarching tension for the whole narrative. Pericopes having their own point become parts of a coherent narrative. In this way all the pericopes acquire an underlying surplus of meaning. They are all about the Son of God, even when people do not notice it. In principle, it is possible to think of pericope literature as biography. This is evident from Lucian of Samosata's *Demonax*. But here the mysterious double structure through which smaller and larger genres are overlaid is unique. The Gospel of Mark, unlike the Sayings Source, is not a prophetic book whose form is exploded by the message of a unique prophet. It is the tradition of one who is more than a prophet, and that tradition has been reshaped into the form of biography.

Therefore it has rightly become a consensus among scholars that the Gospel of Mark is a variant of the flexible ancient genre of biography.[6] This genre does not emerge from the Jewish world, where there were only two biographical texts: Philo's *vita* of Moses, written to make Moses known to non-Jews,[7] and Josephus's *vita*, which is not a real autobiography and was written by Josephus to defend himself against the accusation that he compromised himself in the war against the Romans. Neither of these writings is addressed solely to Jews.

Precisely the same is true of the gospels. Although the historical Jesus addressed himself only to Jews, all the gospels extend his proclamation to Gentile audiences. In Mark the Gentile mission begins already in Jesus' lifetime. There a healed man begins to preach in the Decapolis about Jesus' deeds (Mark 5:19-20).[8] Matthew's Gospel programmatically restricts Jesus' earthly activity to Israel (Matt 10:6; 15:24) but ends with a universal command to mission in which it is deliberately emphasized that everything Jesus taught applies to all peoples.[9] The Gospel of Luke shows in its continuation, the Acts of the Apostles, how the universal command to mission is carried out. While Paul's letters from the start are addressed to Gentile communities (but only to individual congregations), Jesus' proclamation was addressed to all Jews, yet in the gospels was expanded secondarily to all Gentiles (i.e., all people). Only in the redactional layer of the gospels was this universalizing of Jesus' message fully developed. The addressing of the gospels to all "Gentiles" and the appropriation of the literary form of the biography that was familiar in "Gentile culture" are necessarily related.

This universalizing of Jesus' message is associated in the oldest gospel with the concept of "evangelium/good news" (*euangelion*). Mark introduced it into the Jesus tradition. In two of the passages he created, he emphasizes its universality: one says that the "good news" is to be preached "to all nations" (Mark 13:10); the other that it is to be proclaimed "in the whole world" (Mark 14:9). At the time when Mark's Gospel originated, when someone spoke of "good news" (*euangelia*) for the whole world the thought evoked was that of a new emperor. According to Josephus, the ascent of Vespasian as emperor, which again brought stability to the empire shaken by war, was celebrated in the year 69—that is, precisely at the time when the Gospel of Mark (ca. 70 C.E.) was created—as *euangelia*.[10] Probably the *euangelion* in the Gospel of Mark was an anti-gospel to this political gospel.[11] It says that it is not the Flavians who have saved the world, but the crucified King of the Jews, whom God has raised from the dead. Even before Mark, the concept of "gospel" designated the preaching *about* Jesus as a ruler from the line of David (Rom 1:1-6) and as the crucified Messiah (1 Cor 15:1-11).[12]

But the concept has a second meaning also. Mark probably introduced it everywhere into the Jesus tradition[13] and extended it to the proclamation made *by* Jesus (1:14). Jesus' preaching of the reign of God is "gospel" (*euangelion*). Thus for him what Jesus did and taught is just as much "gospel" as what God did in him in the cross and resurrection. This second meaning of "gospel" as Jesus' message about the coming of the reign of God links to the second root of the concept of "gospel/good news" in the Old Testament:[14] Jesus appears in the role of a prophet like the "messenger of good news" in Deutero-Isaiah (Isa 52:7; 61:1-11; cf. Rom 10:15-16, where Isa 52:7 is quoted). We should not set up an opposition between this second source and the derivation from imperial propaganda or the conscious opposition of the gospel to the political "gospels" of its time, since even Isaiah's messenger of good news brought a political message about the end of the exile and the liberation of Israel.

In both variants the concept of "gospel" acquires an additional significance through its opposition to the Flavians. The noun "gospel" is attested primarily in the imperial ideology. Even with Paul we find it once in opposition to the imperial cult. In Romans 1:3-4 he describes the proclamation of Jesus, son of David, Son of God, and ruler of the world as gospel—perhaps in ironic derivation from the apotheosis of Claudius in October 54. Jesus was "really" ruler of the world, not merely through a state-supportive fiction.[15] Was not the point of Mark's "anti-gospel" against the rise of the Flavians also that Christians should not bow down before the Roman emperor, but rather the centurion, as representative of the Roman superpower, bows before the crucified Jesus?

Thus, the Gospel of Mark adopts the form of biography from the pagan world and fills it with the content of the proclamation of a ruler as good news (*euangelion*). Jesus is the royal Messiah whose entry into power is proclaimed as "gospel," as joyful news. The other Synoptic Gospels follow: Matthew's shows at the beginning, by means of a genealogy, that Jesus is a Jewish royal son, and it proclaims him at the end as ruler of the world to whom all power in heaven and on earth is given (Matt 1:1-18; 28:18). The Gospel of Luke sees the son of David from Bethlehem as the counterpart of the emperor. Here he, like an emperor, ascends after his death and is received into the divine world (Luke 2:1-21; 24:50-53).

The twofold character of the concept of gospel fits well with our literary-historical classification of the Gospel of Mark. The early Christians first attempted to collect traditions about Jesus in the form of a prophetic book, something familiar to them. The oldest of these attempts is the Sayings Source. Even there the Jesus tradition exploded the form of a prophetic book. But in Mark's Gospel the tradition of the prophet Jesus is shaped even more firmly according to pagan models: the evangelist writes a biography. The image of a prophet is still influential: he does without a birth story, beginning with Jesus' commissioning; he summarizes the essentials as a message of good news brought by Jesus as a prophet—but he himself is its essential content, as crucified king and Son of God. This last does not fit any prophet's life.

In the gospels, then, a group stemming from Judaism makes use of literary forms adopted from non-Jews in order to address non-Jews. A tradition that people had attempted without much success to edit in analogy to a prophetic book was transformed into an ancient biography. To that extent we are dealing with an intercultural literature, one that crosses boundaries between peoples. Even in its creative first phase, then, this is not "primitive literature" in the sense of having arisen on the soil of early Christianity before it had any contact with the world, as Franz Overbeck thought. Instead, it is part of Jewish-Hellenistic literature arising out of the soil of the Septuagint.

We can distinguish two currents within Jewish-Hellenistic literature.[16] One adheres closely to the Septuagint in style and form: it includes novellas like Tobit and Esther or 1 Maccabees.[17] Another stream of tradition sought to follow the forms of elevated pagan literature; this included the tragedian Ezekiel, the poet Pseudo-Phocylides, but above all the religious philosopher Philo and the historian Josephus.[18]

Based on its language and style, early Christian literature belongs to the first line of tradition; based on its adaptation of pagan forms, however, it belongs to the second. Even in Philo and Josephus we found the beginnings of a biographical form—but with an important difference: what for these Jewish aristocrats was a form of expression of a literary upper class we encounter in early Christianity as a literature for ordinary people. In adopting biography, the first Christians took over a form of expression proper to the upper class. They even took hold of a form of communication belonging to the imperial upper class when they called its content a "gospel." In doing so, they crossed boundaries both upward and downward: by placing a crucified man at the center they offered an identification to all those lower on the social scale.[19] The same is true of the general tendencies of early Christianity: to a downward transfer of the values of the upper class, which are now adopted by ordinary people—for example, when the first Christians made their own the humane ideal of the ruler as one who brings peace (Matt 5:9).[20] When, in addition, they emphatically turned with their "gospel" to all nations (or all Gentiles), their literature became "intercultural." This fits with the opening of an originally Jewish group to non-Jews, an opening associated with Paul and with the second beginning of early Christian literature.

However, the first beginning of early Christian literature clearly lies with Jesus: his preaching and his work. The preaching was first written down in the Sayings Source—according to the model of a prophetic book, although the prophet depicted in this prophetic book was far more than a prophet. Jesus' work and suffering were first recorded in the Gospel of Mark, on the model of a biography (something well known in the non-Jewish world). We do not know who did it. Papias traces both these beginnings to an apostle, Matthew, and an apostle's disciple, Mark. He also sees clearly that the tradition of the words had a much closer affinity to the Jewish world than the Gospel of Mark. The words had to be translated. The Gospel of Mark is itself based on a process of translation. It is not impossible that Papias accurately retained for us the historic names of the two oldest Christian writers—even though we have to reckon with subsequent concretizations that grew up around these traditions.

B. The Charismatic Phase of Paul's Epistolary Literature

Many works treat the letters of Paul as the oldest written sources for early Christianity before the gospels.[1] But the oral Jesus tradition is older than Paul, and fragments of it are quoted by Paul himself. If we consider oral as well as written "literature" there is no reason to begin with Paul, in contradiction to this clear chronological order. Apart from that, Q could be just as old as the letters of Paul. The oldest *surviving* written document need not be the most ancient writing of all. The Synoptic apocalypse, that is, the tradition behind Mark 13, could stem in its written form from the Caligula crisis of 38/39 and be older than the oldest Pauline letter, the one to the Thessalonians, written about 51 C.E.! The decisive reason for treating the origins of the gospels before the letters of Paul, however, lies in the literary-historical conception of this proposal, which has a biographical component: the two basic forms of the New Testament literature rest on two prominent charismatic figures. Jesus gave the impetus to the construction of a tradition that led to the Sayings Source and the Gospel of Mark. Paul created the form of the community letter. If one holds this personal factor in high regard, one must begin with Jesus and the history of his activity before treating Paul.

4 The Historical Conditions for Paul's Letters

The second literary-historical impulse for the origins of the New Testament comes from Paul, who developed the private letter of friendship into a community letter.[1] This took place in Asia Minor and Europe, where letters and letter collections were a familiar phenomenon. Here his letters were later published as a collection—without any model in Judaism.[2] His letters were instruments of the Gentile mission and not least weapons for its defense against attacks. Without a counter-mission against him, Paul would scarcely have developed the community letter within the space of only five to seven years.

Paul was called to be an apostle in about 32 C.E. He understood his call from the outset as a commission to the Gentile mission. Immediately after his conversion he engaged in missions in Arabia, then in Syria and the southern parts of Asia Minor; only after his separation from the community in Antioch did he engage in missions in Europe and the Aegean. In terms of literary history it is a mystery why his surviving literary production began so late—only after eighteen years of missionary activity. All his letters were written in the Aegean region, or possibly in Rome as well. Had Paul written no letters previously, when he was a missionary from Antioch to the East? Hardly! First Thessalonians cannot be his first letter. He doubles some stylistic elements of the letter that must have been familiar to his scribe already. What we experience before our eyes in this letter and the other Pauline letters is how Paul developed the personal letter into an instrument for linking congregations together. The fact that the letter is the second fundamental form of early Christian literature is due to him.

The period of origin of the epistolary literature—the 50s C.E.—points to the conditions in which Paul's letters originated. They arose out of a crisis in his mission that made it necessary for him to develop the community letter in order to secure his mission. The crisis developed on three fronts:

(1) Conflicts with the non-Christian world led to Paul's having to flee or to his imprisonment. Therefore (because of his flight) in 1 Thessalonians and (because of his imprisonment) in Philippians and Philemon he could make contact with his communities only through letters. The fact of imprisonment is encountered later also, in the fictive Pauline letters (Colossians; Ephesians; 2 Timothy). (2) Conflicts with a counter-mission led to energetic interventions by means of letters in Galatia, Philippi, and Corinth. The fact that Paul and his mission were conflictual has given us these letters. Likewise his last testament, Romans, is shaped by his desire to secure his work against opponents and misunderstandings beyond his possible death. (3) We obtain a deeper insight into conflicts in his communities through these letters, especially 1 Corinthians. These were consequences of the Pauline preaching itself. Now Paul's own enthusiasm had become a problem; there were tensions between groups in the community that were associated with tensions between the community and Paul.

The place of origin of the epistolary literature is no accident. That all the letters were written in Europe could be connected with the fact that letters were a familiar form of literature there. We may think of the letters of Plato, Cicero, the Cynics, and Seneca. The Old Testament, in contrast, offered no suggestions for making letters into texts for the grounding of communities! While it contains letter forms, quotations from letters, and allusions to letters, it holds no letter in independent form.

The following sketch of a literary history of the Pauline letters is thus shaped by this basic idea: Early Christian epistolary literature was evoked by a crisis in which Paul discovered the letter as an instrument for the direction of communities. His letters are expanded private epistles. We can see in them a development from occasional writings directed to particular situations (1 Thessalonians) to the beginnings of early Christian publications (Romans).

The literary-historical relationship to the line of tradition stemming from Jesus can be summarized as follows: the Sayings Source and the Gospel of Mark document the tradition of Jesus' sayings and narratives about him; in Q it is handed on from the perspective of the itinerant charismatics, and in Mark from the perspective of local communities. Q is Jewish Christian, while Mark's Gospel is Gentile Christian, but still close to the mentality of Jewish Christianity. Paul, in contrast, represents the Gentile mission. In his letters we directly experience the interaction between an itinerant missionary (Paul) and his local congregations. Here the two perspectives found separately in Q and Mark are reduced to one (Figure 2).

Figure 2: Jesus Tradition and Pauline Letters

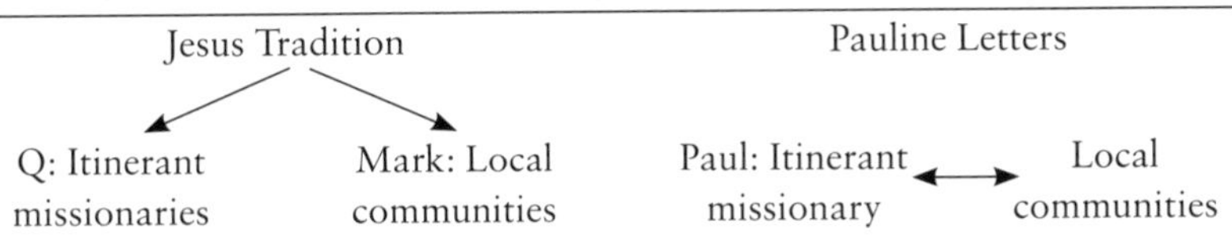

An important difference between the Jesus and Paul traditions is also that Q and Mark are "collected writings." They consist of small units that have been integrated into a framing genre through redactional work. These small units arose independently of the framing genre and are still discernible as independent traditions. The genre of the collected writing is overlaid on the forms of the small units and give these writings, especially in Mark, a mysterious depth. The framing genre and the small forms both retain their formative power.

The Pauline letters, on the other hand, are "whole writings." They do indeed draw on oral traditions, but they only occasionally have recourse to them. Most of the pre-Pauline units (with the exception of the hymn in Philippians) are scarcely imaginable as independent traditions. They are not forms, but formulae. They do not consist of complete texts, but of brief expressions and phrases. The letters as a whole are complete written creations and far more than collections and redactions of oral traditions. The formative power here belongs only to the genre of the whole writing: the letter. It establishes a framing genre in which the beginning and ending are more strictly regulated. What lies in the middle, in contrast, is variable, even though there are two tendencies and formal traditions in Paul's letters (see below). The transfer of the form-critical search for oral traditions to the letters was fruitful, but it suggests an inappropriate picture.

5 The Pre-Pauline Oral Tradition

For Paul also, oral tradition precedes the letters, and his letters, even after their composition, remained embedded in oral communication. They were read aloud, since many members of the communities could not read. Paul knows Jesus traditions and is dependent on early Christian traditions. Overall, where we encounter the same formulae and expressions in early Christian literature independent of Paul, we may conclude to a stream of oral tradition.

Jesus Traditions in Paul

What would we know about Jesus if we had nothing but Paul's letters? More than nothing, but astonishingly little. Of his origins we would know that he came from a Davidic family (Rom 1:3-4), had a number of brothers (1 Cor 9:5) including one named James (Gal 1:19; cf. 1 Cor 15:7) who later played a leading role in the community. Of his teaching we would be sure of only two sayings of Jesus that Paul cites explicitly: they are always rules with normative force—perhaps the reason why he here appeals to the authority of the *kyrios*. In both cases he represents a small deviation from the original meaning of Jesus' sayings: like Jesus, he forbids a husband and wife to divorce (1 Cor 7:10), but he tolerates their separation with the aim of reconciliation. In the case of marriages between pagans and Christians he permits divorce if the non-Christian partner desires it. He quotes Jesus' advice to missionaries to get their living from the gospel (1 Cor 9:14), but interprets this command of the Lord as a privilege of the missionary to be supported by the community, and he is proud that he has refused this privilege for himself. In the context of 1 Corinthians 9 there is an echo of other key sayings from Luke 9 and 10: apostle, authority, work, reward, harvest.[3]

It is possible that Paul knew other Jesus traditions that yield an explicit reference to Jesus: (1) He speaks of the law of Christ (Gal 6:2) that is fulfilled by bearing others' burdens. He has previously quoted the love commandment (Lev 19:18 = Gal 5:14). The law of Christ could mean the love commandment for him. (2) In Romans 14:14 he probably alludes to Mark 7:15: "I know and am persuaded in the Lord Jesus that nothing is unclean in itself; but it is unclean for anyone who thinks it unclean." (3) There is some dispute over a saying "of the Lord" in 1 Thess 4:15/16-18, which could also be a prophetic word spoken in the name of the Risen Lord, since Paul speaks in the third person about "the Lord": "For this we declare to you by the word of the Lord, that we who are alive, who are left until the coming of the Lord, will by no means precede those who have died. . . ."

Other implicit references to sayings of Jesus, without specific mention of his name, are concentrated in Romans 12–14: the general paraenesis is dominated by the love commandment (chs. 12–13), the special paraenesis (14:1–15:13) by the command not to judge one another—thus by the two primary commands in the Sermon on the Plain. Here (Jesus) traditions could in fact have been the structural elements of the text. The admonitions recall the ethos of the Sermon on the Mount: "Bless those who persecute you; bless and do not curse them" (Rom 12:14); "Do not repay anyone evil for evil" (Rom 12:17); "Do not be overcome by evil, but overcome evil with good" (Rom 12:21); "Why do you pass judgment on your brother or sister? Or you, why do you despise your brother or sister?" (Rom 14:10). There may be, in Romans 13:7, an echo of the dispute over taxes in Mark 12:17: "Pay to all what is due them—taxes to whom taxes are due, revenue to whom revenue is due, respect to whom respect is due, honor to whom honor is due." The warning against putting stumbling blocks in the path of another echoes in Romans 14:13-14: "Let us therefore no longer pass judgment on one another, but resolve instead never to put a stumbling block or hindrance in the way of another" (cf. Mark 9:42). In 1 Thessalonians 5:2 Paul uses the phrase about the "thief in the night" that we encounter in (genuine?) Jesus sayings (Matt 24:43; Luke 12:39). It is not marked as a saying of Jesus, but it is probably genuine Jesus tradition as reinterpreted by Paul!

Paul is aware of parts of the story of Jesus' passion: Jesus celebrates a last meal during which he interprets his death as an offering for the sake of others (1 Cor 11:23-26). When in this context Paul speaks of the night in which Jesus was handed over, he indicates that he also knows a tradition about Judas's betrayal. According to 1 Corinthians 15:7 he seems to prefer the Johannine chronology of Jesus' last days: Jesus is slaughtered as a Paschal lamb, and therefore could not have celebrated the Passover meal. He also knows about Jesus' being mistreated (Rom 15:3). He is certainly aware of his death on the cross. His burial is briefly mentioned in 1 Corinthians 15:4. Thus, Paul must have known passion traditions that included the Last

Supper, betrayal, mistreatment and insult, crucifixion, and burial. But these need not have been the Synoptic traditions. Regarding the resurrection he offers not only formulaic expressions but also a list of witnesses based on old tradition. Here he mentions three individual appearances, two group appearances, and a mass appearance before five hundred brothers and sisters (1 Cor 15:3-8).

On the whole, however, Paul does not say much about Jesus. Why this silence? The first reason we may mention is biographical: Paul did not know the earthly Jesus. Other apostles drew their authority from the fact that, as Jesus' disciples, they were handing on his words. Paul could not compete with them in that regard. He devalues their knowledge of the earthly Jesus as knowledge from "a human point of view" (2 Cor 5:16). But Paul, like the other apostles, had seen the Risen One. In that he was their equal. No wonder he presents faith in the Risen One as central!

Add to this a social-historical reason: the words of the earthly Jesus were of such a radical nature that they would have been out of place in his communities. Jesus called his followers to abandon everything. Paul admonishes people to remain in the roles in which they had been called (1 Cor 7:17-18). Jesus promised toll collectors and prostitutes that they would enter the reign of God ahead of the pious (Matt 21:31). Paul excluded the immoral from the reign of God (1 Cor 6:9). Jesus commanded his disciples to abandon acquisitions and property (Matt 10:9; 6:25-34). Paul is proud that he supports himself by his own labor (1 Thess 2:9; 4:11). Paul's ethical teachings are oriented to the needs of local communities, while Jesus' ethos is shaped by itinerant radicalism.[4]

We may also mention form-critical reasons: Very few sayings of Jesus are quoted in early Christian letters—not even in places where the gospels were known (cf. the Johannine letters with the Gospel of John or the letters of Ignatius with the Gospel of Matthew). The letters differ in function from the Jesus tradition.

What may be conclusive, however, is a theological reason, namely, the fundamental monotheistic problem of the new faith: through the Easter appearances, Jesus had been experienced as a divine being. That was only supportable in Judaism by excluding any possible suspicion that Jesus himself had claimed that position. He could only owe it to divine action. Paul was convinced of that. For someone crucified and dead, any thought of a self-apotheosis is out of the question. God alone had exalted him above every name. While in the Sayings Source the temptation story had insured that any suspicion of a self-apotheosis on Jesus' part was excluded, Paul achieved the same goal by concentrating on the cross and resurrection.

Pre-Pauline Christological Formulae

Paul sketches only broad strokes of a picture of the earthly Jesus. He has clearer ideas about a mythical preexistent being from heaven who was crucified on earth and exalted to God. This "Christ myth" is retained in some pre-Pauline formulae. At its center is what God has done and said through Jesus, especially through the cross and resurrection. Both are embedded in a history beginning with preexistence and reaching its goal with Jesus' exaltation. For Paul this kerygmatic Christ, not the historical Jesus, is the object of faith. But he had already received this Christ-faith in his tradition; he did not create it. This is shown by the many pre-Pauline formulae and expressions in the whole of which a much broader stream of oral tradition is visible, as it is in Paul.

Some pre-Pauline formulae concern preexistence and mission: "But when the fullness of time had come, God sent his Son, born of a woman, born under the Law, in order to redeem those who were under the Law, so that we might receive adoption as children" (Gal 4:4-5); comparable to this is Romans 8:3: "God . . . by sending his own Son in the likeness of sinful flesh, and to deal with sin, he condemned sin in the flesh. . . ." Other pre-Pauline formulae deal with death and resurrection. The following schema gives an overview of these formulae (Table 6).[5]

Finally, we encounter pre-Pauline formulae about the Exalted One: In the *Kyrios* acclamation (Rom 10:9; 1 Cor 12:3; Phil 2:11) the divine name *Kyrios* is applied to Jesus. This title appears also in the *heis* acclamation (*heis* = a single one): The one *Kyrios* corresponds to the one God and is contrasted with the many *kyrioi* in heaven and on earth (1 Cor 8:6). The monotheistic formula is thus christologically augmented. The personal formula in Romans 1:3-4 is based on an adoptionist formula about Jesus' installation as Son of God because of the resurrection, but Paul understands it in the sense of his preexistence Christology. We encounter here, not accidentally, the Son of God title. Paul designates with this title both mission and preexistence—two elements coupled with closeness to God.

Thus, Paul from time to time uses both Jesus traditions and community traditions in his letters. Many traditions will be heard to echo in them, though not specifically noted. He speaks a language he did not have to invent, even if he gave it his own accents. The letters as a whole, however, unlike the gospels, are not collections of small units, but complete creations within which now and then small traditional units are adapted, their language following an early Christian tradition of language that already existed. But as a whole they represent something new. How can we classify it in literary-critical terms?

Table 6: Pre-Pauline Formulae

Death		Resurrection
Submission Formula	*Death Formula*	*Resurrection Formula*
Son	Christ	*Kyrios*
Rom 8:32	Rom 5:8; 14:15	Rom 10:9
Gal 2:20	1 Cor 8:11	2 Cor 4:14
(Gal 1:4)	1 Thess 5:10	Rom 4:24
	Redemption Formula Rom 3:25	

Rom 4:24-25:	1 Cor 15:3-5:
Jesus, our *Kyrios*,	*Christ* died
. . . who was handed over to death for our trespasses	for our sins in accordance with the scriptures, and . . . was buried,
and was raised for our justification.	and . . . was raised on the third day in accordance with the scriptures,
	and . . . appeared . . .

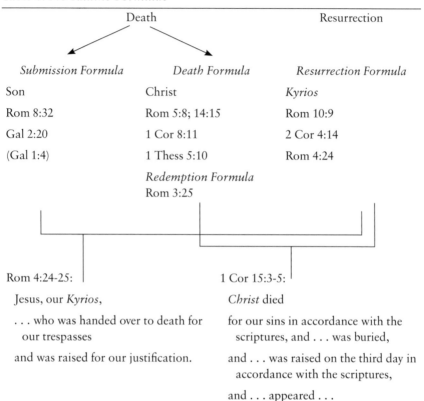

6 The Pauline Letter as Literary Form

Paul has employed forms and formulae in letters whose only fixed element was the frame. As regards the letter corpus, the ancient tradition of letter writing allowed great freedom, and Paul made use of that openness. He altered the letter of friendship by giving it an elevated claim by means of a twofold purposive shaping: on the one hand, his use of liturgical forms made it a worship text, and, on the other hand, his rhetorical shaping gave it a public character. We will first locate the Pauline community letters within the forms of ancient letters and inquire about their models and predecessors; then we will show how Paul developed the letter of friendship into a community letter by the use of liturgical formulae and public rhetoric.

The Form-Critical Location of Paul's Letters: Models

Ancient letters may be broadly divided into three groups: utility, diplomatic, and literary. Diplomatic and literary letters were meant to be public from the outset. Utility letters were unknown to the public. They include private letters as well as letters of friendship, recommendation, and consolation, but also official letters such as administrative or petitionary letters, complaints, receipts, and orders. Diplomatic and literary letters have rarely been retained in their originals. They were copied or perpetuated in inscriptions. Utility letters, on the other hand, have been retained in their papyrus originals. There are no copies. The basic form is the letter of friendship. Three aspects of their typical formulae and motifs may be distinguished: *philophronesis*, *parousia*, and *homilia*.[1]

Philophronesis, the attitude of friendship, is evident in that Paul addresses his audience with respectful epithets: "Philemon our dear friend and co-worker" (Phlm 1). It is further expressed in wishes for health (the *formula valetudinis*) and in the *proskynema* formula, the assurance of prayers and remembrance. Although Paul developed the private letter into the community letter, he holds fast to the formal language of friendly association. His addressees are friends. This is true even when he addresses and reproaches them with his apostolic authority. Through this authoritative address he continually introduces a foreign note into the letter of friendship.

A second motif is *parousia*, the presence of the author of the letter. The letter is an exchange between people who are separated. It is like a visit: it begins with a greeting and ends with a farewell. The absent person is present in his or her words. We find this idea in Paul's writing, in 1 Corinthians 5:3: "For though absent in body, I am present in spirit . . ." (cf. Col 2:5). The *parousia* motifs also include the desire to see the addressees in the future, which is found in almost all of Paul's letters (1 Cor 16:5-12; 2 Cor 12:14—13:10; Rom 15:23-29; Phil 2:19-20; Phlm 22). What is unusual in Paul is that he introduces *parousia* motifs even where, because of existing tensions, his presence is not desired.[2] In spite of conflicts, Paul wants to maintain contact—if necessary through a letter instead of his personal presence. This expansion of the *parousia* motif is foreign to the letter of friendship, and clearly marks its further development into a community letter.

The third characteristic of the letter of friendship is the *homilia*, the friendly conversation, which does not allow for any high style! A relaxed and chatty tone is considered appropriate. Paul often drops that style. The Corinthians sensed it when they called his letters "weighty and strong" (2 Cor 10:10). Paul fills his letters with a powerful rhetoric that explodes the form of the letter of friendship. This rhetoric signals to the hearers of his letters that Paul's words make a public claim. Rhetoric is the language of public discourse. It contributed to making Paul's letters a literature addressed to everyone.

All three aspects of the letter of friendship are retained in Paul's letters, and yet we sense how they take on a different character. Paul develops the letter of friendship into a community letter, with the two public forms of the ancient letter—the diplomatic and the literary—as models. A third influence comes from Jewish tradition: it seems that in that tradition there were already letters designed as directives for communities.

Diplomatic letters were often public. They were intended to be read aloud in a popular assembly and were secondarily replicated as inscriptions in stone or in historical works. Three arguments speak in favor of Paul's letters having borrowed from the ruler's letter (or diplomatic document): The increasing emphasis on titles in the *superscriptio* (prescript) in Paul's letters is striking; there are no titles at all in the earliest Pauline letters, but simply "Paul, Silvanus, and Timothy to the church of the Thessalonians" (1 Thess 1:1). In the captivity letters, Philippians and Philemon, we find titles of humility: "slaves of Christ Jesus" (Phil 1:1) or "prisoner of Christ

Jesus" (Phlm 1). The other letters begin with titles of dignity: Paul is an apostle through the will of God (Gal 1:1; 1 Cor 1:1; 2 Cor 1:1). In Romans he combines humility and dignity in his introductory self-presentation: "Paul, a slave of Jesus Christ, called to be an apostle, set apart for the gospel of God, which he promised beforehand" (Rom 1:1). He proceeds to describe the content of his apostolate and in doing so bursts through the form of the prescript by summarizing his whole message in a brief formula. If we consider the letter beginnings in their chronological sequence he increasingly emphasizes that he writes as the one sent by his Lord. Likewise striking is the address of all the letters to an *ekklēsia*, that is, a collectivity. Even Philemon is addressed not to a private person, but to his house church. Only in Romans is there no *ekklēsia* as addressee; instead, Paul there emphasizes all the more the universal nature of his writing: it is directed to all human beings, not only to the community in Rome. First he mentions all the Gentiles, and then the Romans. The literary model is an edict to the whole world. Paul characterizes himself as the legate of the world ruler. An allusion to writings carved in stone in 2 Corinthians 3:3 shows that Paul was aware of the way his epistles borrowed from public letters: "and you show that you are a letter of Christ, prepared by us, written not with ink but with the Spirit of the living God, not on tablets of stone but on tablets of human hearts." In the same letter Paul describes himself as a diplomat: "So we are ambassadors [*presbeuomen*] for Christ, since God is making his appeal through us; we entreat you on behalf of Christ, be reconciled to God" (2 Cor 5:20). If Paul sees himself as an ambassador and legate, we may suppose that he adopts forms of the "diplomatic letter." He probably also had copies of his letters made. Diplomatic letters were intended to be copied, often in the form of public inscriptions. Copies would explain the rapid spread of Paul's letters. In any case, Paul's growing self-awareness as the author of his community letters found a model in political and diplomatic letters.

The second model that may have played a role in the development of the letter of friendship into a community letter is the literary letter.[3] Characteristic of literary letters is that they are much longer than utility letters and official documents. They contain small tractates and were often published in letter collections. The letters of Plato are famous examples. In the seventh letter Plato presents his theory of oral and written teaching. This letter is longer than any of Paul's. The letters of Epicurus are three instructional epistles, the most famous of which, the letter to Menoikeus, contains Epicurus's ethics. Cicero was the greatest letter writer of antiquity. Over seven hundred of his letters have survived, edited by his slave-scribe Tiro. The letters of Seneca to Lucilius present his moral philosophy and were intended to preserve his teaching for the world after him. They were published in about 64/65, that is, at about the time when people began to collect Paul's letters. Paul must have been inspired by such literary letters. Three indicators favor this: first, the length of his letters. No private or official letter is as long as the Corinthian letters and Romans. Diplomatic letters cannot have served as models in these cases. The second indicator is that Paul's critics in Corinth ridiculed him: "His letters are weighty and strong, but his bodily presence is weak, and his speech contemptible" (2 Cor 10:10). Paul concedes that he may be untrained in speech, but not in knowledge (2 Cor 11:6). The Corinthians apparently measure his letters against a rhetorical ideal, and so treat them like literary letters. The third indicator is the rapid collection of Pauline letters. Such collections are known only in the case of literary letters. This does not exclude the possibility that Paul himself began collecting his letters or that the Corinthians (or Ephesians) hit on the idea while he was still alive. Thus, the literary letter was the force at least behind the length of his letters and the larger volume of his letter collection.

There may also have been a Jewish model for the Pauline epistolary literature: the letter for community direction. The Old Testament and LXX repeatedly mention letters (for example, in the books of Maccabees). But very seldom is an entire letter, such as that of Jeremiah to the exiles (Jeremiah 29), quoted. Jeremiah wanted to give direction to the community in exile about accepting their exiled situation. We also know the letter of a leader of the Qumran community (4QMMT) and those of Bar Kochba. Nevertheless, the letter never became an independent genre in the Old Testament or the LXX, nor is there such a literary genre in the extracanonical literature of Judaism. There are certainly no letter collections. The letter form did not function as a component of literature in Judaism, with very few exceptions. Those, however, may be important, for precisely in these few letters we discover an intention to lead and direct communities.[4]

1. In the letter of Jeremiah to the exiles in Babylon (Jer 29:1-23), Jeremiah urges them to "seek the welfare of the city" in their foreign land. The exile will last for seventy years. Form-critically speaking, this letter was influential in Judaism. In the Old Testament it became part of the book of Jeremiah. The LXX contains an *epistula Jeremiae* (Letter of Jeremiah) as an independent writing. It is only formally an imitation of the letter of Jeremiah; its content is a polemic against idolatry and idols.[5] Apocalyptic literature from the second century C.E. contains a further expansion of the Letter of Jeremiah, its content a letter of consolation in light of the destruction of the temple,

which fictionally refers to the first destruction, but in reality to the second (*Syr. Bar.* 77–87). This letter is part of *Syriac Baruch*.[6] Likewise, the letters in the *Paraleipomena Ieremiou* (also second cent. C.E.) are part of the historical influence of the book of Jeremiah. They, too, are not independent letters, but enclosures.

2. More important, however, is a second group of letters: the festal letters in the books of Maccabees (2 Macc 1:1-9; 1:10-19) urge celebration of the feast of Hanukkah, commemorating the dedication of the temple after the religious persecution of Antiochus Epiphanes (second cent. B.C.E.). Here we find (as with Paul) the intention to offer leadership to a community. Letters on cultic questions are also found in Elephantine in the Persian period; this was the exchange of letters between a Jewish military colony in Egypt and the governor in Jerusalem. They concern, among other things, questions about the Passover feast. Irene Taatz has concluded from these letters to a genre "letter for community direction" in early Judaism, one continued by Paul and including the tradition of letters of Jeremiah.[7] One should mention here also the letter, which she does not treat, of a leader of the Qumran community (4QMMT = 4Q394-399): it discusses the cultic deviations that led to the break between the separate Essene community and the temple.

There was, then, a Jewish letter culture. For that very reason it is striking that letters did not become a genre of sacred scripture. We can say only this much about Paul: as a Jew he had already learned to write letters. His prescript corresponds to the two-part Jewish and not the one-part Greek prescript. He may have found a model for his letters in the Letter of Jeremiah and the festal letters insofar as they were addressed to a community. Perhaps he was already familiar with such community-directing letters in his pre-Christian period. In Acts 22:5 the Lukan Paul reports that the high priests and elders had given him letters to Jewish communities in order to intervene in the conflicts between the newly organized Christian communities and the other Jews. These were intended to help him to combat the new "heresy." We do not know whether this account is historical. But independently of its historicity it may affirm a general tradition of community-directing letters in Judaism. The letter composed at the apostolic council (Acts 15:23-29) and directed to communities is part of that formal tradition. Did Paul also activate that tradition when he developed the community letter as a means of community direction in conflicts with his environment and opponents? Does this explain the fact that it was first of all his conflicts in Asia Minor and Greece that challenged him to become a letter writer with an enduring influence?

We thus come to the conclusion that Paul created the community letter by reshaping the ancient letter of friendship, borrowing from official and "literary" letters.[8] He may at the same time have activated a tradition of community-leadership letters already extant in Jewish tradition. The borrowing from official letters explains his self-awareness of authority as the letter writer, while attention to literary letters shows why his letters were of exceptional length; modeling on the letter of community leadership explains the direction to a group of addressees. Using such models, Paul gave the letter of friendship an authoritative weight, a collective address, and a significant content, all of which explains the length of his letters.

Development from Letter of Friendship to Community Letter by Means of Liturgical Stylization

The further development of the letter of friendship into a community letter is revealed in the letter formula. This is largely established by convention: the opening consists of a prescript and a proemium, corresponding to the epilogue and postscript at the end. Within these, the greeting and farewell are shaped by the formal language of the letter. Paul recreated this formal language independently by developing the two-part Eastern prescript through the addition of certain elements (Table 7).[9]

All the letter formulae of the prescript are expanded by Paul. In the *superscriptio* Paul always, except in Romans, mentions coauthors. In the *adscriptio* Paul always addresses himself to a community that—except in Romans—is called *ekklēsia*. Even in Philemon he mentions the house church together with the individual addressee, Philemon! His plea for good treatment of the slave Onesimus is not a petition to a private person. The *adscriptio* in 1 Corinthians is expanded ad hoc by an ecumenical formula: Paul writes to the Corinthians "together with all those who in every place call on the name of our Lord Jesus Christ" (1 Cor 1:2). This ecumenical expansion appears in a different form in Romans: Paul writes it for all Christians, including the Romans as well. In 1 Thessalonians the *adscriptio* is augmented theologically by means of a prepositional phrase: "to the church of the Thessalonians in God the Father and the Lord Jesus Christ." The profane *salutatio*—a simple *chairein*— is transformed, in accord with Jewish tradition (*Syr. Bar.* 78:2) into a full, rounded blessing: "grace to you and peace from God our Father and the Lord Jesus Christ" (1 Cor 1:3). The similarity between *chairein* (greetings) and *charis* (grace) would have made this change easy.

Table 7: Greek and Eastern Epistolary Prescripts

	The Greek prescript is made up of an infinitive clause	The Eastern prescript consists of two sentences	A Pauline letter has two sentences
Superscriptio	*Apion*		*Paul, Silvanus, and Timothy*
Adscriptio	*to Epimachos*	*To our brothers who dwell in Lower Galilee.*	*to the church of the Thessalonians . . .*
Salutatio	*greetings (chairein)*	*May your joy increase!*	*Grace to you and peace.*
	(Letter of Apion)	(Letter of Gamaliel, *Sanh.* 11b)	(1 Thessalonians)
	The sender appears in the nominative. The infinitive retains a remnant of oral messenger language: "So speaks NN, that it may go well with you."	The sender need not be named, but sometimes appears in a prepositional expression: "To NN from NN."	Paul combines Greek and Eastern traditions. He names the sender(s) in the nominative and formulates two sentences, as in the Eastern prescript.

The *salutatio* can also be expanded, as in Galatians 1:4-5, where Paul gives a short summary of his message: "grace . . . from God our Father and the Lord Jesus Christ, who gave himself for our sins to set us free from the present evil age, according to the will of our God and Father, to whom be the glory forever and ever. Amen." All these expansions lend the prescript a liturgical sound and shift the expectation of the hearers toward a liturgical text.

The proemium serves to establish contact, and in ancient letters consists of a wish for the recipient's well-being, thanksgiving, assurance of remembrance, petitions for the recipient, and an expression of joy. For the most part, Paul introduces the proemium as a prayer: "I give thanks to my God. . . ." Once, in 2 Corinthians, he begins with praise: "Blessed be the God and Father of our Lord Jesus Christ. . . ." Paul usually gives thanks for the faith of the community, that is, for the good things he finds in it (e.g., Rom 1:8). He also assures the community that he is thinking of it and praying for it: here he also addresses what he wants and what could be better: "For God, whom I serve with my spirit by announcing the gospel of his Son, is my witness that without ceasing I remember you always in my prayers, asking that by God's will I may somehow at last succeed in coming to you." The travel wish is then further developed (Rom 1:9-13). At the transition from the proemium to the body of the letter is a self-recommendation.[10] In Romans it reads: "I am a debtor both to Greeks and to barbarians, both to the wise and to the foolish—hence my eagerness to proclaim the gospel to you also who are in Rome" (Rom 1:14-15). This self-recommendation varies widely in its form.

The epilogue at the end of the letter corresponds to the proemium in its numerous motifs of contact. These include, in 1 Corinthians, the closing admonitions regarding the collection (1 Cor 16:1-4), alertness and love (1 Cor 16:13), travel wishes, and the announcement of a visit. The last is connected with the collection, which Paul hopes if possible to bring to Jerusalem in person. Added to these are recommendations and attitudes toward certain persons: Timothy (1 Cor 16:10-11), Apollos (16:12), and Stephanas (16:15-18).

The postscript's formulaic nature corresponds to that of the prescript. Here we find greetings (*aspasmoi*), either the extension of greetings in the third person, "the churches of Asia send greetings . . ." (1 Cor 16:19), or a request to greet in the third person: "greet one another with a holy kiss" (16:20b), or a direct greeting in the first person, such as "I, Paul, write this greeting with my own hand" (16:21). The note about writing with one's own hand is a kind of signature, giving the letter legal validity. In Galatians he takes this occasion to emphasize that his handwriting differs from that in the previous letter: "see what large letters I make when I am writing in my own hand!" (Gal 6:11). At the end of the letter are requests for blessing. In the ancient private letter they take the form of "may it be well with you!" (*errōsō* or *eutyxei*). Paul expands on this. In 1 Corinthians the blessing is combined with a conditional curse: "let anyone be accursed who has no love for the Lord. Our Lord come! The grace of the Lord Jesus be with you. My love be with all of you in Christ Jesus" (1 Cor 16:22-24).[11]

Such liturgical elements appear not only in the letter frame, but also in the body of the letter. In the course of the letter we come upon blessing formulae, confessional formulae, and hymns, which we discussed above as oral tradition. In a literary history the most interesting questions are: Were these formulae liturgically significant? Did they shape the overall character of the letters? Are the Pauline letters something like an exegesis of tradition?[12] Did the numerous small forms and formulae have structural significance for the construction of the Pauline letters?

This is, in fact, true for some formulae and traditions: for 1 Thessalonians we can recognize a structure-determinative significance in the formula "faith, love, hope." All three are named in the proemium, where the Thessalonians' "work of faith and labor of love and steadfastness of hope" are praised (1 Thess 1:3). At the end, Paul repeats this triad in the image of spiritual armament when he speaks of the "breastplate of faith and love" and the "helmet of hope" (5:8). This triad may have an outline function here and there in the letter: at the beginning the Thessalonians' faith is praised (1:6-10); in 4:9-12 they are exhorted to love and in 4:13-18 to hope.

First Corinthians begins with the cross and ends with the resurrection, as if the two-part formula of death and resurrection (1 Cor 15:3-4) were the basis and frame for the whole letter. In between, practical questions are discussed and are frequently to be resolved according to the criterion of love. Otherwise, the letter consists of a series of thematic units that are loosely arranged in sequence. At least four units rest on traditions and explain or apply them: the remarks on meat sacrificed to idols emerge from a traditional monotheistic formula (1 Cor 8:6) that is expanded in terms of Jesus the *Kyrios*: because there is only one God, there can be no such thing as meat sacrificed to gods. The remarks on the spiritual gifts rest on the confession "*Kyrios* Jesus Christ = Jesus Christ is Lord" (12:1-3). This confession is evidence of possession of the Spirit; glossolalia is only one gift among others. In 1 Corinthians 15:1-5 Paul starts from a traditional formula of the resurrection of Jesus in order to strengthen the assurance of resurrection in Corinth. The assurance of resurrection of the individual and hope for the resurrection of all are mutually related.

Clearest of all is the literary function of traditional formulae in Romans. Here Paul writes to a community with which he is unacquainted and therefore he must link all the more firmly to what is familiar. The first three sections all begin with traditional formulae: that of the son of David (1:3-4) occurs in the prescript. Jesus is the Messiah for the Jews and Lord of the whole world. The theme of Jews and Gentiles is already to be heard here. The redemption formula in 3:25 serves to name the reason for justification: Jesus' death is the overcoming of the sins of all. Paul develops the theme of the transformation of the human being on the basis of baptismal formulae that recall the traditions of Christ's death and resurrection (6:1-4; cf. 1 Cor 15:3-7).

The traditions of formulae from the communities could also have had a limited significance for the structure of 1 Thessalonians, 1 Corinthians, and Romans. One cannot explain the form of Paul's letters solely on that basis, but the formulae gave them a solemn sound. Thus we may say that not only the frames of the letters but the whole of the letters themselves were laden by Paul with religious expressions. It is true that ancient letters did not lack references to the gods, but Paul strengthened the reference to God and Christ.

Hence there is a kernel of truth in Ernst Lohmeyer's thesis when he saw entry and concluding formulae of worship services in the letter formulae.[13] After all, the letters were read in the common assembly. By solemn opening and closing expressions the reading became an act of worship even if the formulae of the letter frame did not constitute the frame of the worship service. But in the frame itself, in particular, this was "performative" language, like that of blessing. The model for the reading of apostolic letters was the public common assembly, which was called *ekklēsia*. In the popular assembly, letters from the emperor or his legate were read aloud. Analogously, in the Christian "popular assembly" the letters of the apostle Paul were read. Consequently, an important conclusion regarding the form-critical location of the letters of Paul is that these are liturgically stylized letters with an aura of public worship. We may suppose that when they were read they took the place of preaching. But that is not all that needs to be said about their special form-critical character.

Development from Letter of Friendship to Community Letter by Means of Rhetorical Stylization

The expansion of the letter of friendship into a community letter was effected not only by the liturgical shaping of the letter but also by Paul's enrichment of it with elements of public rhetoric.[14] The letter allowed considerable freedom for this. Only the frame was determined by a number of variable formulae. The body of the letter itself could be very differently shaped. Paul used this freedom to endow his letter with major significance by, among other things, adding rhetorical elements. The community letter created by Paul is, form-critically considered, a rhetorically enhanced letter of friendship with a liturgical frame.

This thesis assumes that there was a difference between letters and speeches, but not so great a difference that the two forms could not be open to one another. Pseudo-Demetrius, in his work *De elocutione* (second cent. B.C.E.–first cent. C.E.) distinguishes various stylistic types and requires that letters have a simple style; elements of festal and judicial oratory he found inappropriate there.[15] He defines the letter as a friendly conversation that retains only the voice of one partner in the dialogue. In such letters, he says, there is no place for everything that would be appropriate to a public speech. Cicero also emphasizes that "a letter is not a judicial proceeding or a speech to the public" (*Fam.* 9.21.1). Likewise, letters and speeches are clearly different in their origins:[16] from a form-critical perspective Paul therefore undertook to cross a boundary when he outfitted a letter with stylistic and formal elements that belonged not to the simple style of the letter of friendship but to public rhetoric. However, he was not alone in this. The establishment of boundaries quoted above was directed in part against stylistic boundary violations that were common at the time. Demetrius concedes (§234) that letters to cities and rulers should be more elevated in style. He mentions "diplomatic" and "literary" letters as forms in which the simple letter style is abandoned. And Paul must have had precisely those two forms in mind when he abandoned the simple letter style and assumed the role of a speaker sending his communities theological tractates and apostolic advice—and at the same time appealing to them for friendship and recognition.

What is certain is that Paul had no rhetorical education (he calls himself an amateur in speaking in 2 Cor 11:6), but a person gifted in language and its forms could also acquire rhetorical competence by listening. The rhetorical analysis of the Pauline letters may have led only to disputed results on individual points, but on the whole so many echoes of the rhetorician's art are found in Paul that we must reckon with an amateur education in rhetoric on his part.[17] What would be the content of such a rhetorical education? Rhetoric includes knowledge of particular genres of speech and the mastery of five steps in preparing a discourse: *inventio*, that is, the search for particular *topoi* that one may use as a collection of materials; *dispositio*, the application of outline schemes to direct the structure of the speech; *elocutio*, the ornamentation of the speech with tropes and figures. The last two steps are *memoria* and *pronuntiatio*, learning the speech by heart and translating it into oral discourse. These were primarily important for the "performance" of the speech. In addition, rhetoric distinguished three types of speeches or texts:

1. The *genus deliberativum* or *deliberative* speech. Its locus is the public assembly, and its aim is advice about how to decide and act. Undoubtedly Paul offers suggestions to a community in his letters. They are largely made up of deliberative speech—not in the *ekklēsia* of the city, but in the *ekklēsia* of God.
2. The *genus demonstrativum* or *epideictic* speech. Its locus is the festal assembly. It dispenses praise and blame. The *laudatio* is epideictic. With Paul it is not human beings who are praised, but God and Jesus Christ. The liturgical parts of his letters are religious, epideictic speech. The hymn in Philippians is especially beautiful; it has been understood as an *encomium*, a speech praising a single person.
3. The *genus iudiciale* or *judicial* speech. Its locus is the court; its purpose is defense and accusation. Paul repeatedly defends

> himself in his letters. The letter to the Galatians in particular can be understood as a defense speech (Betz), but sections of 1 Thessalonians and Philippians also sound like apology.[18]

When one of Paul's letters was read, then, it on the one hand signaled friendly association with the communities by means of elements and motifs of the letter of friendship. Paul wants to have contact with them and struggles for a personal relationship—but at the same time he confronts them with public rhetoric. Thereby it is clear from the outset that Paul is not addressing individual persons, but the community. He wants to teach basic questions (as in the literary letter), appears as an authority (as in the official letter), and speaks about God as if he were in a worship space. Can various forms of stylized "public discourse" be demonstrated in Paul's letters? In what follows we will offer a brief overview of the formal shaping of the Pauline letters.

First Thessalonians is a letter of friendship, a letter of those separated against their own will. But here already we encounter a public claim. Paul solemnly orders the community to have the letter read to all (1 Thess 5:27). That would not be necessary if the genre of the community letter were already familiar. Letters were regarded primarily as private. The motif of the parousia stems from the letter of friendship: "Night and day we pray most earnestly that we may see you face to face and restore whatever is lacking in your faith" (1 Thess 3:10). This whole section (1 Thess 2:17—3:13) is imbued with longing and affection. But at the same time the parousia of the Lord is announced—analogously to the proclamation of the arrival of a ruler. This raises a public claim. On the occasion of a parousia the emissaries of the city would go out to meet the ruler. In 1 Thessalonians this parousia is incorporated in the friendship motif: as Paul and the community long to see each other face to face, in a direct encounter, so Christians long for the presence of the Lord, in order to be with him forever.

Galatians is the parody of a letter of friendship, with a rhetoric of defense. The expression of thanksgiving is replaced by an anathema. Paul begins his defensive speech with an *exordium*, a highly polemic introduction (Gal 1:6, 11), and follows it with a *narratio* of his calling and its recognition by the apostolic council (Gal 1:12—2:14); after that he formulates the doctrine of justification in a *propositio* as a means of proof (Gal 2:15-21) and follows it with a *probatio* in two steps (Gal 3:1—4:31). But then he proceeds to an *exhortatio* (Gal 5:1—6:10), which does not belong in a speech to the court and requires a separate explanation.[19] He ends with a *conclusio* (Gal 6:11-18). Elements of a public speech before the court are here incorporated into a letter—but, remarkably enough, no forensic metaphors of the last judgment are developed, even though the doctrine of justification has a forensic frame. Only in Romans will it be developed with the aid of imaginary judicial scenes.

The letters to the Corinthians are letters of friendship with a rhetoric of reconciliation.[20] First Corinthians has as its theme parties and community problems in Corinth that reveal themselves in conflicts: party strife, conflicts between ascetics and libertines, the strong and the weak, charismatics and ordinary Christians, poor and rich at the Lord's Supper, skeptics of the resurrection, and others. Strife and conflict in the *polis* were regarded as endangering its existence. At that time there were many public speeches with admonitions to unanimity (*homonoia*) in the city. Paul takes up that rhetoric, describing himself, not accidentally, as a diplomat in the service of Christ who seeks to create reconciliation—first between the contending parties (1 Corinthians), but then between himself and the community (2 Corinthians). In this he is constantly sustained by the conviction that God himself creates reconciliation.

Finally, Romans is an ambassadorial letter[21] seeking friendship and uniting apologetic features from Galatians with conciliatory rhetoric from 1 Corinthians. Characteristic of Romans is the enhanced employment of the diatribe style, a fictive dialogue that Paul conducts by introducing counter-arguments—and this precisely at crucial points:

> Then what becomes of boasting? It is excluded. By what law? By that of works? No, but by the law of faith. For we hold that a person is justified by faith apart from works prescribed by the law. Or is God the God of Jews only? Is he not the God of Gentiles also? Yes, of Gentiles also, since God is one; and he will justify the circumcised on the ground of faith and the uncircumcised through that same faith. Do we then overthrow the law by this faith? By no means! On the contrary, we uphold the law. (Rom 3:27-31)

7 The Sequence and Development of the Pauline Letters

We have two points of contact for an absolute chronology. The edict of Claudius in 49 C.E. must have been issued shortly before Paul arrived in Corinth. In addition, Paul was accused in Corinth before Gallio, whose term of office may be dated, on the basis of an inscription, to 51 or 52 C.E. With regard to the relative chronology there is a consensus that 1 Thessalonians is the earliest letter of Paul, written from Corinth in about 50 C.E., after his flight from Thessalonica and while he was in the process of founding the Corinthian community. First and Second Corinthians were clearly written after that, since they presume the existence of the community at Corinth. Both the Corinthian letters were written from Ephesus or on the journey from Ephesus to Corinth. Romans was written in Corinth after the struggles with the Corinthians were past and Paul was about to leave for his last journey to Jerusalem. In short, we can easily describe the sequence of the four letters written in and to Corinth. The order of Galatians and the two captivity letters, Philippians and Philemon, remains disputed.

First, as regards the two captivity letters: Paul was in danger of death in Ephesus, probably an imprisonment from which he expected a death sentence (2 Cor 1:9). He looks back on that in 2 Corinthians; consequently, the letters to the Philippians and Philemon, written in prison, could fall into the period between the two letters to the Corinthians. But that is not certain. The captivity letters could also be Paul's last letters before his death—after Romans—and in that case would have been written in Rome during Paul's last imprisonment. However, the close contacts favor a location in Ephesus. Members of the community from Philippi have brought material aid to Paul; the messenger, Epaphroditus, has fallen ill; the Philippians may have heard of this; Paul presumes that they will be worried about Epaphroditus; he sends Epaphroditus, who has in the meantime recovered his health, back with his letter of thanks and intends to visit the Philippians soon, after his release. This does not fit with the great distance between Rome and Philippi. In addition, the letter to Philemon presumes that the slave Onesimus has sought Paul out to beg him to mediate. Onesimus lived in Asia Minor, as we see from the agreement of many personal details with Colossians. That a slave would travel to a nearby city to beg a friend of his master to intercede for him is easy to understand, but not that he would make a week-long (sea) journey to Rome. Hence, in my opinion, there is much more to favor a dating and location of the two captivity letters in the period when Paul was at Ephesus than in his last period in Rome. A late dating of the two captivity letters would be highly interesting in terms of Paul's theological development. In Philippians Paul has changed his ideas about death and eternal life. He hopes to be with Jesus immediately after his death, independent of the general resurrection. Did Paul perhaps reformulate his hopes for life after death at the end of his life? But just as plausible would be a new view of death after Paul had to face the possibility of execution in Ephesus.

Galatians is taken up in Romans as a model and script and is therefore clearly prior to Romans. Romans once again reformulates the doctrine of justification found in Galatians. The main argument for dating it after 1 Corinthians is 1 Corinthians 16:1-2, where Paul writes to the Corinthians that he has given directions to the churches in Galatia that they should make a regular collection. It is concluded from this that at the time when 1 Corinthians was written there were not yet tensions with the Galatians. These must have occurred later, and Galatians, as a witness to those tensions, must be dated after 1 Corinthians.[1] However, form criticism can offer a new argument for placing Galatians before 1 Corinthians: small changes in the prescript and the concluding formula of 1 Corinthians that could have been occasioned by the Galatian situation.

In 1 Thessalonians Paul presents himself in the prescript without any title. In 1 Corinthians (and similarly in all other letters) he emphatically names himself "Paul, called to be an apostle of Christ Jesus by the will of God." The shift from the prescript of a private letter to a prescript with elements of an official letter was brought on by the Galatian conflict: in Galatia Paul found his apostleship under attack. Here he delivers a sharp emphasis: "Paul, an apostle—sent neither by human commission nor from human authorities, but through Jesus Christ and God the Father, who raised him from the dead— . . ." The unusual situation may have been the motive for this change in the form of the prescript. At the end of the letter Paul emphasizes in Galatians that he has concluded the letter with his own hand (6:11). That is understandable in the context of the Galatian conflict: the opponents had said that Paul thought differently on many points, and had not said some things at all. Now Paul wants to give legal validity to his real opinion. He therefore signs his letter like a legal document, in his own hand, and stresses this with a note to that effect.[2] Only in 1 Corinthians 16:21 and Philemon 19 does he emphasize his own handwriting—in Philemon to give emphasis to an affirmation of responsibility, and in 1 Corinthians without perceptible motivation. Here there is an echo of a shift in form already accomplished, and here also the model of Galatians may be having its effect. Add to this that at the end of the letter, in 1 Corinthians 16:22, Paul gives a conditional anathema—an unusual conclusion. In Galatians he had placed an anathema at the beginning. In this anathema also there is an echo of Galatians. Thus, in 1 Corinthians the official stylizing at the beginning and the autograph notice at the end can be explained as brought about by the influence of Galatians. The extreme situation in Galatia can better explain the change of form in the letter formula than can the less tense Corinthian situation. In addition, there is an argument from content: Paul argues in Galatians like an enthusiast, but in 1 Corinthians his task is to correct enthusiasm. In Galatians he relies solely on the Spirit as the power of new life, while in 1 Corinthians he has to oppose Christians who trust too much in the Spirit.[3] If Paul had already had his clash with the enthusiasts in Corinth behind him he could not have spoken so unreservedly in Galatians in favor of enthusiasm in the Spirit.

If the suggested dating is correct, the first and last of Paul's letters (1 Thessalonians and Romans) would have been written in Corinth, and the intervening letters all in the time when Paul centered his work in Ephesus. One puzzle is why he fell silent after that. After Romans, about 56 C.E., he probably lived six more years, most of them spent in prison. This problem would be eliminated by a late dating of the two captivity letters (Philippians and Philemon). Or was he working more through others in this last period when his imprisonment separated him from his communities? Was it then, for example, that one of his disciples wrote Colossians, to which he simply added his signature at the end to authorize it (Col 4:18)? Or was he working with his companions on an edition of his letters? Is a memory of this literary activity of Paul retained in 2 Timothy, when the imprisoned Paul asks that Tychicus (2 Tim 4:13) bring him "the books, and above all the parchments" from Ephesus? Or was he working more from prison through oral messengers? It is hard to imagine Paul being idle.

In any case, the suggested ordering of Paul's letters yields a more meaningful internal sequence. If we consider the thrust of their content and presentation, we can depict the theological development of the Pauline letters (minus Philemon) thus (Table 8):

Table 8: Theological Development of the Pauline Letters

1 Thessalonians
Preservation of Christian identity in the face of the Gentile environment and of the Jews (2:14-16)

Anti-Jewish Letters
Against a wrong understanding of the Law, drawing boundaries toward Israel (Galatians; Philippians 3)

Anti-Enthusiast Letters
Against a wrong understanding of the Spirit, drawing boundaries regarding enthusiasm (1 Corinthians; 2 Corinthians)

Romans
Synthesis of anti-Jewish letters (without drawing boundaries toward Israel) and anti-enthusiast letters (with sympathy for enthusiasm)

The formal development of the letters, however, may be described this way: 1 Thessalonians is a two-part letter. The first part consists of an expanded proemium, the second of an extended paraenesis. Pieces of text that go beyond the making-contact of the proemium and the admonitions of paraenesis are worked into both parts: in the first part there is an apology by Paul (1 Thess 2:1-12) and an attack on the Jews who are hampering Paul in his mission (1 Thess 2:14-16); in the second part there is an eschatological instruction about the resurrection of the dead (1 Thess 4:13-18). Beginning from 1 Thessalonians, we can discern two lines of development: on the one hand, the development toward a systematically structured document such as Galatians and Romans, conceived and written as a unit, and on the other hand a development toward letters that result from an ongoing interaction with the communities they address and hence have an additive structure (1 Corinthians; 2 Corinthians; Philippians). We will initially follow the first of these lines of development. Unmistakably, Galatians served as a script for Romans. Paul repeats its structure, introduces a series of *topoi* in the same sequence, and repeatedly inserts themes and motifs from 1 Corinthians (Table 9).

Themes from 1 Corinthians are then built into this outline established by Galatians and are here revised. Since Paul wrote Romans in Corinth, one may assume that while writing Romans he continued his conversation with the Corinthian community (Table 10).

Table 9: Galatians and Romans

Galatians	Romans
1. Biographical section (Gal 1–2) Paul's call from God and his acceptance by the apostles gives legitimacy to his message.	Description of divine wrath toward all: human history replaces Paul's biography.
2. Systematic section (Gal 3–4) Develops the thesis: *justification by faith* without works (Gal 2:15-21).	The revelation of God's justice culminates in the thesis: *justification by faith* without works (Rom 3:28).
This thesis is demonstrated by a double treatment of the *example of Abraham* (Galatians 3 and 4):	The twofold use of the *example of Abraham* appears again in Romans (Romans 4 and 9):
Abraham is the bearer of the promise and source for the inclusion of the Gentiles in the promise. He is the basis for the union of Jews and Christians in Christ. *Sperma* is interpreted in the singular, as applying to Christ (Gal 3:6-9).	In Romans 4, Abraham is the ancestor of all believers, both Jews and Gentiles, and the physical ancestor of all Jews. New here is the plural interpretation of "seed," which does not deny to Jews their descent from Abraham.
The *baptismal theme*: In order that Abraham's blessing may benefit all the Gentiles through his "descendant" (= Christ), all must be identified with Christ. Through baptism all have put on Christ (3:26-29). All are one person in him.	In Romans 6, the *baptismal theme* follows the example of Abraham in Romans 4 (interrupted by other themes). Here, however, it stresses not the unity of all people but their transformation to new life.
Sending and Bestowal of the Spirit: Gal 4:1-7 describes the transition from being immature children to the status of heirs through the sending of the Son and the Spirit, who enables us to call God "Abba" (Gal 4:6).	The same motifs also follow in Romans 8: *sending* of the Son (Rom 8:3-4), bestowal of the status of sons/daughters and of the *Spirit*, who enables us to cry "Abba," and who ensures our status as heirs (Rom 8:12-17).
Second application of the example of Abraham: Abraham is the ancestor of two opposing *sons*: Ishmael persecutes Isaac. This explains the opposition of Jews and Christians (Gal 4:21-31).	In Romans 9 the two *sons* of Abraham are used to demonstrate the distinction between election and nonelection. What is new in Romans is the salvation of Israel in Romans 11.
3. Paraenetic section (Gal 5:13-26) The paraenesis is summarized in the love commandment, which is seen in both letters as the fulfillment of the Law (Gal 5:14). In Galatians the love commandment follows a paraenesis on freedom.	*Paraenetic section (Rom 12:1—15:13)* In Romans also the love commandment (Rom 12:9-21; 13:8-16) is a summary of the paraenesis, but it does not follow an appeal to freedom, but instead to subjection to state authorities.

Galatians	Romans
Concern for the weaker: If charismatics discover a brother or sister transgressing, they should deal with one another gently: "bear one another's burdens" (Gal 6:2).	This *gentleness* recalls the admonition to the strong and the weak. They should welcome one another as Christ has welcomed them (Rom 15:7).

Table 10: 1 Corinthians and Romans

1 Corinthians	Romans
Both letters are introduced by a *theologia naturalis*. In 1 Cor 1:18-25 this shows that human wisdom by itself cannot find the way to God. Therefore God chooses the way of the foolishness of the cross in order to save humanity.	Similarly, the failure of the wise is depicted in Rom 1:18-32. Although God can be known from the world by a *theologia naturalis*, they do not worship God. They become fools and worship creatures. The consequence is their surrender to horrible transgressions.
The *Adam-Christ typology* is found at the end of 1 Corinthians. In 1 Corinthians 15 it contrasts the nature of the earthly human Adam with that of the heavenly human, the risen Christ.	In Romans 5 the *Adam-Christ typology* concludes a fundamental section of the letter. The act of the earthly Adam, his transgression, is contrasted with the act of the earthly Jesus, who was obedient through his self-surrender to death.
Glossolalia: In 1 Corinthians 12 Paul relativizes the value of glossolalia. Angelic speech (1 Cor 13:1) is measured by what it accomplishes as speech between humans: it is of little value unless it is translated.	In Rom 8:18-27, when he speaks of "sighs too deep for words," Paul is probably referring to *glossolalia*. It is not seen as the expression of positive, enthusiastic feelings, but as the lament of the tortured creature.
The *image of the Body of Christ* appears in 1 Corinthians 12 as an argument for relativizing the especially charismatic gifts, especially glossolalia. In the community, all gifts are of equal value.	In Rom 12:3-8 there is no mention either of the *pneuma* or of glossolalia in connection with the *Body of Christ*. The ideas in 1 Corinthians 12 are generalized: no one should think more of herself or himself than she or he is, but should exercise sober judgment.
The theme of *strong and weak* is applied in 1 Corinthians 8–10 to the eating of meat offered to idols. Paul argues in terms of conscience; there is no mention of the concept of faith.	The theme of *strong and weak* is applied in Rom 14:1—15:3 generally to questions of eating meat, drinking wine, and calendrical observances. Paul argues on the basis of faith, not using the concept of conscience.

The relationship between Galatians and Romans shows that Paul could adapt the basic scheme of one letter for use in another. There are some traces of this also in the relationship between 1 Thessalonians and 1 Corinthians, as the following table shows (Table 11):

Table 11: 1 Thessalonians and 1 Corinthians

1 Thessalonians	1 Corinthians
1:1 Prescript	1:1-3 Prescript
1:2-10 Proemium, with thanksgiving for the faith of the community and prospect of the parousia.	1:4-9 Proemium, with thanksgiving for the wealth of gifts and prospect of the parousia.
2–3 First section: expanded proemium with exclusion of deceivers and assurance of relationship and longing for contact.	1:19—4:21 First section: party strife and theology of the cross, with announcement of Paul's coming in a threatening tone.
4:1-12 Second section: holiness paraenesis, sexuality. Acquisitions (*pragmata*).	5–6 Second section: holiness paraenesis, sexuality, distancing from evil in general, judgment on everyday things (*biōtika*), immorality (*porneia*).
	7:1-24 (*peri*) marriage 7:25-40 (*peri*) the unmarried 8:1-13 (*peri*) flesh offered to idols 11:1-34 worship questions 12:1—14:40 (*peri*) spiritual gifts
4:13—5:11 Final section: instruction regarding the resurrection.	15:1-58 Final section: those who deny the resurrection; instruction about the "that" and "how" of the resurrection.

If we look closely, we will see that the formal "model" of 1 Thessalonians leaves off after 1 Corinthians 7:1, that is, at the very moment when Paul for the first time refers to a written letter from a community and in what follows, with segments introduced by *peri* (what . . . concerning), replies to that letter. It is very likely that the community's letter arrived while 1 Corinthians was being written. The letter was thus created interactively and could for that very reason not be in the form of a unified composition. The arrival of the community's letter shifted the conception of the letter in new directions. If the community's letter had been there from the start, it is likely that Paul would have referred to it at the very beginning of his letter. But in 1 Corinthians 1 he probably had nothing but the news brought by Chloe's people (1 Cor 1:11).

With 1 Corinthians begins a special development continued in 2 Corinthians and Philippians. These letters, too, are constructed additively. The lack of unity in 2 Corinthians may also be the result of the repeated arrival of new pieces of news.[4] Paul writes the first part, 1 Corinthians 1:1—2:13, on the way from Ephesus to Macedonia. In 2 Corinthians 2:13 he has arrived in Macedonia and is awaiting news from Corinth. But he finds no rest in his *mind*, that is, his *spirit* (2 Cor 2:13). The situation is still open. He writes an apology for his apostolate (2 Cor 2:14—7:4) until Titus arrives with good news from Corinth, to which Paul reacts with conciliatory and heartfelt words. But in the meantime he has also been under external pressure: he finds no rest in his *flesh* because he is afflicted not only from within, but also from without (2 Cor 7:5). Before he himself can come, he sends messengers to Corinth to prepare for the collection (2 Cor 8 and 9) and (on the basis of more recent news) again writes a bitter section of the letter (2 Cor 10–13)—now that he is certain that the community is basically accepting of him he wants, before his arrival, to use a letter and the messengers bearing it to take care of the problems outstanding between him and the Corinthians: "So I write these things while I am away from you, so that when I come I may not have to be severe in using the authority that the Lord has given me for building up and not for tearing down" (2 Cor 13:10).

An interactive history of origins is also probable in the case of Philippians.[5] In favor of this is the well-documented intensive interaction with the community at Philippi to which the letter attests: members of the community have brought Paul a material gift; Paul begins to write them a letter (Phil 1:1—2:18), but its dispatch is delayed as Epaphroditus, one of the messengers from Philippi, who is to bring the letter of thanks back to them, falls ill. Paul decides therefore to send Timothy, and also hopes to be able to come to Philippi soon in person (Phil 2:19-24). But in the meantime Epaphroditus recovers his health, and Paul can, as originally planned, send him back with a letter of thanks (Phil 2:27-28). It is silently assumed that Timothy need no longer go. Therefore Paul adds to the letter already begun, to be brought by the now-healthy Epaphroditus, with a polemic that Timothy would probably have delivered in person, since he was someone Paul often sent in difficult situations (Phil 3:2—4:1). The polemic was probably occasioned by new information: since rumors that the Philippians were worried about Epaphroditus's illness have reached him (Phil 2:26), it may be that in fact new reports about opponents in Philippi have reached Ephesus. After this polemic, for balance, Paul adds conciliatory admonitions and blessings (Phil 4:2-9), and he thanks the Philippians for the support brought by Epaphroditus (Phil 4:10-19). The interactions could have been different in details, but what is crucial is that a series of contingent interactions may explain the strangely composed letter.

Thus—starting from 1 Thessalonians—we can observe two form-critical lines of development in the Pauline letters (Table 12):

Table 12: Form-Critical Development of Paul's Letters

1 Thessalonians
Two-part letter, proemium + paraenesis

1 Corinthians / 2 Corinthians / Philippians	*Galatians / Romans*
Additively structured letters created interactively. The two-part structure is eliminated.	Systematically structured letters, unitively conceived. The two-part structure is here retained.

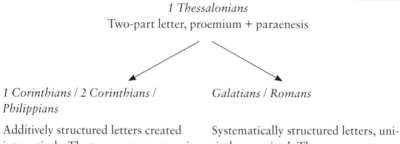

In general we can readily trace the development from private letter to community letter on the basis of the external form of the development. The oldest Pauline letter that is preserved is meant to maintain a disrupted communication despite a forced separation. The letter is altogether determined by the situation. The (possibly) last letter of Paul, Romans, from the year 56/57, is almost a tractate. It is addressed to the community at Rome, with which Paul was unfamiliar. In his letter he announces his coming visit to them. But at the same time Romans has three additional addressees:[6] first, the community in Corinth, which values his letters so highly (2 Cor 10:10) that Paul must certainly have read his letter to Rome aloud to them before sending it. A second associated addressee was the community in Ephesus. Part of the Roman community had been driven out of Rome by an edict of the emperor Claudius in 49 C.E. and had regathered in Ephesus. Paul sent them, as part of the Roman community, a copy of Romans with additional greetings. The third additional addressee is the Jerusalem community: when writing, Paul is already with them in thought, since he wants to visit them even before he goes to Rome. We see this from how he reflects on the fate of Israel in Romans 9–11. As a result of the Jerusalem journey about to take place, Romans became Paul's testament,[7] since Paul feared he would be killed in Jerusalem. Before that he wants to summarize his teaching once more, defend it against accusations, and secure his work beyond his death. Thanks to its broad circle of addressees, the letter to the Romans stands on the threshold of early Christian public literature, yet it is still, like its predecessors, a genuine letter with a concrete addressee.

We can sense in Romans the role into which Paul slips in order to create a general hearing for his letter. Only here does he present himself with his full title: "Paul, a servant of Jesus Christ, called to be an apostle, set apart for the gospel of God. . . ." He then defines the gospel as the proclamation of a person from the Jewish royal house who, after his death, has as Son of God risen to be the world's ruler, and to whom all peoples owe "the obedience of faith." Here, at the beginning of the letter to the Romans, Paul presents himself as did Roman officeholders in official letters, giving their titles. We again encounter the word "gospel" (*euangelion*)—here once more as the proclamation of a ruler. Romans borrows formally from the letter of an emissary, that is, a political message.

After Paul's death his disciples added other letters to his testament, the letter to the Romans, and issued them as a letter collection.[8] In this way Paul's letters became literature with a public claim—more or less simultaneously with the Gospel of Mark, in which the Jesus tradition was shaped into a biography with a literary claim. The motives that drove Paul to develop the letter of friendship into a community letter are obvious. They are those of a missionary who wants to shape and strengthen his communities. In doing so he was presented, as is every leader, with five tasks:

1. *Building consensus*: Paul repeatedly refers in his formulae and expressions to common Christian convictions. He quotes familiar bits of tradition. In relating a central piece of tradition about Jesus' death and resurrection (1 Cor 15:3-7), he explicitly emphasizes his agreement with all other apostles on this question (1 Cor 15:11). Likewise, for the legitimacy of the Gentile mission he appeals emphatically to his agreement and consensus with the other apostles (Gal 2:1-10). Consensus building also serves his argument. He not only reaches back to an already existing consensus, but in some questions (including that of male circumcision) he seeks to create a new consensus.

2. *Orientation within the environment*: Paul conveys an ambivalent attitude toward the surrounding world. On the one hand, Christians are in it as "children of God without blemish in the midst of a crooked and perverse generation, in which you shine like stars in the world" (Phil 2:15). In the same letter he admonishes them to respect and obey the norms of the world around them: "whatever is true, whatever is honorable, whatever is just, whatever is pure, whatever is pleasing, whatever is commendable, if there is any excellence and if there is anything worthy of praise, think about these things" (Phil 4:8). He appeals to his addressees simultaneously not to be conformed to this world (Rom 12:2) and to respect its norms of good and evil (Rom 13:1-7).

3. *Defining identity*: Every group must give its own account of how it differs from others—especially in situations like the division between Christians and Jews. This process of separation is already in progress with Paul, even though it is not completed. Paul grounds the separation from traditional Judaism with harsh alternatives between Moses and Christ, law and promise, works and faith (Galatians; Romans). But he also defines Christian identity in contrast to the Gentiles (1 Thessalonians; 1 Corinthians). In this, Paul's greatness consists in his effort to maintain continuity with Judaism despite the break, and in his ability also to recognize positive values in the Gentile world.

4. *Regulating conflicts*: Paul is almost always busy regulating conflicts within the communities. First Corinthians offers us an especially good insight: Paul mediates conflicts between followers of various apostles, between ascetics and non-ascetics, strong and weak, poor and rich. Especially in the conflict between the strong and the weak he develops a new model for reaching solutions: respect for the attitudes of other people, even if one must in such cases set one's own convictions aside. This model developed for the community in Corinth was so important to him that he presents it again to a community unfamiliar to him and emphatically recommends it (Rom 14–15).

5. *Structures of authority*: Paul lives out of a charismatic authority that he has received in a singular way on the basis of the revelation given him outside Damascus, but he begins to institutionalize this authority and separate it from his own person: scripture, Jesus traditions, and early Christian statements of faith are for him likewise given authority, to which he refers in his argumentation. Above all, he develops the idea of the Body of Christ in which all members have equal value but exercise different functions. The different tasks of leadership are gifts ("charismata"); access to them is not institutionally regulated, but they are not restricted to a few charismatics. In principle every member of the community has an individual leadership task.

One may say of Paul's letters that they are literature of community leadership. Paul developed the letter into an instrument for forming and directing his communities even in his absence, in fact even beyond his death. The letter to the Romans is Paul's community-leadership testament.

Paul and the Markan evangelist are thus the crucial figures in the first phase of early Christian literature. Each created a literature related directly to a person—the gospel concentrated on Jesus, the letters on Paul. This literature derived its authority in early Christian groups entirely from these two charismatics. This concentration on one charismatic in each form of literature had no model in Jewish-Hellenistic literature. Both (independently of each other) shaped their writings according to pagan models of letter and biography. Both laid claim to the public nature of their message by calling the content of their writings "gospel."[9]

Certainly there is some need to explain why the letter form arose before the gospels, Romans coming about fifteen years before Mark's Gospel. The Jesus tradition, rooted in the land, was transmitted orally by ordinary people. Paul's mission, however, led him very quickly into an urban milieu familiar with written communication. Nevertheless, this difference should not be overemphasized: Romans (from the year 56 C.E.) is just on the threshold of public literature. At about the same time the Jesus tradition was first formulated in writing, in the Sayings Source, which has not survived—a document that stood on the threshold of gospel writing. The synchrony of the development in both areas is perhaps greater than appears at first glance.

The result of the first phase of early Christian literature was thus two basic forms in which Jewish traditions were shaped according to pagan forms and whose public claim imitated political claims. This claim to a public nature was, in fact, limited. The early Christian writings circulated in networks of small Christian communities. But in principle their content was addressed to all people. The gospel traditions stemmed from the mission to Israel, the letters of Paul from the Gentile mission. Two charismatics, two directions, two basic forms stood at the beginning. Despite their separate origins and different cultural milieus, we can perceive common tendencies that permit us to speak of a (unified) originary phase of early Christian literature.

8 The Collection of Paul's Letters

Paul's epistles were genuine letters, which Paul built up into community letters by means of liturgical formulae and rhetorical stylization. He thus created a new genre that was on the way to becoming public literature. Non-public letters were usually accessible to the public only when they were brought together in letter collections. The collection dissolved their occasional nature. Paul's letters were also collected very early, although we can express some guesses about the first collection of Paul's letters only by way of some "crime-solving" techniques.

The Sequence of Paul's Letters

The first indicator we can evaluate is the sequence of the letters in the textual tradition. Despite some variations, a particular sequence has survived. If we take as our basis the sequence most frequently attested in the manuscripts, we come to the following arrangement of the writings. The figures indicate the number of letters each contains (Table 13).[1]

Table 13: Expansion of the Pauline Letter Collection

Original Collection		First Appendix		Second Appendix	
Romans	34,410	*Ephesians*	12,012	*1 Timothy*	8,869
1 Corinthians	32,767	Philippians	8,009	*2 Timothy*	6,538
2 Corinthians	22,280	*Colossians*	7,897	*Titus*	3,733
Galatians	11,091	1 Thessalonians	7,423		
		2 Thessalonians	4,055		
		Philemon	1,575		

It is immediately evident that as a rule the letters were arranged according to length, but the ordering begins anew two times: with Ephesians and the Pastorals. That probably indicates that at these points an original collection of Paul's letters was twice augmented, sequentially, by the addition of other letters, the first time with the community letters to the Ephesians, the Colossians, the Philippians, and the Thessalonians (1 and 2 Thessalonians), and the second time with the Pastoral Letters, addressed to individual persons, which were inserted before the single authentic letter from Paul to an individual, Philemon (and his house church).

Attestation of Paul's Letters

The second indicator we can evaluate is the attestation of the letters of Paul in other early Christian writings. Here a certain insecurity remains: associations transmitted through tradition history are not literary dependencies. Some similar-sounding formulae could also be explained by the dependence on a common fund of language. On the other hand, we sometimes know for certain that an author was familiar with a letter (*1 Clement* knew 1 Corinthians), but we can show that he deals rather freely with the text of the letter. Our question is: Do we find indications in other early Christian witnesses to a collection of Paul's letters because they are aware not only of a single Pauline letter, but more than one? Can we perhaps even find indications that the original collection of Romans, 1 Corinthians, 2 Corinthians, and Galatians, which we have posited above, was known at a very early date?

Colossians, as a pseudepigraphic letter, certainly presumes other Pauline letters, because it admires them. Otherwise the unknown letter-writer would have had no motive for writing a letter in the name of Paul. What is disputed is which letters he knew. There are indications that the four letters listed were in the original collection.[2] In Colossians 2:12 the author refers to the baptismal theology of Romans 6:1-4: Christians are buried with Christ in baptism; that this author also connects the resurrection with baptism is an understandable development of Pauline statements. Baptism is, beyond what is said in Romans, a "circumcision made without hands" (Col 2:11). This very image, however, could have been developed out of the "circumcision of the heart" in Romans 2:29. It is also certain that the author knew 1 Corinthians: the revelation schema from 1 Corinthians 2:7-10 may have been adopted here. In Christ a long-hidden mystery has been revealed (Col 1:26-27). It is possible, however, that this was simply a common element of tradition. In Colossians 2:5, however, the author clearly imitates

1 Corinthians 5:3-4: Paul is absent in the flesh, but present in spirit. The author of Colossians is also familiar with 2 Corinthians. That the beginning of the hymn in Colossians, "he is the image of . . . God" (Col 1:15), agrees word for word with 2 Corinthians 4:4 does not prove literary acquaintance. But the fact that the prescript of Colossians agrees almost completely with the prescript of 2 Corinthians is a secure indication: it is precisely in the formal frame of the letter that a pseudepigraphic author wants to imitate existing models in order to create an appearance of genuineness. Finally, the author may also know Galatians: the polemic against the "elemental spirits of the universe" (Col 2:20) looks back to Galatians 4:3, 9, even though in Colossians the universal elements have become mythical powers. Beyond the four letters of the postulated original collection, this author would also have known the letter to Philemon, for there are numerous personal references in Colossians 4:7-17 that coincide with that letter. These personal references show that Colossians pretends to have been written in the same situation of captivity as Philemon—thus in Asia Minor, probably in Ephesus. It is in turn the model for the letter to the Ephesians. From all this we may conclude that there must have been a collection of Paul's letters at a very early date in the area where Colossians was written, and it must have included at least our "original collection." It could be objected that this collection could not yet have been known as such.[3] After all, it was still subject to being augmented by new letters. However, an extension by the addition of indisputably genuine Pauline letters (such as Philemon) was certainly unproblematic. It is readily imaginable that when the collection was augmented by the addition of genuine letters, some non-genuine ones might have been incorporated: the first expansion we have posited, in fact, includes two genuine letters (Philippians and Philemon) and three non-genuine ones (Colossians, Ephesians, 2 Thessalonians).

The *Pastoral Letters* are among the indirect witnesses to a Pauline letter collection, because they were written from the outset as a corpus of three letters and imitate an already existing *Corpus Paulinum* containing at least three and probably more letters. Here again it remains uncertain which of Paul's letters those were. Only two can be demonstrated with confidence: Romans is known, as shown by the ideas concerning the Law (1 Tim 1:8; cf. Rom 7:12, 16), the oath formula in 1 Timothy 2:7 (cf. Rom 9:1), the christological statement about Jesus as son of David and Risen One in 2 Timothy 2:8 (cf. Rom 1:3), the idea of dying and living with Christ in 2 Timothy 2:11-13 (cf. Rom 6:3-4, 8), and the influence of the doctrine of justification in Titus 3:3-7. It is very probable that 1 Corinthians is also presumed, since 1 Timothy 5:18 quotes the saying about not muzzling the ox that is threshing grain (Deut 25:4) and applies it to the obligation to support church officials

(1 Cor 9:9). This idea appears only in these two places. Of course, it could already have become proverbial, in which case no literary acquaintance can be deduced from it. Thus the command to women to keep silent in 1 Timothy 2:11-14, which presupposes the *mulier taceat in ecclesiam* in 1 Corinthians 14:33b-36, is a better indicator. While that passage is secondary in 1 Corinthians, for the author of the Pastorals it was either part of the original text or had been interpolated into 1 Corinthians within his own milieu. That in itself would be a certain indication that 1 Corinthians was known in that milieu. The Pastorals are in contact with 2 Corinthians only in the idea that Eve was led astray by the serpent (1 Tim 2:14; cf. 2 Cor 11:3). The wording and tendency of the saying are different in the two passages. Familiarity is possible, but not certain. In my opinion the basis of proof is better with regard to Galatians. It is probable that its autobiographical section, which depicts Paul's turning from persecutor of Christians to missionary to the Gentiles (Gal 1:13-23), was the formal model for 1 Timothy 1:12-17: here, as in Galatians, there appears at the beginning of the letter a section about a change in Paul's life. Our conclusion is that for the Pastoral Letters also the original collection we have posited—Romans, 1 and 2 Corinthians, and Galatians—must have been familiar.

The *Acts of the Apostles* appears at first glance to be unfamiliar with any letters of Paul, who is nowhere described as a letter writer. The text itself contains only a few hints of the Pauline letters themselves. But the historical situation—at the end of the first century—makes it hard to imagine that the author of Acts did not know the letters of Paul. After all, this author was an admirer of Paul who had deliberately gathered information for his historical work. Would he not have come across Paul's letters in the process? According to Andreas Lindemann, Acts knows of Romans and 2 Corinthians (10–13), and perhaps Galatians as well.[4] While that is not certain, it would also point to the original collection we have posited, even though 1 Corinthians is not attested in Acts.

First Clement (Rome, end of the first century) must have been aware of a small collection of Paul's letters, certainly including 1 Corinthians,[5] because *1 Clement* 47:1-3 refers to that letter. However, the exhortation "take up *the* epistle of the blessed Paul the Apostle!" (47:1) appears unaware of a second Corinthian letter, unless one understands the continuation, "what did he *first* write to you at the beginning of his gospel?" as a reference to another letter of Paul to the Corinthians—after his opening proclamation in Corinth. Since *1 Clement* 47:1-3 refers to the party strife in Corinth described in 1 Corinthians 1–4, this could also be a reference to the first pages of 1 Corinthians.[6] But the word "gospel" would be strange in reference to a letter. Probably the author of this letter (as in Phil 4:15) is thinking of Paul's missionary activity, that is, the preaching of the gospel. Probably Romans is known, as well as the Corinthian correspondence; texts from Romans find an echo in a number of passages.[7] Of course, we cannot conclude with certainty from these echoes to an awareness of Romans. It is primarily the supposition that *1 Clement*, written in Rome, must for historical reasons have known the letter to the Romans that causes these echoes to have some demonstrative force. In any case, it seems fairly certain that two letters from the posited original collection are attested in Rome at the end of the first century. In addition, *1 Clement* may have known other of Paul's writings (perhaps Philippians?), but that would be difficult to demonstrate.

Second Peter is a definite witness to a collection of Paul's letters. The author speaks of "all the letters" of Paul as if he were certain of knowing *all* of them (2 Pet 3:16). It is all the more surprising that he makes no use of Paul's letters. We could, of course, question whether the image of the master who comes like a thief in the night stems from 1 Thessalonians 5:2-3, but it is already familiar in the Synoptics (Matt 24:43-44) and would not indicate knowledge of 1 Thessalonians.

In *Marcion's collection of letters* (Rome, mid-second century) the Pastorals are missing—although the Marcionites later used them. Did Marcion deliberately ignore the Pastorals? Could he do so because he knew that they were not yet accepted everywhere? Or did he not know them? That would confirm the supposition that the Pastorals were a secondary addition and is also an argument for supposing that the renewed beginning of a "principle of ordering by length" in the Pauline collection does in fact point to an addition.

Ignatius of Antioch, according to Annette Merz, attests as early as about 110 to the complete Pauline letter collection, including the Pastorals.[8] For besides Ignatius's self-stylization as a disciple of Paul, including in the writing of letters, and besides many individual text references in his letters, we find a "systematic reference," that is, an imitation of the structure of the entire *Corpus Paulinum*: Ignatius, like Paul, besides writing community letters, also pens a pastoral letter to an individual community leader, that is, a letter to Polycarp, as well as the letters to various communities. He must have had a model for that, but in that case he must have known the Pastorals.

Thus, quite early we find indications of knowledge of a number of Pauline letters in one place, including letters of Paul not addressed to that place: our original collection may be known even by the author of Colossians. The individual conclusions are, of course, associated with uncertainties in the various cases. An overview is revealing (Table 14):

Table 14: The Earliest Attestations of the Letters of Paul

Letter	*Letters Attested*
Colossians	Romans, 1 Corinthians, 2 Corinthians, Galatians, Philemon
Pastorals	Romans, 1 Corinthians, 2 Corinthians(?), Galatians(?)
Acts of the Apostles	Romans, 2 Corinthians, Galatians
1 Clement	Romans, 1 Corinthians, 2 Corinthians(??)
2 Peter	An extensive collection of Paul's letters
Ignatius	Collection of Paul's letters including the Pastorals and Hebrews
Marcion	Romans, 1 Corinthians, 2 Corinthians, Galatians, Ephesians, Philippians, Colossians, 1 and 2 Thessalonians, Philemon

One interesting conclusion that may be drawn from this overview is that around 100 C.E. a more extensive collection of Paul's letters may have been known in the East (as attested by Ignatius) than in the West (as shown by *1 Clement*). Does this indicate that the place where Paul's letters were collected is also to be sought in the East—where Paul himself founded communities?

The Place Where Paul's Letters Were Collected

In conclusion we must ask: Where were the most Pauline letters accessible, and where could there have been interest in editing them? Two places present themselves: Corinth and Ephesus. Corinth was both the recipient and the place of origin of important letters, while Ephesus was only the originating point a number of the letters.

The first letter to the Thessalonians was written in Corinth, before or during the founding of the Corinthian community. Romans was written later in Corinth. In addition, the community there was the addressee of more than one letter to the Corinthians. If we do not suppose an interactive origin for 2 Corinthians, which I consider probable, 2 Corinthians could have been assembled by the Corinthian community out of a number of Paul's letters in order to place a second and equally weighty letter alongside 1 Corinthians. If the receiving community itself was behind the "artificial product" of 2 Corinthians it would be understandable why all the letters that contributed to 2 Corinthians have not been individually preserved. Who was in a better position to give the stamp of authenticity to a somewhat artificial product of redaction and editing than the recipient community, if not the author himself, in case 2 Corinthians was put together by Paul personally?[9] In that case, three letters from the posited original collection would certainly be attested in Corinth, and only the fourth, Galatians, would have no discernible relationship to Corinth. One would have to suppose that Paul himself brought a copy of the letter to the Galatians to Corinth. In Galatians he emphasized the legal character of his writing, certifying it through a personal signature. Certified documents are given to both parties. Thus, Paul must have had a copy of Galatians in particular. If Paul still had Galatians at hand in Corinth when he was writing the letter to the Romans that would also explain the considerable contact between the content of Galatians and Romans, without having to date Galatians immediately before Romans. In writing Romans, Paul may well have had a copy of Galatians before him. A high estimation of Paul's letters is attested in Corinth even in Paul's lifetime (2 Cor 10:10). This could, then, be the place where Paul's letters were first collected. Possibly this oldest collection was an authorial edition by Paul himself (so David Trobisch), or an edition by Paul's circle, either authorized by Paul or undertaken only after the end of his activities there. Unfortunately, we do not know.

The second candidate for the place of origin of the oldest collection of Pauline letters is Ephesus; here originated 1 Corinthians, Philippians, and Philemon, and possibly Colossians and Ephesians as well. A copy of Romans may also have been available there, because Roman exiles who fled to Ephesus may have been among the additional addressees of the letter to the Romans. Paul could have sent them a copy of Romans with the greetings meant especially for them in Romans 16. The same considerations apply to Galatians, as we have indicated above: Paul could have had a copy of that writing with him. In addition, if we accept the early dating of Galatians we prefer, Galatians itself might have been written in Ephesus. We must also suppose that copies of 1 and 2 Thessalonians were available in Ephesus. In fact, Ephesus may have been the location of a Pauline tradition that cultivated his memory after his death. The original collection could have originated here—and especially the expanded collection of Pauline letters, since Colossians was certainly written in Asia Minor, and Ephesians presumes its existence. An indication of the special significance of the community in Ephesus for Paul's heritage is also found in the fact that the Acts of the Apostles presents Paul's theological testament as an address given at Miletus to the presbyters from Ephesus (Acts 20:18-35). He insists to the presbyters that he has declared to them the *whole* purpose of God (Acts 20:27). They possess the entire Pauline tradition. Nothing is said here about letters, but in any case Acts is silent on that subject altogether.

It would be an appealing thought that an original collection of four letters had been made in Corinth and went from there to Rome (*1 Clement*). An expansion with two addenda could have been completed in Ephesus and traveled from there to Antioch in the East. But we must admit that these historical processes will always remain in the dark.

Part Two

The Fictive Self-Interpretation of Paul and Jesus

The Pseudepigraphic Phase

At the end of the first generation there already existed a literature with a high claim to authority: Paul had created the community letter through his own authority, and the Jesus tradition had found a form for the future in the Gospel of Mark. At the same time (i.e., in the 60s) the three most important early Christian leadership figures—Paul, James, and Peter—died violent deaths. Who was to exercise authority in the communities after them? The early Christian structure of office was not yet fully developed. Recourse had to be had to already recognized authorities. There were two possibilities: writing pseudepigraphic letters in the name of Paul (or the other apostles), or referring directly to the authority of Jesus and shaping his traditions redactionally in gospels in such a way that they served the purpose of community guidance.[1]

Recourse to the authority of the apostles was obtained through the epistolary literature. This had a major advantage: the apostles possessed an authority derived from Christ, but in this they did not differ from the church's officeholders. They were therefore suitable models for church offices and other authorities in the community. The letters to the Colossians and Ephesians support the authority of the household fathers, the Pastorals that of the community leaders—always with an appeal to Paul, that is, with recourse to the fictive self-interpretation of Paul created in the Pastorals and used in other pseudepigraphic writings.

However, recourse to the authority of Jesus in the gospels had the advantage that the superior authority of Jesus could be employed even against the newly created community offices. Here people who wanted to exercise influence in the communities independently of bishops and presbyters by a direct appeal to Jesus seized their pens. Their intentions were disseminated in the gospels in the form of a fictive self-interpretation by Jesus—most clearly in the Gospels of John and Thomas, where this self-interpretation saturates not only a redactional layer but the whole text, and led to a transformation of the Jesus tradition.

9 Pseudepigraphy as a Literary-Historical Phase in Early Christianity

The second phase of New Testament literary history falls under the rubric of a fictive self-interpretation of Paul and Jesus in epistolary literature and gospels.[1] With pseudepigraphy something new begins: the creative period of early Christian literary history was replaced by an imitation of existing Christian models. Mark's Gospel and Paul's community letter were prescriptive of the forms used in the further development. Hence we can only speak in the preceding phase of development, from oral tradition to the written gospels, from concrete letters to the general public character of the letter to the Romans, of "primitive literature" as formative in Franz Overbeck's sense—corresponding to his two criteria of form-critical creativity and social interactivity between author and addressee. Pseudepigraphic literature was neither creative nor did author and readership interact. The real author remained invisible to the readers, hidden behind the writing, which is form-imitative literature (Table 15).

Both the basic New Testament forms, the gospel and the letter, contain particular opportunities for founding intra-community authority after the death of the first generation: the apostles had built up the communities. What they had said and done was therefore a model for community leaders. The letters written in their names supported their authority (this was particularly true of the Pastorals). The gospels, on the other hand, could also bring into play the authority of Jesus, even against disciples and other intra-community authorities. In all the gospels we find a critique of community authorities: in Mark in the form of the disciples' lack of understanding (Mark 8:14-21, and frequently), in Matthew by emphasis on the fact that Jesus is the sole legitimate teacher (Matt 23:8-10), in the Lukan corpus by critique of community leaders who allow themselves to be supported (Acts 20:33-35), and in John through the devaluation of Peter, who, as shepherd, is the epitome of the community leader (John 13:8-10, and frequently). The

Table 15: Charismatic and Pseudepigraphic Phases of the History of Early Christian Literature

	Charismatic Phase: Earliest Literature Determinants: Jesus and Paul	**Pseudepigraphic Phase: Imitative Literature** Determinants: Anonymous Authors
First Criterion: Creative character of the form	*Creative literature* with new forms adapted from pagan models: Gospel as creative adaptation of the ancient *bios*. Community letter as creative adaptation of the letter of friendship.[2]	*Post-creative literature* adapted from early Christian models. Expansion of the gospel form through redaction (Synoptics) and *relecture* (Gospel of John); Imitation of the community letter and its development into a pastoral letter.
Second Criterion: Presence of the author in the work	*Presence of the author*, who can interact with the readers either through writing and personal presence (in the letters) or through the work (in Q and Mark) without the evangelist's retreating behind a particular figure in the writing.	*Concealment of the author*: The true author does not wish to be known: Authors hide behind Paul and desire no interaction with the addressees. Evangelists conceal themselves behind fictive personae: the we-sections in Acts and the Beloved Disciple in the Gospel of John.

letters are therefore potentially "more conservative" than the "more critical" gospels; their authority is derived only from the apostles and does not go back directly to Jesus, whose authority is the standard for criticizing all others.

Thus the existence side by side of the two basic forms of early Christian literature reflects a conflict over the internal authority structure of the communities in that period. Was the (more radical) Jesus tradition the norm regulating the authority of living community leaders, or should the (more moderate) attitude of community leaders be decisive? The conflict is again repeated within the epistolary literature: here we can recognize a bolder (Colossians; Ephesians) and a more moderate wing (Pastorals) within the Pauline school. But in both forms early Christian authors say that "Jesus or Paul, rightly understood, already intended what I am saying," or "Jesus and Paul already said what I think." In fictive self-interpretations the two fundamental authorities, Jesus and Paul, are presented as speaking the authors' own theology. That is a new beginning.

This presupposes one thing: that not only Jesus, but Paul as well, the *Kyrios* and his apostle, had become defining authorities by the end of the first generation and the first phase of an early Christian literary history, that they remained unique, and that thereby the time of the first generation was recognized as fundamental and normative. In fact, at a later time only those writings were canonized that were believed to go back to this early time. They had to be apostolic, that is, stemming directly (like Matthew or John) or indirectly (like Mark and Luke) from an apostle. While Overbeck sees the end of the "primitive literature" only with the transition from early Christian to patristic literature in the second century, in my opinion at this point already a decisive break within early Christian literature had occurred, namely, at the transition from the creative, charismatic first phase to a pseudepigraphic, imitative second phase.

But is it justified to call this phase "pseudepigraphic"? This is true of the letters, but for the gospel literature? In fact, we must make an important distinction here: the letters are primary, the later gospels secondary pseudepigraphy. The non-genuine letters are primary pseudepigraphy. The authors wrote under another's name from the start. They interpreted Paul or another apostle by writing fictive letters in their names. The gospels, on the other hand, are secondary pseudepigraphy. It is possible that they were originally anonymous. The *Didache* cites Matthew's Gospel four times as "the" gospel, without using the name of Matthew. The gospels drew their authority from Jesus, not from their authors.[3] As long as each was the only gospel that was not a problem. It was only the collecting of the gospels that necessitated a distinction between a gospel "according to Mark," "according to Matthew," or "according to Luke." Only then were the gospels attributed to particular authors. Even though the originality of the *inscriptiones* has been defended by serious scholars,[4] they are probably secondary. That, however, does not exclude the possibility that the authorial attributions reflected there rest on older, perhaps even accurate traditions.[5]

However, the disciple Matthew was certainly not the author of Matthew's Gospel, because that gospel was assuredly not written down by an eyewitness. Such a one would scarcely have tied himself down to another source, the Gospel of Mark, if he himself had shared in all the events. It is possible, however, that the author, to whom at one time the Sayings Source was attributed, was promoted to author of the Gospel, since Papias testifies to a tradition that Matthew wrote down the *logia* of the Lord. That may originally have referred to the Sayings Source. This tradition was then transferred to the Gospel of Matthew, in which in fact the words of the Lord collected in Jesus' five discourses play a central role. We would have here a name transfer that could have been performed in good faith.

Luke could scarcely have been the author of the two-volume Lukan work. We cannot imagine that a companion of Paul could have written it, since Luke never calls Paul an apostle. The two exceptions can be explained: in Acts 14:4 and 14:14 Paul and Barnabas are called "apostles"—apparently to emphasize, especially in this narrative, that they are not gods, as the people of Lystra suppose, but only messengers from a deity. Otherwise, however, the title of "apostle" is withheld from Paul. But Paul repeatedly and emphatically fought for just that: that people recognize him as an apostle. The author of Luke-Acts denies him that recognition. But since the "we" accompanies the apostle to Rome and, according to 2 Timothy 4:11, Luke alone remained there with Paul, people astutely concluded that the anonymous companion of Paul in Acts must have been Luke the physician.

In the case of Mark and John, a similarity of names may have occasioned a secondary identification of the evangelists with well-known persons in early Christianity. The John Mark from Jerusalem could scarcely have been the author of Mark's Gospel. But it is altogether possible that an unknown "Mark" wrote the Gospel of Mark. After all, if it was possible to freely invent an author, it would have been more attractive to attribute the gospel to an apostle, not merely to an apostle's disciple. Later, then, this Mark was identified with the Jerusalemite John Mark, who was familiar from other writings. Not pseudonymity, but homonymity, eventually led to this authorial attribution.

The same may be true for the Gospel of John. John the son of Zebedee can hardly be the author of the gospel, since according to Mark 10:38-39 John died even before 70 C.E., if not at the same time as his brother James. Possibly the Gospel of John comes from a like-named "presbyter" John, who like the author of the letters 2 and 3 John bore the title "elder" and might even be identical with him. According to Papias he may have been an apostle's disciple. But the identity between the names of "John" and an apostle led an editorial group astray into implying direct apostolic origins for the Gospel of John.[6] At the beginning, then, there was no pseudonymity here either, but only homonymity, the sameness of the name "John" for two people that was, however, applied in such a way that the reader was meant to think of John the apostle.

However, the inclusion of the gospel redaction in the pseudepigraphic phase of early Christian literature is not dependent on authorial attribution. All the gospels are pseudepigraphic in the sense that, together with the preservation of Jesus tradition, they present a fictive self-interpretation by Jesus: they interpret Jesus in a new way, the Synoptic Gospels through a redactional editing of his tradition, the Gospels of John and Thomas by a profound transformation of his message. In both cases the gospel authors place their own convictions on the lips of Jesus. They themselves, meanwhile, could retreat into the background. In the case of the gospels, secondary false attributions of the documents were more likely a mistake spread in good faith (and in which we are sometimes uncertain whether it did not strike on truth, as in the case of Mark).[7] In the case of the pseudepigraphic letters, in contrast, we must assume that the authors intended to deceive.

We can exclude the possibility that there was a silent agreement between authors and readers that religious pseudepigraphy, as pious deception, was legitimate. Falsifications were rejected in antiquity. It was expected that the content of a text belonged to the author to whom the text was attributed. It could deviate, but only in its wording.[8] In early Christianity, moreover, falsifications were in contradiction with the ethos of truth in the same documents. What should we think when the letter to the Ephesians warns its readers: ". . . putting away falsehood, let all of us speak the truth to our neighbors" (Eph 4:25), and at the same time deceives its readers by suggesting it was written by Paul? It is disputed whether there was such a thing as open pseudepigraphy, that is, pseudepigraphy as a literary game that everyone saw through and therefore was not a pious fraud since no one was deceived by it. In the New Testament one might at most reckon with that in regard to 2 Peter.

How could there be such a thing as pseudepigraphy in good conscience in a group that was aware of its obligation to the truth? That is one of the greatest problems in a literary history of the New Testament. The attempted solution sketched below may be summarized in advance as follows: Early Christian pseudepigraphy is explained by a unique encounter between Jewish and Greek tradition, orality and literature, education and lack of it. It can be explained as a behavior in conformity with culture, but not solely by the idea that falsifications were generally practiced at the time; the only adequate explanation lies in factors that were characteristic only of early Christianity.

Early Christian Pseudepigraphy between Jewish and Hellenistic Cultures

Early Christian pseudepigraphy was based in the first place on a combination of Jewish traditional literature with the literature of individual authors in the Greco-Roman world.[9] Many documents in Jewish literature were written under the names of great figures from the past: apocalypses under the names of Enoch, Abraham, Moses, Baruch, and Ezra; wisdom literature under the name of Solomon. Pseudonymity was almost the rule in Jewish literature. Add to these the anonymous historical books such as Kings,

Chronicles, and Maccabees. Only quite late do we encounter individual authors: Jesus Sirach, at the beginning of the second century B.C.E., is the first author to write a wisdom book under his own name. He was influenced by Hellenism. In the field of Hellenistic influence more and more individual authors appeared, including Aristobulos and Philo. With Josephus, historical writing also acquired the name of an individual author.

Early Christianity combined orthonymous and pseudonymous writings: the authentic letters of Paul, Ignatius, and Polycarp and the apocalypses of John and Hermas, appearing under individual names, are orthonymous; in contrast, the deutero-Pauline and catholic epistles are pseudonymous writings, and secondarily pseudonymous are the gospels, which were originally anonymous. Much favors the supposition that many traditions of early Christianity could have remained anonymous in a Jewish environment. This is true especially of the gospels. But as soon as early Christianity penetrated a non-Jewish milieu, an unavoidable tendency to literature by individual authors imposed itself. Early Christian authors translated the pseudonymity that had been oriented in Judaism to figures of the past into pseudonymous letters by apostles of the present. The apostles had a superior authority comparable only to that of the great figures of the past. At the same time, these authors translated the Hellenistic tendency to orthonymy by individual authors of the present into apocalyptic. Only in early Christianity do we find apocalypses published under genuine names: John and Hermas! In this respect as well, early Christian literature crossed cultural boundaries. And yet the marginal situation of early Christian literature, between Jewish and Hellenistic culture, cannot by itself offer a satisfactory explanation for pseudonymity. Most of the pseudepigraphic writings in the New Testament are letters. There are no models for pseudonymous letters in Jewish-Hellenistic literature. But in non-Jewish literature of the time they were anything but rare.

Early Christian Pseudepigraphy between Oral and Literary Cultures

Early Christian literature stands on the threshold between oral and written literature; this is true both of the gospels and of the letters. In oral literature different "criteria of authenticity" apply. Oral tradition is variable and open to expansions. The oral messenger never formulates the message of the one who sent the message in exactly the same words in which it was received, but feels assured of delivering the message accurately, even though the words are changed. The authors of early Christian literature also stood within this tradition of oral proclamation. They lived in a messenger culture. The messenger represents the one giving the assignment.

Early Christian writers translated this awareness of being a representative that characterized the oral messenger into the literature they created. Jesus had sent out his disciples to spread his message. He told them: "Whoever hears you, hears me!" (Luke 10:16). After his death the accent in the disciples' awareness of being messengers shifted. Now it was: "Whoever hears *us*, hears him!" The same was true for writings, because these were not merely read, but read aloud. The communities still for a long time received the texts of the gospels and those from Paul as oral words of the Lord and of the apostle. The *viva vox* oral tradition was even valued more highly than written witness, as Papias attests in the second century (Eusebius, *Eccl. hist.* 3.39.4). Oral tradition, however, can never be finally fixed in writing. Its living nature is evident particularly in the variation of the wording. Even the gospel writers felt free to reformulate traditions when they thought they could give them a shape more in accord with Jesus' intention. They probably knew from their own experience how variable words and narratives in the oral tradition were in their details.[10]

In the realm of epistolary literature, Paul's coworkers were often his messengers and were named by him as coauthors of his letters. In the last phase of Paul's life, when (after his imprisonment in Jerusalem) he was imprisoned without interruption, it may be that Paul worked even more than previously through representatives and messengers who took his place. Why should they have stopped speaking and writing in his name after he was dead? They were also in possession of many oral traditions of Paul and could again and again bring forth new treasures from those traditions. They therefore "faked" letters of Paul with disarming innocence and in good conscience. It may be that Titus and Timothy themselves wrote the Pauline letters addressed to them—basing them on oral Pauline traditions, that is, on what they had heard from Paul.[11] We can now and then recognize, or at least suspect, such Pauline traditions in the letters. The hymn in Colossians could have been a piece of Pauline tradition. Perhaps Paul wrote it himself. The letter to the Colossians exegetes it and applies it to the current situation (the conflict with a philosophy). The schema of revelation is modeled on 1 Corinthians 2:6-16. It recurs in a number of places in the deutero-Pauline letters: a hidden wisdom is revealed to the privileged (Rom 16:25-27; Col 1:26-27; Eph 3:3-4; 1 Pet 1:20; 2 Tim 1:9-10). In the Pastorals we find statements with an introduction such as "the saying is sure [*pistos ho logos*] . . . that Christ Jesus came into the world to save sinners—of whom I am the foremost" (1 Tim 1:15; 3:1; 4:9; 2 Tim 2:11; Titus 3:8). The language of the Pastorals certainly has a Pauline shape. Only minute studies of the vocabulary show that there are, nevertheless, some major differences.

The messenger's consciousness and dependence on tradition are parts of oral culture. But pseudepigraphy has already crossed the threshold of written culture. Here it encountered a motif of epistolary ideology, that of the *parousia*. Hans-Josef Klauck uses it to explain pseudepigraphy:

> The "parousia," the enablement of the presence of someone absent, is a leading idea of letter writing that Paul knew how to exploit when he allowed himself to be represented in his communities through his letters, and in addition by his coworkers, who often carried, accompanied, prepared, and commented on such letters. It was not a very great step to the idea of transforming the geographic distance into temporal distance; then Paul and other authority figures from the first Christian generation could remain present even after death through letters, ideally letters of their previous coworkers.[12]

Early Christian Pseudepigraphy between Educated Authors and Uneducated Addressees

Early Christianity was a colorful social collection made up of educated and uneducated people. Authors were educated, or they could not have written. Their addressees were largely uneducated. Authors had to be able to imitate other writings, something they could learn in school. There people deliberately practiced imitating other authors. They learned the technique of *prosōpopoia* (Latin *sermocinatio*), which consisted of transposing oneself into a person from the past and formulating a speech that person might have given in a particular situation. What, for example, might the king of Syria, Antiochus Epiphanes, have said when he wanted to persuade Jews to eat pork, and what would the priest Eleazar have answered? In 2 Maccabees 7 we learn very little about that, but in 4 Maccabees we can read an extended discourse on it.[13] The authors of the New Testament writings, on the basis of their education, were thus practiced in writing speeches in the name of another person—according to the motto, "what would XY have said in a familiar situation?" It was only a small step to writing texts under the motto "what would XY have said in a situation unknown to her or him?" Since in antiquity only a relatively small number (20 to 30 percent?) of the population could write, and only a few of those possessed any literary competence, those capable of literary composition were members of a vanishing minority. Some of them must have belonged to the early Christian communities, if only a few (1 Cor 1:26). The astonishing scope of the early Christians' literary productivity presumes people with a certain degree of education. Must we, then, abandon the socio-romantic idea that the lower orders left us their voices in early Christian literature? That is how it often seems today. But we can give good reasons to the contrary.

Literature does not simply belong to its authors, but to its addressees as well. The latter exercise a preventive censorship by deciding what is received and what is not. To that extent they are co-authors. Their expectations constitute genres and forms and play an important role in the production and reception of texts. The New Testament authors may have belonged to educated circles capable of literary production, but a majority of the addressees of the early Christian writings were surely members of classes far removed from literature. The genre expectations one may presume in regard to these groups were minimal. They were familiar with the personal authority of Jesus and the apostles. What came from them was acceptable to simple believers. Therefore Paul's letters were imitated, and gospels were written. Both these things were done in order to make possible a literary communication within a milieu that in itself was non-literary.

In the first phase of early Christian literature we can observe the adoption of communicative forms used by the upper classes by groups far removed from literature. In the second phase we see the reverse process: the penetration of the oral culture of ordinary people into literature, on the one hand in the messenger consciousness of the authors, on the other hand in the limited familiarity of the addressees with genre. Both explain pseudepigraphy in good conscience. Because the ordinary people in the community accepted a gospel or a letter of Paul but were unfamiliar with many other genres, those genres with which they were acquainted were imitated and new gospels and new Pauline letters were written. The authors' motive was the effort to gain authority through an already acknowledged charismatic author.[14] They placed themselves fictively in a position of authority that in actuality was far above them.[15]

Open Pseudepigraphy in Early Christianity?

Did the first Christians know that many early Christian writings were pseudepigraphic? Was there a tacit understanding on that subject? Was there an open pseudepigraphy minus the *pseudos*? As regards the communities as a whole we would have to say "no," but as regards small groups of educated Christians we must say "yes." At least the real authors of pseudonymous early Christian writings saw through what was going on: anyone who publishes writings under another name would have to suppose that others did so as well.

It is true that in early Christianity we find very few approaches that point to such a transformation of pseudepigraphic fiction into transparent fictionality. When, in 2 Peter, the fictive Peter formulates his theological inheritance before his death and asserts that later false teachers will appear and say that the fathers have died without the parousia having occurred, he opens a window on the situation of the real author in a much later generation. The fictive Peter speaks openly of the fathers who have died (a long time ago), among whom he himself (paradoxically) belongs (2 Pet 3:4). But he does so within a prophecy. Did early Christian readers see through this, realizing that the real author lived much later than Peter? But there is also open pseudepigraphy when, in the Gospel of John, the post-Easter period is anticipated as transparent to the reader. Thus, the Johannine Jesus says in the concluding high-priestly prayer of his farewell discourse that he is no longer in the world (John 17:11), although he *is* in the world and is about to take leave of his disciples. Every reader realizes immediately that the post-Easter Christ is speaking here, after he has already left the world. A third example is found in the Muratorian Fragment, where the Wisdom of Solomon is traced not to Solomon but to his friends, and yet it is counted among the canonical scriptures. A naïve reader could scarcely be aware that the author could not be Peter, the earthly Jesus, or the historical Solomon. But would an early Christian author not have had to reckon also with educated hearers who would see through his authorial hide-and-seek? Hans-Josef Klauck in fact assumes that one must count on there having been two groups of addressees of early Christian literature, those who saw through the names game, and others who naïvely took the fictive authorial names for the real ones.[16]

The fact that some educated persons saw through the pseudepigraphic game is indicated by the ancient view of the relationship between teachers and students. In school traditions it was accepted that students would publish writings under the name of their master. Iamblichus writes of the Pythagoreans: "If, as we may admit, the writings currently in circulation partly stem from Pythagoras, are partly derived from his oral discourses (wherefore the Pythagoreans have not asserted that these writings are their own property, but have attributed them to Pythagoras as his own work), it is clear from all this that Pythagoras was sufficiently experienced in all wisdom" (*De vita Pythagorica* 158). "It is also honorable that they attributed everything to Pythagoras and only very seldom claimed personal fame for their discoveries: there are but a vanishing few of whom personal writings are known" (ibid., 198). Tertullian applies such figures of thought to the gospels: Mark and Luke were students of the apostles, but their authority rests on that of the apostles. It is asserted "that the [gospel] published by Mark is from Peter, whose interpreter Mark was. Likewise, Luke's narratives are often attributed to Paul. That is, it is allowable to regard what students have published as the work of their teachers" (*Adv. Marc.* 4.5.3-4). We need not presuppose such a school consciousness throughout early Christianity, but only among certain educated persons who consciously cultivated Paul's heritage and thus might be able to understand themselves as a kind of school.

Our overall conclusion: we find in early Christianity a pseudepigraphy in good conscience. In the broad uneducated classes it was conditioned by the oral culture familiar to everyone, but among the small groups of educated persons it was potentially an "open pseudepigraphy" that these people saw through. Early Christian pseudepigraphy is not a morally objectionable phenomenon, but it can easily be explained in historical terms. The suggestion that we should call it "deuteronomic" instead of "pseudonymous" is justified, but it is an unnecessary deviation from well-understood usage. We can today assert the fact of pseudepigraphy without indignation. After all, we ourselves recognize fictive elements in the most trusted scientific truths and can as a consequence recognize elements of truth in fictive texts as well.

10 Paul's Fictive Self-Interpretation in the Deutero-Pauline Writings

The pseudepigraphic letters of Paul can be divided into two groups: first, the non-genuine letters that were appended as a first addition to the original collection of Romans, 1 and 2 Corinthians, and Galatians: 2 Thessalonians, Colossians, and Ephesians. These three letters are "deutero-Pauline" in the stricter sense. They include the oldest pseudepigraphic writings in the New Testament. The second group is made up of the Pastorals, which came as a second addition to the collection of Pauline letters: 1 Timothy, 2 Timothy, and Titus. Occasionally these are called "trito-Pauline" to distinguish them from the older deutero-Pauline letters. In terms of form criticism, these two groups continue the two lines of development we have worked out in the genuine Pauline letters:

The deutero-Pauline letters (2 Thessalonians, Colossians, and Ephesians) are systematically constructed letters and have a two- or three-part structure; they give the impression of being complete compositions. In this they are less closely related to the later systematic letters of Paul, namely, Galatians and Romans, than to the earliest Pauline letter, 1 Thessalonians: they are often written in two parts. In 2 Thessalonians this comes about through dependence on 1 Thessalonians itself. But Ephesians also consists of an expanded thanksgiving for saving knowledge (Ephesians 1–3) and a paraenesis (Ephesians 4–6). Such an expansion of the proemium finds its structural model in 1 Thessalonians. Colossians has the same form, but the paraenesis is expanded by a polemic against the philosophy it combats. It may have been formally influenced by Philippians in this regard, because Philippians also contains a polemical section in the center. The letters in the first expansion of the Pauline collection, as we have posited them, made up of both genuine and non-genuine letters—Ephesians, Philippians, Colossians, 1 Thessalonians, 2 Thessalonians, Philemon—are thus formally related to the extent that they continue the two-part Pauline letter. That also speaks in favor of their belonging together.

The trito-Pauline letters, on the other hand, continue the additively composed letters of Paul. They treat practical themes in serial form, but they differ from genuine Pauline letters in that the loose structure indicates no interaction between writer and recipient. Especially in 2 Timothy the suggestion of genuineness is built up in detail. "Paul" asks that someone bring his mantle and books from Troas (2 Tim 4:13). Here we are at the threshold of deliberate falsification, unless one supposes that in 2 Timothy 4:9-17 the author was editing in a fragment from a genuine Pauline letter or historical Pauline traditions. The Pastorals would then have been created not in interaction with their readers, but in an imagined interaction with the historical Paul, in that they edited and incorporated fragments from his writings or isolated traditions about him.

The deutero- and trito-Pauline letters are further distinguished by their intertextual links to the genuine Pauline letters. In the first group we find letters that were each created as an individual letter of Paul: 2 Thessalonians is related only to a single letter, namely, 1 Thessalonians, and could have been inspired by oral Pauline traditions left behind by Paul's visits to Thessalonica. Colossians and Ephesians, in contrast, do not merely interpret a single letter, but continue and expand on the whole of Pauline theology: a broad stream of Pauline theology culminates here in two single letters in which there are echoes of many genuine Pauline letters. The Pastorals, on the other hand, from the outset imitate the collection of Paul's letters *as* a collection; they were created as a corpus of three letters.

The Eschatological Theology of 2 Thessalonians

Second Thessalonians has only one letter as its model, namely, 1 Thessalonians. It shares the latter's two-part structure: an expanded proemium (2 Thess 1:3–2:16) is followed by a paraenesis (2 Thess 3:1-18). Nothing indicates that it used or evaluated several of Paul's letters. It holds rigidly to the structure of 1 Thessalonians and deviates in only a few places, including especially the eschatological instruction in 2 Thessalonians 2:1-12. But 2 Thessalonians imitates 1 Thessalonians only formally; its content says the opposite: namely, 1 Thessalonians represents an expectation of an imminent end, while 2 Thessalonians warns against such an expectation[1]—precisely in the section that goes beyond 1 Thessalonians. Here "Paul" reminds the readers that when he was with them he taught that before the end a "lawless one" must come (2 Thess 2:3) who "opposes and exalts himself above every so-called god or object of worship, so that he takes his seat in the temple of

God, declaring himself to be God" (2 Thess 2:4). Before he appears, what "is now restraining him" must be eliminated (2 Thess 2:6). The end-time has not yet come because first the great fall must happen and a contrary "one who restrains it" is at work; this is represented as both neuter (*to katechon*, v. 6) and personal (*ho katechōn*, v. 7). This is probably a relic of experiences with Gaius Caligula, who wanted to have his statue set up in the temple at Jerusalem in 39/40 C.E. but was prevented from carrying out his intentions by being murdered. The end-time was now seen as delayed, but still expected. Ideas of this nature could therefore go back to the 40s or 50s. Paul certainly did not present them in that way during his initial stay in Thessalonica, but he visited the community one more time (2 Cor 2:13; Acts 20:1-5). During this second visit the community would have asked him why the imminent end announced in 1 Thessalonians had not come. Paul could then have orally corrected his first letter by teaching about a mystery that was delaying the end. Later someone felt justified in setting down this oral self-correction by Paul in written form and publishing it in 2 Thessalonians. Therefore 2 Thessalonians 2:5 recalls what Paul said when he was in Thessalonica and warns openly against reading an imminent end from 1 Thessalonians: "we beg you . . . not to be quickly shaken in mind or alarmed, either by spirit or by word or by letter, as though from us, to the effect that the day of the Lord is already here" (2 Thess 2:1-2). It is not the intention of 2 Thessalonians here to declare the competing 1 Thessalonians ungenuine. The quotation inserted is not found word for word in 1 Thessalonians. In addition, the community is to hold fast to Paul's traditions—whether in oral or in letter form (2 Thess 2:15). Thus 1 Thessalonians is explicitly affirmed; it is only its meaning that is to be corrected.

The Cosmic Wisdom Theology of Colossians and Ephesians

Colossians and Ephesians differ from 1 Thessalonians in that they presuppose a number of Pauline letters and draw on them. But they do not imitate them as a collection as the Pastorals do. These two letters were written in succession and were not conceived from the outset as a pair. Both are systematically structured: in Colossians we find a basic systematic section (Col 1:9—2:4) in which the Colossians hymn is quoted and prayed as a common liturgical heritage. It is followed by a polemic section (Col 2:6-23) in which the theology of the Colossians hymn is played off against the false teachers. It concludes with a paraenetic section (Col 3:1—4:6). Ephesians follows this structure, but also takes up the fundamental building blocks of 1 Thessalonians: an expanded proemium constitutes the first section, an expanded paraenesis the second (Eph 1:3—3:21; 4:1—6:20). Where Colossians has a polemic against false teachers we find in Ephesians a praise of the peace-bringing power of faith in Christ, which overcomes the ancient hostility of Jews and Gentiles by bringing the two together in one community. Formally and in their content Colossians and Ephesians represent a transformed theology—in Colossians with a polemic aim, in Ephesians with an irenic one.

In Colossians a group of Paul's coworkers battles a "philosophy" (Col 2:8) that is in competition with the revelation in Christ. This must be a philosophy in which the world is religiously transfigured. It calls for submission to the elements of the world. We do not know what philosophy this may be, but there must have been the kind of religious turning in it that we can observe in a number of philosophical currents at the time: the late Stoa was imbued with a warm devotion; Neoplatonism and Neopythagoreanism were filled with longing for the divine. Colossians opposes this self-sacralizing philosophy: it regards as unconditionally empowered to compel obedience not the numinously interpreted world but only a crucified and risen Human Being. Only in him can be reconciled what in this world is in conflict (Col 1:20). Only Christ overcomes its destructive power (Col 2:15). Being tied to him means freedom from all the world's powers. This religious pathos of independence is, however, only effective in an initial form in social life. It is true that among Christians there are no longer Greeks and Jews, foreigners, Scythians, slaves, and free (Col 3:11). The divisive power of social differences is overcome. But Colossians (in its so-called household code) emphasizes all the more the obligation of women, children, and slaves to subordinate themselves, even though it draws some limits for men, fathers, and masters (Col 3:18—4:1). One has the impression from the (relatively extensive) admonition to slaves that the letter to Philemon has been somewhat withdrawn. Had it awakened too many expectations among slaves?

Ephesians took Colossians as its model. Unlike Colossians, it contains no polemic, but instead emphasizes that Paul's message overcomes the hatred between Jews and Gentiles (Eph 2:11-22). Paul, who throughout his life was a strain on social peace between Christians and Jews, is here portrayed as the great apostle of peace. Paul's disciples sensed that only as a peacemaking apostle could Paul become an acknowledged teacher for the whole church. These disciples, in Ephesians, continued Paul's message of justification in a manner appropriate to the subject, but they turned his ambivalence toward the law into a one-sided overcoming of the law (Eph 2:15), and the transformation of people in faith, which spontaneously produces good works, into a predestination to good works (Eph 2:10). Otherwise, however, Ephesians softens Paul's awkward teaching. Thus for Paul there was an unbridgeable tension between marital and religious obligation (1 Cor 7:32-35). In

Ephesians, by contrast, marriage is the image of the relationship between Christ and his church. It is important for Ephesians to state that everyone can live a holy life in marriage, whereby the sexual union is sanctified as the image of the mystery of the church (Eph 5:22-33). Seldom in the New Testament is sexuality so highly regarded as here, where, as also elsewhere in Ephesians, a longing for greater harmony and unity shines through. Christ is the one who encompasses the universe in himself and brings unity. The church is the predecessor of this unity among humans, and sexual union is symbolic of it.

There are some features common to Colossians and Ephesians that may allow us to infer a sort of Pauline school. Both letters contain a cosmic sense of threat from hostile and unreconciled powers: in Colossians the elements of the world (*stoicheia tou kosmou*, 2:8), in Ephesians the satanic "ruler of the power of the air" (2:2). These are involved in strife with one another, but they also display hostility to human beings. This feeling of threat is transformed in both letters into a feeling of being cared for, namely, a cosmic awareness of reconciliation: Christ has not only conquered and deflated these powers, but has reconciled them instead of destroying them. He is a cosmic power, head of all the world's powers—and at the same time the head of his body the church, which has universal dimensions. Knowledge of this cosmic Christ has redemptive power. We find in both letters a soteriological concept of knowledge: a Christian participates in this process of reconciliation through wisdom and insight into the cosmic mysteries. Christ is the epitome of all wisdom. The revelation of a mystery hidden from remotest ages (thus the revelatory schema of Col 1:24-29; Eph 3:1-13) is therefore the great revolution, and it has already happened! Both letters contain a present eschatology in spatial categories: already now the Christian has been placed in a heavenly sphere of power; in baptism Christians are not only raised with Christ (Col 2:12), but also "seated . . . with him in the heavenly places" (Eph 2:5-6), and thus have access already, in secret, to an extraordinarily elevated status. A conservative love-patriarchalism in the household codes links to this fundamentally enthusiastic concept of faith. Colossians and Ephesians thus not only bend the historical Paul, but carry further what Paul had announced in Corinth as "wisdom theology for the mature" (1 Cor 2:6-16). It is clear, however, that Paul's reticence toward enthusiasm has been abandoned, insofar as the awareness of being already "in the heavens" is associated with the church. This is a socially oriented enthusiasm. Entry into the community is entry into heaven already here and now. Paul himself had battled enthusiasm because of its socially destructive sides. He fought against the "egoistic" dangers of enthusiasm. His disciples, in contrast, activate enthusiasm for the community. Paul's harsh, polemic sides are "retouched." The apostle of peace in Ephesians is ecclesially "usable." Paul's potential for division is defanged, and his radical ethical features are withdrawn: the moderate ethics of the household codes replaces a deviating way of life.

It is possible that Ephesians was conceived from the outset for a collection of Pauline letters, since if we organize Paul's letters in the best-attested sequence the principle of ordering begins anew with Ephesians. This points to an appendix to an already existing collection. Ephesians could from the outset have been conceived as an introductory letter for this appendix. This explains why in the best manuscripts its opening names no addressees. It is directed to "the saints in that place." The "in Ephesus" represented in the translations is text-critically secondary. In his collection of Paul's letters the author read the superscriptions (before the opening of the letter) "to the Romans," "to the Corinthians," "to the Galatians," and continued the series by writing "to the Ephesians." This superscription thus stems from the author of the letter, so that the ascription was introduced, consistently but secondarily, into the prescript as well. Because Ephesians from the outset was designed to continue the collection of Pauline letters it could be content with a reference back to this superscription and address itself to the "saints in that place" (namely, the Christians among the people of Ephesus; 1:1). The introductory letter for the appendix, addressed to Ephesus, probably also points to the place where the first augmentation of Paul's letters was undertaken.

The Theology of Office in the Pastorals

The ordering principle of the Pauline letter collection begins anew with the Pastorals: once again, in a third edition, an addition was made to an already existing collection of Paul's letters. Unlike the first addition, it consists solely of pseudepigraphic letters. The three "Pastoral Letters" thus imitate the *Corpus Paulinum* as a collection. It is true that they could have been written separately, as individual letters. But probably they were planned as a trilogy.

Where did they originate? Who wrote them? We find indications pointing to Ephesus: in 1 Timothy the fictional letter situation is that Paul has left Timothy in Ephesus (1 Tim 1:3) and now instructs him on how he should lead the community. In Titus the fictional Paul has left his disciple in Crete (Titus 1:5). In 2 Timothy there is a suggestion that the place of composition is Rome, since Paul is a prisoner approaching his martyrdom: 2 Timothy is a testament. The separation of the places of composition is deliberate: the Pastorals underscore that they are meant not simply for individual communities, but for all Christianity. The suggestion of having been written in Rome is meant to give them weight as Paul's testament. They were most likely written in Ephesus. According to Acts 20:17-38 the elders (*presbyteroi*) in Ephesus, whom Paul had installed as bishops (*episkopoi*) for the community, could have understood themselves to be successors of Paul: the Pastorals presume presbyters who are also bishops, and so in their designations of office correspond exactly to Acts 20:17, 28. We do not know who was the author of the Pastorals. Perhaps Timothy and Titus (the supposed recipients of the Pastorals) may have at some point taught what is contained in the Pastorals. In that case we would have not so much Pauline tradition in these letters as Timothy- and Titus-traditions. Perhaps Timothy and Titus were even the authors of these letters.[2] It is understandable that they are written not to communities but to individuals. A fake letter to an individual is more easily put into circulation.

What is crucial is this: What do the Pastorals want to achieve? They are instructions for community leaders in the form of letters from Paul to his disciples. They are intended to motivate them to work in the community. In the background is an optimistic theology of creation and redemption. Everything enjoyed with thanksgiving is good (1 Tim 4:1-5). Ascesis in food and sex is rejected. God wants everyone to be saved (1 Tim 2:4). The idea of judgment retreats.

The institutionalization of offices in the community is carried out according to the "household" model. Induction into office was regulated by ordination. Not everyone has a charism, but only the bishop, who receives his charism by the imposition of hands. He is to preserve it not by ascesis, but by readiness for martyrdom (2 Timothy). The basis for the legitimacy of office is sound teaching, which is regarded as an objective body of tradition, and not administration of the sacraments! A succession (Paul—disciples of apostles—community leaders) is coming into being. The ideas about the community, however, are not very Pauline: the image of the household, headed by a single *paterfamilias*—the bishop, who has deacons with him and at the same time is embedded in a college of presbyters within which he is the leading presbyter. The Pastorals thus meld two notions of community: one stemming from the Pauline field, with a bishop at its head, and another derived from Jewish Christianity, with a presbyterium as leadership organ. In any case, community leadership is institutionalized and restricted.

The model of the patriarchal household leads to a suppression of women: marriage and raising children become an obligation and a soteriological "work." The right to teach, which qualifies one for office, is denied to them. The "widows," who were in the process of being recognized as holding office alongside the presbyters, are newly defined as "social objects."

They are to be supported, subject to strict criteria, but they are to have no influence. Only men may stand at the head of the community, since women are not to teach (1 Tim 2:12) and a bishop must be "an apt teacher" (1 Tim 3:2). Paul regarded celibacy as a form of life superior to marriage. The Pastorals, in contrast, want to obligate women to marry, and they battle against sexual ascesis—probably because it gives women too much independence. Precisely where the Pastorals, in their views on the role of women, go directly against statements in the genuine letters of Paul, the author has his "Paul" speak in the first person. He knows that on these points he cannot persuade through a new interpretation of the Pauline texts, but only through a (supposed) cancellation of them by Paul himself. The two most important of these "fictive personal textual references"[3] speak for themselves: "I permit no woman to teach or to have authority over a man; she is to keep silent!" (1 Tim 2:12). "So I would have younger widows marry, bear children, and manage their households, so as to give the adversary no occasion to revile us!" (1 Tim 5:14). It is undoubtedly an important concern of the Pastorals to keep women away from community leadership. They are not to teach, but to marry and bear children. Without the Pastorals the New Testament would be much more friendly to women. The Pastorals alter the image of Paul in some places, contrary to the historical Paul. The exaltation of teaching and the fundamental affirmation of creation link them to the authentic Paul, but the anti-ascetic Paul is unhistorical. The historical Paul valued celibacy more highly than marriage. The Pastorals almost attempt to impose a kind of marriage obligation. The patriarchal Paul thus cannot be found in the historical Paul: the expulsion of women from community leadership has no basis in the Pauline letters, which often reveal a great deal of significance on the part of women in the building up of communities.

Paul's Fictive Self-Correction in the Deutero-Pauline Letters

In his letters Paul not only developed a theology that would endure through time but responded to many concrete problems. The transformation of the charismatic early Christian movement of the beginnings into a self-institutionalizing religion brought new problems with it, in the overcoming of which one might fall into a contradiction of Paul. There were two solutions: either Paul had to correct himself in non-genuine Pauline letters or he had to be corrected by other apostles such as James, Peter, John, and Jude, for which purpose one must activate them literarily against him. We can show through examples, some of which were already mentioned, how the non-genuine letters correct the historical Paul. Of course, the corrections could succeed only if these letters all gave the impression of being from Paul. Only then would they have a chance to be accepted as his letters. To that extent pseudepigraphy was also a tradition-stabilizing element, and yet the small corrections of the genuine Paul spoke volumes.[4]

No one could deny that the historical Paul had asked in the letter to Philemon that slaves be treated as brothers and sisters. The fictive Paul must therefore emphasize all the more in Colossians that Christian slaves should respect their masters; still, even this fictive Paul admonishes the masters also to act fairly (Col 3:22—4:1). The Pastorals then offer only a one-sided admonition to slaves to be obedient and give as a reason for this that otherwise Christianity will be maligned (1 Tim 6:1-2).[5]

It is undeniable that the historical Paul preferred freedom from marriage to marriage. For him, married people were torn between human and religious ties (1 Cor 7:33) and were altogether imperfect humans who did not have full control of their sexual impulses (1 Cor 7:9, 37). The fictive Paul, however, can praise marriage in the household codes as an image of the relationship between Christ and the church (Eph 5:25-33). It is not in tension with the new faith. Sexual *unio* is ordered to a cosmic tendency toward unity.[6]

One cannot deny that women behaved independently in the world of the historical Paul. The fictive Paul of the Pastorals, in contrast, intervenes twice in the first person to restrict women to the traditional female role: "I permit no woman to teach or to have authority over a man; she is to keep silent" (1 Tim 2:12); "I would have younger widows marry, bear children, and manage their households . . ." (1 Tim 5:14).[7]

It is undeniable that for the historical Paul every member of the community had a charism and was an equal member of the body of Christ. But the fictive Paul in the Pastorals acknowledges charism only in the community leader (2 Tim 1:6) and replaces the model of the body of Christ with that of the household of God, in which only a single household father is the head (1 Tim 3:15)!

The conservative tendency of the non-genuine Pauline letters, overstepping Paul, did not remain uncontradicted. The *Acts of Paul and Thecla* represented the counter-position. Here a quite different, equally fictive Paul preaches ascesis and freedom from marriage. Thecla is commissioned to proclaim the word and baptizes herself. She is meant to show that preaching the word and administering the sacraments are also entrusted to women.[8] The *Acts of Thecla* were disclosed as falsifications even in the early church,[9] but the non-genuine letters of Paul have for centuries, as supposedly genuine Pauline letters, shaped the image of Paul.

Excursus: The Correction of Paul by the Catholic Epistles

Correcting the real Paul through the fictive Paul was only one strategy. The "catholic" epistles written in the names of other apostles could also correct Paul, his doctrine of justification, his theology of suffering, his imminent expectations of the end, his freedom toward angelic powers. In my opinion the three Johannine letters are the only ones that reveal no critical references to Paul. They continue Johannine theology and exist in their own right. In all the other catholic epistles, however, we can find indications of a correction of Paul.

There is a broad consensus on this point as regards the letter of James. According to Paul it is faith alone that justifies, and not the works of the law. Paul extended this antithesis between faith and works from ritual actions (such as circumcision and food laws) to ethical actions as well. The letter of James protests against this: faith without ethical works is for him a dead faith, and he uses the example of Abraham to demonstrate this, the same example to whom Paul appealed for his antithesis of faith and works (Jas 2:14-26).[10] It is possible, however, that the critique of Paul and his followers was continued in many other passages: the letter of James corrects an image of Jewish Christianity that must have been evoked by the Pauline letters, especially Galatians, 2 Corinthians, and Philippians, namely, that Jewish Christians were proud of their status, were fixated on ritual questions, had not emancipated themselves from the burden of the law, and sought conflict with other Christians.[11] In contrast, the letter of James emphasized the independence in principle of Christian attitudes from human status (Jas 2:1-10). The law, for him, consists not in ritual demands but in ethical commandments of human solidarity. It is a law of freedom (Jas 1:25; 2:12). The wisdom of Jewish Christians is practical wisdom for life that does not seek conflict (Jas 3:1-18).[12] On the whole, the letter of James presents a sympathetic image of an ethically exalted Jewish Christianity that offers a necessary counterweight to Paul's polemically distorted statements about his Jewish-Christian opponents.

The first letter of Peter is written in the spirit of Paul, as if intended to spread his theology in Asia Minor in the name of Peter and to emphasize the consensus between the two apostles. This letter gives Christians an orientation in their society, where they were discriminated against as "strangers." To this end it develops a theology of suffering with six motifs:[13] Christians' suffering is purification (1 Pet 1:6-7); innocent suffering leads to future glory (1:8-9; 2:20); it is part of the messianic travails that precede the end (4:17); but above all it is part of being disciples of Christ (2:21-23; 3:18; 4:1); still more, it is a participation in Christ's suffering (4:13) and can be borne in surrender to God's will (4:19). Slaves are the models for all Christians: their suffering is presented primarily as discipleship of Christ (2:18-25); only in a second step is it applied to the whole community (3:8-22). We can see a correction of Paul in the fact that Paul developed a theology of suffering as discipleship of Jesus primarily for his own person. When he considers the suffering of the community, he emphasizes his own distress. One of Paul's followers could even interpret his sufferings as completing the suffering of Christ (Col 1:24). To this apostle-centered theology of suffering, 1 Peter offers the contrast of a community-centered theology of suffering. The supposed Peter is, of course, writing in Rome (= Babylon; 1 Pet 5:13). The reader is meant to think of Peter's martyrdom. But Peter wastes not a single word on a description of his own suffering. Rather, he accomplishes a "democratization" of the theology of suffering: it is, above all, slaves who are the models of Christian life. Their suffering may often be trivial and ordinary, but it is precisely here that 1 Peter finds value: it is not primarily martyrdom that is discipleship in suffering, but bearing everyday humiliations and discrimination. The intent of 1 Peter is not only to console but to appeal to the surrounding world through the conscious acceptance of suffering: "that, when you are maligned, those who abuse you for your good conduct in Christ may be put to shame" (1 Pet 3:16). Suffering as followers of Christ is a demonstrative self-stigmatizing by means of which one will shake and convert the world.

The second letter of Peter emphasizes that in every one of his letters Paul admonishes to eschatological patience (2 Pet 3:15-16), that is, he does not propose an expectation of the imminent end. This turns the matter on its head. Paul, from his first letter to his last, is expecting the imminent end of the world. The fictive Peter of the second Petrine letter asserts the contrary: everyone who reads Paul's letters as the expression of an imminent expectation, which meanwhile has become outdated, is distorting their meaning.

In the letter of Jude a Jewish Christian, writing in the name of Jude, the brother of the Lord, addresses false teachers, reproaching them: "[they] reject [the] authority [of the Lord: *kyriōtēs*] and slander the glorious ones" (Jude 8). Such a critique of the super-earthly powers was widespread in the Pauline realm. In Colossians, Jesus triumphs over the angelic powers (*kyriōtētes*, Col 1:16). Colossians warns against the worship of angels (Col 2:18); the letter of Jude rejects such impiety. Even the archangel Michael, it says, did not dare to slander the devil (Jude 9).

Had the Pauline letters not possessed a great deal of authority at an early date there would have been no need to write pseudepigraphic letters to correct Paul through a fictive self-interpretation by Paul himself and by other apostles.[14] On one point they are all dependent on Paul, and this is decisive for their literary history: without Paul, the letter form would not have achieved literary status in early Christianity. All early Christian letters are form-critically dependent on him. But they were not only his form-critical successors. Their very origin was occasioned by the same social motive that inspired the creation of Paul's letters. As the augmentation and correction of those letters, they were intended to be a basis for community life. Their intent was to provide leadership for congregations. We can discern the following functions:

Building consensus: Within the Pauline letters, consensus rests almost exclusively on Paul. The Pastorals nowhere mention the other apostles. Colossians and 2 Thessalonians are silent about them. They do not appear even to exist. Only Ephesians links Paul to the other apostles: it is apostles and prophets who have laid the groundwork for the community (Eph 2:20; cf. 3:5). It is understood that such a *Corpus Paulinum*, from which the authority of a single apostle emerges one-sidedly, was augmented by the catholic letters from other apostles. Paul himself had not emphasized any consensus with other apostles: agreement with the Jerusalem pillar apostles, James, Peter, and John, was for him a recognition of his own mission. It is precisely these three apostles who dominate the collection of catholic letters, with the addition of Jude, the brother of the Lord. He is introduced in Jude 1 as the brother of James, and thus subordinated to him. The augmentation of the collection of Pauline letters by the catholic letters was intended to represent the consensus of the apostles and counter the preponderance of the Pauline letters.[15]

Orientation within the environment: First Peter engages with the situation of Christians in society. The political paraenesis in 1 Peter 2:11-17 introduces new accents in contrast to Romans 13:1-7; here there is no prohibition of resistance. The state is an order fashioned by humans. Its task is to punish evil and promote good. Christians should cooperate freely. The emperor is treated like all other human beings: the admonitions "honor everyone" and "honor the emperor" (2:17) use the same verb. But how are Christians to act as free people within their society? They are to do so as the elect, priests, and kings (2:9). They have made a break with futile traditions (1:18), but at the same time they are obligated to be patient in bearing discrimination in a world that rejects them, so that "[those who] malign you as evildoers . . . may see your honorable deeds and glorify God" (2:12). The tension between interior superiority to the surrounding world and "submission" to its discrimination is great and leads to a differentiated theology of suffering—also as a means, nevertheless, to convince the world.

Defining identity: The acceptance of the letter to the Hebrews, which we will discuss in detail later, can best be understood as a contribution to the definition of identity on the part of the young Christian community. We find in it a principled differentiation of the new Christian service of worship from the Old Testament cult. Indirectly, however, the critique of the sacrificial cult in Jerusalem could refer to the whole ancient exercise of religion. The end of the Jewish sacrificial cult (in my opinion silently presumed) is transparent to the outdatedness of all religions, since religion existed in the ancient world as a sacrificial service. The letter to the Hebrews, however, on the basis of the one and unique self-sacrifice of Jesus, declares all other sacrifices passé.

Regulating conflict: The beginning of the first expansion with Ephesians at its head is meant to portray Paul as a peacemaker. The historical Paul, as we encounter him in the seven genuine letters, was always associated with conflict and strife. Not every such strife was constructively resolved. First Corinthians is followed by Second Corinthians, in which it is clear that in the meantime Paul has aroused everyone in Corinth against him. In Ephesians, however, the apostle appears as someone who successfully overcomes the hostility between Jewish and Gentile Christians in the community. In many other letters more or less clearly evident conflicts are resolved: in Colossians a dispute with a religiously colored philosophy that lays claims to revelations; in the Pastorals (2 Tim 2:18) a conflict with a present eschatology; in the Johannine letters a confrontation with a docetic Christology that is convinced that the redeemer only appeared to become human.

Structures of authority: The second major expansion of the Pauline letter collection was the addition of the Pastorals. Here again the community-leadership purpose is unmistakable: the Pastorals establish an ecclesial system of offices independent of individual charisms. They define the necessary qualities of a church officeholder in order to make the choice easier, and they touch on precautions before his ordination.

Not only the genuine Pauline letters but all the post-Pauline letters as well are thus shaped by the same community-leadership functions, which is why they were added to the genuine letters. Probably this happened—independently of the origins of the individual letters—in successive steps, as we have shown above: an original collection of Pauline letters (Romans, 1 and 2 Corinthians, Galatians) was augmented by a first addition headed by Ephesians (and including Colossians, Philippians, 1 and 2 Thessalonians, and Philemon). The letter to the Ephesians, which dominates here, reveals the intention to present Paul and Pauline theology as yielding not potential conflicts but rather reconciliation. The second addition was the Pastorals; here the dominant interest was the securing of internal church authority by means of a practicable theology of office. The final addition to the *Corpus Paulinum* may have been the letter to the Hebrews. Here the leading interest is the securing of Christian identity over against all ancient Jewish cults. A counterweight to the gradually accumulating collection of Pauline letters was created by the catholic letters. Alongside Paul now stood the brothers of the Lord and apostles James and Jude, as well as Peter and John. The leading interest here was securing a consensus within a pluralistic early Christianity in which many theological currents existed alongside one another.

11 Jesus' Fictive Self-Interpretation through the Redaction of the Jesus Traditions in the Synoptic Gospels

As there was struggle within the Pauline school over the correct interpretation of Paul, and each approach claimed that it possessed the right understanding of Paul—for "Paul, rightly understood, always said what I think"—so there was in early Christianity a struggle over the correct image of Jesus. The Synoptic Gospels can certainly be understood as collections and editions of Jesus traditions, but in them outstanding theologians and authors also used the image of Jesus they had developed in order to place their own emphases. We will sketch certain tendencies in the respective Jesus-images in each of the three Synoptic Gospels, as a literary history of the gospels thus seeks to develop the historical motives and situations that led to each new shaping of the image of Jesus. Certain common motifs can be detected in all three Synoptic Gospels: as the letter was developed as the first basic literary form in early Christianity as a result of the Judaist crisis, so the second basic form, the gospel, was evoked by the crisis of the Jewish War and its consequences. All three gospels reveal a relationship to the Jewish War. We still sense something of the shock brought by the war, but also the transformation of that shock into positive motivation: Jesus had predicted the destruction of the temple. This prophecy had been fulfilled. The memory of everything he said and did was thus immensely exalted in value. Certainly that was not the sole motive for writing down the memories of him. With the passing of the eyewitnesses there was an obvious necessity to secure the Jesus tradition in writing—not only for future generations but also for Christians outside Palestine, especially after the flight of Jesus' followers from the land. Even in the first generation, Christianity had already spread among non-Jews within the large cities of the Mediterranean world. Hence, all the gospels formulate Jesus' message and meaning in such a way that he directed his mission not only to the Jewish people but to all nations.

The universalizing of his message as a gospel to all peoples (Mark 13:10) and the whole world (Mark 14:9) is thus an important motive for gospel writing. Behind these and other single motives for writing we can discern an overarching motivation for the gospel writers: they write their gospels for the same reason Paul had in writing his letters. He wanted to influence his communities according to his own thinking in critical situations, even in his absence and beyond his possible death. This required that he become an author. The same literary-creative motive impelled the evangelists. They, too, wanted to guide communities in and after crises. They did not do so by giving direct instructions in letters, but by telling a story of Jesus and giving impulses to their communities by indirect means. In Jesus they activated the highest authority in early Christianity for leading the communities according to their own understanding. If we ask about the duties of a community leader, we again discern the five tasks whose mastery we can find in all the gospels as constitutive factors:[1]

1. The community leader must express the *consensus of the community*. Only one thus rooted can exercise influence. The three Synoptic Gospels gather traditions and sources about Jesus and shape them into an image of Jesus capable of producing consensus.
2. The community leader must convey to the community an *image of its surrounding world* in order to lead it also through crises and conflicts with that world. All three gospels present compelling ideas for how Christians are to behave in the crisis after the Jewish War.
3. The community leader must define for the first Christians their *Christian identity in distinction from the mother religion*. The leader must answer the question: Why have we separated from the Jews, and to what extent are we still part of them? All three Synoptic Gospels deal with the problem of the relationship to the surrounding world: the Roman Empire and Judaism.
4. The community leader must *regulate conflicts in his or her own community* and make it possible for various groups to live together in it. That is always a balancing act. On the one hand he or she must uphold the common norms—and possibly carry out the exclusion of members who defy them. But the leader must also be flexible so that there are no unnecessary divisions. Here again we can show that all the gospels deal with internal tensions.

5. The community leader must create a *structure of authority within the community* that is independent of persons and generations. This includes the formulation of criteria for legitimate authority that can be accepted by everyone, if possible. This task has also left its traces in the gospels. In them Jesus is, ultimately, the sole legitimate authority.

If we apply these terms to the three Synoptic Gospels we see that they exercise all these functions of a community-directing literature. The same is true of the Gospel of Mark, which we already discussed above.

The Gospel of Mark

It is much harder to discern the intention of Mark's Gospel than that of Matthew and Luke, because we cannot compare Mark with its sources and traditions. Such a comparison is possible for Matthew and Luke, even though it can lead us into error: not every deviation from Mark or the reconstructed text of Q can be traced to a deliberate alteration on the part of the evangelist. Matthew and Luke may just as well have been following a different version of the tradition. Despite these difficulties, the tendencies of the gospels are clearly discernible: for Mark, the overall picture composed of small units is his own work. This overall picture, compared with the other gospels, reveals what is characteristic of Mark's Gospel, and here we encounter the five factors in community leadership through authorship we have described above:[2]

Building consensus: Mark means to create an image of Jesus that can achieve consensus by combining two traditions about him, the miracle stories and the passion narrative. In the miracle stories Jesus is the one who overcomes misery and suffering. The passion narrative, in contrast, shows him as powerless, exposed to suffering. Mark combines these two traditions and unites two images of Jesus. The motifs of secrecy during Jesus' ministry signal to the reader: only when one has read the gospel to the end will one fully understand Jesus. Only then does one have access to the mystery of his person. It is not enough to know only the miracle stories. Cross and resurrection are also part of the whole.

Orientation within the environment: The Gospel of Mark projects a dark image of the world. It was written much closer to the war than any of the other gospels. We could interpret it as an anti-gospel to the gospels of the Flavians after the Jewish War. Jesus, not Vespasian, has saved the world. The community stands in opposition to the world and must prepare itself for conflicts. Mark's Gospel comes to their aid when it says that Christians need not reveal their identity in public without necessity. Even Jesus wanted at first to remain secret and unrecognized. But when God leads Christians who follow Jesus into conflicts they should self-confidently hold fast to their identity.

Defining identity: Mark formulates the identity of Christians in relation to and in distinction from Judaism. On basic ethical questions there is no difference (12:28-34), but only on matters of ritual. The temple (the ritual center of the Jewish religion) has been destroyed. The old ritual commandments—the Sabbath and the purity laws—are openly criticized in Mark's Gospel. In their place Mark introduces two new Christian rites, baptism and the Lord's Supper, thus distancing it ritually from Judaism. In doing so, Mark's Gospel perhaps deliberately separates itself from the image of Jesus we encounter in the Sayings Source,[3] where there is no passion narrative and only very few miracle stories. It is precisely these two genres that shape Mark's Gospel.

Regulating conflict: We sense in Mark some internal tensions between the itinerant charismatics and the local communities. Therefore the Markan evangelist reinterprets discipleship. It consists not only of following Jesus in the literal sense, but also of table fellowship (2:15), readiness to suffer (8:34), and care for others (15:41). In contrast to the a-familial ethos of the itinerant charismatics, family values are newly esteemed: obligations to one's parents (7:8-13), spouse (10:2-12), and children (10:13-16). At the same time, the disciples are criticized as lacking understanding. It may be that this is a criticism of a different image of Jesus propagated by Jesus' itinerant disciples.

Structures of authority: Mark's Gospel is a witness to the process by which the local communities separated themselves from the authorities of the first generation, the itinerant charismatics. Material criteria for community leadership are emphasized, such as were also fulfilled by those who did not lead an itinerant life as missionaries and disciples: whoever wants to be first must be prepared to be last. This is shown in the dialogue with the sons of Zebedee (10:35-45). The duties of community leaders include care for (orphaned) children (Mark 9:33-37). Here itinerant disciples have no place; on the contrary, Jesus' disciples even try to keep children away from Jesus (Mark 10:13-16). In Mark, the legitimation of authority lies in readiness to serve and suffer.

Matthew and Luke both augment the Gospel of Mark by the addition of infancy narratives, though in this they do not follow a common tradition. Matthew sets Jesus' infancy against a dark background. Jesus' family must flee to Egypt as political fugitives and wait for Herod's death before they can return to Palestine. The Lukan infancy narrative feels more relaxed: Jesus' family need not flee. On the contrary, Mary and Joseph behave like model taxpayers and travel to Bethlehem to be taxed. And yet here there is also a perceptible tension between Augustus, the ruler of the world, and the newborn king in the city of David. By beginning with Jesus' birth these gospels are made to correspond, in form-critical terms, to the ancient *bios*, since in that genre it was simply a matter of course to begin with birth.

At the same time, however, this is associated with an alteration in the image of Jesus: Matthew and Luke agree in saying that Jesus was begotten by the Holy Spirit. His birth through the Holy Spirit makes all the miraculous things he later says and does appear as expressions of a nature that existed in him from the beginning. This corresponds to the ancient idea of a *bios*. The life makes visible what shapes a person from within. In Mark, by contrast, the earthly Jesus is transformed into a new being, while in Matthew and Luke he develops a majesty inherent within him.

The uniqueness of Mark's Gospel, in contrast to its two "heirs," is especially clear in this instance. In Mark, Jesus does not have a hidden heavenly "nature" from the beginning. He is adopted as Son of God and at the transfiguration is temporarily changed into a divine being. What he is, in a sense, does not emerge from within but is given him from above—through the divine voice, which the reader hears twice, at Jesus' baptism and transfiguration, and with which she or he is confronted in the form of the angelic message before the empty tomb.

The Gospel of Matthew

The Matthean evangelist wrote in Syria, where his gospel is quoted by Ignatius (*Smyrn.* 1.1) and in the *Didache*. The first quotation of a work is often an indication of the place of its origin. There are other indicators as well: Matthew calls Jesus a "Nazorean" (Matt 2:23), which is what people called Christians in Syria. He has Jesus' reputation sound as far as "Syria" (Matt 4:24), so that people from Syria are also present at the Sermon on the Mount. Matthew's Gospel was written about 80–100 C.E., that is, before Ignatius's letters (ca. 107/110 C.E.) and after Mark's Gospel (ca. 75 C.E.). His sources are Mark and Q, both of which were accessible in Syria. Mark was written there, and the Sayings Source in Palestine or its neighborhood, but emigrants (during the Jewish War) may have brought it from Palestine to Syria.

This evangelist is at home in the Jewish-Christian theology of the Sayings Source. The very structure of his book, based on five discourses, shows that he attributes decisive weight to Jesus' words. These words represent a Judaism open to the world. Matthew abrogates the mission to Israel alone

(Matt 10:5-6) through the words of the Risen One (Matt 28:19-20). He affirms a universal mission, but indicates that for him it began only after the destruction of the temple. In the parable of the great banquet, for example, the outsider guests (= Gentiles?) are called only through a second invitation after the king has burned the murderers' city (Matt 22:1-10). We find here a Jewish Christianity that has, in a second stage, opened itself to the Gentile mission and yet conducts it out of conviction. But Matthew also corrects the Gentile-Christian Gospel of Mark, which had declared all foods clean (Mark 7:19). That is omitted in Matthew 15:17. Jesus' Sabbath conflicts are presented in such a way that they do not signify any breaking of the law (Matt 12:1-14). Matthew gives the disciples' hunger as motive for plucking heads of grain and legitimates it, in addition, by arguments from the law and the prophets. That God desires mercy and not sacrifice (Hos 6:6) is for Matthew an important basic principle; he cites it twice in his gospel (Matt 9:13; 12:7).

Since Matthew's Gospel joins together a Jewish-Christian and a Gentile-Christian source it is probable that his intention was also to unify Jewish and Gentile Christians in reality.[4] The common element is a universal ethic in which Matthew sees the Jewish tradition summarized, but in which he also finds an ethos capable of evoking consensus among all people. He presents Jesus as the true teacher of the Law, giving a humane interpretation of the Torah accessible to all. He claims not to abandon anything in Jewish tradition in his interpretation of the Torah—he will keep it to the last *yod*. But *de facto* he offers a universalist interpretation that silently relativizes all the ritual laws. One may practice the latter, but they are not what is most important (Matt 23:23). The issue for him in his ethical interpretation of the Torah is stated in four formulations that acquire more and more branches in the course of his gospel:

1. In the *golden rule* he already, in the Sermon on the Mount, summarizes the most important content of that sermon in a single sentence: "In everything do to others as you would have them do to you; for this is the law and the prophets" (Matt 7:12). The golden rule is a universal maxim attested in antiquity even before Jesus.
2. A second summary is the *twofold love commandment*: "'You shall love the Lord your God with all your heart, and with all your soul, and with all your mind.' This is the greatest and first commandment. And a second is like it: 'You shall love your neighbor as yourself.' On these two commandments hang all the law and the prophets" (Matt 22:37-40). This is said (in Matthew) to a critical scribe. The twofold love commandment

corresponds to the ancient canon of two virtues: devotion to God and justice to fellow human beings.

3. The *most important thing in the law* appears again in Matthew 23:23: "justice and mercy and faith." This trio is more important than ritual demands, such as tithing the three culinary herbs, mint, dill, and cumin. One should do the former and not neglect the latter. In context this is spoken against the Pharisees and scribes. Matthew is silent regarding male circumcision. Was it for him also part of the ritual ordinances that were not to be neglected—but are less important? At Jesus' baptism he emphasizes that with this ritual act of baptism "*all* righteousness" is fulfilled (Matt 3:15). Circumcision would then really be no longer necessary (as an initiation rite for male Gentile Christians).
4. At the end of Jesus' final discourse stands a listing of *six works of mercy*. Here the judge of the world encounters all humankind. Independently of whether they are Jews, Christians, or Gentiles, all will be measured by whether they have helped the Son of Man in his least sisters and brothers. The righteous do not know that they have been of help to him in person. Jesus explains to them: "I was hungry and you gave me food, I was thirsty and you gave me something to drink, I was a stranger and you welcomed me, I was naked and you gave me clothing, I was sick and you took care of me, I was in prison and you visited me" (Matt 25:35-36).

In Matthew's Gospel we encounter an ethical Christianity with a Jewish-Christian stamp. Matthew requires, as conditions for salvation, the readiness to forgive (Matt 6:14; 18:23-34) and elementary aid like the works of mercy. Everyone can do that. No one needs, in addition, to be transformed by a miraculous power like the Spirit (thus Paul). Only Christians who shared Paul's pessimistic anthropology experienced Matthew's ethical demands as excessive. Matthew, in contrast, shared the ethical optimism of the Jewish tradition: the human being is created to fulfill the Law, and how much more the Christians, for whom Jesus interprets the law in humane fashion so that it is no longer a heavy burden (Matt 11:28-30). God demands the impossible of no one. Who has not helped a hungry person at some point? Who has not visited a sick person at least once? And who would be so blind as not to forgive others, when one is not perfect oneself?

The search for an overall ethos for Jews and Gentiles, however, is only one side of the Matthean agenda. It was precisely through his new ethos that Jesus and his followers wanted to surpass all others. The agenda of the Matthean Jesus is to "fulfill" the law and the prophets (Matt 5:17). If Matthean Christianity distinguishes itself from Judaism, it does so through a better interpretation and realization of their common tradition. The decisive motif is programmatically formulated in the Sermon on the Mount: "unless your righteousness exceeds that of the scribes and Pharisees, you will never enter the kingdom of heaven" (Matt 5:20). Even where the scribes and Pharisees are models for the interpretation of the commandments (Matt 23:1-3), Christians are to do and obey what they teach, "but do not do as they do, for they do not practice what they teach" (Matt 23:3). This ethic of greater righteousness distinguishes itself not only from the Jewish world, but also from the Gentile. This is emphasized in the command to love one's enemies. What would be special about being kind only to one's brothers and sisters? "Do not even the Gentiles do the same?" (Matt 5:47-48). In the same way, one must distinguish oneself from the Gentiles in prayer (Matt 6:7) and dealing with everyday concerns (Matt 6:31-32). In both directions, regarding Jews and Gentiles, the intention is to make real a superior righteousness. The Gospel of Matthew thus represents a markedly "aristocratic" morality. It is not the good that is the goal of its ethics, but the better.

But in what does this *better* or *greater* righteousness consist? The answer is in the Sermon on the Mount. Here we encounter the concept of "righteousness" five times, probably all passages created by the Matthean redaction (Matt 5:6, 10, 20; 6:1, 33). In addition, it is twice associated with John the Baptizer (Matt 3:15; 21:32)—indicating how little the Matthean community claimed righteousness exclusively for itself. It shares its ideas of righteousness with others, but it strives for more, for greater righteousness.

The Sermon on the Mount, in its three principal sections, develops the content of this greater righteousness. The antitheses (Matt 5:21-48) demonstrate great freedom toward the tradition—independently of whether the powerful "but I say to you" is directed against Moses (i.e., the Torah) or only its interpreters, of whom Matthew was probably thinking. The antitheses teach a great deal of freedom toward inner affects (such as aggressivity and sexuality), but also in dealing with aggression experienced passively.

The devotional rules (Matt 6:1-18) instruct in a particular way of giving alms, praying, and fasting—namely, in a consistent freedom from social controls. If one fasts in secret and gives alms in secret, the surrounding social world has no opportunity to influence one's behavior through positive or negative sanctions.

The social paraenesis (Matt 6:19—7:11) demands sovereign freedom toward material ties. Seeking the reign of God and its righteousness consists in having no concern for food, drink, and clothing. Between God and mammon there is only either–or.

This praxis of greater righteousness is even tied to a striving for perfection. Matthew twice links this word with concrete behavior: once with love of enemies, when those who love their enemies are promised: "[you will] be perfect . . . as your heavenly Father is perfect" (5:48); the same is true of radical abandonment of possessions and discipleship. The rich young man who wants to follow Jesus is told: "If you wish to be perfect, go, sell your possessions, and give the money to the poor, and you will have treasure in heaven" (Matt 19:21).

Matthew thus represents an aristocratic ethos. Seeking the good is not sufficient for him, but only striving for what is "better," even what is "perfect." The disciples who make that effort are "salt of the earth" and "light of the world" (Matt 5:13-15). And in fact their "better" ethos applies to the whole world. With it they distinguish themselves both from Jews and from Gentiles. They want to surpass both, in teaching and praxis. This is evident in the case of Judaism, but it is palpable with regard to the Gentile world as well. Jesus' teaching is to be proclaimed to all nations. Jesus rises from Jewish son of David to be a world ruler who does not subject the world by means of armies, but governs through his teachings, through "everything that I have commanded you" (Matt 28:19). Jesus' ethical teaching is superior to the ethos of the nations.

We can localize this concept of a universal ethos stemming from Jewish roots in its cultural context. The Jewish War is over (Matt 22:7). The expectations of a Jewish or Eastern world ruler that had been circulating in the East among Jews and Gentiles have been destroyed. During the war not only Jews, but other peoples of the East had been seized by the expectation that a ruler from the East would achieve world dominance. Josephus is aware of an ambiguous oracle that was found *also* in Jewish scriptures, according to which one from their land would achieve world dominance; however, many sages had been deceived in their conclusions (*B.J.* 6.312-13). Josephus himself applied the prophecy to Vespasian, who came from the East and rose to be emperor (*B.J.* 3.351-54). After the war, Matthew dealt with such expectations.[5] His thesis is: Jesus of Nazareth is this new world ruler from the East whom Jews and Gentiles await. Matthew shows that Jesus, the royal son from the tribe of David, has risen to world domination. He further shows that Jesus exercises this world rule not through military might but through his ethical teaching and the ethical obedience of his followers. His teaching is a universalized Judaism, which in the view of Matthew's Gospel is superior to other proposals. He thus competes in his own time with the reorganized Judaism that began in the synagogue at Javneh after the catastrophe of 70

C.E. There, too, people were aware that the loss of the temple was not the end of the true worship of God. The great teacher Yohanan ben Zakkai consoled his Jewish contemporaries with Hosea 6:6: "Once, as Rabban Yohanan ben Zakkai [d. ca. 80 C.E.] was coming forth from Jerusalem, Rabbi Joshua followed after him [as his disciple] and beheld the temple in ruins. 'Woe unto us!' Rabbi Joshua cried, 'that this, the place where the iniquities of Israel were atoned for, is laid waste!' 'My son,' Rabbi Yohanan said to him, 'be not grieved. We have another atonement as effective as this. And what is it? It is acts of loving kindness, as it is said, 'For I desire mercy and not sacrifice'" (*Abot R. Nat.* A 4).[6] The works of love could thus replace the sacrificial cult in the temple. It can be no accident that the Gospel of Matthew twice quotes this favorite saying of Yohanan ben Zakkai, each time in a redactional addition to the Markan text, in Matthew 9:13; 12:7. The Gospel of Matthew competes with the contemporary rabbinic movement in its efforts to realize the "greater righteousness" on the basis of their common Torah.

To what extent can we say that the Matthean evangelist has concealed himself behind this image of the Matthean Jesus in order to present his own theology? That is the pseudepigraphic element, or the fictive self-interpretation of Jesus, which is really an interpretation of the Jesus tradition by the evangelist. First of all we should emphasize that the Matthean image of Jesus corresponds to genuine Jesus traditions. The historical Jesus belonged to Judaism. He wanted to work on the basis of the Torah. To that extent Matthew's Gospel constitutes an actualization of possibilities already laid down by the historical Jesus. And yet there are also fictional elements in his image of Jesus, for Matthew, through his image of Jesus, intervenes in an "interpretive dispute." He struggles with rabbinism over the right interpretation of the Torah, and with Gentile Christianity over the right interpretation of Jesus.

In the confrontation with the beginnings of rabbinic Judaism, Matthew represents an approach that was not hopeless. Matthew's Gospel fits within the renewal of Judaism through emphasis on a more profound ethics after 70 C.E. Precisely like contemporary rabbinic Judaism, he values mercy above cultic worship. This had little to do with a Judaism influenced by Pharisaism, and much more with a rabbinic Judaism that distanced itself from the Pharisees as much as Matthew does.[7] The rabbis after 70 C.E. may often have come in fact from among the Pharisees and followed their teachings, but they wanted to have nothing to do with them. The Pharisees (*perushim*) were in their tradition a notable sectarian group. The Gospel of Matthew is similarly ambivalent in its judgment of them: one should follow their teaching but not their praxis. After 70 C.E., in my opinion, Matthew's Gospel renewed the effort to revitalize Judaism on the basis of the Torah as interpreted by Jesus. Its sharp separation from the Pharisees is thus an attack not on Judaism as a whole but on a recently much-calumniated group, and this attack would have found sympathy among many Jews. This is Matthew's answer to the catastrophe of 70 C.E. For him, the destruction of the temple was punishment for rejecting Jesus. The consequence, for him, is an appeal to recognize Jesus as the true interpreter of Torah.

At the same time, Matthew engages in an inner-Christian conflict over the true image of Jesus. In Gentile Christianity, Jesus had become someone who overcame and surpassed the Torah. Many of its commandments were no longer kept. Paul was the chief representative of this "law-free" Gentile Christianity. It is improbable that Matthew, located in the region of Syria, had not heard of him. In his first period Paul had remained in Syria and its neighboring territories and his base was in Antioch. It is altogether possible that the Matthean evangelist knew the rumors about Paul. But he never polemicizes directly against Paul. An analogy may clarify this. Luke, as can be demonstrated, admired Paul and tells a great deal about him in the Acts of the Apostles—and yet in his gospel we find not a single allusion to him. The little "stabs" in Matthew are thus much more obvious. Besides, they occur in all five discourses:

In the *Sermon on the Mount* Matthew polemicizes against the idea that Jesus had come to abolish the Law (Matt 5:17): this logion argues explicitly against that opinion. Can this be a reference to the Pauline position? It is true that there is dispute over whether according to Paul (Rom 10:4) Christ is the "end" or the "goal" of the Law. But in substance Paul recognizes a time limit for the Law, until Christ (Gal 3:19). Theologically, he got the reputation of wanting to abolish the Law. The polemic against an anonymous scribe who annuls minor commandments and therefore will be the "least" (*elachistōs*) in the reign of God could thus be aimed at Paul. The keyword *elachistōs* recalls his self-designation in 1 Corinthians 15:9. He considers himself the least of the apostles. It is not a counterargument that Matthew 5:19 speaks only of lesser laws, while Paul abolished not only such minor laws. The logic is: if someone who annuls the least of the laws will be the least in the kingdom of heaven, how much more status is lost by the one who abolishes greater commandments!

In the *mission discourse* Matthew makes the commandment to abandon possessions into a command not to acquire anything. He does not say that the disciples should not take gold, silver, or copper with them on their journeys, but instead: "Do not *acquire* for yourselves gold, silver, or copper!" (Matt 10:9). Who in early Christianity financed his missionary journeys through his own earnings? Barnabas and Paul did. Is there a criticism here of the type of missionary they represent?

In the *parables discourse* we encounter a hostile person in the parable of the weeds among the wheat (Matt 13:24-28, 36-43). Is this "hostile person" Paul? There is no doubt that this is a description of the growth of communities. Is Paul, then, the disturber of the peace who sows weeds among the wheat? Is Matthew's Gospel saying that one must tolerate such people in the community and leave the judgment of them to God? In the *epistula Petri* placed as a preface to the *Clementine Homilies,* the "enemy" is clearly Paul (*Clem. Hom.* 2.4).

In the *community discourse* a woe is spoken over people through whom stumbling blocks come (Matt 18:6). Is this also a warning against Paul? Did he lead the little ones astray? In that case this would be an expression of a very ugly hatred, held in check only by the fact that Peter is admonished to forgive without measure.

In the *Pharisees discourse* there is an interesting polemic against Pharisees who go on mission: "Woe to you, scribes and Pharisees, hypocrites! For you cross sea and land to make a single convert, and you make the new convert twice as much a child of hell as yourselves" (Matt 23:15). That is usually regarded as polemic against a Jewish mission about which we otherwise know nothing. But it could also be an indirect slash at Paul. He had been a Pharisee. He crossed sea and land. In his communities he had difficulty establishing a minimum of ethics.

If the reference is really to Paul, the immoderation of this polemic would be disturbing. But we must consider that the author makes no explicit identification of Paul. One can lambaste anonymous opponents without any holding back. Perhaps they remain anonymous precisely so that one can polemicize against them all the more sharply. Paul used the same tactics. In any case, the Matthean picture of Jesus, despite indisputable continuity with the historical Jesus, is a piece of "interpretation conflict" over Jesus. The author uses the image of Jesus to influence his contemporary communities on behalf of his own ideas. In doing so he exercises "church politics." In conclusion, we can compare his intention with that of Mark's Gospel by demonstrating the five factors of community leadership through gospel writing in Matthew's Gospel and so refer back to some of the tendencies described above.[8]

Building consensus: While the Gospel of Mark joins miracle and passion narratives, in Matthew we find a synthesis of Jewish-Christian and Gentile-Christian traditions. Strongly Jewish-Christian material from Matthew's special source is combined with the Gentile-Christian Gospel of Mark. The basis of this synthesis is a moderate Jewish Christianity such as we find in the Sayings Source.

Orientation within the environment: Matthew proclaims the world rule of a Jewish king and thus transforms hopes for a world ruler coming from the East to abolish the rule of the Romans. In doing so, he joins Jewish messianic expectations with Gentile hopes as embodied in the Magi from the East (Matt 2:1-12). He radically redefines the messianic character: in the place of a militant messiah there appears a peaceful king who desires to rule the world only through his commandments.

Defining identity: Matthew formulates an ethical framework in place of the ritual framework of Judaism. Christians should practice a "greater righteousness" than the Pharisees and scribes (Matt 5:20). Matthew emphasizes that Christians have much in common with Jews: the Torah (Matt 5:17), the scribes (Matt 23:1-12), the messianic hope. The loss of the temple affects Jews and Christians in the same way and the response to it is the activation of the ethical side of Judaism (with Hos 6:6).

Regulating conflicts: Matthew's Gospel works through tensions between Jewish and Gentile Christianity. For this purpose Matthew proposes an image of the community as a *corpus mixtum* in which groups of different origins live together. Therefore he works out an ethos of mutual forgiveness (Matt 6:14) with which one can overcome even sharp tensions in the community. As he joins Jewish- and Gentile-Christian literary traditions in his gospel, so he desires to unite Jewish and Gentile Christians in the social reality of his community.[9]

Structures of authority: The Matthean community is an egalitarian one. There is one supervening authority in it: "you have one teacher, and you are all students" (Matt 23:10). His teaching is formulated in Matthew's Gospel in the way that will be valid until the end of the world. With this emphasis on the overall authority of Jesus, the Matthean evangelist fundamentally grounds the authority of his gospel. Through it he influences the communities—outside the structures of authority that existed in his time.

Matthew's Gospel was successful. It quickly became the most beloved Gospel and well into the nineteenth century was *the* gospel of the church. But many of its purposes were not fulfilled: Jewish and Gentile Christians did not live as equals in the Christian church. Alongside the Matthean voice of the one teacher, many other voices arose. The dialogue with Judaism over righteousness on the basis of a Torah interpreted critically and humanely broke off. But the radicalism of Matthew's Gospel has repeatedly, throughout the church's history, created unrest. His ethical teaching made an impression. And that began very early. The *Didache* could have seen itself as a continuation of Matthew's Gospel. That Gospel concludes with Jesus' missionary command to the disciples: "Go therefore and make disciples of all nations, baptizing them in the name of the Father and of the Son and of the Holy Spirit, and teaching them to obey everything that I have commanded you" (Matt 28:19-20). The reader spontaneously asks: What are the disciples to teach these people they baptize? The *Didache* fills in this gap. It refers four times to a gospel that must be identical with Matthew's, and points to what is taught there. But on the whole the *Didache* presents a teaching of the apostles that goes further: the instruction about the two ways to life and death, directions for baptism and the Lord's Supper as well as for common life in the community. Perhaps this was originally intended to be a continuation of Matthew's Gospel.

The Gospel of Luke and the Acts of the Apostles

This tendency to augment gospel writing through another writing was carried further in Luke's Gospel. He expanded his depiction of Jesus' activity not with a "teaching of the apostles," as the *Didache* did for Matthew's Gospel, but through his history of the apostles, later dubbed "the Acts of the Apostles." In doing so he created something new in the growing literature of early Christianity, and with it a major problem: there was nothing controversial in depicting human beings as transmitters of a teaching authorized by God, as messengers and missionaries of Jesus, as was the case in the *Didache*. But it was a problem to depict human beings as active agents, as missionaries and miracle workers continuing the work of Jesus. There was the danger that human beings would become surrounded with an inadmissible divine aura and be placed on a level with Jesus, the son of God. Luke recognized this danger. No other author besides the author of the Johannine apocalypse so often criticizes human self-apotheosis.[10] He rejects not only the satanic invitation to attempt it in the temptation story (Luke 4:5-8), but also the blasphemous apotheosis of rulers and apostles (Acts 12:21-23; 14:8-20); he corrects the mistaken divinization of apostles (Acts 10:25-26; 16:25-34), and nevertheless he tolerates at the end of Acts an apotheosis of Paul in the people's imagination when, on the basis of his miraculous rescue and his miracles, the people of Malta say that he is a god (Acts 28:1-6). Luke knows that people sense some truth when they affirm that the apostles have divine powers, but they are mistaken when they direct their worship to the apostles and not to the Lord who sent these apostles. But what kind of divine power is this? And what links these people to Jesus? What distinguishes them from him?

Luke resolves this problem by writing a history of Jesus and the apostles in which they are linked by the action of the Spirit and yet are separated by a periodization of the history of salvation. He wants to distinguish Jesus from the apostles and nevertheless to present their story as a continuing history!

The significance of the Spirit and the periodization of salvation history have previously been interpreted differently by exegetes: Hans Conzelmann reads the Lukan two-volume work as the expression of a theology of salvation history by means of which Luke offered an answer to the delay of the *parousia* and the lapse of time.[11] Luke, he says, replied with the concept of a three-part salvation history: Jesus comes not at the end of time, as Christians previously expected. Rather, he is the middle of time. With his passion begins the time of the church. Luke looks back, "historicizing," at the "middle of time," which is bounded on the one side by the prophets until (and including) John the Baptizer, on the other side by the time of the church. Its characteristic is that it is a Satan-free time in which Jesus is the sole bearer of the Spirit. Because Christians in the time of the church had a positive task in this world until the end, Luke could manage the delay of the *parousia*: Christians should not wait passively for the coming of the Lord but should actively go out to all peoples and missionize the world. Luke sees good opportunities for this in the Roman Empire. For that reason he is said to show readiness to engage more actively in this world and its circumstances than Paul, who expected the immediate end of all things.[12] In schematic form, the periodization of salvation history in the Lukan two-volume work looks like this (Table 16):

Table 16: The Salvation-Historical Conception of the Lukan Work

The time of the Old Testament until John is a time of expectation.	The time of the prophets "until John": *The prophets are bearers of the Spirit.*	• 3:19-20: The death of the Baptizer is mentioned before Jesus' baptism. • The Baptizer is not identified with Elijah (different in Mark 9:11-13).
4:13: The Satan leaves Jesus: the Satan-free time begins.	The time of Jesus (3:21—23:56): *Only Jesus is bearer of the Spirit.* The gathering of the witnesses in Galilee (3:21—9:17): Jesus' messianic awareness.	• Public proclamation of Jesus as Son of God at his baptism (3:22). • Rejection in Nazareth (4:16-30).
	The journey to Jerusalem (9:18—19:27): Jesus' awareness of his suffering.	• Announcement of passion and transfiguration (9:21-36). • Rejection by the Samaritans (9:52-56).

The Satan enters Judas: end of the Satan-free time.	Jesus' teaching in the temple and his suffering in Jerusalem (19:28—23:56): Jesus' royal awareness.	• Jesus' entry into Jerusalem: acclamation as king (19:28-40). • Rejection by the Pharisees (19:39).
Acts 1:5: Fulfillment of John's prophecy of baptism with the Spirit (Acts 11:16).	The time of the church: *All Christians are bearers of the Spirit.*	• Acts 1:6-8: The question of the *parousia* is answered by reception of the Spirit and commissioning for mission.

This fascinating proposal requires correction on one point. Luke divides history not into three but into two phases: a time of expectation and a time of fulfillment. Programmatically, he says in his prologue: ". . . many have undertaken to set down an orderly account of the events that have been fulfilled among us" (Luke 1:1). Luke thus moves within the two-part early Christian conception of history. Luke 16:16, a primary passage for the three-phase interpretation of Lukan salvation history, distinguishes only two phases: the time until John and the time after him. The time of fulfillment began with John the Baptizer. What is correct in the three-part interpretation of salvation history, however, is that Luke depicts the time of which he tells as a "three-part time of fulfillment." It began with a prelude featuring John the Baptizer, has its center in Jesus, and is continued in the history of the church. Despite all the criticism of the three-phase interpretation of salvation history, it does contain some truth. The observations made within this framework could be placed in a different frame. But the Lukan historical work is not so much "salvation historical" as it is "pneumatic." For Luke, the key to history is the Holy Spirit. He places the activity of the prophets, the life of Jesus, and the mission of the apostles on a single level, and at the same time separates them by means of historical periodization. Luke writes a history of the Spirit. The Spirit is both the objective dynamic that drives history forward and the subjective means of insight that makes its inner dynamics perceptible.

Luke thus gives an original answer to the problem of how a theological account of history is possible. In the Old Testament we find two other models that Luke thought inadequate: the models of intervention and motivation. In the Pentateuch God intervenes directly. He causes signs and wonders to occur, reveals himself in promises to the patriarchs and to the whole people through his law on Sinai. History is direct divine intervention. In the books of Samuel, on the other hand, God works only indirectly through

Nathan's promise (2 Samuel 7). He either likes or dislikes human actions (2 Sam 11:27; 12:24); he foils plans. God works through human motivation, without direct intervention. He works in secret and guides human beings from within. Luke's historical work goes its own way, combining motifs of the intervention and motivation models. Luke writes history as a history of the Spirit. The Spirit is a motivating power that God, through miraculous intervention, has placed in human hearts. The Spirit thus on the one hand motivates human beings from within; their "normal" deeds and words are caused by God through the Spirit. At the same time, however, the Spirit is a power coming from God that enables people to "super-normal" deeds: miraculous works, speaking in tongues, and precognition. Finally, the Spirit is the power that subjectively reveals the meaning of history. Luke can thus write a history in which human beings are subjects and in which, nevertheless, God is present and can be recognized through his Spirit in the form of human motivation and an irrational force. The story of Jesus and the apostles is linked by this inner dynamic of the Spirit, but also separated by it because the Spirit works in Jesus in an altogether unique manner: Jesus is begotten by the Spirit; the Spirit of God continually works in him and, during the time of Jesus, exclusively in him. Apostles and prophets, however, have received the Spirit; it is not part of their "natural" equipment and they share it with one another. Jesus ascends into heaven and sends the Spirit from there. The disciples, however, work on earth and are filled by this heavenly power. Jesus is therefore rightly worshiped as divine, the apostles incorrectly so.

How is this salvation history effected by the Spirit to be recognized? It is revealed through the Spirit: with the aid of scripture, through living prophets, and through extraordinary revelations. The Holy Spirit effects knowledge through all these three methods of revelation.

God's saving will is visible in scripture. The whole of sacred scripture is understood as prophecy, including Moses and the Psalms: "everything written about me in the law of Moses, the prophets, and the psalms must be fulfilled" (Luke 24:44). Isaiah, and especially Deutero-Isaiah, is most frequently cited. The Holy Spirit spoke through him: "The Holy Spirit was right in saying to your ancestors through the prophet Isaiah . . ." (Acts 28:25). Further examples of scriptural prophecy caused by the Spirit are Acts 1:16 and 4:25.

Besides scriptural prophecy in the past, a living present prophecy emerges in the Lukan work. The Holy Spirit seizes human beings and enables them to speak prophetically of the future. The spirit of Pentecost is a spirit of prophecy accessible to all: young and old, men and women (Joel 3:1-5 = Acts 2:17-21). Numerous prophets speak in the Holy Spirit throughout the Lukan work:

1. In the first phase of the Lukan history of fulfillment, the infancy narrative, Zechariah and Simeon speak prophetic words in the Spirit (Luke 1:67; 2:29-32): Jesus is announced and greeted as the one who brings salvation to Gentiles and Jews. Anna is a prototype of the widow living an ascetic life, dedicating her life to the Spirit, even though nothing is said directly about the Spirit: she is waiting for Jesus as the redeemer of Jerusalem (Luke 2:36-38). John the Baptizer, according to Acts 13:25, ended his "course" with the messianic prophecy of the one who will come after him, who will baptize with the Spirit.
2. In the middle of the time of fulfillment Jesus is presented as a prophet: after the raising of the young man of Nain the crowd says: "A great prophet has arisen among us" (Luke 7:16). The disciples on the road to Emmaus call him a "prophet mighty in deed and word" (Luke 24:19). In Acts he appears as the prophet promised by Moses (Deut 18:15-20; cf. Acts 3:22; 7:37).
3. The third phase of the time of fulfillment is introduced by the statement that the prophetic Spirit will be poured out on all Christians. The statement "I will pour out my Spirit; and they shall prophesy" is a Lukan addition to Joel 3:1-5 and a repetition of Joel 3:1. Agabus, an early Christian prophet, foretells a famine under Claudius (Acts 11:27-29) and Paul's imprisonment (Acts 21:10-11). The daughters of Philip have a prophetic spirit (Acts 21:9).

Revelation also occurs through angelic messengers and visions. Sometimes such appearances occur in parallel and are mutually affirming: the angel's message to Zechariah (Luke 1:13-17) correlates with the one to Mary (Luke 1:30-33, 35). The angel's Easter message to the women (Luke 24:1-7) confirms the appearance of the Risen One to the disciples at Emmaus. The appearance of Christ before Damascus (Acts 9:1-8) corresponds to the revelation to Ananias (Acts 9:10-19). The angelic appearance to Cornelius (Acts 10:3-6) correlates with Peter's vision (Acts 10:10-16).

All three ways for revealing the will of God—scripture, present prophecy, and appearances—are pneumatic experiences. The prophets have spoken "in the Spirit" (cf. Acts 28:25). The living prophecy of the present speaks in the name of the Spirit: "Thus says the Holy Spirit . . ." (Acts 21:11). The appearances are experiences effected by the Spirit. Corresponding to the Joel quotation, those gifted with the Spirit see "visions" (Acts 2:17).

But the Spirit not only conveys revelation about history; it is above all the force and power that drives people onward within it. God's power is at work within them. God works in history through people who are convinced by God's working and act by God's power.

1. This working of the Spirit begins again in the prelude to the history of fulfillment. In the angel's announcement to Zechariah it is said of the work of John the Baptizer as precursor of Jesus that "even before his birth he will be filled with the Holy Spirit" (Luke 1:15). Other prophets are always seized by the Spirit on particular occasions, but John the Baptizer will possess the Spirit at all times. That alone exalts him above all other prophets.
2. This is even more the case with Jesus himself. He not only possesses the Spirit from the womb but is begotten through the Spirit. This Spirit is called "power": Mary will be overshadowed by "the power of the Most High" (Luke 1:35). Jesus owes his existence to God's power and Spirit. This is true above all of his mission: the Spirit of God rests upon Jesus. He has been anointed at his baptism (Luke 4:18 = Isa 61:1). In Acts this is referred to as anointing with God's "power" (Acts 10:38). In his inaugural discourse Jesus traces his work for the poor, prisoners, the blind, and the oppressed to the power of the Spirit (Luke 4:18-19). This power is effective as healing power in the cure of the lame man (Luke 5:17). It is transmitted by touching the sick and makes them whole (Luke 6:19).
3. Finally, the Spirit is also the motive power of Christians: In Luke 24:48 the promise of the Spirit to the disciples is proclaimed as a gifting with "power" from on high. This is repeated at the beginning of Acts: "But you will receive power when the Holy Spirit has come upon you" (Acts 1:8). From then forward, at every crucial point in the history of the church, the Spirit is active. As the cause of the miracle of tongues, the Spirit is the legitimation for the mission to the Gentiles in all nations. The Spirit is the power for miraculous healings, prophecies, and glossolalia; that is, the Spirit is apparent in visible phenomena.

The so-called salvation historical interpretation of history in Luke thus consists primarily in the fact that God is present in history through the divine Spirit and steers it toward its goal. Luke wants thus to make the Spirit alive in his readers, or to sharpen their sense of its significance. God not only intervenes in history from without or is restricted to influencing human motivation from within: God intervenes through the Holy Spirit by placing it within the hearts of people. Through the Spirit, God gives human beings the power to work miracles and to prophesy. The Spirit was present in Jesus in a unique way in that he was begotten through the Spirit. But the history of the Spirit continues after his death.

This new view of a sectioned time of fulfillment is based on a perception of time's extension, but it does not as such imply an abandonment of the traditional expectation of the imminent end. Precisely because so many phases of the time of fulfillment have already passed, it can be that the end will break forth at any moment. Now, when the mission has founded Christian communities throughout the world, that world is ripe for the end. It is correct to say that the idea of a successively realized fulfillment makes it possible to continue to live with ongoing time and to see it positively as a mission in which God is at work through human beings. It is unmistakable that Luke is thus struggling with the problem of imminent expectation of the end. Redactional changes to the Markan text show that he deliberately suppresses it, and even rejects it as heresy when it is proclaimed in and for the present time—without excluding the possibility that it will be acute later on. Three examples may suffice (Table 17):

Table 17: Correction of Imminent Expectation of the End in Luke's Work

In Mark, Jesus proclaims: "The time is fulfilled and the kingdom of God has come near" (Mark 1:15).	Luke replaces this summary with the statement: "Today this scripture has been fulfilled in your hearing" (Luke 4:21). Today, with Jesus, begins a "year of the Lord's favor" (4:19).
Mark speaks of false prophets who will appear in Jesus' name: "Many will come in my name and say, 'I am he!' and they will lead many astray" (Mark 13:6).	Luke 21:8: "Beware that you are not led astray; for many will come in my name and say, 'I am he!' and, 'The time is near!' Do not go after them." Imminent expectation is branded as heresy.
In Mark, Jesus says to his judges: "I am; and 'you will see the Son of Man seated at the right hand of the Power,' and 'coming with the clouds of heaven'" (Mark 14:62).	Luke is silent about the *parousia* of the Son of Man: "But from now on the Son of Man will be seated at the right hand of the power of God" (Luke 22:69).

Programmatically, at the beginning of Acts, Luke formulates the question of the disciples as "'Lord, is this the time when you will restore the kingdom to Israel?' He replied, 'It is not for you to know the times or periods that the Father has set by his own authority. But you will receive power when the Holy Spirit has come upon you; and you will be my witnesses in Jerusalem, in all Judea and Samaria, and to the ends of the earth" (Acts 1:6-8). The assignment to mission replaces the imminent expectation of the end as the presence of the Spirit replaces the presence of Christ. Nevertheless, there are some examples of such an imminent expectation in Luke's two-volume work, all of which, however, are corrected in characteristic fashion. The Baptizer proclaims the imminent end in his preaching: "Even now the ax is lying at the root of the trees" (Luke 3:9). Jesus corrects this expectation in Luke 13:6-9: the barren fig tree gets another reprieve. Precisely in this, Jesus distinguishes himself from the Baptizer. In the mission discourse the disciples are told to preach in the places they visit: "The kingdom of God has come near to you" (Luke 10:9). Here the coming of the reign of God is understood in spatial terms. With Jesus' missionaries the reign of God has come to particular places, and it goes away again with them, just as their peace goes with them when they are rejected in such places (Luke 10:6). In the parable of the pleading widow, Jesus promises: "[God] will . . . quickly grant justice to [his chosen ones]" (Luke 18:7-8). This parable is less directed to imminent expectation than to a continual present expectation; it is meant to admonish its hearers to pray *always* (Luke 18:1). When God hears a prayer, he intervenes within history.[13]

A great many passages show that Luke in fact is thinking of a *constant expectation*, that is, a readiness to reckon with the end at any time: he presents two eschatological discourses, first the little apocalypse in Luke 17:20-37 from Q, and then the Synoptic apocalypse in Luke 21 from Mark. The reader encounters the Q apocalypse first and is meant to read the Markan apocalypse in light of it. What does one learn from the Q apocalypse? According to Luke 17:20-21, the reign of God does not come with external signs. Thus the question about signs that the disciples ask in the apocalypse derived from Mark (Luke 21:7) is rejected from the outset as inappropriate. The reign of God, rather, is a reality "among" or "within you" (*entos hymōn*). Philologically, the most plausible interpretation has always been that this refers to an inner reality: the faith of the disciples, previously mentioned, would be such an inner reality; here it is a saving power (Luke 17:19). The reader also learns from the Q apocalypse that the disciples will one day long to see the day of the Son of Man, and they will be led astray by people who identify the Messiah: "'Look there!' or 'Look here!'" (Luke 17:23). Thus Luke says from the outset that all expectations that identify particular concrete figures as the One who returns are false. The *parousia* will break in suddenly and will be cosmically visible. Finally, the reader learns from Luke 17:26-30 that the *parousia* will break in on a peaceful world. But in Luke 21 it is expected in a world torn apart by wars. The reader knows from the previous passage that this is an error. Luke is here contending with false expectations of the imminent end derived from the period of the Jewish War. He wants to create a constant awareness that expects the *parousia* at any time but does not prophesy it with specific dates or identify it with particular figures. Therefore he adds, at the end of the Q apocalypse, the parable of the pleading widow to illustrate the admonition to constant prayer (Luke 18:1). For the same reason he ends the Markan apocalypse with the redactional words: "Be on guard so that your hearts are not weighed down with dissipation and drunkenness and the worries of this life, and that day does not catch you unexpectedly, like a trap. For it will come upon all who live on the face of the whole earth. Be alert at all times, praying that you may have the strength to escape all these things that will take place, and to stand before the Son of Man" (Luke 21:34-36).

But how can one live in constant expectation? It corresponds to the existential situation of human beings, who may individually die at any time and then stand before God to give an account of their lives. So we find in Luke's Gospel an individual eschatology that replaces the seriousness of early Christian expectation of the imminent end of all things. In the parable of the foolish rich man (Luke 12:16-21) and that of the unjust manager (16:1-8), Luke considers the death of the individual. Lazarus is taken to Paradise immediately after his death (Luke 16:19-31). The same is true for the repentant sinner on the cross: "Today you will be with me in Paradise" (Luke 23:42-43).[14]

Here again the question arises: to what extent is Luke, in this approach, hiding behind Jesus in order to further his own theology? He is undoubtedly using a new approach, and yet with Luke as well we must emphasize the continuity with Jesus. It is true that Jesus held an imminent eschatology, which Luke opposes. But on one point he could appeal to Jesus: he had interpreted the present as a joyful time, a positive task with opportunities. Precisely in this Jesus differed from the ascetic John, the preacher of repentance. Luke, two generations after Jesus' death, again interprets his own present in a positive manner. It offers opportunities. In it, in continuity with Jesus but in clear distinction from him, the Spirit is at work in Christians. He offers this message to a community in a concrete situation. With Luke, too, we find the intention to guide communities. With him, too, we can recognize the five functions every community leader must perform. Therefore let us quickly review the five functions with regard to Luke's two-volume work.[15]

Building consensus: Luke combines, as does no other evangelist, the authority of Jesus with that of the apostles, by devoting a book to each. The preaching of Jesus and the preaching of Jesus' apostles are depicted together in a single work and thus harmonized. What Luke tells of Jesus is also told by the apostles in short summaries of his life (Acts 2:22-24; 10:28-43; 13:26-37). Within the apostles' preaching, however, he creates in Acts a balance between the dominance of Peter in the first part (to Acts 15) and that of Paul in the second part. The contrasts between the different currents in early Christianity are described in harmonizing fashion: his ideal is the primitive community that was one heart and one soul (Acts 4:32). The primary consensus-building power is the Holy Spirit. Therefore the apostles at the apostolic council could formulate their consensus as follows: "For it has seemed good to the Holy Spirit and to us . . ." (Acts 15:28). The unity of the community is, for Luke, a work of the Holy Spirit.

Orientation within the environment: Luke proposes a differentiated image of the world, avoiding black-white depiction. It contains good and evil officials, sympathetic and hostile Pharisees, an unrepentant and a repentant "thief" on the cross. This world offers the opportunity to be able to preach the gospel without hindrance. But that freedom must, when necessary, be defended through civil disobedience. This attitude marks Luke more clearly than any other New Testament author (with the exception of the Johannine apocalypse). To be rejected above all is any apotheosis of human power. Here Luke distances himself from corresponding tendencies in the period of the Flavians. He may be writing shortly after the fall of Domitian (96 C.E.). He has Mary sing revolutionary songs about the fall of the mighty (Luke 1:46-55) and yet is certain that in this he will also find positive resonance in the upper class of the Roman Empire: shortly after Domitian's fall there was a sympathetic ear for such. His ending also created in the empire's upper levels a certain understanding of the fall of those who exalted themselves. Jesus was different from those. The Holy Spirit had created him in his mother's womb and presented him visibly in public as the Son of God.

Defining identity: Luke, in his two-volume work, proposes the image of a stepwise separation between Jews and Christians. At the beginning, the promise of salvation was extended also to Gentiles, to the benefit of Israel (Luke 2:31). Jesus addresses himself only to Israel, but causes within it a split between people and leaders. After Easter, the Holy Spirit successfully begins anew the gathering of Israel, as the mass conversions in Acts show. It is only the Gentile mission that leads to a definitive rejection of the message by Jews. At the end there remains a tiny ray of hope, if we translate the conclusion of Acts 28:27 literally, in the future tense: "and I will heal them." The ritual distinction in Mark's Gospel and the ethical division in Matthew are, however, augmented in Luke's work through a historical delimitation. He tells how division came about, thus showing that while it is understandable, it was not necessary, and it need not exist for all time. If one had asked him what, then, constituted the identity of Christians, he could have given a clear answer: Christians are people endowed with the Holy Spirit.

Regulating conflicts: The Lukan two-volume work is characterized by tensions between poor and rich. Luke does not want to transcend these tensions only through a vertical accommodation, by donations from the rich, but also through a horizontal equalizing among all. The Baptizer already warns in his preaching that even ordinary people should share their food (Luke 3:10-14), and Paul encourages hardworking people to support others (Acts 20:32-35). Offenses against this intra-community solidarity are offenses against the Holy Spirit. Ananias and Sapphira are therefore sharply criticized: they have lied to "the Holy Spirit" (Acts 5:3). The Spirit sees to it that people support one another with money, but is not against having money, as the story of Simon Magus shows (Acts 8:4-25).

Structures of authority: Luke opposes the financial support of itinerant charismatics and local officeholders, but also the charitable acts of the powerful and rich by which they secure influence in the community (Luke 22:25). For him, authority is bestowed not through riches but through legitimate succession. Through the work of the twelve apostles, the Samaritan Christians acquire legitimacy (Acts 8:14-17), and through the work of the thirteenth witness, Paul, the disciples of John the Baptizer in Ephesus are integrated into the church (Acts 19:1-7). In all this the Holy Spirit plays the decisive role. The Spirit is, of course, closely connected with the ecclesial offices through the laying on of hands, but in principle is independent of the authority of church office. The Spirit works where it will, and can also be given to people without ritual actions.[16]

If the evangelists wanted to act as community guides through their writings, they thus filled the gap in authority left by the passing of the first generation. They wanted thus to strengthen the authority of Jesus, in contrast to which every other authority paled. The Gospel of Luke thus also proposes an image of Jesus in order to affect the present. In comparison to Matthew we find in it a closer approach to the Gentile world, but still an admiration of Judaism. In the birth stories he presents Jews awaiting the Messiah with great sympathy. Perhaps this author was one of the "God-fearers," Gentiles who sympathized with the Jewish synagogue but had not completed a full conversion to Judaism. As one who understood the Gentile world, he knew about people's inclination to surround themselves or others with a divine aura. He depicts Jesus and the apostles as people who are endowed with the Spirit in clearly different ways. The former is Son of God in a unique way through the Spirit; all others are simply human beings moved by the Spirit. But the same divine power is at work in all of them.

Gospel and Acts, life of Jesus and life of the apostles can therefore be shaped together into a continuous two-volume work. In fact, they play out on a single level, though in clearly distinguished periods of salvation history. For later Christians this equation was too bold. In the canon the Lukan work was taken apart, and Acts was separated from Luke's Gospel by the Gospel of John. As a rule, in the text tradition the Acts of the Apostles introduces the catholic letters. Sometimes these are placed after Paul's letters and sometimes before them. The "deeds of the apostles" thus, in the various canonical orderings of the books, do not necessarily stand immediately after the deeds of Jesus (the gospels), but in any case they precede the apostles' letters.[17]

12 Jesus' Fictive Self-Interpretation through the Transformation of the Jesus Traditions in the Gospels Associated with Gnosis

With the Johannine and Thomas Gospels, Jesus' fictive self-interpretation acquires a new quality. The Synoptic Gospels, like the Jewish-Christian gospels, applied their own accents within the Jesus tradition by means of selection, ordering, small additions and excisions. But form-critically they drew on the potential already present in the Jesus tradition: Q retained the formal language of Jesus' sayings, Mark the formal language of the first narratives about Jesus: apophthegms, miracle stories, passion narrative, in which the two streams of tradition overlapped. In the two oldest written presentations of the Jesus tradition (Q and Mark), as in the great Synoptic Gospels (Matthew and Luke), it was a matter of redacting the Jesus tradition, not transforming it. We can also speak of redaction in the way that, through the gospel form, the Jesus traditions narrated within this framework were illuminated by a different light. In Mark's Gospel that light shines above all on the end of gospels, from the darkness of the cross and the light of the resurrection. The dignity of the Son of God revealed through the Easter events streams over the individual traditions as a secret revelation accessible only to the reader but remaining hidden from the persons within the text. In the Gospels of Matthew and Luke this light shines on the story of Jesus from the very beginning: the infancy narratives give the whole a new quality. Even today a fascinating glory streams from the star of Bethlehem and the child in the manger, one that has inspired artists through many centuries. Everything becomes an unfolding of the hidden divine nature of the Son of God begotten by the Holy Spirit, whose miraculous gifts and revelatory power betray his supernatural origins.

The Gospel of John

In John's Gospel the redaction of the Jesus traditions constitutes a far-reaching transformation of them. This can be shown in the altered formal language. The genres of the Jesus tradition are transformed by the idea of the Redeemer's self-revelation. The narratives become symbolic narration on two semantic levels: the miracle stories become masterful self-revelations of Jesus (*semeia* and signs), the stories in the passion narrative a paradoxical glorification of Jesus. Jesus' words are transformed into long revelatory discourses centered on "I am" sayings. Parables become images in which the Redeemer reveals himself as sent by God. In addition, however, Jesus' words and deeds contain a self-commentary produced by a constant *relecture* or a hermeneutic in stages leading from a superficial level of understanding to a comprehension in depth.[1]

Hermeneutic in Stages as Overall Formative Principle

The prologue contains the program for a "hermeneutic in stages" as a reading guide for the whole gospel. It begins directly with God. The revealer comes straight from the heart of the Father and brings exclusively authentic knowledge of God. No one else has seen God (John 1:18). All reality is his hidden "word," which is "spoken" in him. He existed before all things. Moses and the Baptizer have received their light and truth from him. He is recognized in two stages, corresponding to the two strophes of the prologue (John 1:1-13, 14-18). Both strophes begin with a statement about the Word, or *Logos*: John 1:1 with "In the beginning was the Word . . ." and John 1:14 with "And the Word became flesh." The first strophe is formulated in the first person singular, the second primarily in the first person plural. John the Baptizer appears in both strophes. The statements about him were probably inserted by the evangelist, because their prosaic style sets them apart from the surrounding hymnic phrases. The Baptizer has to appear twice because the faith he is to induce through his testimony develops in two stages, as the following schematic overview shows (Table 18).

It is not hard to discern the "stages": the first strophe speaks of faith, the second of seeing. The first witness of the Baptizer speaks of the light, the second of Jesus' preexistence. In the first strophe the light enlightens every human being; in the second strophe the glory of God is accessible only to a "we" group. It is also clear that the whole prologue represents a path from not understanding to understanding. John 1:5 says, "the darkness did not comprehend (or overcome) it (the light)." At the end, in John 1:18, complete understanding is possible: "It is God the only Son . . . who has made him

(God) known." Since no one has ever seen God, it is only through him that there is access to God.

Table 18: The Johannine Prologue

1-5	Creation of the world by the *Logos*, who was with God in the beginning, and the inability of darkness to understand him:
6-8	*The Baptizer's witness to the light: through his testimony all are to come to believe.*
9-11	Rejection of the light and
12-13	acceptance of the light by those who "believe" in his Name.
14-18	Revelation of God through the *Logos* in the flesh and the beholding of his glory:
15	*The Baptizer's testimony to preexistence: Jesus existed before the Baptizer.*
16-17	Moses and the law are surpassed by the revelation of "grace and truth."
18	The authentic revelation of God through Jesus, who is the "only-begotten God."

What is the purpose of this hermeneutic in stages? At first glance one might say it is about believing in the Preexisting One, by means of which the Gospel of John reaches beyond the faith in Christ of the Synoptic Gospels. In John's Gospel Jesus has become a heavenly being, coming from heaven to walk on this earth for a time and then return to the Father. But beyond that content, what is crucial for the Johannine hermeneutic in stages is the self-founding and self-legitimation of the new Christian religion from its christological center: Jesus is the one who defines himself. God is the one who is self-revealed in Jesus. Those whose faith is fixed on God and the One whom God has sent do not belong to the world but are guided by God alone: the internal autonomy of Christian faith is the goal of the Johannine hermeneutic in stages.

This stepwise hermeneutics shapes the structure of the Gospel of John. Revelation proceeds in two stages corresponding to its two parts. The public activity of the Revealer (John 1–12) is surpassed by his revelation within the group of disciples (John 13–17, 20–21). But even within these two parts we find advances in recognition and understanding. In the public section the readers of the Gospel of John repeatedly move from an initial faith oriented to the visible to faith in the revelation of what is invisible. So Jesus' miracles are interpreted symbolically, and Jesus' words acquire a deeper sense through being misunderstood. The same is true of the non-public revelation in the group of the disciples in the second part of John's Gospel: an initial farewell discourse is followed by a second that treats the themes of the first anew on a higher plane. This *relecture* of previous texts culminates in the high-priestly prayer (John 17), in which the whole mission of Jesus is newly interpreted in retrospect.

This hermeneutic in stages, however, shapes not only the overall structure of the Gospel of John but also the sequence of texts in each part. Themes and texts are repeated again and again in order to be interpreted on a deeper level.

In the first part of John's Gospel Jesus repeatedly encounters human expectations of salvation that he fulfills and surpasses. The first disciples come to him because they see the traditional expectations of a redeemer fulfilled in him. They have found in Jesus the "Messiah" (John 1:41) and "Son of God" (John 1:49). While in the Synoptic Gospels the disciples win through to a knowledge of Jesus' dignity only with great difficulty, in John's Gospel they have access to that knowledge from their first encounter with Jesus. But they thus represent only a first stage of knowledge. Jesus promises Nathanael still more: "You will see greater things than these . . . you will see heaven opened and the angels of God ascending and descending upon the Son of Man" (1:50-51). All expectations are exceeded through a "seeing" of the immediate union of Jesus with the heavenly world. Jesus is thus not yet perfectly known when one expresses his dignity with traditional titles of majesty. What is crucial is how the Redeemer defines himself. He does this in the "I am" sayings through which the Christology bound to titles is surpassed by a metaphorical Christology in images: I am the bread of life, the light of the world, the door, the good shepherd, the resurrection and the life, etc. In all these images the Revealer defines himself in a way that transcends the traditional roles of Redeemer and Revealer.

In the farewell section (John 13–17) Jesus deals with the sorrow and fear of his disciples. He prepares them for life in the world without him. As his mission in his public work was the revelation of life, he has a different mission here: the revelation of the love commandment. He speaks explicitly of a "new commandment" he has to give. But even this "new commandment" is revealed in stages. We find it the first time in the dialogical farewell discourse (John 13:34-35), the second time in the farewell monologue (John 15:12-17). The evangelist gives a clear indication in the text that with this the most important thing in the Johannine Gospel has been spoken. Jesus had often announced before *that* he says what he has heard from the Father. But we never hear *what* he has heard. Only once does the gospel explicitly emphasize that now Jesus has said *everything* he has heard from the Father, namely, after the second formulation of the love commandment:

> This is my commandment, that you love one another as I have loved you. No one has greater love than this, to lay down one's life for one's friends. You are my friends if you do what I command you. I do not call you servants any longer, because the servant does not know what the master is doing; but I have called you friends, because I have made known to you everything that I have heard from my Father. (John 15:12-15)

Here it is said explicitly that with the love commandment everything, really *everything* that Jesus has to communicate from the Father on the basis of his familiarity with him, has been said. The whole Gospel of John has been written in order to bring the love commandment and love itself from heaven to earth. All previous revelation is thus surpassed, for until now the disciples were servants (slaves) in relationship to God and Jesus, but now they have become Jesus' friends. The decisive factor is religious knowledge.

Changes to Formal Language in Detail

The literary *relecture* of the existing Jesus tradition by means of a hermeneutic in stages leads to a clear transformation of traditional small forms.

In the *narrative traditions* we find some remarkable characteristics in contrast to the Synoptics. There are no exorcisms among the miracle stories. The passion narrative is reinterpreted as a paradoxical glorification and a way to the Father. In the apparent victory of the world over Jesus, Jesus triumphs over the world because it cannot touch him. Other changes are connected: through the elimination of exorcisms the struggle with Satan is concentrated entirely in the passion. Here the prince of the world is overcome, after his apparent victory in Jesus' crucifixion. He is not overcome in the many individual miracles Jesus does (as in the Synoptics), but through the one great miracle done in and for Jesus himself: the resurrection. The other miracle stories become symbolic narratives. This development had already begun to a degree in the Synoptic Gospels. The miracle of insight for the "blind" disciples is represented symbolically in the miracle stories: the healing of a blind man, also to be understood symbolically, precedes Peter's confession of Jesus as Messiah (Mark 8:22-26). In the story of the stilling of the storm the disciples' doubts as followers of Jesus are symbolically represented: they are afraid of sinking in the waves of history. The boat in which they are sailing is the ship of the church, threatened by storms and waves

(Matt 8:23-27). The miraculous catch of fish points to the gathering of the church by the many "fishers of people"; in one case the thought is of the mission (Luke 5:1-11), in the other the task of holding the church together (John 21:1-14). The symbolic deepening of the miracle stories begun already in the Synoptics always begins with the disciples: their blindness, their discipleship, their gathering are symbolically represented in the stories. In John's Gospel, on the other hand, everything is concentrated on Jesus himself. The healing of the blind man (John 9:1-38) attests above all to the saying of Jesus that preceded it: "I am the light of the world" (John 8:12). The bread miracle (John 6:1-15) leads to Jesus' subsequent saying: "I am the bread of life" (John 8:35). And the raising of Lazarus (John 11:1-46) reveals that "I am the resurrection and the life" (John 11:25).

The *sayings tradition* is completely changed. We do find here and there some pointed expressions, but they are embedded in long discourses with many repetitions that often seem like an eternal bell-ringing in heaven. At the center are the "I am" sayings, in which Jesus reveals himself as the one sent by the Father. His image is unmistakably modeled after the then-widespread idea of the figure of the messenger or envoy. The "mission Christology" of John's Gospel contains six motifs:

- The messenger is sent. The most frequent designation of God in John's Gospel is even connected to this act of sending: God is "the Father who sent me."
- The messenger must legitimate himself. Jesus has a better witness than John the Baptizer, consisting of three "testimonies": his works, God's voice, and scripture (John 5:31-47).
- A messenger must present himself. The heavenly Sent One does this in his "I am" sayings: I am the bread of life, the light of the world, etc. (John 6:35; 8:12; 10:7, 9, 11; 11:25; 14:6; 15:1-5). The sequence of the sayings makes sense: people come to Jesus (John 6:35), follow him (8:12), find life here and now in his community (John 10:1-18), and for all eternity beyond death (John 11:1-27). All this is repeated again in the farewell discourses: Christians come through him to the Father (John 14:6) and through him they remain in the love of Jesus and the Father (John 15:1-11).
- A messenger has an assignment or "commandment": Jesus defines this assignment twice, once as a task, the revealing of life (John 12:50), then as a "new commandment" of love (John 13:34).
- Ultimately, the messenger returns to the one who sent him. Jesus speaks repeatedly of going to his Father. To Mary Magdalene he

says: "I am ascending to my Father and your Father, to my God and your God" (John 20:17).

- After his return, the messenger gives an account of how he has fulfilled his assignment. In John's Gospel this occurs even before the return to the Father, in the high-priestly prayer. There Jesus says to God: "I glorified you on earth by finishing the work that you gave me to do" (John 17:4).

The unique character of this "messenger" from heaven is that he himself is the essential content of his message. John thus quite clearly goes beyond Jesus and Paul: the historical Jesus proclaimed the reign of God theocentrically; this is still clearly visible in the Synoptics. Paul, in contrast, preached the Crucified and Risen One. In John's Gospel the preaching of the earthly Jesus himself is already christocentric: he proclaims himself. Salvation and damnation are determined in the encounter with his self-revelation. What he reveals about life in the present cannot be surpassed for eternity. What he conveys of salvation cannot be retracted by the last judgment. It is ultimate, eschatological salvation in the midst of time. This salvation is a deep tie to Christ, which has been called the Johannine Christ-mysticism, a Christ-mysticism that surpasses even the mission Christology.

The Relationship of John's Gospel to the Synoptics

Once we have recognized the hermeneutic in stages as an internal structural principle of the Gospel of John, a number of knotty literary-critical questions about that gospel, while not resolved, are at least relativized in their significance.[2] Staged hermeneutics presuppose that a Jesus tradition that preceded the Gospel of John is being newly interpreted. John's Gospel takes a critical look at traditional images of Jesus and is a witness to the hermeneutical unrest that has existed throughout the history of Christianity. It documents a dissatisfaction with an image of Jesus shaped by the Synoptics. But in that case it is altogether improbable that this is the oldest gospel,[3] especially since both conclusions to the book reckon with the existence of other gospels—probably in the first conclusion, at John 20:30-31, and certainly in John 21:25. Also favoring knowledge of a Synoptic Gospel is the gospel form itself. It is improbable that the gospel form developed two times, independently of each other, solely on the basis of immanent developmental tendencies in the Jesus tradition. The narrative beginning with the preaching of John the Baptizer, the still visible turning point with Peter's confession, the division of the passion narrative into a farewell and a judicial section—the least forced explanation for all this is that the Johannine evangelist had become acquainted with Mark's Gospel. He need not therefore have had it open before him for use as a source in writing his gospel. It suffices if he had heard it read, or if he himself had once read it, or read it aloud. A general knowledge of the other Synoptic Gospels is less likely, though not excluded. What is decisive is that the Johannine evangelist very certainly followed his own tradition with a unique stylistic and theological shape. He knows other gospels, but presents an autonomous Jesus tradition. Even the Lord's sayings in the Gospel of John, often so synoptic-sounding, cannot be traced with certainty to the Synoptic Gospels; they are independent variants of the traditions.[4] Knowledge of other gospels probably inspired the Johannine evangelist to write down his own tradition in a gospel also, in order to trump all of them through the valid testimony of the Beloved Disciple.

The Situation of John's Gospel

What kind of church situation is visible in this gospel? In John's Gospel Jesus is the sole emissary from God. All other such envoys are dependent on him. At the same time, church offices are criticized. The competition between the Beloved Disciple and Peter presents a conflict between the authors and the community leadership. Peter appears as inferior, limited, and lacking understanding. Jesus himself undertakes a slave's office when he washes the disciples' feet. Peter, the representative of office, protests (John 13:1-17). Peter thinks in hierarchical categories. The Beloved Disciple says in his writing, on the contrary, that all Christians should have as direct a relationship with their Lord as he himself has: all branches are directly connected to the vine (John 15:1-8). The true disciples are Jesus' friends and not slaves (John 15:15). Between the vine and the branches, between Jesus and his friends, there is an immediate relationship. No bishop and no office stands between them.

This immediacy of relationship to Jesus is connected with the awareness that Jesus is immediately present in Christians through the Paraclete. The farewell discourses refer to him in five sayings about the Paraclete (John 14:16-17, 26; 15:26-27; 16:5-11, 12-15). The last of these summarizes the latter's mission as follows: "I still have many things to say to you, but you cannot bear them now. When the Spirit of truth comes, he will guide you into all the truth; for he will not speak on his own, but will speak whatever he hears, and he will declare to you the things that are to come. He will glorify me, because he will take what is mine and declare it to you. All that the Father has is mine" (John 16:12-15). Here we find a legitimation of inspired discourse. It originates with the exalted Jesus who shares everything with the Father. In addition, two parts of the content of that discourse are named: the announcement of the future, which is the classic task of prophecy, and the glorification of Jesus. The discourse inspired by Jesus is in the first person, as we find it everywhere in John's Gospel. It encounters us later in Montanist prophecy.[5] This first-person style is characteristic of John's Gospel. Hence, in form-critical terms, we can interpret the typical speech of the self-revealing Christ as a further development of early Christian inspired prophetic speech. To understand the uniqueness of the Gospel of John, however, one must also take into account a new religious-historical context within which this prophetically marked tradition accomplished a new interpretation of Christian faith.

John's Gospel stands at a turning point in the history of religion. We sense in it the rise of "Gnosticism," which combined three underlying motifs: (1) a radical devaluation of the world as the work of a subordinate, either unconscious or evil demiurge, who is distinct from the true, transcendent God. Added to this was (2) a radical exaltation of the human self as a heavenly spark lost in this world. These two were linked by (3) the conviction that salvation happens through intuitive knowledge (*gnōsis*), an identity of the human self with the transcendent God. Gnosticism is a variant of mystical religion. In John's Gospel Jesus is the sole Gnostic: only he has come from heaven and knows he will return there (John 8:14). The image of the creator God at one point almost reverses itself into that of a Satan (John 8:37-47). The Gnostic temptation can be sensed throughout. But as a whole the Gospel of John is a clear rejection of the Gnostic temptation: the world was created by the Redeemer himself (John 1:1-18). Human beings cannot satisfy their longing for God through "knowledge" of being identical with God. Only in Christ is God, whom no one else has seen, made visible (John 1:18). Only in him does the transcendent God touch the earth. Only in him is the religious longing of all people satisfied. But the Gnostic temptation we can already sense in John's Gospel continued its influence. The Johannine letters attest to conflicts into which it drove groups within the Johannine movement. The result must have been a division among the groups responsible for this gospel.

John's Gospel can also be interpreted as the writing of an early Christian theologian who hoped to influence the community through his depiction of the Johannine Christ. Here again we can demonstrate the five functions of community leadership:[6]

Building consensus: John knows the Synoptic image of Jesus, either from the Synoptic tradition or from his familiarity with one or several of the gospels, and he reconciles it with a spiritual image of Christ for "advanced Christians." However, he does so in the knowledge that with this image of Christ he is producing a depiction for everyone, containing everything a believer needs in order to live (John 20:31). He legitimates this subtle Christ image by means of the Beloved Disciple, who is regarded as the author of the gospel and who is said to have had a privileged relationship with Jesus. While his testimony to Christ does not exclude other Christ imagery, it contains, in contrast to them, a definitive truth.

Orientation within the environment: John asserts a profound dualism between the "ruler of this world" and Jesus. The mythical ruler of the world is closely associated with the Romans, the real world rulers. Therefore Satan acts through Judas and a Roman cohort under his direction (John 14:30-31; 18:3). Satan is active only in Jesus' crucifixion; the Romans are responsible for it, because they alone have the right to impose a death sentence (John 18:31). Jews aim at the crucifixion of Jesus only because they have become subject to the Romans (= Satan). The resurrection, however, is Jesus' victory over his enemies. The Gospel of John teaches the community to view the world as hostile, a place where Christians are hated. Their mutual love is all the more to be a light in this dark world.

Defining identity: The Gospel of John maintains a great deal of ambivalence toward the mother religion, Judaism. On the one hand, salvation comes from the Jews (John 4:22); on the other hand, the Jews are seen as possessed by Satan insofar as they work for Jesus' crucifixion (John 8:44). This outward dissociation may have had an internal function in John's Gospel: it exalts the unity of Johannine Christians and elides deep tensions among them.

Regulating conflicts: We sense in John's Gospel the tensions between simple and advanced Christians. The gospel intends to overcome these tensions by presenting a spiritual image of Jesus that can speak also to ordinary Christians. Peter symbolizes the *simplices*. At present he does not yet understand who Jesus really is and what he does for the disciples in washing their feet. But in the future he will understand. The Beloved Disciple, his competitor and contrasting figure, symbolizes the pneumatic Christians who have a deeper understanding of Jesus.

Structures of authority: In John's Gospel, Jesus is the sole authority, and even he does not want to be "Lord," but a "friend." Nevertheless, a lack of institutional regulations caused the development especially in the Johannine milieu of a monocharismatic situation, that is, a group climate in which individual gifted people claimed great authority for themselves. Within the Johannine milieu we may mention Peter, the Presbyter who wrote 2 and 3 John, and Diotrephes. Weak group structures, paradoxically, favor individual charismatics. To that extent, the development toward the monarchical episcopate of Ignatius of Antioch is easily imaginable in this environment.

Since the five functions of community leadership can also be found in John's Gospel, we may conclude that this gospel was intended to furnish the basis for the life of a community. The case is different in the *Gospel of Thomas*, in which it is primarily "individuals" who are addressed, people who have found the way to God through mystical knowledge.

The Gospel of Thomas

Comparable to the Gospel of John is the fictive self-interpretation of Jesus in the *Gospel of Thomas*, discovered in 1945. While John's Gospel was about an advanced Christianity of love, the *Gospel of Thomas* represents a Christianity of higher knowledge. It is a collection of sayings of Jesus in which Synoptic-sounding words stand alongside profound revelatory sayings of a transcendent redeemer. The formal language of the Jesus tradition is much more closely preserved here than in John's Gospel. We find brief sayings of Jesus and a few longer similitudes placed one after another. But these "simple" words of Jesus are to be read in light of a new revelatory thought added to the Synoptic-sounding sayings. The beginning of the *Gospel of Thomas* gives the reader an introduction to understanding these words: "These are the secret sayings that the living Jesus spoke and Didymos Judas Thomas recorded. And he said, 'Whoever discovers the interpretation of these sayings will not taste death'" (*Gos. Thom.* 1).[7] Readers are promised eternal life if they rightly understand the words that follow. For what they find in these words is self-knowledge, the awareness that the human being has within himself or herself a spark of divine light that is only awakened by a call from without. The *Gospel of Thomas* has retained for us an individual early Christian mysticism. The book cannot fall under the verdict against Gnosticism, even though it offers a Gnostic reinterpretation of Jesus' words. It is not aware of a second world creator distinct from the true God, and it does not present a docetic Christology. On the contrary: it embodies a pure form of the message of the infinite value of the individual human soul. The reign of God is the place from which human beings come and to which the redeemed return—and at the same time it is the inmost self. Knowledge of the reign of God is therefore knowledge of the self: "the (Father's) imperial rule is within you and it is outside you" (*Gos. Thom.* 3). The Redeemer, who conveys knowledge, is likewise not radically transcendent with respect to this world: Jesus says, "in flesh I appeared to them" (*Gos. Thom.* 28). He is omnipresent: "I am the light that is over all things. I am all: from me all came forth, and to me all attained. Split a piece of wood; I am there. Lift up the stone, and you will find me there" (*Gos. Thom.* 77). Despite all devaluation of the world, it remains the medium of revelation. We find traces of a cosmic piety. The stones will serve the disciples (*Gos. Thom.* 19). What distinguishes the *Gospel of Thomas* from all other early Christian writings is its radical individualism. No community is visible. It addresses individuals and those who are alone, and it offers them a mysticism of union with God: a return to the origin of all things.

The Gospels of John and Thomas are internally related by their affinity with Gnosticism, but for that very reason their differences are all the more evident. One sometimes has the impression that there is a material alternative: in John, the dominant revelatory word is Jesus' "I," and it culminates in the "I am" sayings. On the other hand, there are very few sayings about the reign of God (John 3:3, 5; 18:36). In the *Gospel of Thomas*, however, as in the Synoptic tradition, the reign of God is the central revelatory word, but this reign is radically reinterpreted: it becomes a symbol for the self within the individual human being. It is not the person of Jesus but a message of Jesus reinterpreted as mysticism that is the center of this gospel. This corresponds to the formal difference between the two gospels: John's is a biography framed by narratives. Even the discourses are contextually situated revelatory speeches. The *Gospel of Thomas*, in contrast, is a collection of sayings without narrative elements. Characteristic for these two gospels is the difference between the two "guarantors" of these transformations of the Jesus tradition: the Beloved Disciple is clearly presented as a recipient of revelation with a privileged closeness to Jesus. Jesus' love distinguishes him from all others. Thomas, however, is introduced as Didymos, that is, as Jesus' twin, and thus is even more closely tied to Jesus. He is more than a disciple; he is related to Jesus and thus stands symbolically for every Christian who, through knowledge of the heavenly self, is to become a relative of the Revealer who has come from heaven. The difference between the two is on the one hand a consistently community-oriented christocentrism in John, and on the other hand a consistently individualistic mysticism in Thomas.

The date of origin of the *Gospel of Thomas* is disputed. Some want to see it as older than the Synoptics and hope to find here an access to the historical Jesus through which they can fundamentally correct the traditional image of Jesus. A great deal more, however, favor the position that the *Gospel of Thomas* presupposes the canonical gospels, even if it offers autonomous Jesus traditions independent of them. It contains many parallels to bits of Matthew's and Luke's special material.[8] Often elements in the Synoptic traditions that may be due to redactional work are presupposed. Only the sequence of the sayings was for a long time impossible to derive from the Synoptics, but here there may be a new solution: the wording and sequence of Jesus' sayings can often be explained from Tatian's *Diatessaron*. In that case, the *Gospel of Thomas* could not have originated before the end of the second century.[9]

The Gospel of the Egyptians

We may consider yet a third variant of a Gnostic transformation of the Jesus tradition, in the *Gospel of the Egyptians*. Unfortunately, we have only fragments of it through Clement of Alexandria. He argues with the *Gospel of the Egyptians* because he knows ascetics who appeal to this gospel. Hence he cites from it, one-sidedly, only sayings that have an ascetic character. In the *Gospel of the Egyptians* the mission of Jesus is also summarized in a saying about Jesus' having come: "I came to destroy the works of the female" (Clement, *Strom*. 3.63.1). This develops the idea that through ascesis one can remove the limitations of gender, an idea that has had widespread influence in Christianity. Thus, in *2 Clement* 12.2 we find a saying of the Lord that is also attested in the *Gospel of the Egyptians* (Clement, *Strom*. 34.92.2–93.1): "For the Lord himself being asked by someone when his kingdom should come, said: 'When the two shall be one, and the outside (that which is without) as the inside (that which is within), and the male with the female (neither male nor female).'" Clement of Alexandria defends the *Gospel of the Egyptians* against a radical ascetic interpretation. Although he gives precedence to the four canonical gospels, he can cite other gospels, such as the *Gospel of the Hebrews*, in a positive sense.

13 Jesus' Fictive Self-Interpretation through the Continuation of the Synoptic Jesus Tradition in the Jewish-Christian Gospels

Besides the gospels that were later canonized, there was also a series of other gospels of which we have nothing but fragments. These can be divided into two groups: the Jewish-Christian gospels are continuations of the Synoptics. Others, however, harmonize Synoptic and Johannine traditions and presuppose the simultaneous existence of the Gospel of John and the Synoptics. In both groups we can observe a comparable tendency, independent of each other: the Jesus tradition is increasingly imbued with ideas having a Gnostic effect, though this is very much muted in the Jewish-Christian tradition. The Jewish-Christian gospels are reworkings of Synoptic-flavored traditions, just as Matthew's and Luke's Gospels were reworkings of Mark and other traditions of unknown origin. Hence, we refer to the Jewish-Christian gospels as continuations of the Jesus traditions. In them these traditions were not exposed to a fundamental transformation, but were newly edited and redacted. Unfortunately, only a few quotations from these Jewish-Christian gospels have survived in the writings of the church fathers. Since they contain three different accounts of Jesus' baptism they are usually assigned to three Jewish-Christian gospels, those of the Nazareans, the Ebionites, and the Hebrews, even though there are some voices in favor of accepting the existence of only two Jewish-Christian gospels. We can observe individual accents in the fragments of each of these three gospels.[1] Since Jerome and Epiphanius both regarded the Jewish-Christian gospels known to them as variants of Matthew's Gospel, it is probable that the Jewish-Christian gospel literature is in large part a continuation of Matthew, which does not exclude the possibility that here and there some older features have been retained.

The Gospel of the Nazareans

What strikes us in the fragments of the *Gospel of the Nazareans* is above all the social motifs. Here Jesus heals the man with the withered hand so that he can earn his livelihood. The sick man asks for healing so that he need no longer beg (*Gos. Naz.* frag. 10). In the pericope on the rich young man, the one rich person becomes two. This makes it clear that Jesus directed his call to abandonment of possessions and discipleship not to a single person, but that in principle he appeals to many wealthy persons, if not all. Abandonment of possessions is motivated by the social distress of Jewish brothers and sisters. It is fulfillment of the Torah (namely, the commandment to love one's neighbor) and not an additional task for the perfect (*Gos. Naz.* frag. 16). The parable of the talents is also shaped in more humane terms. The servant who buried his talent is not punished but only admonished. It is another servant, who has squandered his property in loose living, who is thrown into prison (*Gos. Naz.* frag. 18). All that is more morally illuminating than the punishment of the fearful servant. These bits of information cause us to regret the loss of this gospel: its ethical sensibility is a valuable voice for further work on the image of Jesus in the early Christianity of the second century.

The Gospel of the Ebionites

Similarly, the absence of the *Gospel of the Ebionites* from the canon deprives us of an important voice, that of an early Christian vegetarianism that we encounter already in Romans 14:2, 21, where Paul pleads for consideration for Christians who refuse in principle to eat meat. The *Gospel of the Ebionites* retains for us the original voice of such Christians. In it the Baptizer eats "wild honey, the taste of which was that of manna, as a cake dipped in oil" (*Gos. Eb.* frag. 2). It is not compatible with the vegetarianism of the *Gospel of the Ebionites* that the Baptizer eats locusts. Jesus refuses to celebrate the Passover, because that would mean eating meat (*Gos. Eb.* frag. 7). This fits with the idea that his whole mission is summarized in his having come to abolish sacrifices (*Gos. Eb.* frag. 6). Sacrifices were primarily of animals, and many were associated with eating meat because of the community meals that followed. As the *Gospel of the Nazareans* reveals a special sensibility for fellow humans who are poor, the *Gospel of the Ebionites* shows sensitivity toward all creatures. Abandonment of possessions and vegetarianism are protests against the harshness of a life in which people live at the expense of others. It is thus understandable that some attribute the fragments of these two Jewish-Christian gospels to a single document.

The Gospel of the Hebrews

The *Gospel of the Hebrews* differs from the two other Jewish-Christian gospels in that it is filled with a spirit close to Gnosticism. Here the motif of rest plays a role that unites God and the human: through the voice at his baptism, God identifies with Jesus: "My son, in all the prophets was I waiting for thee that thou shouldest come and I might rest in thee. For thou art my rest; thou art my first-begotten Son that reignest forever" (*Gos. Heb.* frag. 2). Here God is longing for a place of rest, and through Jesus he promises every person rest and glory. What God finds in his Son, the human being will find through Jesus: "He that marvels shall reign, and he that has reigned shall rest" (*Gos. Heb.* frag. 4a; cf. 4b). This fulfillment of divine and human longing is, however, closely tied to care for fellow human beings: "And never be ye joyful, save when ye behold your brother with love" (*Gos. Heb.* frag. 5). Among the worst crimes is to have "grieved the spirit of [your] brother" (*Gos. Heb.* frag. 6). We can only guess that in these Jewish-Christian gospels the voices of a very impressive Christianity have been lost to us, a Christianity not less valuable than the one so close to Judaism that we find in the letter of James or the Gospel of Matthew. The *Gospel of the Hebrews* already indicates the beginnings of a harmonization between the Synoptics and the Gnostic-influenced gospels. This will be still clearer in the gospels to be discussed next.

14 Jesus' Fictive Self-Interpretation through the Harmonizing of the Jesus Tradition in Other Apocryphal Gospels

The multiple images of Jesus and Jesus traditions brought about a tendency very early to accommodate the various images of Jesus. This was at work already in the Synoptics, when Matthew and Luke, each in his own way, accommodated the Jesus images in their two sources, Mark and Q. This tendency reached its climax in Tatian's *Diatessaron*, a gospel harmony from the second half of the second century that circulated in Syria. The same tendency is evident in the fragments of gospels in which Johannine elements are combined with traditions from all three Synoptic Gospels. Certainly one could also interpret these as if they stemmed from a time before the separation of the Synoptic and Johannine traditions.[1] But there are a number of indications that what we have before us in these gospels is a reworking of Synoptic and Johannine traditions and gospels. What had been shaped and refined in different ways in the individual gospels is now recombined. In this process the relationship to the canonical gospels rested not only on the direct use of literary sources but also on secondary oral tradition—that is, a knowledge of the gospels derived from listening as they were read aloud that had retrospectively affected the oral Jesus tradition. In addition, Jesus materials were incorporated that stand in none of the gospels that later became canonical.

The Egerton Gospel

In Papyrus Egerton 2, edited in 1935, we have four fragments of an unknown gospel that was then augmented with a bit of fragment 1 (Papyrus Cologne

255) that was edited in 1987. The manuscript is now dated around 200 C.E. It contains a controversy dialogue with teachers of the law shaped in Johannine style (frag. 1) and a Johannine-sounding attempt by the Jews to stone Jesus (frag. 2). After that (still in fragment 2) follows the healing of a leper in Synoptic style: the leper who is healed had become infected because he lived with lepers. His human compassion is rewarded by his miraculous healing. Fragment 3 contains a variant on the Synoptic question about the tax, which is answered polemically with the accusation of hypocrisy (following Isa 29:13 = Mark 7:6-7). The fourth, a very damaged fragment, is an unknown seed miracle with motifs parallel to those of an infancy gospel of Thomas: Jesus sows in water—a metaphor for vain action transformed into narrative?—and yet is successful. This unknown gospel presupposes the Synoptics and John. The certainty of this was cemented by the addition of the text from Papyrus Cologne 255. The acquaintance with the canonical gospels could be a literary one or could rest on secondary orality. But, in addition, the Egerton Gospel draws also on other sources, perhaps even primary oral Jesus traditions.

The Gospel of Peter

Eusebius writes in his church history (*Hist. eccl.* 6.12.1-6) that Bishop Serapion of Antioch, at the end of the second century, permitted the neighboring community in Rhossos to read a gospel of Peter without knowing it. When he heard that Docetists appealed to this gospel for their doctrine of the illusory body of Jesus, he recalled his permission. In 1886–87 parts of this *Gospel of Peter* were discovered in upper Egypt (or, to be more cautious, we can say that these fragments are as a rule identified with the *Gospel of Peter*). All that remains is the passion narrative, beginning with the scene of Pilate's washing his hands and breaking off when the disciples, after the resurrection, return to their work as fishermen. It is not impossible that this gospel once told also of Jesus' work and preaching before his passion—especially if one assigns Papyrus 4009, which contains some sayings of Jesus (the earthly Jesus? the Risen One?), to the *Gospel of Peter.* The gospel is a first-person account by Peter, though this is not consistently maintained. The first disciple among the Twelve is not only named directly as an eyewitness but called upon in support of many details. This tendency to confirm eyewitness character is also shown in the fact that the *Gospel of Peter* depicts the resurrection itself: the guards placed by Pilate see how the stone is rolled away from the tomb by two men, the grave opens, and the two men come back out of the tomb with a third whom they are supporting, followed by a cross.

When one reads the gospel no docetic features are immediately apparent, but it is understandable that some passages could be interpreted docetically: Jesus is silent at his crucifixion, "as if in no pain" (*Gos. Pet.* 4.10). At the end he cries aloud: "My power, [my] power you have abandoned me" (*Gos. Pet.* 5.19). Immediately after that he is "taken up." This can undoubtedly be interpreted to say that Jesus' soul departed from him before his death, so that it did not need to experience death. However, one can clearly say that the *Gospel of Peter* represents a secondary stage of tradition. It contains echoes of all four canonical gospels. It is, of course, not impossible that here and there a feature independent of them has been retained, but everything speaks against our having access here to an older passion narrative.

The Unknown Berlin Gospel

The unknown Berlin Gospel (= UBG) was first published in 1999.[2] It is a Coptic text translated from Greek. The Greek fragment is a section of the passion narrative between the Last Supper and the crucifixion and consists of dialogues of Jesus with the "apostles." Here we have an analogy to the farewell discourses in the Gospel of John: conversations with Jesus reported by the apostles in the first person plural. Interiorly, Jesus is already with the Father, but even before his death (and not only after his resurrection) he leads his followers to higher mysteries. The apostles experience a journey to heaven together with him, arriving at the throne of God. Probably this is a continuation of the *Gospel of Peter.* The canonical gospels are presupposed. John's is paraphrased directly: "Yet I am the good shepherd. I will lay down my life for you. You yourselves also lay down your lives for your friends in order that you might be pleasing to my Father. For no commandment is greater than this, that I lay down my life for people. Because of [this] my Father loves me, for I completed [his] will. For (although) I [was] divine, I became [human]" (UBG §4).[3]

The unknown Berlin Gospel resembles another form of gospel that spread with enormous rapidity in the second century: it bleaches the dialogical gospels with dialogues between the Risen One and his disciples. These were produced in great numbers in Gnostic circles, but not only there. If we include the oldest of the infancy gospels, which also goes back to the second century, one may say that century was a time of blossoming for Jesus literature. It appears in four genres: the "canonical" gospel form and sayings, dialogical gospels, and infancy gospels. Understandably, modern scholarship hopes to obtain a new access to Jesus, or at least to the origins of the canonical gospels, with the aid of this Jesus literature, which has often survived only in fragments. But all these gospels presuppose either the Synoptics or all four canonical gospels, including John. John's Gospel probably motivated and legitimated the production of these gospels, for there the author of the final form of John's Gospel writes in his book's conclusion: "there are also many other things that Jesus did; if every one of them were written down, I suppose that the world itself could not contain the books that would be written" (John 21:25). That is not an indication of a four-gospel canon; quite the contrary. Here it is considered possible that there will be a multitude of other potential gospels about Jesus' works and deeds. This legitimates more gospels about his life and death. Since the Johannine Christ also promises the Paraclete to the disciples, who (after Easter) will lead them into all truth (John 16:13), further post-Easter revelations are also legitimated. The many dialogical gospels could have been motivated by the Gospel of John. They share the dialogue form with the Johannine farewell discourses and contain a hermeneutic in stages comparable to that of John's Gospel. One can at least understand very well that many Christians read more gospels beyond the four that circulated very early, and did so in good conscience. They were convinced that Jesus had said and done far more than stood in the gospels later canonized.

The literary history of the gospel form reveals two tendencies: on the one hand we repeatedly find a tendency to differentiation and on the other hand a move toward harmonization. From the very beginning there was a genre-conditioned plurality in the Jesus tradition: the sayings tradition and the narrative tradition offered different images of Jesus and were also written down, at first, in two different literary forms, the Sayings Source and Mark's Gospel—whereby Mark already contained a balancing of miracle stories and passion traditions, even though it placed its own accents. Matthew and Luke continued these tendencies of their two sources and smoothed them out: in doing so, Matthew followed more closely the theology of the Jewish-Christian Sayings Source, and his work was continued in Jewish-Christian gospels, while the Gentile-Christian Gospel of Luke is more a continuation of the Gospel of Mark, addressed to Gentile Christians. Besides these gospels, John appears with a more profound image of Jesus than that of the Synoptic tradition: this is a gospel for more perfected Christians. This gospel, too, is in itself a balancing act: Jesus here becomes the preacher of the Christ image presupposed by Paul. He speaks of himself as the preexistent Son of God sent into the world. In subsequent years, we sense, in the gospel literature of the second century, an effort to harmonize Synoptic and

Johannine traditions. This is true of the Egerton Gospel, the *Gospel of Peter*, and the unknown Berlin Gospel. The harmonization takes place not only through new gospels but, in the case of Marcion, by concentrating on a single gospel (that of Luke), and with Tatian by the composition of a gospel harmony. The generally accepted solution, however, was found in the establishment of a canon in the form of a fourfold gospel in which four different gospels, despite their contradictions, stand alongside one another.

With our discussion of gospels from the second century we have greatly anticipated the process of development. The second phase of early Christian literature begins already in the first century with the redaction of the Synoptic Gospels and the composition of John's Gospel, with its affinity for Gnosticism. The fictive self-interpretation of Jesus begun here through redaction and continuation of the Jesus tradition was practiced for a long time after that period. In the second century it experienced a brief flowering in the "apocryphal" gospels, often retained only in fragments,[4] and continued even after the origin of the idea of a canon at the end of the second century.

In the second phase of New Testament literature also there were common features in the development of the gospel and letter corpuses. These have in common both the fictive self-interpretation of major authorities and a high claim to revelation. In the letters this appears as a "revelation schema," a statement about revelation in the present. This "schema" says: until now the truth was hidden from the world, but now it has become accessible in Christ.[5] This corresponds in John's Gospel to the programmatically formulated claim to revelation: "No one has ever seen God. It is God the only Son, who is close to the Father's heart, who has made him known" (John 1:18). The Jesus of the *Gospel of Thomas* laments: "I took my stand in the midst of the world, and in flesh I appeared to them. I found them all drunk" (*Gos. Thom.* 28). He alone brings true knowledge. If the divine mystery is first revealed in Jesus, it would appear that as far as these writings are concerned the preceding Old Testament history of revelation has been extinguished. A new religion announces its claim to bring the ultimate, valid revelation, in the face of which everything that preceded it pales. In other words, both the fictive self-interpretation of Paul in the post-Pauline letters and the fictive self-interpretation of Jesus in the gospels heighten the authoritative claims of the new message. It is not only (as *euaggelion*) comparable to a political claim to power, but instead it embodies a cosmic revelatory event.

Such a high claim to revelation, in fact, presses toward a different form of literary vehicle. Mysteries concealed in heaven and to be revealed on earth were conveyed in Jewish-Hellenistic literature by visionaries who ascended into heaven to experience the divine mysteries there. Some of them heard of these divine mysteries audibly in heaven or on earth. But only a few early Christian writings chose that form. These writings draw their authority directly from heaven. They can therefore name their author on earth—as the writing of the seer John, exiled to Patmos, or of the freedman Hermas in Rome. While the Jewish apocalypses appeared under false names, early Christian literature occasionally broke through this pseudepigraphic tradition and made the place and time of the origin of apocalyptic writings transparent.[6]

On the whole, however, early Christianity increased the number of pseudepigraphic writings. This was connected with the fact that for early Christianity the crucial revelation took place not in heaven but on earth: in the story of Jesus of Nazareth. It was possible to make contact with him through eyewitnesses. Pseudepigraphy denies that contact with him in the second generation was only possible in mediated fashion. It fabricated a closeness to him that had been irrevocably lost. As an alternative there were only heavenly journeys and direct visions, by means of which one could obtain revelations directly from Jesus in heaven. The two early Christian seers we encounter individually under their own names, John the apocalypticist and Hermas, took this path—the one as an exile on Patmos, the other as a Christian freedman in Rome. But in the long run that was a risky path. Who could control such ecstatics and heaven-travelers? The Montanist movement in the later second century shows how much difficulty could be created in a church by radical prophets.

Pseudepigraphy showed itself, paradoxically, to be a means of securing the tradition. In order to be accepted as apostolic writings, pseudepigraphic documents had to reproduce convictions that were generally accepted. A non-genuine Pauline letter must seem Pauline. Only then could the fictive Paul in it correct the real one. A gospel had to agree with the image of Jesus. Only then could it reinterpret his message from its own point of view.

PART THREE

The Authority of the Independent Forms

The Functional Phase

The three genres represented only once each—the Acts of the Apostles, the Johannine Revelation, and the letter to the Hebrews—have great weight from their length alone. Taken together they represent a quarter of the New Testament. They stand in isolation there, but from a formal point of view they correspond to a broader tendency in late early-Christian literature. The two basic forms of early Christian literature were essentially large "collection boxes": the gospels collected small forms, while the letters took up more ancient formulas. These small forms and formulae sometimes made themselves independent in the later New Testament period as separate texts.[1] The genres represented only once each in the New Testament are, from a form-critical point of view, just such partial forms rendered independent. It is no longer the charismatic power of persons but substantive and functional demands that increasingly shape these texts and establish their authority. The authority of person and tradition continued in effect, but a new element was added: the authority of the form. Acts, Revelation, and Hebrews are indeed isolated in the New Testament, but they correspond to more general tendencies in ancient Jewish literature and find their continuation in apocryphal early Christian literature. We will first give an overview of the tendency to make partial texts independent in this third phase of the literary history of the New Testament, and then we will treat each of the three once-only genres for its own sake.

15 The Independent Differentiation of Partial Texts and Tendencies

Preaching

Paul adapted fragments of sermons into his letters. He begins First Corinthians with a "message about the cross," *logos tou staurou* (1 Cor 1:18). The text introduced by this phrase constitutes one of those "sayings" or "messages" with which gifted preachers could approach the community, be it an "utterance of wisdom" or an "utterance of knowledge" (1 Cor 12:8). But this sermon is only a small part of his long letter. The letter to the Hebrews, by contrast, is from beginning to end a discourse with an artistic structure and the best Greek in the New Testament. An incomplete letter frame has been placed around this discourse; its beginning is missing. Only the ending has the character of a letter. Paul is nowhere said to be the author, but when the name of Timothy appears it suggests to the readers that this letter should be attributed to Paul and no one else: the author intends to visit the community together with him (Heb 13:23). Hebrews would thus be secondary pseudepigraphy if the letter ending was added only later—but even in that case it would be only a very indirect pseudepigraphy, since the readers are supposed to carry out the false attribution themselves; it is not imposed on them. Thus, in its final form, Hebrews is a kind of "noble falsification." Important for us is that here we find as a whole document something that was otherwise only a sub-genre. What is thus in preparation, as far as form criticism is concerned, is brought to its conclusion in *2 Clement*. The latter is pure preaching. A letter frame with prescript and postscript is completely absent. In the *Gospel of Truth* we have a Gnostic homily. The line between this and patristic literature was crossed in the *Paschal Homily* of Melito of Sardis, in which the formal language of popular rhetoric shapes Christian preaching.

Congregational Order

In Matthew's Gospel a little community order regulates conflicts within the congregation with the "little ones" and the "sinners" (Matthew 18). It constitutes one of the five major discourses of Jesus. In the pseudepigraphic Pastorals the congregational order expanded. It now encompasses large portions of the letters but remains embedded in a letter frame. Only in the *Didache*, the "Teaching of the Apostles," do we find, at the beginning of the second century, a literarily independent congregational order with instructions for teaching, baptism, Eucharist, and dealing with various "offices." The model of ancient association orders encouraged making this genre independent and also influenced the further church orders in patristic literature: the Syrian *Didascalia,* Hippolytus's church order, and the *Apostolic Constitutions.*

Collections of Sayings

All the gospels are filled with sayings of Jesus. Many of these come from the Sayings Source, a collection of Jesus sayings that is tentatively embedded in a narrative frame, since it tells at the beginning about the temptation of Jesus and later about the centurion at Capernaum. At the conclusion there are sayings about the end of the world. The Sayings Source, with its still incomplete narrative embedding of Jesus' preaching, is a preparatory stage for the shaping of a gospel. The *Gospel of Thomas* and the later *Gospel of Philip,* in contrast, are pure collections of sayings. Here sayings have been deliberately made into an independent genre. In the development of this form also, then, there is an accommodation to ordinary pure sayings collections. We can see such a form also in the *Sayings* of Sextus, the little handbook of an early Christian Stoicism that stands on the threshold between early Christian and patristic literature.

Secret Teachings of Jesus

Another small form in the gospels is that of Jesus' secret teachings. In Mark we find short discourses by Jesus to his disciples in the open and in the house.[1] John's Gospel contains long farewell discourses by Jesus stylized as secret teaching: the disciples are enlightened on the meaning of Jesus' departure. But it is only the Gnostic gospels that built up these secret dialogues of Jesus into an independent genre, as dialogues of the Risen One with his disciples. At the beginning there is an appearance account, and this is followed by dialogues between Jesus and the disciples. These "dialogical gospels,"[2] like that of John, contain a hermeneutic in stages, but they transfer the higher stages of knowledge into the time after the passion. What takes place in John's Gospel in the farewell discourses as a separate revelation of Jesus to his disciples before the passion[3] happens here after the passion. The intention is to augment, not to suppress, the other gospels. Even non-Gnostic Christians made use of this genre of dialogue between disciples and the Risen One, especially in the *Epistula Apostolorum*.

Historical Writing

The gospels are the expression of a historiographical interest, here concentrated on Jesus. But now and again both gospels and letters contain sketches of historical sequences of events even after the time beyond Jesus' death. Matthew arranges three parables in Matthew 21:28—22:14 into a summary of salvation history: the parable of the two sons depicts the appearance of the Baptizer as precursor of Jesus, the parable of the vinedressers Jesus' work and his end, and the parable of the great banquet the mission to the Gentiles and the destruction of Jerusalem. Paul, in Galatians 1–2, offers the beginnings of an autobiographical narrative. This historical interest was able to establish itself independently: the Acts of the Apostles and the lost *hypomnemata* of Hegesippus are the only historiographical writings in early Christianity. It is uncertain, however, whether Hegesippus's writing is correctly classified as historiography. It contains historical materials but was probably not a description of history. To that extent the Acts of the Apostles is isolated in early Christianity, and yet the independent establishment of a particular literary interest in writing was a general early Christian trend. The borrowing from ordinary historiography begins already in Luke's two-volume work, but only much later was it again form-critically influential in Eusebius of Caesarea's church history. But by that time we are already in patristic literature.

Apocalypses

Finally, we must mention the apocalypses. There are brief apocalyptic texts in the gospels and letters. Before his death Jesus delivers an apocalyptic discourse in which he predicts the future and the end of the world. Apocalyptic texts are contained also in 1 and 2 Thessalonians. But not all these texts reveal an awareness of resting on an extra-normal "revelation." This is true in the strict sense only for Romans 11:25 and 1 Corinthians 15:51.[4] Nevertheless, the texts in Mark 13, 1 Thessalonians 4:13-18, and 2 Thessalonians 2:3-12 contain so many apocalyptic motifs that one can in good conscience count them among the apocalyptic texts. In the Johannine apocalypse, this form has become independent. Here not only is the content apocalyptic through and through, but so is the form: this is about a supernatural revelation. The development of the independent form of the apocalypse was not unique. Besides the Revelation to John, other apocalypses such as the *Shepherd of Hermas* and the *Apocalypse of Peter,* as well as the *Ascension of Isaiah,* were written, but these writings were not accepted into the canon.[5] In the apocalypses, too, Christianity later borrowed from pagan forms. Christians inserted their end-time expectations into the *Sibylline Oracles,* thus opening the way to the transition to patristic literature.[6]

The following overview is restricted to the forms that were also accepted into the New Testament (Table 19); canonical writings appear in boldface:

Table 19: Sub-Genres and Their Establishment as Independent in the New Testament and Early Christianity

Sub-Genres in the New Testament Literature	**Independent Establishment in Later Early-Christian Literature**
Discourses	*Discourses*
1 Corinthians 1–4: message of the cross	**Letter to the Hebrews**
Five discourses of Jesus in Matthew	*2 Clement*
Farewell discourses in John 14–16	*Gospel of Truth*
	Melito of Sardis, *Paschal Homily*
	Tatian, *Address to the Greeks*
Apocalyptic Texts	*Apocalypses*
Synoptic apocalypse: Mark 13	**Revelation**
2 Thessalonians 2:3-12	*Shepherd of Hermas*
	Apocalypse of Peter
	Ascension of Isaiah
	Christian Sibylline Oracles
Historiographical Texts	*Historical Writing*
Galatians 1–2	**Acts of the Apostles**
Beginnings of historical writing in the gospels	Transformed into other genres:
	Hegesippus's *hypomnēmata*
	Apocryphal Acts of the Apostles

This brief overview shows that most of the sub-forms that became independent, which belong to the third phase of the history of early Christian literature, are no longer represented in the canon. But they developed in other early Christian literature, where they experienced a brief flowering. Only three writings from this group of forms made it into the New Testament. The Acts of the Apostles continues the Synoptic narrative tradition, the letter to the Hebrews the Pauline epistolary literature, and Revelation the Johannine writings. All lean on powerful currents in contemporary Jewish literature: Acts on Jewish-Hellenistic history writing, Revelation on the revelatory writings of apocalyptic, and Hebrews on the rhetoric of the synagogue.

16 The Acts of the Apostles

The two-volume Lukan work further developed Old Testament historical writing by adopting the formal language of secular Hellenistic histories. We sense this dependence in the proemium, where the author refers to his sources and predecessors and is intent on establishing that he is worthy of confidence (Luke 1:1-4). And yet the Lukan proemium has only a limited similarity to other ancient forewords: most ancient authors presented themselves differently from Luke, giving their own names; they seldom name their sources, and they write longer forewords. Dedications are unusual. The language and style of the Lukan proemium have more analogies in "professional literature," which did not advance such high literary claims as did written history. Hence, we can say that in the case of the two-volume Lukan work we have to do with a popular account of history, somewhat distanced from great literature.[1] Nevertheless, historical writing is his model: this is evident in the synchronisms by which Luke locates the narrated events within history: Zechariah experienced the announcement of his son in the time of Herod (Luke 1:5); Jesus was born at the time of a worldwide census under Augustus (2:1); John the Baptizer appeared in the fifteenth year of the reign of Tiberius (3:1). But these are only minor accents: we would have expected more synchronisms in Acts. When we hear of a worldwide famine under Claudius (Acts 11:28) and his expulsion of "all the Jews" from Rome (Acts 18:2), these are not synchronisms, but events that are part of the overall narrative. In the speeches in Acts, composed by Luke, the author interprets events, just as other ancient historians did. These speeches often transcend the immediate occasion: Stephen gives a summary of Jewish history in order to prepare for the transition of the mission to the Gentile world, but he does not defend himself against the accusation that he has predicted the destruction of the temple. Paul is offended by the idols in Athens (17:16) but praises the Athenians for their piety: unknowingly they worship the true God in the god unknown! Before the presbyters in Ephesus, Paul defends himself in his farewell discourse (20:18-35) without any accusation being raised against him, etc. These discourses make sense only in the context of the whole work. Finally, in the we-sections, the author suggests that he is an eyewitness (16:10-17; 20:5-8, 13-18; 21:1-18; 27:1—28:16). It is true that there are no genuine analogies to such we-sections, but eyewitness accounts are of great significance for ancient historians. Finally, we may mention fragments of instruction, which the author scatters in a number of places. These include the *topos* of friends who have everything in common, applied here to the community (Acts 4:32), the *clausula Petri*, recalling Socrates, according to which one must obey God rather than human beings (Acts 4:19; 5:29), or the quotation from the poet Aratus: "For we too are his offspring" (Acts 17:28). This positive (though still very tentative) linkage to the style of the secular world corresponds to the content: Acts describes how Christianity penetrated the Roman Empire and grew within it. Despite all its critique of that empire, it shows that in it Christianity has a chance. It will pervade this empire. Even though Paul is in chains at the end, it can still be said that he is preaching the gospel unhindered (Acts 28:31). This message endowed Acts with its narrative concreteness. In the city of the first Christian community in Europe, the Roman colony at Philippi, the local citizens emphasize that as Roman citizens they are not permitted to introduce new religions into their city (Acts 16:21). But in the end they have to acknowledge that Paul is a Roman citizen. When he brings his new message to Philippi he does not violate the law; it is the Philippians who do so when they scourge and imprison him, a Roman citizen. He is led respectfully out of prison (Acts 16:37-39). Paul has to go to Rome in order to offer his message there, too. A shipwreck and his rescue from the storm at sea show that God is leading him to Rome in order that he may proclaim the message there.[2]

The form-critical problem with the two-volume Lukan work is that its two books constitute a single work, even though they belong to different genres.[3] Luke's Gospel is a biography of Jesus, while Acts is a historical monograph about the spread of the church. It is true that both genres fall under historical writing, but we have no model in literary history for their joining in a single work. The only thing certain is that the author wanted both to be understood as a single unit. This is clear from the proemium of Acts: "In the first book, Theophilus, I wrote about all that Jesus did and taught from the beginning until the day when he was taken up to heaven" (Acts 1:1-2). Unfortunately, he does not describe the content of the second book, so that we can only guess that in it he will tell of more deeds and teachings of Jesus—now the deeds of the Risen One from heaven! In that case we would have just *one* genre in the two books: a two-part biography continued in heaven. But that would be a unique genre. Equally plausible is that the author composed Acts not so much as a continuation of a biography, but just the opposite: he understood the gospel as the history of a community. It began, then, with the birth of Jesus. Before that an expectation is awakened among pious Jews, through psalms and anthems, that the decisive turn in history for the sake of God's people is imminent. A saving king has been born to this people. He gathers Israel. Jesus and his twelve disciples shape this history, which is continued in Acts: in the church the fallen dwelling of David is rebuilt (Acts 15:16 = Amos 9:11). In that case we would have a continuous work of history intended to tell the story of the people of God. But neither of these simplifications of the form—one starting with the gospel or one beginning with Acts—is consistently maintained by the author. On the contrary, he intends, through his two- or three-phase theology, to separate clearly the time of Jesus from the time of the church, even though the two are united by the work of the Holy Spirit: in the time of Jesus a divine being begotten by the Holy Spirit is at work on earth, but in the time of the apostles it would be a huge misunderstanding to regard the apostles as divine because they work miracles through the gift of the Holy Spirit.

Therefore, we should see the form-critical *proprium* of the Lukan work in the combination of the two related but distinguishable genres of biography and history: Luke tells of the expansion of Christianity in the form of a continuation of his biography of the Messiah of Israel. For Franz Overbeck that was a "tactlessness of historical dimensions";[4] "Luke treats historiographically what was not history and was not handed down in this form."[5] For Jesus, the end of history had arrived. Luke, on the contrary, has history continue. But that can also be seen differently: Luke uses a genre intended to describe the history of kings or nations for the history of the tiny early Christian communities. Their history is the continuation of the history of the messianic king from the house of David. In it the salvation of the world is realized. But unlike in the time of Jesus, in this period there is no divine Son at work on earth; only his apostles are acting. To venerate them as divine would be absurd.

How can we locate Luke's historical writing within the history of literature? The two-volume Lukan work was written at about the same time as the works of Josephus. After the Jewish War, the writing of Jewish history enjoyed a new springtime. Besides Josephus, his competitor Justus of Tiberias was also writing. Since Josephus composed his depiction of the Jewish War for the purpose of impressing the Eastern nations and the Greeks and to warn them against rebellion, his work may have been known in many places. The author of Luke and Acts may have heard of this description of Jewish history. Did that, perhaps, spur him to write a history of the Christians? In any case, he continues Jewish-Hellenistic history writing as we know it from

1 and 2 Maccabees. His work belongs within the context of Jewish historical writing after the Jewish War, but as a result it also belongs with it in ancient historiography, so long as we keep in mind the great breadth of variation within that genre: besides informative, pragmatic historical writing intended to enable the reader to make a judgment there was a tragic form of history meant to cause the reader to experience the events emotionally, like an audience in a theatre. Acts is part of that tragic historical form, the influence of which is also perceptible in Josephus.[6] This type of historical writing is intended to move the reader emotionally. For this purpose it makes use of a dramatic, episodic style repeatedly leading to emotionally laden climaxes. In addition, he adopts motifs from novelistic entertainment literature. While the Lukan historical work may be unique within the New Testament and found no followers in early Christian literature, it is by no means isolated within the history of biblical, Jewish, or ancient literature. Above all, the rooting of this genre in the biblical tradition was probably one reason why Acts, despite its singularity, was adopted into the canon.

There was another reason as well. Acts probably linked, from one point of view, with familiar forms of oral communication in early Christianity. It reports on the success of the mission. Luke was certainly not the first to have done that. Early Christian missionaries would have reported their experiences to their communities, especially when they were sent out by those communities. Acts sometimes lets us see that kind of situation. In Acts 11:4-17 Peter reports to the Jerusalem community about his experiences with the acceptance of Gentiles into the community in Caesarea. According to Acts 15:3, Paul and Barnabas told in the communities of Phoenicia and Samaria about the "conversion of the Gentiles, and brought great joy to all the believers." This is repeated in Jerusalem: "And they reported all that God had done with them" (Acts 15:4; cf. 15:12). Paul's farewell discourse in Miletus is an accounting of what he has done (Acts 20:18-35). When he arrives in Jerusalem "he related one by one the things that God had done among the Gentiles through his ministry" (Acts 21:19). The author of Acts presumes such reports as an obvious part of community life. This is not an exotic genre, but a variant on the report of a messenger that plays an important role in every oral culture. It is also "projected back" into the gospels. According to Mark 6:30 the apostles returned to Jesus after he had sent them out "and told him all that they had done and taught." According to John's Gospel, Jesus is the sole Sent One. His high-priestly prayer is an accounting for his mission (John 17:1-26). Wherever missionaries or messengers were sent, people would have been familiar with such reports. If the form of Acts had a predecessor in community life it must have consisted of such reports from messengers. If we look at Acts in those terms we can see that it tells of a great mission, beginning with Jesus' promise: "you will be my witnesses in Jerusalem, in all Judea and Samaria, and to the ends of the earth" (Acts 1:8). This mission indicates the structure that will be followed in Acts: it begins in Jerusalem, reports on the mission in Samaria (Acts 8), and beginning with Acts 13 it turns to the mission to all nations. When people are sent out, they have to give an account afterward. Perhaps such an accounting is hinted at in the structure of Acts: the problematic "we-sections" begin in Troas, with the transition from Asia Minor to Europe, and end only in Rome at the conclusion of Acts (16:10-17; 20:5-8, 13-18; 21:1-18; 27:1—28:16). They may have been parts of a letter of accountability on the part of the delegation with the collection that Paul accompanied to Jerusalem.[7] But the question naturally arises why the author of Acts adopted the "we" from this account. Perhaps when he was writing he had in mind the account of the successes and failures of the mission as a subconscious model. The missionaries sent out by the Holy Spirit recount in Acts "all that God had done with them" (Acts 15:4)—not to a community gathering but to a broader public. The we-style of an accounting would fit well with that. The author of the Lukan two-volume work would have oriented himself generally to models in ancient historiography when shaping his literary account of the mission, but with his work he was introducing something new in historical writing by linking it to oral forms of communication. This new thing corresponded to the life of his communities: those who had again and again heard oral accounts of the mission in community assemblies could accept that the gospel was continued in an Acts of the Apostles with missionary accounts and that Acts should also be read aloud in community assemblies alongside the gospels and letters.

17 The Revelation to John

The book of Revelation is the only independent apocalypse in the New Testament. Besides this there were only isolated apocalyptic texts such as Mark 13. But the apocalypse too, developed into an independent genre, combined a variety of traditions and forms: apocalyptic and prophecy, apocalypse and letter.

First, let us consider the linking of apocalyptic and prophecy in Revelation. Apocalypses are revelatory literature. Through dreams, visions, or hearing they offer an insight into the mysteries of the end-time. Now and then we find fictive overviews of history that are intended, by their accurate depiction of history up to the present time of the apocalypticist, to make the genuine prophecies of the future plausible. The recipients of the revelation depicted in apocalypses are always great figures from the past: Enoch, Abraham, Moses, Ezra. Only one of these apocalypses was accepted into the Old Testament canon: the book of Daniel. Because the real author must conceal himself behind a seer from the past, it is constitutive of apocalyptic literature that it be written. The Revelation to John, by contrast, clearly reveals its location in oral prophecy. Its content consists of "words of prophecy" (Rev 1:3; 22:7, 10, 18-19). The author regards himself as one prophet among others (Rev 22:9; cf. 19:10). He is exiled and cannot reach his addressees directly; therefore he uses the written medium of a letter and addresses himself to them in seven of these. These seven brief letters are prophetic words in the first person singular with messenger formula, invective, threats, and promises.[1] The prophet appears personally under his own name. Different from other apocalypses, this one does not ascribe the revelation to a great figure from the past. Theoretically the author could be concealing himself behind another figure in present-day history.[2] But it is more probable that because of his prophetic self-awareness he is able to do without any pseudepigraphic game of concealment. For he has immediate access to the exalted Christ, whom he has seen in his "call vision" (Rev 1:12-20). Other early

Christian prophets, such as Agabus (Acts 11:28; 21:10) and Hermas (*Herm.* 1.1-4) are also known to us under their own names.

The apocalypse of this prophet from Asia Minor borrows from the letter genre. Epistolary elements appear above all in the introduction to his writing and in the central section in the seven letters. After a general introduction there follows an epistolary prescript: "John to the seven churches that are in Asia: Grace to you and peace from him who is and who was and who is to come" (Rev. 1:4). The prescript corresponds to the Pauline letter style. At the end, as with Paul, there is a blessing: "The grace of the Lord Jesus be with all the saints" (Rev 22:21; cf. Rom 16:20, 24; 2 Thess 3:18). In the first part of the apocalypse the seven letters are addressed directly to the seven churches (Rev 2:1—3:22). They oppose the "Nicolaitans" and a prophet called Jezebel because they act immorally and eat flesh offered to idols (Rev. 2:14-15; 2:20). Probably some Christians claimed the Pauline freedom to eat meat offered to idols. The seer wants to drive a wedge between them and the world—among other means by demonizing the world. Revelation is a prophetic declaration of war on the *imperium romanum*. Christianity and the imperial cult are as irreconcilable as God and Satan. The language and style are shaped accordingly, for the language of the apocalypticist John, with its barbarisms and solecisms, is also a declaration of war on Greek grammar.

The two tradition- and form-critical features, the linkage of prophecy and apocalyptic in a revelatory writing without pseudonymity and the reliance of this revelatory writing on the letter form, are closely connected. A letter presumes an author with whom one can interact. Therefore, an attribution of the apocalypse to a figure from the past is inappropriate. The author openly declares his historical location in the present time. He probably emigrated, with other early Christian prophets (cf. 22:9), from Palestine to Asia Minor during the Jewish War (66–74 C.E.). Revelation 11:1-2 quotes a prophecy that could come from the end of the Jewish War, when the temple court had already been captured by the enemies and the Jews in the inner temple were still hoping for a miracle. The prophetic circle behind Revelation experienced the Roman Empire as a destructive power, and that continues to affect the fears and hopes depicted in Revelation.

In its content, the great theme of Revelation is therefore God's own victory over all opponents, especially the political and economic power of Rome. While others at that time expected Rome to remain forever—*Roma aeterna*—these prophets expected Rome's collapse. For them Rome is a bloodthirsty beast. Against it is placed the blood of the Lamb that "was slain."

From a form- and literary-critical perspective the intermediate point between oral prophecy and written apocalyptic is if great interest. Oral prophecy was familiar to the communities (1 Cor 11:5; 12:28-29; 14:1-5). It was a recognized genre. The apocalypticist of Revelation wants to transfer something of the authority of a recognized oral genre to his written "work of art." For a work of art is a writing very carefully composed, even if it goes against classicist norms. Since the prophet is prevented by his exile from speaking directly, his writing takes the place of his speech and demands the same recognition as his oral word. At the same time, however, the author is a member of a literary writing culture: he makes books an object of his apocalypse. We can recognize three such "books within the book": the book with the seven seals, the angel's little book, and the book of life.

The book with the seven seals is the key to understanding world history. The seven letters are followed by a magnificent vision of a throne room. The author imagines God's sphere of power as the counterfoil to the imperial court (Rev 4:1—5:14). The problem in heaven is the book with the seven seals. The question, typical of commissioning visions, is: "Who is worthy to open the scroll and break its seals?" (Rev 5:2). Only the Lamb is able to do it. First, he is addressed directly: "You are worthy to take the scroll and to open its seals, for you were slaughtered and by your blood you ransomed for God saints from every tribe and language and people and nation; you have made them to be a kingdom and priests serving our God, and they will reign on earth" (Rev 5:9-10). Then follows praise of the Lamb in the third person: "Worthy is the Lamb that was slaughtered to receive power and wealth and wisdom and might and honor and glory and blessing" (Rev 5:12). Unmistakably, the ability to open the book is associated with power and status. The composition of the whole book is determined by this "book within the book": it is a scroll written on the outside and on the inside, so that it can be read from without and from within.[3] The seal visions introduce the most important actors: the apocalyptic riders, the first martyrs, the godless, those who are sealed, and at the end the seven angels who set the further events in motion (Rev 6:1—8:1). After the book with the seven seals has been opened, its inner side is also legible. The same phases of eschatological history are repeated again, like a nightmare. The trumpet visions that follow the seal visions have a proclamatory character (Rev 8:2—11:19): trumpets are signaling instruments. The seven angels blow the trumpets and seven plagues terrify the world. But at the end these seven angels appear again and announce what is to happen not only with trumpet blasts: they themselves pour out the seven bowls of divine wrath on the earth (Rev 15:1—16:21). After the proclamatory depiction of the eschatological plagues, this is the final and ultimate depiction.

To this book with the seven seals is added a second "book within the book," the angel's little book, which the seer has to "eat" (Rev 10:2, 8-11).

Not all the predictions are in the book with the seven seals, for the trumpet visions are followed by a battle between God and the satanic trinity consisting of the dragon, the beast from the sea, and a second beast from the land—the great conflict between the Roman Empire and the Christians (Rev 12:1—14:20). The prophet cannot read that in the book with the seven seals; he sees it directly in visions. He is capable also of such direct prophecy. The author has already made this clear: as the sixth trumpet is blown, an angel gives the seer a book. The seer is to swallow it, and he says: "So I took the little scroll from the hand of the angel and ate it; it was sweet as honey in my mouth, but when I had eaten it, my stomach was made bitter. Then they said to me, 'You must prophesy again about many peoples and nations and languages and kings'" (Rev 10:10-11). The prophet has so deeply internalized the prophetic words handed down in writing that he is capable of new prophecies, independent of any book. He can proclaim, beyond the visions of the seven seals and the trumpets, his prophecy of the great battle between Satan and God, Rome and the Christians (Rev 12:1—14:20). And in the same way, beyond the visions of the seven bowls, he can prophesy the destruction of Rome as the whore of Babylon (Rev 17:1—18:24). He does this on the basis of his own authority in oral form, but as a prophet "nourished" by written prophecy.

A third "book within the book" appears as the book of life. It is first mentioned in the letter to the community at Sardis: "If you conquer, you will be clothed . . . in white robes, and I will not blot your name out of the book of life; I will confess your name before my Father and before his angels" (Rev 3:5). After this the book appears a number of times. It is the book of life in which, since the beginning of the world, the names of the saved have been written (Rev 17:8), and in which the works of human beings are inscribed for judgment (Rev 20:12, 15). It is the Lamb's book of life (Rev 21:27).

This self-reflexive thematizing of the book within the book says something about the literary culture of Revelation: when a redeemer figure must be employed to open a book we are not in a literary milieu. Rather, it is made clear in an impressive image that the author is writing for groups whose books are as a rule "books with seven seals." His addressees live in a nonliterary milieu. Only in such a context can the idea that the key to world history is a closed book be so persuasively presented. But the author himself is a writer who has deeply internalized written tradition. He writes in the language of Old Testament prophecy, even though he does not explicitly cite his written traditions.

It remains a mystery why Revelation is included in the canon as part of a group of Johannine writings. Perhaps the author or an editor deliberately linked it to the Johannine writings through its introduction (Rev 1:1-3):[4] the author had his revelation, written down in Revelation, from God, mediated to him by Christ and an angel, so that the result is a revelatory sequence: "God—Christ—angel—John—book of Revelation." We could construct a parallel chain of revelation from John's Gospel: "God—Christ—Paraclete—Beloved Disciple—Gospel of John,"[5] even though this sequence does not precisely correspond to that in the Gospel of John in which the Beloved Disciple is immediately next to Jesus. Much closer is the relationship of the two writings at their respective ends. When Christ promises at the end of Revelation, "Surely I am coming soon" (Rev 22:12, 20), this seems to link to the end of the Gospel of John: there was a promise associated with the Beloved Disciple that Christ would come before he died. He was to experience the *parousia* (John 21:23). This recalls the author of Revelation, to whom Jesus reveals that he will come soon. However, this relationship is not certain.

Despite this later (?) connection between Revelation and the Gospel of John, there is a contrast between the content of the two writings: Revelation is full of religious aggressivity, while John's Gospel represents a theology of love. But despite the disparity in their content, it may be that both portray the history of their supporting groups: behind Revelation could be an early Christian prophetic group who had fled from Palestine to Asia Minor. Likewise, the Gospel of John could have been brought to Ephesus by emigrants from Syria. These emigrants brought a variety of theologies with them, but in a "foreign land" they felt they belonged together despite their theological differences. Thus, there may have been a limited exchange between them.

- In terms of literary history we observe a converging development: the group behind the Gospel of John adapted the letter form secondarily in the three Johannine letters, which was an accepted move because of the Pauline mission. The same occurred in the group behind Revelation: the author of Revelation formulated his prophetic sayings in the seven letters secondarily in the letter form accepted in Asia Minor (Rev 2:1—3:22) and shaped Revelation's beginning and end to make it a letter.
- Despite all the contrasts, there is a structural commonality in the theology, namely, the opposition to the world. In John's Gospel this appears as a "metaphysical" dualism between light and darkness, truth and lie, God and Satan, the "ruler of this world" behind whom sometimes the current world rulers, the Romans, are visible. Corresponding to this in Revelation is a mythologically encoded power struggle between the Roman Empire and the community. The Roman Empire is Satan.

- Added to this there are a few individual motifs that link Revelation to the Gospel of John: the image of "living water,"[6] the identification of Jesus with the "Word of God,"[7] and his designation as "Lamb of God."[8] In both writings "testimony" plays an important role (Rev 1:2; John 5:31-47; 8:13-19).
- The church order reveals parallels: the apocalypticist intervenes in the communities through his letters, bypassing the local authorities. John the evangelist ignores them in his image of the vine. Here there is no place for a bishop between the branches and the vine; all Christians are directly linked to Christ.

Thus when, in the canon, the Johannine corpus is regarded as a unified group of writings despite theological differences among those writings, this may retain memories of emigrant groups from Syria and Palestine who shaped the history of early Christianity in Asia Minor. In that sphere there may have occurred a limited exchange of motifs and attitudes.

For Revelation also, as for the other individual genres, it is true to say that it is isolated within the New Testament. We may find individual apocalyptic texts, but there is only one independent apocalypse. In the wider sense, however, it belongs within the broad current of Jewish apocalyptic. It is a processing of the Jewish War and therefore belongs, in terms of literary history, in the neighborhood of *4 Esdras* and *Syriac Baruch,* even though the reaction to the war is very different in these three apocalypses: *4 Esdras* is a desperate lament posing questions of theodicy about guilt and justice. The reaction is intra-punitive, that is, this apocalypse seeks guilt within its own people. By contrast, Revelation is extra-punitive, finding guilt in the *imperium romanum*, the beast from the depths. Revelation is more accusation than lament. In any case, its embeddedness in a broad current of apocalyptic literature that had already penetrated the Old Testament canon certainly eased Revelation's acceptance into the New Testament canon. But the primary reason for its canonization was its subsequent attribution to the author of the Gospel of John. It entered the canon on a towrope attached to the Johannine writings. A further reason was that it was the literary reworking of a form of oral communication in early Christianity: it made early Christian prophecy, which had always had an acknowledged place in worship, into a literary genre.

18 The Letter to the Hebrews

In the case of Hebrews we can also assert that, on the one hand, here a genre is being emancipated from its embeddedness within other types of texts; Hebrews is an independent discourse. On the other hand, it is adapted to the acknowledged Pauline letters. The superscription "to the Hebrews" shows that Hebrews was placed, as a Pauline letter, alongside Paul's letters "to the Romans," "to the Corinthians," "to the Galatians." Only Paul's letters had this kind of superscription. However, the superscriptions "to the Romans" and "to the Galatians" correspond most closely to the address "to the Hebrews," since only in the case of Romans and Galatians could one think of a whole people and not only a particular city. There is nothing text-critical to indicate that the superscription of Hebrews is secondary. It could be original, or it may have been secondarily formulated when Hebrews was related to the *Corpus Paulinum*. The discourse is, indeed, concluded in proper style in Heb 13:21 with a doxology; the subsequent letter conclusion may therefore be a secondary addition: "I appeal to you, brothers and sisters, bear with my word of exhortation, for I have written to you briefly. I want you to know that our brother Timothy has been set free; and if he comes in time, he will be with me when I see you. Greet all your leaders and all the saints. Those from Italy send you greetings. Grace be with all of you" (Heb 13:22-25). These sentences are meant to suggest that we should see Paul as the author of the letter without his being mentioned by name. This indirect reference to Paul links the letter's conclusion to the superscription, according to which the letter is addressed to "the Hebrews"; according to the conclusion, "Paul" intends to visit them together with Timothy. Timothy was a Hebrew, the son of a Jewish mother and a Greek father. Paul himself circumcised him (Acts 16:1-3). That his name is placed in a letter to the Hebrews may not be accidental. In any case we have in Hebrews an incomplete letter frame (without a prescript) around a skillfully developed discourse. How should we interpret this finding?

An initial possibility even brings the historical Paul into the process. The whole letter cannot possibly be from him; it is too independent in its content and style. But the historical Paul could have authorized someone else's writing by means of a postscript, so that the letter conclusion retains a "genuine Pauline text." In that case, since Paul could not write such a comprehensive letter, he would have written "only briefly" (Heb 13:22). The postscript from him was in fact short. But this thesis does not fit with the fact that the letter was probably written after 70. It speaks of the way to the sanctuary not being free as long as the first part of the tabernacle still exists as a parable for the present time (Heb 9:8-9). In the interim the way to the sanctuary has been opened by the high priest, Christ. Thus the first part of the tabernacle and its earthly counterpart have disappeared. The time to set things right has come (Heb 9:10). Of course, the end of the temple and the ancient cult is presumed only implicitly and indirectly.

A second possibility is that the "letter" was originally just a speech (Heb 1:1—13:21), its author unknown. Later an editor desired to include this speech in the sequence of Pauline letters because in that way it would have a chance to be accepted into the canon. The superscription and epistolary conclusion would then be secondary and come from an editor. The speech was secondarily made by this editor into a pseudepigraphic writing. But here, too, there is a difficulty: beginning with 13:1, Hebrews resembles a letter. We find a typical epistolary paraenesis such as is often found at the end of a letter. Can we, then, really separate the epistolary conclusion from what precedes it? Although this thesis supports our proposal that Hebrews reveals a tendency to render forms and genres independent, we must consider that it could have been otherwise.

For there is still a third possibility to consider: that the letter was a unit and was from the outset composed as a (pseudepigraphic) Pauline letter. The author had to date it to the time before the destruction of the temple; hence, there is no reference at all to the temple's end, which would have made the letter implausible. Its goal is to write a letter to the "Hebrews" in Rome to stand alongside the letter to the Romans, addressed to the Gentile-Christian community in Rome. Therefore he has "those from Italy" send greetings at the end (Heb 13:24). That only makes sense if he wants to suggest that Christians from Italy are with him. If he were sending greetings from Italy, "those from Italy" would not be a definable group. The author clearly wants us to believe that he is writing from outside Italy. In that case, however, we may be able to recognize the situation the author has in mind: after the leading Jewish Christians were driven out of Rome by the edict of Claudius, some of the exiles from Italy were with Paul. The latter is in Greece, separated (as in 1 Thessalonians) from Timothy and awaiting his arrival. He admonishes the Jewish Christians in Rome: "Let us then go to him outside the camp and bear the abuse he endured" (Heb 13:13), thus referring to their expulsion. The Christians who are addressed have lost their possessions as a result of being banished by Claudius (Heb 10:34). But the author knows that they have not yet resisted to the point of shedding blood. There were as yet no martyrs like those later ones in Nero's persecution (Heb 12:4), of whom the author was probably aware. So he suggests a situation in the life of Paul that is imaginable in principle. If the letter, including its superscription and conclusion, is from a single hand it would have been written from the start as an addition to the Pauline letter collection. It was to stand alongside the letter to the Romans: while Romans sets the new Christian religion apart from Judaism through a new interpretation of the Law, Hebrews intends to strengthen that separation in terms of cultic categories.

References to the Roman community are probable for other reasons as well. Hebrews and *1 Clement*, which was also written in Rome, share some traditions without being dependent on each other.[1] In *1 Clement* 36:1 Christ is addressed as the High Priest "who being the brightness of his majesty is so much greater than angels, as he has inherited a more excellent name" (*1 Clem.* 36:2). This recalls Hebrews 1:3-4. There follow in *1 Clement* 36 three psalm quotations from the LXX: Psalms 103:4; 2:7; 109:1. These appear in Hebrews in a different sequence (2, 1, 3) and are augmented by further scriptural citations (Heb 1:5-14) that come from outside the Psalter (2 Sam 7:14; Deut 32:43 LXX).[2] It is difficult to decide whether *1 Clement* quotes Hebrews, as most exegetes think, or whether *1 Clement* and Hebrews independently refer to the same liturgical tradition. The concept of the high priest appears in both letters, in any case, in a different place and independently of each other in liturgically colored traditional material—a confession (Heb 4:14), a prayer (*1 Clem.* 61:3), and a blessing (*1 Clement* 64). The contacts between *1 Clement* and Hebrews are not to be explained only in literary terms, but also through tradition criticism. This is confirmed by the series of paradigms in Hebrews 11 and its parallels in *1 Clement* 9–12, for here no literary dependence can be demonstrated. These contacts with *1 Clement* allow us to suppose that Hebrews knew traditions that were also current in the Roman community. It may itself come from Rome, even though it pretends to have been written outside Rome.

The epistolary elements constitute only an external frame. Essentially Hebrews is a discourse, a "word of exhortation" (*logos tēs paraklēseōs*, Heb 13:22). This expression appears in Acts 13:15 also to designate a synagogue sermon. Within Hebrews we find repeated references to oral speech, to speaking and hearing (Heb 2:5; 5:11; 6:9; 8:1; 9:5; 13:6). Over long stretches it interprets the Old Testament. Consequently, its formal language adheres to the forms of Jewish-Hellenistic synagogue preaching.[3] Not much of that tradition has survived: the speech in *4 Maccabees* about mastery over the passions and three sermons by Pseudo-Philo on Jonah, Samson, and the designation of God as a "refining fire."[4] All these can be dated to the first or second century C.E.,[5] and thus are more or less contemporary with Hebrews. Despite this sparse documentation, synagogal preaching was a powerful formal tradition at the time, since it was alive in every synagogue. We should not underestimate it. The letter to the Hebrews should be classified within it. The sermon contained in it need not have been delivered orally. The artistic structure points from the beginning to the greater probability of a written form. But a writing can also be oriented to oral genres. In addition, sermons were an oral genre recognized in early Christianity. They were a part of worship. Hence, alongside letters and gospels, a sermon in literary form could easily obtain recognition.

Hebrews also has as its content the fundamental situation of Christianity in this world. All other cults possessed temples, sacrifices, and priests. The Christians, however, gathered in private houses, celebrated a simple meal as a sacrament, and had no priests. Hebrews gives young Christianity an identity as a religious-cultic community separate from all other cults—and especially the Jewish cult: the Christians' temple is heaven and the entire cosmos; they have a high priest in heaven. Its worship is based on his unique self-sacrifice. Hebrews defines the social identity of Christians. Its two basic images reveal both a distancing from and an affirmation of the world. The image of the wandering people of God in the wilderness, on its way to the otherworldly city, interprets the present as a pilgrimage in a foreign land. The image of the cosmic temple into which not only the high priest, but all Christians, enter witnesses on the contrary to an affirmation of the world as the place of a constant worship of God. The path through the wilderness becomes a celebration of entry into the Holy of Holies. And it happens here and now.

As with the other two individual genres, Acts and Revelation, we can say that in Hebrews an artistically and skillfully shaped genre becomes the independent vehicle of a message. It is no longer legitimated solely through the authority of the two great dignitaries, Jesus and Paul, no longer solely through tradition, but also by its form. As a discourse it was part of a Jewish synagogal preaching tradition, only fragments of which have survived. This tradition was revivified every week. In early Christianity as well, preaching followed that model. Although Hebrews, as an individual genre, now stands in relative isolation within the canon, it was embedded in a broad formal tradition. That was one reason why it was received into the canon. The second was that on the basis of its incomplete epistolary frame it was regarded as a letter of Paul. But that was only a secondary motive. The beginning of the letter reveals a greater degree of self-confidence. It begins as "the word of God," and not as a letter from Paul: "Long ago God spoke to our ancestors in many and various ways by the prophets, but in these last days he has spoken to us by a Son, whom he appointed heir of all things, through whom he also created the worlds" (Heb 1:1). We find a comparable beginning only in the Gospel of John (1:1): "In the beginning was the Word, and the Word was with God. . . ."

We can now venture a few summary observations regarding the three individual genres in the New Testament in order once more to emphasize why a new phase in early Christian literature began with them, even though this phase overlapped in time with the preceding one.

These three individual genres convince by the authority of their forms and not solely that of their authors and traditions, although they rely on the support of those authorities. Their forms and intentions are nothing completely new. They were always already present as sub-genres and tendencies in the letters and gospels: Luke was not the first to bring an interest in writing history to early Christianity; the gospels are themselves an expression of that interest. Hebrews is not the first witness to early Christian discourse. Fragments and descriptions of such speeches have been retained in the letters and in Acts. Apocalyptic texts existed as a sub-genre even before Revelation. The successful and formally accurate shaping of a genre according to the norms immanent within it created for these three individual genres both assent and their ability to be disseminated.

Therefore the characteristic of the second phase, pseudepigraphy, could fade or disappear: Revelation does not conceal itself behind a figure from primeval times. It appears under the name of John, a contemporary on Patmos. That it uses a pseudonym is improbable. The author of the two-volume Lukan work places himself in his proemium in the third generation of early Christianity and thus suggests that he is not an eyewitness to what he reports; he acknowledges his dependence on tradents and sources (Luke 1:1-3).[6] Although he dedicates his work to one Theophilus, he conceals his own name. Possibly his two-volume work was anonymous, as were the Old Testament and Jewish historical works, before it was secondarily attributed to one "Luke." With Hebrews also, the game of pseudonymous concealment fades away. The author does without an epistolary opening and nowhere names Paul as the author of his work. He is pseudonymous only in a limited sense, inasmuch as in the epistolary conclusion he suggests Paul as the author by mentioning Timothy. That this pseudonymous epistolary conclusion stems from the author of the whole letter to the Hebrews is probable, but disputed. We must also take account of the possibility that Hebrews was originally an anonymous writing that the author himself (or an editor) secondarily converted into a pseudonymous writing by means of the epistolary conclusion. In any case, its beginning makes clear that his writing ultimately is "the word of God." In view of that, the human author can readily retreat into the background.

The three individual genres could also achieve acceptance on the basis of their form, because despite their relative isolation in the New Testament they were embedded in a broad literary movement. They fulfilled expectations placed on a writing of their genre within that tradition. Either they belonged to biblical Jewish apocalyptic (Revelation), or biblical Jewish historical writing was revived in them (Acts), or they continued the preaching tradition of the Hellenistic synagogue (Hebrews). Associations with the history of contemporary Jewish literature are always evident: Luke's two-volume work was created at the time of a renaissance in Jewish historical writing, attested by the work of Flavius Josephus. Revelation belongs among the Jewish apocalypses (*4 Esdras; Syriac Baruch*) that reacted against the Jewish War. Hebrews is a part of the largely vanished rhetorical and homiletic culture of the Jewish synagogue. This embeddedness in a broader history of Jewish literature distinguishes the three individual genres from the letters and gospels, for those two basic forms had no models in biblical and Jewish-Hellenistic literature. They were oriented to non-Jewish models and, through their connection to Jewish traditions, created an original early Christian literature.

The acceptance of the three functional genres was, finally, made easier because behind them lay oral forms of communication in early Christianity that were already part of divine worship. This was true especially of Revelation and Hebrews. In the community assemblies there had always been oral forms such as prophecy and public speaking. Oral prophecy became a written apocalypse in Revelation; oral discourse became written discourse in Hebrews. Regarding Acts we can only suppose that it, too, built on a form of oral communication: it speaks of the sending of missionaries by the Spirit. Messengers had to give an accounting of their task in a subsequent report. The mysterious "we" in Acts could have been formulated in imitation of stylistic characteristics of such reports, with which early Christians were familiar.

But all this did not achieve an unchallenged validity for these writings—neither the authority of their forms nor their embeddedness in the context of biblical-Jewish literature nor their links to forms of oral communication. All three individual genres also adopted features of the basic forms of the New Testament: Hebrews and Revelation, the letter; Acts, the (Lukan) gospel. All three combine their forms with a second that was already recognized. All three locate themselves within accepted currents of tradition: Hebrews entered the canon on a towrope from the Pauline letters; Acts was towed by the Gospel of Luke, and Revelation was attached to the Johannine writings. Without links to the authorities—Paul, John, and Luke—they would not have found their way into the canon.

In conclusion, we still must ask whether correspondences between form and content can be detected in this phase of early Christian literature as well. The message content of the gospels and letters was a proclamation of lordship, an "evangelium" (*euaggelion*). This was as true for Mark as it was for Romans. The gospel was an independent variant of the ancient biography, the community letter an independent development of the letter of friendship. Early Christianity had created new genres here. In the individual genres, by contrast, the dependence on existing forms of historiography, apocalyptic, and homiletic is stronger. The forms of the "world" outside Christianity left clear traces in these three genres. This is reflected in their content. The attitude toward the world revealed in New Testament formal language is clearest, and most fully revealed in all its dimensions, in the three individual exemplars in the New Testament: we find the confidence in a missionary saturation of the Roman Empire in Acts; we hear an abrupt declaration of war on the apotheosis of the emperor in Revelation; and we experience the ambivalence of Christian existence as a wilderness wandering and a road to the eternal sanctuary in Hebrews. The first phase of early Christian literature was shaped by the impulse to preach the gospel throughout the world. The second phase secured continuity with Jesus and Paul through pseudepigraphic writings. In the third phase emerged the necessity to orient oneself to this world and find a unique path between shaping the world and maintaining distance from it.

These three texts, which convince by means of their content and genre, in any case point to a growing genre-competence in the later early Christian communities: interest and feeling for public speaking, writing history, and revelatory literature must have increased among them—tied to a social ascent of early Christianity in the first century and a developing internal literary culture in its communities. If we also consider that the three individual genres in the New Testament were accompanied by a much greater number of independent genres in early Christian apocryphal literature—church orders, dialogues, collections of sayings, hymns, and infancy gospels—we may see the clearly expanding multiplicity of literary forms as an indication of the development of a differentiated literary culture in early Christianity.

Despite all these factors that eased reception of the individual genres, two of them remained in dispute for a long time: Revelation in the East, Hebrews in the West. Thus we come to the last phase of a literary history of the New Testament, the construction of a canon.

PART FOUR

The New Testament on Its Way to Becoming a Religious World Literature

The Canonical Phase

The construction of a canon is always ambivalent. It is at the same time the rescue of tradition from oblivion and its mummification; it gives some writings the highest worth and excludes others from enduring influence. Both are necessary for living religions: on the one hand, stability of tradition as the basis for a consensus that also draws boundaries; on the other hand, a flexibility of tradition that reacts to new challenges by deviating from the received consensus. In Judaism we find this balance in the existence of law and prophets together. The Law assures a basic consensus; living prophecy develops it further through revelations. But the prophets were also codified. After them came secret apocalyptic revelations and wisdom writings that made possible a further development and flexibility in the religion until fixed texts and living interpretation achieved in Judaism a balance of stability and flexibility. Analogously, it is true of early Christianity that it began on the basis of the Jewish Bible as the guarantor of stability and normativity, but that basis was augmented by new revelations in the words of the Lord and the letters of the apostles. For a long time "scripture" was accompanied only by the "oral" words of the Lord as the superior authority in early Christianity, with the letters of Paul subordinated to them. Only little by little was the authority of the "Lord" assigned also to writings that contained his words. Through their canonization in the New Testament writings this formerly flexible element became fixed. Therefore new factors had to ensure the vitality of the tradition: a continuing production of writings alongside the New Testament and beyond the New Testament—those writings that we summarize today as apocryphal, as well as a hermeneutics of the Bible that by means of interpretation can draw new meaning from ancient texts. With the construction of a canon, exegetes became responsible for the further development of belief and ethos. It is no accident that the first representative of a theology of the canon was also one of the first theologians who developed his theology out of exegesis: Irenaeus of Lyons.[1] In this section we will discuss first the origin of the canon as a securing of a consensus ensuring stability, and then the ongoing creation of new writings that only became "apocryphal" as a result of the construction of the canon.

19 Canon as a Means to Stability Based on Compromise and Demarcation

The construction of the canon was the climax of the history of the New Testament literature. The path from a pre-literary oral tradition and letter correspondence to a definitive literature was thus concluded. As a New Testament canon, the writings of the New Testament became a religious world literature. The other early Christian writings, however impressive, did not enter into the history of the influence of the New Testament and only achieved some effect in modern times in association with the New Testament, as enhancements or counter-readings of it. At the same time, the construction of the canon is one of the most obscure phases in the history of New Testament literature, containing many questions that are unresolved and subject to contentious discussion.[1] But we can indicate the period of time in which the idea of a canon arose and the basic boundaries of its extent were laid.

Since at the beginning, besides scripture (the Old Testament), only the *oral* authority of the Lord and the apostles existed, their words were not quoted as scripture as was the Old Testament. This changed toward the middle of the second century C.E. The second letter of Clement, which repeatedly introduces Old Testament quotations with the words "thus scripture says," once, after the Old Testament citations, includes a saying of Jesus (Matt 9:13b), introducing it with the formal "and another scripture says: I did not come to call the righteous, but sinners" (*2 Clem.* 2:4). At about the same time the *Letter of Barnabas* introduces the Jesus saying from Matthew 22:14, "many are called, but few are chosen," with the formula usually used for Old Testament texts, "as is written" (*Barn.* 4:14). Here the authority of the words of Jesus has been transferred to writings in which they are attested. They are on the same level as the Old Testament. This corresponds to what we find in Justin Martyr. In the mid-second century C.E. he is familiar only with sayings of the Lord and "memoirs of the apostles" alongside the Jewish Bible. He attests that these "memoirs," which he also calls gospels, were read in worship alongside the prophets and thus were treated like the Old Testament (*1 Apol.* 67.3). With Irenaeus (ca. 180 C.E.) and in the Muratorian Fragment at the end of the second century there is then the idea of a canon: Irenaeus regards the four-gospel collection as definitively closed, and in the Muratorian Fragment the collection of Paul's letters is a completed entity. But a good deal is still open.

With the construction of the canon the New Testament writings entered the history of ancient literature, not as a positively evaluated enrichment, but as a foreign and irritating phenomenon: in about 176/180 C.E. the philosopher Celsus published his attack on Christians, in which he accuses Jews and Christians of having fallen away from the "true teaching" (thus the title of his book) held by all nations in common. His writing is retained through Origen, who quotes it sentence by sentence in his *Contra Celsum* before attempting to refute it. Celsus presupposes a collection of Christian writings made up of a number of gospels and letters of Paul. He certainly knows the gospels of Matthew and Luke, referring, for example, to the genealogy of Jesus in both Matthew and Luke (*Cels.* 2.32); from John, he knows about the marks of the wounds in the body of the Risen One (*Cels.* 2.55) and of his appearance to a woman (*Cels.* 2.71). There is no certain reference to Mark's Gospel, apart from the fact that Celsus may have learned from Mark 6:2 that Jesus was a carpenter (*Cels.* 6.34).[2] At one point he accuses Christians of changing the wording of the gospels for tactical reasons "three times, four times, and more" (*Cels.* 2.27). That could be interpreted to mean that he knows of a collection of three or four gospels, but of a number of other gospels as well. The number four is probably not yet "canonical." What is important is that he has also read Paul, and thus probably knows of a collection of Christian writings made up of gospels and letters, for he accuses the Christians of thinking that human wisdom is foolishness before God (*Cels.* 6.12), and quotes Galatians 6:14 directly: "the world is crucified to me and I to the world" (*Cels.* 5.64)—according to Origen the only passage he has noted from the Pauline letters. Besides the "canonical" sources he refers also to Jewish traditions about Jesus as a bastard child of a soldier named Panthera (*Cels.* 1.32), and he knows Gnostic teachings (e.g., *Cels.* 5.54, 61). Whether, as Origen says, he also knew the *Letter of Barnabas* is uncertain (*Cels.* 1.63). In any case this writing by the philosopher Celsus is the first evidence that early Christian literature was studied by literati from outside. This indirectly illuminates a motif that played a role in the construction of the canon: by editing their normative writings the Christians were able to present their identity to the outside world and clarify their teachings. Only thus could Celsus identify them with their writings. When in Carthage in the year 180 C.E. Christians from Scilli were asked by their judge about the contents of a box they had with them, one of them answered that these were "books and letters of Paul, a righteous man" (*Acts of the Scillitan Martyrs* §12). They, too, knew of a two-part canon consisting of books (= gospels?) and Paul.

It is uncertain whether early Christian literature at that time evoked a positive echo in the Gentile world as well as criticism. In the nineteenth century a counter-project to the gospels was sometimes seen in the biography of the miracle-worker and itinerant philosopher Apollonius of Tyana (first century C.E.) by Philostratus (ca. 170–245 C.E.). Philostratus was supposed to have written this biography at the request of the empress Julia Domna, who came from Syria. The birth and end of Apollonius were surrounded by miracles. A god speaks to his mother in a dream before his birth (*Vit. Apoll.* 1.4). The child thus born is declared by the people of the land to be the son of Zeus (1.6). The growing boy is outstanding, possessing brilliant mental powers and beauty (1.7). Later he travels as a philosopher throughout the land. He works miracles, including an exorcism (4.20) and the raising of a dead person (4.45). His end is mysterious: he disappears suddenly, then appears to an unbelieving disciple (in a dream?). His grave cannot be found. There is a scene of an ascension into heaven during which a choir of virgins sings: "Leave the earth behind and come to heaven" (8.30-31). Was Apollonius of Tyana depicted as a counter to Christ? Or were there only unconscious transfers of motifs from individual traditions?[3] The biography of Apollonius shows in any case that the gospels were not foreign to the contemporary literary landscape. Even if they are more "primitive" in their language and style than the work of the educated rhetor and Sophist Philostratus, they surpass it in depth and content.

The construction of the canon by no means took place in isolation from the overall history of literature. The Mishna was codified at the end of the second century. It took its place in Judaism alongside the Hebrew Bible as its interpretation, as in Christianity the New Testament took its place as expansion and completion of the Old Testament. These were two deutero-canonical expansions of an already existing canon.[4] We can observe a similar process in pagan antiquity: in the Hellenistic-Roman period (over a long stretch of time) a corpus of classical authors was established to be used in training and education. Thus, for example, we read in Quintilian (in the second half of the first century C.E.) a list of the Greek and Latin works he recommends for education in rhetoric (*Inst.* 10.46-84, 85-131). That is also a deutero-canonical expansion of an already existing canon of Greek authors by the addition of Latin authors. Atticism and classicism led to an orientation to a few great authors who were regarded as unsurpassable models.[5]

Despite this embedding in general tendencies in the history of literature, the New Testament remained a foreign body within ancient literature. Christian canon-building did not incorporate tested ancient classics and add to them, but clearly valued the New Testament writings above the Old Testament scriptures. Celsus attacks the Christians sharply for despising the ancient traditions. For him they are irresponsible "rebels" against the tested ancient truths. The collection of canonical writings could not root out this "blemish" of the new. There were other disadvantages: the New Testament was literature written in non-literary language. When the church fathers justified its style as *sermo humilis* they did not incorporate the New Testament into an existing system of styles, but expanded that system with a new category. They excused the simple Greek with the idea that revelation made use of a language addressed to ordinary people. It was a treasure in earthen vessels.[6]

The construction of the canon itself is a historical puzzle inasmuch as in the second century C.E. there were no central institutions that could have decided which writings were to be read in worship. The idea of the canon, however, as we have said, is already present with Irenaeus around 180 C.E. The basic lines of its extent were also determined, for him; he cites nearly all the canonical writings of the New Testament, with the exception of the three shortest: Philemon, 3 John, and Jude. Second Peter is probably missing as well. Whether one may conclude from this silence to a lack of knowledge, or that in his time these writings were not part of the canon, is not so certain. It could be an accident, since the frequency of citation of the New Testament writings correlates with their length, and Irenaeus also fails to cite short Old Testament books that were certainly part of his canon.[7] His silence about 3 John is striking because he had a special fondness for the *Corpus Iohanneum*. Probably he was unfamiliar with this letter, as with Jude. Beyond our canonical writings, he cites the *Shepherd of Hermas* (*Haer.* 4.20.2) and *1 Clement* (*Haer.* 3.3.3), but both in such a way that they are distinguished from the canonical writings. The scope of the canon is, in any case, somewhat open for him with regard to the non-Pauline letters, but by no means with the gospels, for the four-part gospel (*tetramorphon euaggelion*) is for Irenaeus as much a necessity as the four points of the compass, the four beasts in Revelation 4:9, and the four covenants of God with humanity (*Haer.* 3.11.8). He is so emphatic in giving his reasons for the number four that it was probably not yet a matter of common consent. But for him it is absolutely certain: there are no other canonical gospels. The collection of Pauline letters he had in a form that was, in fact, complete. But he says nothing about their completeness. In contrast, the "Muratorian Fragment" (end of the second century C.E.) presumes for the first time that the collection of Pauline letters is also closed: Paul wrote to seven communities, just as the seven letters in Revelation are addressed to seven communities. The seven communities are representative of all Christians.[8] The catholic letters, however, are still not a closed part of the canon even in the Muratorian Fragment. The statements in Irenaeus and the Muratorian Fragment match the general conclusion: gospels, Acts, and thirteen Pauline letters have been undisputed since the second century. The scope of the catholic letters remained open; of these, only 1 Peter and 1 John were accepted everywhere,[9] but not 2 Peter, 2 John, 3 John, James, and Jude. Among the more extensive writings, there was dispute over Hebrews in the West and Revelation in the East.

Eusebius (ca. 260–340) described the status of development at the beginning of the fourth century; he divided the writings into three groups but was uncertain where he should put Revelation (*Hist. eccl.* 3.25.1-7). The canon of twenty-seven writings is clearly visible with him, even though five writings from this canon were still rejected in some communities (Table 20):[10]

Table 20: Canonical and Apocryphal Books according to Eusebius

A. Orthodox Books

Canonical Books:
- a. Recognized books (*homologoumena*)
  - 22 books: 4 gospels, Acts, 1 Peter, 1 John, 14 letters of Paul, Revelation (?)
- b. Disputed books (*antilegomena*)
  - James, 2 Peter, 2 and 3 John, Jude

Extracanonical Books:
- c. Spurious books (*notha*)
  - *Acts of Paul, Hermas, Apocalypse of Peter, Barnabas, Didache, Gospel of the Hebrews,* Revelation (?)

B. Fictions of Heretics

Gospels of Peter, Thomas, Matthias, Acts of Andrew, Acts of John, other Apostolic Acts

The twenty-seven writings in our New Testament are attested for the first time in the thirty-ninth *Easter Letter* of Athanasius, written in Egypt in the year 367—but only for the region for which Athanasius was responsible as a bishop. Besides the canonical writings, he recommends as reading for catechumens the Wisdom of Solomon, Jesus Sirach, Esther, Judith,

Tobit, the *Didache*, and the *Shepherd of Hermas*. What is important for us is that there was never a formal decision about the canon, and yet with the exception of a very few writings the extent of the canon was already fixed in its essentials by the end of the second century C.E., as if it had been self-determined.[11]

There is a consensus among scholars that, in fact, two criteria for choice played their parts: canonical writings must, first, come from apostolic authors, that is, from apostles or their disciples, and, second, they must contain the apostolic "orthodox" teaching. Orthodoxy was evident if a writing was generally accepted. To that extent one may add a third, dependent criterion of "catholicity," that is, general circulation of the writings as the expression of an ecclesial consensus. Writings were disputed if there was doubt that they came (directly or indirectly) from an apostle or contained unacceptable teaching. These were undoubtedly reciprocal conditions. Those who rejected the content of a writing soon postulated as well that it could not be apostolic.

We can see this with regard to the Gospel of John. The Montanists appealed to the predictions about the Paraclete in that gospel, which they saw as fulfilled in their prophecy. Following Revelation, they expected the descent of the heavenly Jerusalem. Probably their opponents, as a result, disputed the apostolicity of John's Gospel and of Revelation, saying they came instead from the heretic Cerinthus (Epiphanius, *Haer.* 51.3). Epiphanius calls the *Corpus Iohanneum*'s opponents *alogoi*: they deny the Logos and are therefore "irrational" (*alogoi*). Gaius was their spokesman in Rome. Their argument against the Gospel of John was that it taught the incarnation of the Logos and "immediately" thereafter his baptism. This reminded them of the teaching of Cerinthus that the heavenly Christ first descended on the earthly Jesus at his baptism.

With regard to Hebrews, the rejection of a second repentance was a stumbling block especially in the West, where the sacrament of reconciliation was developing step by step. Rigorists could appeal to Hebrews. No wonder that well-founded doubts about its Pauline authorship were uttered! Eusebius reports that "some dispute the epistle to the Hebrews in view of the Roman church's denial that it is the work of Paul" (*Hist. eccl.* 3.3.5). Where Hebrews was accepted, it was considered a Pauline writing, though it was often proposed that someone else had translated Paul's Hebrew text into Greek.

The Johannine apocalypse was greeted with reservations in the East: its imminent expectation of the end and its palpable-earthly ideas about a new heaven and new earth did not accord with the subtle theology of the Eastern church fathers. Dionysius of Alexandria vehemently denied that it could have been written by the author of the Gospel of John (Eusebius, *Hist. eccl.* 7.25). But Revelation was accepted into the canon only because it was attributed to John the evangelist.[12]

We can now turn again to the historical puzzle of the establishment of the canon: How can we explain the amazingly broad consensus about its extent? It was an unforced consensus, at least without any application of power by formal authorities. The most probable hypothesis, in my opinion, is that the construction of the canon was prepared for in a number of places, independently of one another, but the approach that triumphed was based on compromises between the two most important Christian regions in the second century C.E. and was facilitated by the fact that they had a common enemy, namely, Marcion.[13]

Marcion came to Rome in about 140 C.E. and, after his separation from the Roman community in 144 C.E., founded his own church with its own canon. He regarded the Old Testament as the revelation of another God, a God of righteousness who was fundamentally different from the God of love in the New Testament. He published a book called "Antitheses" on the clashes between the two testaments. His New Testament consisted only of a single gospel, that of Luke, and the letters of Paul (without the Pastorals). He had purged all these writings of supposedly secondary interpolations. His indirect influence on the establishment of the canon can be summarized in this way: the first Christians had no common authority, but they did have one heretic in common. Distancing themselves from him made it easier for them to unite. While Marcion did not create the first canon, he was a catalyst for a consensus about the canon already in process and independent of him. Let us consider the various parts of the canon from this point of view, beginning with the gospels.

The Four-Gospel Canon

In the second century many communities knew only one gospel. That was probably the norm for a long period. In Syria the tie to a single gospel was so much a matter of course that there a single gospel was created out of the four canonical gospels by means of a gospel harmony (Tatian's *Diatessaron*). There was a general tendency in antiquity to see truth as one. It would have been attractive to vary Ephesians 4:5-6 to read "One Lord, one faith, one baptism, *one gospel*, one God and Father." Instead, early Christianity acknowledged four gospels. How did the four-gospel canon come about?[14]

In discussing this question we must distinguish between the concepts of gospel collection, gospel reading, gospel codex, and gospel canon, even though the four forms are connected. When a gospel collection in a community's archive serves the liturgical purpose of reading, those gospels have a normative status for that community and belong to the "canon" of the scriptures read publicly in worship. We can then speak of a (local) "gospel canon." But we should only speak of a "New Testament canon" as a whole when the structure of the canon, with all four parts (gospels, Pauline letters, canonical letters, Revelation), is visible, even though the question of which individual writings are part of it remains open. In this sense the canon is present in Irenaeus's writing. But the "construction of the canon" was only ended when a supra-regional consensus about the extent of the canon was reached. That took a long time.

Collections of four gospels must have existed as early as the first half of the second century. In that period there were many writings that presupposed all four canonical gospels: the non-genuine long ending to Mark's Gospel (first half of the second century) combines the Easter appearance to Mary Magdalene (John) with the appearance to the disciples at Emmaus (Luke) and the sending of the disciples throughout the world (Matthew) with their mission to the whole world according to Acts (Mark 16:9-20). All four gospels may also be adapted in the *Gospel of Peter*, the *Egerton Gospel*, the *Epistula Apostolorum*, and the *Gospel of Truth*. Celsus also probably knew all four gospels. It is therefore improbable that such collections of gospels were first made in reaction to Marcion.

The reading of a number of gospels in worship is first directly attested by Justin around 150 C.E. Justin calls the gospels "memoirs . . . drawn up by his apostles and those who followed them" (*Dial.* 103.8). These "memoirs" he also calls "gospels" (*1 Apol.* 66)—the first attestation to the plural "gospels" as a designation of a genre. Justin thus distinguishes apostolic gospel writings from the gospels written by their disciples. Since he speaks of both in the plural he presupposes at least two apostolic gospels and two from their followers.[15] Demonstrably, he knew Mark and Luke, that is, the two gospels attributed to disciples of the apostles. Of the apostolic gospels he certainly knew Matthew, but probably John as well (cf. John 3:3-5 in *1 Apol.* 61.4). It is only striking that he scarcely uses John's Gospel, nor does he make use of the Pauline letters, which were almost surely known to him. Thus we can say that the gospels had canonical validity in Rome at the time of Justin, but that does not mean that the whole New Testament canon already existed. Justin uses neither Paul's letters nor the catholic letters as sacred scripture.

The oldest codices of the gospels containing all four that we have must be dated later. As a rule, the four gospels were not contained together in a single papyrus. The famous Chester Beatty Papyrus, 𝔓45 (third century), with fragments of all the gospels and Acts, is an exception. 𝔓75 (third century) has parts of Luke and John. The late 𝔓44 (sixth-seventh century) has fragments of Matthew and John, while 𝔓84 (sixth century) has two fragments of Mark and John. It is possible that some other fragments belong together. If we suppose that 𝔓64, 𝔓67, and 𝔓4 were parts of a single codex we would be able to demonstrate a four(?)-gospel codex at about 200 C.E. It may be an accident that we have no older manuscript evidence.

In any case, the four-gospel canon is certainly attested with Irenaeus around 180 C.E. as part of the whole New Testament canon. When Irenaeus gives his reasons for the necessity of a fourfold gospel he presumes that there are four. He did not create the four-gospel canon.[16] He wrote in the knowledge that his canon agreed with that of the church in Rome. How did this consensus arise and spread so quickly? Three historical factors aided its breakthrough: an immanent development in Rome, a compromise with Asia Minor, and a common "front" against Marcion.[17]

The internal development in Rome is attested by Justin and his disciple, Tatian.[18] Justin assumes four gospels as the basis for the church lectionary but uses almost solely the Synoptics, which he quotes in harmonizing fashion. That his harmonizing tendency may rest on a harmony of the Synoptic Gospels prepared by himself, which found its continuation in the gospel harmony of his disciple, Tatian, is an appealing idea, but hard to document. More important for us is that Tatian's gospel harmony took precisely the Gospel of John, which Justin scarcely used, as its basis, and organized the Synoptic Gospels within a Johannine frame. We can no longer determine whether Tatian wrote his gospel harmony in Rome or only after his return to his home in Syria, but that his gospel harmony was a response to Marcion's reduction of the gospels to a single one is very likely. What is certain is that between Justin's *First Apology* (ca. 150 C.E.) and Tatian's gospel harmony, John's Gospel had gained in influence (in Rome).

A very pragmatic compromise contributed to this. In Asia Minor the Paschal feast and Easter were celebrated according to the chronology of John's Gospel, and in Rome according to Synoptic chronology. In about 155 C.E. representatives from Asia Minor and Rome, Polycarp of Smyrna and Anicetus of Rome, met there to seek a compromise on this disputed question. Neither was able to persuade the other. They agreed instead that each region should follow its own tradition. As it was decided to allow the different times of the festival to stand alongside each other, so probably the same decision was reached regarding the different gospels, without thereby breaking the communion between the churches (Eusebius, *Hist. eccl.* 5.24.16-17). In this way the equal value of the Synoptics and John was indirectly acknowledged. That John's Gospel had difficulty achieving acceptance in Rome is evident not only from the fact that we can find no certain reference to that gospel in

Justin's writings, but also because, in reaction to Montanism, John's Gospel was rejected in Rome also by Gaius and the later so-called *alogoi*.

The compromise between Asia Minor and Rome was decisively advanced by the circumstance that the two could distinguish themselves from Marcion through their confession of four gospels. The Roman community had to engage intensively with Marcion precisely at the time of the dispute over Passover and Easter. Marcion's flourishing took place under Anicetus (Irenaeus, *Haer.* 3.4.3), and he was able at that time to persuade "many" (Justin, *1 Apol.* 58.2). Justin (according to Eusebius, *Hist. eccl.* 4.18.9) composed a writing against him. Polycarp also clashed with him during his visit to Rome or previously in Asia Minor. Irenaeus reports on this without giving the location: "And Polycarp himself replied to Marcion, who met him on one occasion, and said 'Do you know me?' 'I do know you, the first-born of Satan'" (Irenaeus, *Haer.* 3.3.4). One may conclude from these reports that the two representatives of Rome and Asia Minor, Anicetus and Polycarp, were able to mutually agree in their rejection of Marcion. That improved the position of John's Gospel: the Logos-Prologue of John must have appeared to be a refutation of Marcion: the Creator and the Redeemer are identical. Therefore there is reason to suppose that the four-gospel canon became a mark of orthodoxy because Marcion acknowledged only one gospel. The Gospel of John, received with reserve in Rome, was made more acceptable by the closing of ranks against Marcion.

This is not to say that the four-gospel canon was first created in reaction against Marcion. We can only say that it has been demonstrated that the four-gospel canon existed in Rome in the second century C.E. and also that since that time the Gospel of John, which had been accepted only with reservations there, has belonged to the Roman canon. Even before that time there would have been gospel collections in other locales containing the four gospels, which were later canonized. The writings mentioned above, from the first half of the second century, point to this because they presume our four gospels: Mark 16:9-20; 2 Peter; the Gospel of Peter; the *Epistula Apostolorum*; Papyrus Egerton; the *Gospel of Truth*. But in the second century there were many other gospels in addition to the four that later succeeded in being canonized. The second century was a fruitful period for "Jesus literature," as we will see. Should we conclude that at that time the selection of gospels was still altogether open? Or should we say that the four gospels later canonized had to have had an advantage from the beginning since these many new gospels did not make their way into the canon with them as the fifth, sixth, or seventh gospel?

From Asia Minor, Papias would be the earliest evidence for the four-gospel collection if we could presume that, besides Matthew and Mark, he also knew of other canonical gospels. But that is uncertain.[19] When Eusebius, despite his interest in demonstrating the existence of the canonical scriptures as early as possible, does not mention that Papias knew Luke and John, it means he found no reference to them in his sources. Did he not have a complete copy of Papias at hand? Or did Papias only report what he had received as tradition from the elders? That tradition may have known only the two oldest writings about Jesus: Mark and the Sayings Source, which was attributed to Matthew. If a knowledge of Mark and Q was all the tradition Papias received, he himself may have been aware of other gospels without mentioning them explicitly, because in what he says about Mark and Matthew he intended only to repeat what he had received as tradition. As regards Papias's knowledge of Luke and John, there are only deductions that are not fully persuasive but that have a certain probability at least as regards the Gospel of John:

1. General historical arguments favor Papias's knowledge of John's Gospel. That gospel was already broadly accepted in Asia Minor. Papias, who came from Asia Minor, had to have known of it. Since it is evident that he knew the first letter of John (Eusebius, *Hist. eccl.* 3.39.17), he should have been familiar also with the central document of the *Corpus Iohanneum*. Or is this only evidence that in some regions 1 John was accepted before the gospel? Many communities were familiar with the idea that there was only one gospel, and they may have been more reticent toward new gospels than toward apostolic letters. After all, it was obvious that there had been many apostles and many letters from them.
2. Papias (or his source) accuses Mark's Gospel of a deficiency in the "ordering" of its material (Eusebius, *Hist. eccl.* 3.39.15). But dependence on the order of John's Gospel cannot be deduced from this. It is true that Papias mentions the disciples Andrew, Peter, Philip, Thomas, James, John, Matthew, etc. in the same order as in John 1:40-44 (Eusebius, *Hist. eccl.* 3.39.4). But John 1 also includes an anonymous disciple and Nathanael. Apart from that, John's Gospel deviates less from the Synoptics in organizing material than in the altogether different style of its traditions and discourses.

Later witnesses cannot establish Papias's knowledge of John's Gospel with certainty: a gospel prologue (the *Argumentum secundum Iohannem* = Frag. 20) appeals to Papias's fifth book for the assertion that John the evangelist dictated his gospel to Papias. In an Armenian source, Papias is made the author of the story of the woman caught in adultery (John 7:53—8:11), probably on the basis of a mistaken conclusion by Eusebius (*Hist. eccl.* 3.39.16), who says he read this or a similar story in Papias and in the *Gospel of the Hebrews*. This note is of no more value than the tradition in Eusebius, and he says nothing of Papias's knowledge of John's Gospel.

It is possible that Papias knew John's Gospel in about 120/130 in Asia Minor, but not the four-gospel canon, which Justin assumes twenty to thirty years later in Rome, for there is no evidence of his knowledge of Luke's Gospel, other than vague echoes of its proemium that are scarcely adequate evidence.[20] Since until the middle of the second century C.E. the gospels were generally quoted without the name of an author there is much to favor the supposition that shortly before the middle of the second century the four-gospel canon was created, breaking through the tendency toward a single gospel, and was quickly accepted in opposition to Marcion's one-gospel canon.[21] For it was only with the creation of gospel collections that it became indispensable to designate the gospels according to their authors.[22] In any case the four-gospel canon was as much of a "revolutionary innovation" in the second century as was Marcion's one-gospel canon. The fourfold gospel was then more easily accepted in reaction to Marcion.

Canonical Collections of Letters

A comparable process may be inferred as regards the letters. Marcion added to his gospel a collection of Pauline letters, consisting of ten letters of Paul, without the Pastorals and Hebrews. Here again it is true that there had been collections of Pauline letters before Marcion. Paul's letters were read during worship in many communities and thus had an authoritative value. But when they are quoted in the oldest Christian writings they are not equated with sacred scripture. Here it was Marcion, at the latest, who brought attention to the equal canonical value of Paul's letters, since Justin, in his apologetic writings (directed outward) in the middle of the second century, does not yet cite the letters of Paul. Thirty years later, they were authentic Christian literature both for the outsider Celsus and for the church father Irenaeus, who cites them alongside the gospels as canonical scripture.

Marcion did not deliberately exclude the Pastorals; he probably was not aware of them. That in itself helped them to find a place in the canon. Here again an agreement between Asia Minor and Rome may have played a role. The Pastorals are probably writings from communities in Asia Minor. Two of them are addressed to Timothy in Ephesus. For Polycarp of Smyrna in Asia Minor they were part of the canon. Here again, then, Rome and Asia Minor were able to agree on a common opposition to Marcion, for the Pastorals were extremely well suited for enemies of Marcion. In 1 Timothy 6:20 idle chatter and the "antitheses" of what is wrongly called Gnosis are rejected. That could be understood as a counter to Marcion's antitheses, as if Paul, who was Marcion's principal witness, had rejected his teaching.[23]

The augmentation of Paul's letters with those of other apostles (the so-called catholic letters) was also advanced by the common front of the Christian communities in Rome and Asia Minor. First John and First Peter were acknowledged in Asia Minor. Papias knew both these writings (Eusebius, *Hist. eccl.* 3.39.17). Polycarp of Smyrna makes clear allusions to 1 Peter (*Pol. Phil.* 1.3; 2.1-2; 5.2; 7.2; 8.1-2; 10.2) and adopts the central statement of 1 John: "For everyone who does not confess that Jesus Christ has come in the flesh is an anti-Christ" (*Pol. Phil.* 7.1). If the dispute over Passover and Easter between Rome and Asia Minor aided and witnessed to the recognition of John's Gospel in the West, so in principle 1 John and 1 Peter, as letters belonging to the communities of Asia Minor, were also acknowledged—that is, the two letters that, among all the catholic letters, have ever since been an undisputed part of the canon. Marcion's concentration on the *Corpus Paulinum* probably advanced the recognition of other letters from other apostles as well. The cornerstone for the acknowledgment of a collection of catholic letters was perhaps laid at that time.

One may probably say the following of the whole process of constructing the canon: whatever the two Christian centers in Asia Minor and Rome could agree upon had a chance to succeed in becoming part of the canon. Their distancing of themselves from Marcion solidified a consensus that was being built independently of him: his canon was thus not the positive model for the newly growing canon, but rather a negative counter-model whose rejection bound people together. Through him the pluralistic canon became a mark of orthodoxy. Why is that so important? Herein is reflected a bit of the social dynamics of early Christianity, namely, the coming into existence of a religious community with ecclesial rather than sectarian features. Ecclesial and sectarian structures are found in all religious communities. Church and sect constitute a continuum within which one can categorize all religious communities.[24] One criterion for distinguishing them is the amount of tension in relationship to the world and society; another is the pressure for homogeneity within. A church is pluralistic within, while a sect is homogeneous. It is true that Marcion created his own "church," but in its internal structure it was more a sect. The tensions with the world were emphasized there; readiness for martyrdom was demanded; inner variety was limited. In opposing Marcion's canon and the community structures he established, the church became aware of its ecclesial character. The literary plurality of the canon corresponded, in terms of social history, to the origination of a religious community of the ecclesial type.[25]

Canonical Clusters of Gospels and Other Genres

If Marcion was not the creator of the canon but only, as a negative model, the catalyst for the establishment of a canon, it must be demonstrated that there had already been a development toward a canon before him. In fact, we can observe a tendency, independent of Marcion, to link a gospel to another writing. The combination of gospels and letters was successful, but combinations with other writings were also in progress, so that we can discover a variety of canonical (or pre-canonical) clusters in early Christianity. Wherever we can demonstrate a combination of "gospel + other type of text" first steps were being taken in the direction of a canon.[26] This happened in a number of places independently of one another. From this point of view Marcion represents only a general trend. One need not have recourse to his canon to explain this trend.

The Johannine literature is a canon-in-becoming, with the gospel at its center. In tow is 1 John, which defends the ideas of the gospel against dissidents. The Johannine literature was thus the first to combine a gospel and a letter in a connected group of writings. There is a reason for this continuation of the Johannine literature in letters that is grounded in the Gospel of John itself. In his farewell discourses Jesus promises that he will send the Paraclete who will lead the disciples into all truth—even beyond what they have thus far been able to bear (John 16:12-15). Their joy will in the future be complete (John 16:24; cf. 15:11; 17:13). First John has been written "so that our joy may be complete" (1 John 1:4). It is oriented to "truth" as the criterion of a Christian life (1 John 1:6, 8; 2:4, 21). Was it written to convey something of the onward-leading revelation of the Paraclete? Later, Revelation was connected to the Johannine gospel and letters. The *Corpus Iohanneum* was thus a preliminary stage of the canon consisting of the canonical cluster of "gospel + letters + apocalypse." An openness to further work on the canon is seen in the fact that there is reference at the end of John's Gospel to other potential gospels. This made it possible to set the Gospel of John alongside other gospels. This approach to canon construction is attested in Asia Minor. In the second century, the Gospel of John was regarded as the gospel originating in Ephesus. Papias of Hierapolis knew the first letter of John and may have been familiar with John's Gospel, but that is not certain.

A second approach to constructing a canon is found in Luke's two-volume work. As in the *Corpus Iohanneum*, here a gospel is augmented by a second work. But Luke, as the author is traditionally called, did not add a letter to his gospel; instead, he gives us deeds of the apostles. The title, "Acts of the Apostles," is first certainly attested by Irenaeus (*Haer.* 3.13.3). However, it is also found in good manuscripts (Vaticanus, Bezae Cantabrigiensis, Y [Athos]). Acts is first quoted by Justin. If it was already known under the title "Acts of the Apostles" (which is not attested), he could have understood it to be a continuation of the "memoirs of the apostles," as he calls the gospels (*1 Apol.* 66). This continuation is prepared for in Luke's Gospel itself, where the Baptizer predicts the coming of Jesus as a figure superior to him, who is stronger than he: "He will baptize you with the Holy Spirit and fire" (Luke 3:16). This promise remains unfulfilled in the gospel, but it is recalled twice in Acts, programmatically in the introduction (Acts 1:5) and again in the Cornelius pericope (Acts 11:16). Acts depicts the fulfillment of the prophecy: at Pentecost the disciples are baptized with the Spirit, who descends from heaven like tongues of fire. Here again the continuation of the gospel is associated with the motif of the Spirit.[27]

A third approach to canonical construction is associated with Matthew's Gospel. Together with the letter of James and the *Didache*, it is part of the Jewish-Christian corpus of writings that experienced a brief flowering after 70 C.E. The *Didache* came about in the wake of Matthew's Gospel as did 1 John after the Gospel of John. Matthew's Gospel ends with the charge to baptize all nations and teach them what Jesus had said. The *Didache*, as a continuation of the Matthean Gospel, contains the instructions for baptism that are lacking in Matthew.[28] It refers four times to a gospel that can only be Matthew (*Did.* 8.2; 11.3; 15.3, 4). Matthew and the *Didache* thus constitute the core of a little canon. The formula of this canonical cluster is: "gospel + *Didache* (i.e., teaching of the apostles)."[29] The Jewish-Christian groups behind Matthew and the *Didache*, however, were not powerful enough to introduce their canon for general use. Syria was at a distance from the regions that shaped the canon: Asia Minor and Rome.

Matthew was also the gospel of Ignatius, the bishop of Antioch. He admired Paul as a martyr and letter writer, and his letters imitate the Pauline collection. Six of them are addressed to communities, one to a community leader, Polycarp. The model is the presence of both community letters and the Pastorals in the *Corpus Paulinum*, the former addressed to congregations, the latter to individual leaders.[30] It is possible that Ignatius hoped that his own letters, following in the wake of Paul's, would achieve the same status.[31] Thus, with Ignatius of Antioch we have the beginnings of a canon with the following shape: "Matthew (and other gospels?) + collection of Pauline letters [+ letters of Ignatius?]." However, it was not his, but the catholic letters that would take their place alongside those of Paul.

We can thus observe beginnings of small (pre-)canonical clusters in various places. The canonical processes converged. The canon that succeeded, however, is more than an organic continuation of these beginnings. It separates things that historically belong together: John's Gospel and the Johannine letters are taken apart, the former grouped with the gospels and the Johannine letters included among the catholic letters. Similarly, Luke's Gospel and the Acts of the Apostles were separated, with John's Gospel coming to stand between them. Acts did not follow the Gospel of Luke, but instead served as an introduction to the catholic letters. The construction of the canon thus continued none of the incipient collections, not even that of Marcion. It is not simply a further development of the small canonical clusters we can find in early Christianity. It had a different model, one that lay outside the New Testament writings—namely, the Septuagint. Thus we arrive at an important characteristic of the incipient New Testament canon: its dependence on the Septuagint. The New Testament is the deuterocanonical continuation of an already existing canon.

The Septuagint as Canonical Model

The Septuagint already presented early Christianity with the idea of a canon, and consequently had from the very beginning a singular significance for the newly formed idea of a New Testament canon. There are three reasons to think that the Septuagint was the godparent not only of the construction of the canon but of its concrete shape: the first of these comes from the inclusion of the Acts of the Apostles and Revelation in the canon. These two writings are isolated genres within the New Testament, but these specific forms (and they alone) had models in the Old Testament. Acts is related to the historical books, and Revelation, as a prophetic-apocalyptic book, found its corresponding partner in the book of Daniel. That one example of each of these two genres found its way into the canon is due to the securing of their places by the already-acknowledged first part of the canon, the Old Testament.

The second reason is that the Septuagint is structured in three parts. At its beginning are historical works about the past, followed by "writings" applying to the present, such as the Psalms and Proverbs. The end is made up of the prophetic books as prediction of the future. In the New Testament we can perceive a similar structure: at the beginning are the historical works, the gospels; the letters provide admonitions for the present; the end is made up of Revelation as a prophetic book. Still, the analogy has its limits: Acts does not fit within this scheme, because in the New Testament manuscripts it introduces the catholic letters, and thus in some manuscripts, though not in all, it is separated from the historical books.

A third reason lies in the superscriptions. At the latest, when the four-gospel collection was formed, the gospels were given the titles "gospel according to Matthew, according to Mark, according to Luke, according to John." Only at that point was it necessary to distinguish them from one another as different versions of the same gospel. The superscription *kata* + author is very rare in antiquity. We know of it only in the case of translations, but it was familiar to Christians because, as a translation of the Old Testament, the Septuagint was called "the scriptures *according to* the seventy translators" (*kata tous hebdomēkonta*). If we start with this idea of the *kata*-superscriptions as a reference to "translators," we see that it is improbable that Papias presumes such superscriptions for *both* of the gospels he describes, since he associates Mark and Matthew with a single process of translation, but in different ways. For him, Mark's Gospel is a translation of Peter's speeches, since Mark was Peter's interpreter. Here the superscription "Gospel according to Mark" could readily be imagined, but the same would not be true of Matthew. This gospel, according to Papias, was translated by someone as he was able. Matthew is regarded as the translated author, not the translator, so that the superscription "Gospel according to Matthew" would be out of place. Therefore the gospel superscriptions as a whole were probably created in connection with a collection; only in the case of Mark does it seem that such a title was given to it at an early date, and when the gospels were collected it furnished the model for the other superscriptions.[32]

Finally, we may take into account also the writing of the *nomina sacra*. Words like *God, Kyrios*, and *Pneuma* were abbreviated. These abbreviations became a *proprium* of Christian writings, and this characteristic usage was not limited to the writings that later became canonical. This signals that from Genesis 1:1 to Revelation these scriptures speak of the same God, with the same aura of holiness. This abbreviation of the *nomina sacra* was a stylistic innovation; it is not simply an adoption of the tetragrammaton from the Hebrew Bible, but it may indirectly have been suggested by it.

The adaptation to the Old Testament (both the Hebrew Bible and the Septuagint) had its limits, however. The Christian manuscripts are not scrolls such as were used in synagogal worship and were the usual form for literary works; they are bound codices. This new form of the book was spread in significant fashion by Christians. It was much more practical for travelers than scrolls, and it became a group characteristic of Christians in distinction from the synagogue. It was only when the New Testament was added to the Jewish Bible as a second part of the canon that the latter became the "Old Testament"—and simultaneously the additional writings were given the title "New Testament." If we ask where this contrast received its terminological form, we arrive once again at Marcion, who systematically contrasted Old and New Testaments in his antitheses. Indirectly the New Testament may owe its name to Marcion, although it is also a further development of Pauline thought (2 Cor 3:14).[33]

A Canonical Edition of the New Testament in the Second Century?

Some of the phenomena thus mentioned have an astonishing unity. Christian scriptures were written as codices and abbreviated the *nomina sacra* in comparable ways. The amazing consensus in the authorial attribution points to a certain degree of unity: the information about authors and addressees in the superscriptions is always the same. If one supposes that some books were anonymous and were only secondarily attributed to authors whose identity was not necessitated by the texts, we should expect a greater variation here. For example, the Gospel of Matthew was anonymous in the middle of the second century, and was cited in the *Didache* as "the gospel." Its content permitted no certain conclusion that Matthew was its author. But it appears in all the manuscripts as the Gospel according to Matthew. The same is true for the other New Testament writings! Is it possible, therefore, that the superscriptions, the abbreviations of the *nomina sacra*, the codex form, and perhaps also the sequence of the New Testament writings are traceable to a unified edition of the whole New Testament?[34] This solution, intriguing at first glance, is improbable. The external characteristics, such as the *nomina sacra* and the codices, quickly dominated all Christian writings (even those that were not canonical). Such abbreviations soon became the mark of Christian writers. The superscriptions point to separate partial collections, because their content and formal shape do not follow unified principles in the various small collections.

For the gospels, writings by disciples of the apostles were accepted alongside the writings of the apostles themselves. The Gospels of Mark and Luke stand between those of Matthew and John on the same level, although Mark, according to early Christian tradition, was only an interpreter for Peter and Luke was merely a companion of Paul. In the epistolary literature, on the other hand, all the writings were regarded as apostolic or as those of the two brothers of the Lord. Among the canonical letters there is not one from an apostle's disciple—although historical-critical scholarship is convinced today that the ten pseudepigraphic letters are probably the work of disciples of the apostles. Only much later (in the fifth century) do we encounter a pseudepigraphic letter of Titus! Does this different evaluation of the apostles' followers not point to independent editions of the gospels and the letters?

But the letters themselves were not edited in unified fashion: the superscriptions of the Pauline and catholic letters are different in structure. Paul's letters name only the addressees: "To the Romans," "To the Corinthians," etc. The catholic letters name only the author, and sometimes enumerate his letters, for example, as the first and second letters of Peter. In Paul's letters, the name of Paul is not given either in the superscription or the *subscriptio* (in the best-attested tradition). We may conclude from this that there must have been a collection of his writings in which it was simply understood that all the letters were from Paul. But then it could not have contained the catholic letters. That collection must have existed before any possible canonical final redaction of the whole New Testament, where the Pauline and catholic letters were joined. The unified character of the authorial attributions is not explained by a unified final redaction, but more simply by various unified redactions of partial collections.

Also favoring such partial collections is the manuscript evidence: the ancient papyri attest only partial collections of gospels and letters. Nowhere do we find a gospel attested together with a letter, nowhere a combination of Paul's letters with the catholic letters.[35] Nor, as a rule, are the four gospels found together in a single papyrus. 𝔓45 and 𝔓75 (third century) are exceptions. But, as a rule, papyri have survived in such tiny fragments that we can say nothing for certain about what was in each of the codices. It is probable that many communities had only a single gospel, and that collections of four gospels only gradually came to dominate. Mark's Gospel was already a shadowy tradition in antiquity. It is attested in only a single papyrus (𝔓45) before 300 c.e.—and then only in combination with the other gospels and Acts, while Matthew is attested by papyri twelve times, Luke seven times, and John sixteen times in that period.[36] If Mark was retained only as embedded in other Synoptic Gospels, that indicates a great significance for these gospel collections in the history of the canon. The New Testament canon was probably put together from partial collections that originated independently of one another. 𝔓45 witnesses to a collection of gospels augmented by Acts in the third century; 𝔓46, the Aberkios inscription, and the Scillitan martyrs witness to separate collections of Pauline letters at the end of the second century. The much later 𝔓74 (seventh century) may indicate a partial collection made up of Acts and the catholic letters. Parchment manuscripts also often contain only the gospels as a partial collection.[37]

The concept of a unified New Testament canon made up of several partial collections may have been in preparation even before the middle of the second century. Second Peter assumes writings from all four parts of the canon and thus gives us an insight into the prehistory of the canon. It refers to the transfiguration story in the Synoptics[38] and a prediction of Peter's martyrdom in John's Gospel (2 Pet 1:14; John 21:18-19), and thus may know four gospels, but certainly Matthew and John. He refers to a collection of Paul's letters regarded as complete, since he speaks of "*all*" the letters of his beloved brother Paul (2 Pet 3:16). In addition, he makes use of a collection (in the process of formation?) of catholic letters, since he appeals to 1 Peter (2 Pet 3:1). The letter of Jude has been used as a source and adapted, but is scarcely regarded as canonical, as witnessed by the corrections made to it. He leaves out all the material that does not come from the Old Testament. Thus, a quotation of a prediction from *Enoch* (Jude 14-15) and the battle between the archangel Michael and the devil over the body of Moses (Jude 9) are omitted.[39] It appears, then, that 2 Peter is aware of a canon-in-becoming in the form "four gospels + collection of Paul's letters + catholic letters (1 and 2 Peter)" and has a sense for what belongs to the Old Testament. He uses this "canon" that is beginning to reveal itself in his battle against heretics. But he is not contending against Marcion and his church.[40] Is this letter then a kind of editorial on a first complete edition of the New Testament? The idea is fascinating at first glance.[41] But the reason for hesitating to associate 2 Peter with the establishment of the canon lies in the fact that its own canonization was so much in dispute. Would, above all, an editorial on the oldest edition of the canon have been canonically in dispute?[42] It is clear only that it reflects a collection of "canonical" writings that is already in the process of being collected and lends it the authority of Peter. It is thus part of the literature that secures the tradition and that accompanied the process of canonization, together with the writings of Hegesippus and Papias of Hierapolis and the Muratorian Fragment.

So we can only say this much: with the building of the canon two formal characteristics of early Christian writings were successfully established: the abbreviation of the *nomina sacra* and the codex form. Both these external characteristics quickly became marks of identity for Christian writings, including non-canonical works. Of course, both were introduced into the tradition for the first time at some point and spread from some center outward. But it need not have been the same center. Group symbols spread rapidly once they have acquired symbolic value as the *proprium* of a group.

Establishment of a Canon as a Recognition of and Limitation on Plurality

The construction of the canon was a process of elimination. There were many writings in early Christianity with a claim to revelation that did not make it into the canon. We may divide them broadly into two groups: on the one hand, orthodox literature, including the apostolic fathers; on the other hand, writings that were increasingly suspected of being heretical: a flood of Gnostic writings with a developed Christology and a few writings with Jewish-Christian convictions that, with their simple Christology, remained behind the general development. Often the establishment of the canon is regarded as a suppression of these writings and the triumph of power, with the canon as a means of censorship. Certainly it cannot be denied that every process of exclusion is an exercise of power. The question is only whether it is a matter of the cultural power of convictions and mentalities or the power of persons and institutions. Here, however, we have a historical puzzle: in the second century, when the basic lines of the canon were becoming visible, there was no institution with the necessary power to establish the canon in its own interest. And yet a consensus over the reception and non-reception of many writings took hold. In what follows we will seek the canonizing factors and strengths that made the consensus possible. We will begin with the most common canonical factors and proceed to more and more specialized ones, ending with contingent circumstances.

a. Cognitive Opportunities for Dissemination as a Strength in Canonization

Investigations of the opportunities for dissemination of religious ideas have intensively occupied "cognitive" religious scholarship in recent years.[43] The chances of dissemination are optimal when two conditions are fulfilled: on the one hand, ideas must be moderately "counterintuitive" in order to impress themselves; on the other hand, they must be interwoven with "intuitive notions" in a coherent whole.[44] Counterintuitive ideas clash with our everyday ontology that distinguishes between natural objects and artefacts, plants, animals, and people. Experiments with repeated retellings show that anything that clashes slightly with this everyday ontology is easily remembered. A story about a nymph hidden in a tree, whose laments can be heard in the fluttering of the leaves, is more memorable than a story about a chattering tree with no "person" hidden in it. But as the counterintuitive features (i.e., the violations of boundaries between ontological spheres) increase, the narrative is separated from the tradition: the story of a nymph who changes herself into a tree (= first boundary violation) and then is transformed by a sculptor into a column (= second boundary violation) is simplified or forgotten. The best chances belong to traditions with moderately counterintuitive features combined with a plausible view of reality: the story of the God who became human and the exaltation of the Crucified is a counterintuitive narrative. Boundaries between human and divine are penetrated in both directions. But this story is tied to a plausible interpretation of the world involving creation and redemption and with a conviction, obvious to many, about the infinite value of the human being as a creature whose worth is restored through the incarnation of God. It is possible to deviate from these "optimal conditions of tradition" in two directions. One direction is toward a reduction of the counterintuitive features, when Jesus is regarded as simply a human being seized by a divine power, as occurred in some Jewish-Christian groups. Or one could regard Jesus as God, never human in the full sense; this happened with the docetic-minded Gnostics. According to István Czachesz's "optimal tradition hypothesis," their writings had no chance of being canonized because the counterintuitive features in them increasingly piled up. In them Christ is a docetic being not tied to the conditions of ordinary humanity. Christ is polymorphous, appearing successively as an old and a young man (*Acts of John* 89), separates from his body before the crucifixion and converses with John in a cave while he is being executed on Golgotha (*Acts of John* 97). This image of Jesus consists of a heaping-up of counterintuitive features: here not only is God incarnate in a human being, thus breaking an ontological boundary, but this human being also exists multilocally and polymorphically and so collides with the ordinary ontology of the body. Such writings had little chance of general circulation: Gnostic writings are found neither in canonical lists nor are they included in manuscripts with canonical texts. They were not "excluded," which would presume that they were once seriously considered as canonical writings. They were always read only in small circles within the communities, a religious elite of "Gnostics" who knew themselves to be different from the *pistikoi*. Only in those circles was their claim to possess a revelation superior to that of the "canonical" books recognized. But they were never accepted into the list of scriptures to be read officially in worship. On the basis of a broad consensus manifested at two points they remained out of consideration. Irenaeus formulated that consensus in his writings, and therein lies his great significance for the history of (early) Christianity: all writings that questioned the unity of the God who is creator and redeemer and saw in this world the work of a bungling and ignorant demiurge had no chance to be accepted in the communities. It denied the plausibility of an interpretation of the world that saw creation and redemption as a unity. The balance between affirmation of the world through the belief in creation and critique of the world by a faith in redemption had great intuitive power because it made it possible to integrate a broad spectrum of good and bad experiences. Add to this, as a second criterion, the reality of the incarnation: all writings that taught that the true God did not really enter into this world and become united with a whole human life (materially with flesh and blood, chronologically from birth to death) had no chance in the communities. This faith in the incarnation was counterintuitive, but it founded a faith in the infinite value of human beings. If God really took on human life, it was thus once and forever hallowed and comprehensively enhanced in value, with body, soul, and spirit, from birth to death. At the latest, the confrontation with Marcion's canon brought these two criteria to awareness, for Marcion (differently from the Gnostics) dissolved the unity of the creator and redeemer divinity and denied the complete incarnation of Jesus in the world formed by the creator god. The flourishing Gnostic literature was thus not secondarily banished from a canon in the process of formation; it never got into it in the first place. It remained the literature of small groups in and near the church; there it may have had group-specific canonical status. The "counterintuitive" features added to them made these writings especially well suited to give elitist special groups a "cognitive" identity separating them from the majority, but by that very fact they minimized the chances of those writings to achieve general circulation. The construction of the canon was undoubtedly a process of exclusion of this Gnostic literature, but the deciding factor was not institutional power—that is, the opportunity to influence other people even against their will. What was decisive was persuasive power: the Gnostics may have dreamed of winning all Christians to their "knowledge," but they could not convince the majority. They lacked the persuasive power for that. Their speculative Christology with its bizarre symbolic constructions may be attractive at first glance, but in the long run no large society could live with it. In the other direction, the Jewish-Christian Ebionites, who saw in Jesus a "mere" human being, reduced the counterintuitive features of Christian faith so that it lost its power to attract. In antiquity it was believed that many people had a divine power at work in them. With such a "low" Christology it was impossible to gain attention among the plurality of traditions and doctrines of salvation, to say nothing of superceding them. That God became a human being and was present in hidden form in a crucified messiah might, in contrast, be foolishness to Greeks and a stumbling block for Jews, but this message had impact. If some obvious truth was hidden in this "counterintuitive" foolishness and stumbling block, it would have to have far-reaching consequences for the whole of life.

b. Social Functionality as a Factor in Canonization

Beyond the general anthropological factors in an optimal transmittal of tradition, in the case of the establishment of the canon we encounter also those social factors we have already observed in the writing of the gospels, the origins of the Pauline letters, and the collection of letters: the canon served the purposes of community leadership and community building. In the construction of the canon as well we can demonstrate the five functions of community leadership we recognized as originating motives for the gospels and the Pauline letters. From this point of view the establishment of the canon brought to a conclusion what had been at work since the beginnings of the literary history of early Christianity.

Building consensus: The canon was constructed to give the Christian movement a normative basis. The consensus expressed in it contained many contradictions: the ethical radicalism of the Synoptic Gospels and the moderate conservatism of the deutero-Pauline letters, the earthly Jesus of the Synoptics and the God sweeping above the earth in John's Gospel, the orientation to the Jewish law rightly interpreted in Matthew and the break with the law in Paul, the optimistic trust in people's readiness for *metanoia* in Matthew and Luke and the anthropological pessimism of Paul, who hopes for redemption only through a transformation of humanity effected by God through the Spirit. Despite this internal multiplicity, at no point was there dispute over the confession of the reality of the incarnation and faith in the one and only God. The Gnostic writings, however, questioned precisely this consensus, as we have seen.

Orientation within the environment: The canonical collection of scripture made it possible for Christians to give a better account of their identity, to outsiders as well. Book religions have the advantage that anyone may study their convictions without participating in their worship. As early as the *Apology* of Aristides, the emperor is twice referred to the Christian scriptures and urged to read them (Arist. *Apol.* 2.7/16.5), without the author applying them concretely. But even Justin argues in his *First Apology* with extensive scriptural quotations. This is the first writing that makes intensive use of the early Christian scriptures. In another writing, his Jewish interlocutor Trypho acknowledges having "read" the teachings of the gospel with interest (*Dial.* 10.2). Celsus studied the early Christian scriptures. Origen, in his dispute with him, enters into concrete exegetical questions. Thus the canon not only was used for internal guidance of the communities but was also indispensable for presentation to the outside world and for apologetics. This cannot be said of the Gnostic writings. They do not appeal to the Gentiles on behalf of Christianity, but to Christians for a higher Christianity. To the outside, some Gnostics, but by no means all, revealed a tendency to "privatize" Christianity radically—to the point of rejecting public confession of Christian faith in order better to survive in a hostile world. The Valentinians, for example, according to Tertullian (*Scorpiace* 10.1), taught that one need not confess Christ before the civil orders on earth, but only before the heavenly *archontes*. In this case, other Gnostics thought differently.

Defining identity: The construction of the two-part Christian Bible made up of Old and New Testaments clarified what linked Christians to Jews and what separated them. With the Jews they shared the Old Testament, and with it faith in the one God and obedience to his commandments. Separating them from the Jews were the New Testament and its faith in Christ as the fulfillment of the Old Testament expectations. Christians added their New Testament to the Old in the awareness that historically the New Testament is the fulfillment and hermeneutically it is the key to the Old Testament. It was regarded as superior to the Old Testament. The Gnostic writings, in contrast, did not place themselves within the existing Jewish and Gentile traditions, but reevaluated all of them boldly as "proto-exegesis." The seductive serpent in Paradise became the voice of the Redeemer, the one and only God a diminished demiurge, Judas the beloved disciple of Jesus. The Old Testament was rather violently reinterpreted. It must have been difficult for the world outside to recognize the religious identity of such Gnostics in relation to the pluralistic religious world known to them.

Regulating conflicts: The canon was also a basis for determining the limits of consensus. It permitted a great variety of convictions but marked criteria for those that were to be rejected. With the construction of the canon, rejection of the Old Testament was disallowed, against Marcion, as well as all attempts to deny the unity of the creator God and the God of redemption. Irenaeus sees it as characteristic of the heretics that they rely respectively on only one gospel, and he makes some fine distinctions: the Ebionites use only Matthew, Marcion mangles Luke, the Docetists prefer Mark to the other gospels, and the Valentinians use John most intensively (*Haer.* 3.11.7).[45] From one point of view, the Gnostic scriptures even intensified conflict by harshly despising ordinary members of the community. The latter were seen as limited *simplices* who think they are praying to the Creator of heaven and earth but in reality are worshiping an ignorant demiurge. We need not imagine any process of repression to make it understandable that the despised members of the community never regarded the Gnostic writings as their sacred scriptures. Those writings lacked any social-integrative feature that could join all Christians together.

Structures of authority: The canon became one of the most important authoritative supports for Christianity, alongside office and the *regula fidei*, that is, the formulations of a consensus of faith by the great theologians of the ancient church. In this the canon was by no means a conservative power; in the course of church history it has often proved to be the basis for critical movements. It contained many unwieldy teachings and traditions that became sacrosanct through canonization and have repeatedly brought about unrest among Christians. For ordinary people that unrest was often caused by the ethical radicality of the Jesus tradition, which was crucial for monks and poor peoples' movements; for theological intellectuals like Augustine, Luther, and Karl Barth, in contrast, the theological upset proceeded primarily from Paul. We find nothing in the Gnostic writings that could have led to the establishment of enduring structures of authority. They applied the same contempt to bishops and community leaders as to ordinary Christians.

All these social factors played a role in the establishment of the canon, which was thus able to succeed without force or compulsion. Writings that could fulfill all five functions had a much better chance of being canonized than did others. In the process, one-sided writings could also be inserted by consensus within the framework of the canon. In any case, the canon contains not only limitations on intra-church plurality but also the acknowledgment of it, without which the church would have become a sect. Against Marcion, the plurality of gospels, the plurality of letter writers, and the plurality of the two testaments was accepted. Without the model of the Septuagint, with its great internal multiplicity, this is scarcely imaginable, since in fact the tendency in antiquity was to see truth in unity.[46]

c. *Contingent Historical Factors as a Force for Canonization*

Optimal cognitive opportunities for dissemination and social functionality do not completely explain the construction of a canon. A good many "orthodox" writings were not considered for inclusion. They were not separated from the canon by suppression, but continued to exist alongside it. Beyond the canonical scriptures that were read publicly in worship there was a growing Christian literature for private reading or the preparation of catechumens. Among these writings, it would have been the *Didache*, the *Letter of Barnabas,* and the *Apocalypse of Peter* that had the best chance of being accepted into the canon, since they claimed apostolic origin: the *Didache* was considered the "teaching of the twelve apostles" and Barnabas was the contemporary and traveling companion of Paul known to us from the New Testament. The *Apocalypse of Peter* was part of the *Corpus Petrinum*. None of these three writings developed offensive heresies, even though the church order in the *Didache* gives the impression of being archaic, the *Letter of Barnabas* deals with the Old Testament in independent fashion, and the visions of hell in the *Apocalypse of Peter* are grotesque. We must suppose here that there were some contingent factors in the construction of the canon. To put it another way: the structuring of the canon could have led to other results. In what follows we will discuss briefly the most important of these non-canonized writings that had a genuine chance of being accepted into the canon.

Eusebius (beginning of the fourth century) includes the *Didache* among the disputed writings, from which we may conclude that it was recognized as canonical in some places (*Hist. eccl.* 3.25.4). It was kept separate from the canon but was not suppressed: Athanasius recommended it (mid-fourth century) as reading for catechumens alongside the canonical scriptures. In the list of the sixty canonical books (seventh century) and that of the *Stichometry of Nicephoros* (ninth century) it appears among the apocryphal writings.[47] How little suppression it experienced is shown by the fact that it was used as a source for the *Apostolic Constitutions* and was copied in a Byzantine manuscript, the Codex Hierosolymitanus 54, written in 1056. It was difficult for the *Didache* to become part of the canon because, as a church order, it would have been unique within the New Testament, without a model in the Old Testament and without parallels among the acknowledged New Testament writings. Like Acts, Hebrews, and Revelation, it would have belonged to the singularly attested genres, but it was not as closely linked to other canonical writings as Acts was with Luke, Hebrews with the *Corpus Paulinum*, or Revelation with the *Corpus Iohanneum*.

The *Letter of Barnabas* was also regarded as canonical in some regions. It is retained as an appendix to Codex Sinaiticus, together with the *Shepherd of Hermas,* which means that it was also used in worship. Its position at the end of the codex, however, shows that there was awareness of its special position in contrast to the other letters. Clement of Alexandria undoubtedly associated it with the biblical writings (Eusebius, *Hist. eccl.* 2.14) and Origen called it a "catholic letter" (*Cels.* 1.63). Otherwise, it is counted sometimes among the disputed writings (Eusebius, *Hist. eccl.* 6.13.6; 6.14.1; *Stichometry of Nicephoros*) and sometimes among the apocrypha (Eusebius, *Hist. eccl.* 3.25.4; list of the sixty canonical books). Its non-canonization limited, but did not prevent, its circulation: it was copied in the eleventh century in northern France in Latin and in the Byzantine Empire in Greek (in the Codex Hierosolymitanus 54, mentioned above). The *Letter of Barnabas* was therefore not so much excluded from a canonical collection; rather, attempts to include it subsequently were not successful. And that is understandable: Barnabas was not an apostle, but the disciple of an apostle. No letter from an apostle's disciple was canonized. All the canonical letters have apostles as their authors. On the other hand, Clement of Alexandria, who counted the *Letter of Barnabas* among the biblical books, regarded him as an "apostle." According to Clement, he was not, of course, one of the twelve apostles, but was one of the seventy whom Jesus sent out according to Luke 10:1-20 (Eusebius, *Hist. eccl.* 2.14).

First Clement is found, together with *Second Clement,* in an appendix to Codex Alexandrinus (fifth century) after Revelation. The two letters are placed in the table of contents alongside the other canonical books, but their separation from the other letters shows an awareness of their special position. In Alexandria and Syria they were regarded by some communities as part of the canon: Clement of Alexandria frequently cites *1 Clement*. For him Clement is an "apostle" (*Strom.* 4.105.1). In one Syrian manuscript the two letters of Clement are placed between the catholic letters and the Pauline letters. Eusebius testifies that *1 Clement* "has been publicly used in a great many churches both in former times and in our own" (*Hist. eccl.* 3.16), but he does not include it among the disputed books. In terms of its content there would be nothing to object to; its grounding of the apostolic succession of offices and defense of the idea that holders of those offices could not be deposed would even have been useful for legitimizing control within the church. And yet the two letters of Clement had no chance in the long run of being accepted into the canon: they did not have an apostolic author. That does not mean, however, that they were suppressed.[48]

Now and again the *Apocalypse of Peter* was counted among the canonical scriptures, for example in the canonical list of Codex Claromontanus and by Clement of Alexandria (Eusebius, *Hist. eccl.* 6.14.1). But as early as the Muratorian Fragment, for Eusebius, and in the *Stichometry of Nicephoros,* it was regarded as disputed. It was handed on in the Ethiopian church. Did the drastic and altogether too vivid depiction of the pains of hell put obstacles in the path of its acceptance? Certainly the moralistic tone of the depiction of hell would not have been as disturbing to ancient readers as to those in modern times; in fact, the document adopted well-known ideas of the world beyond from Orphic-Pythagorean tradition—with long-term consequences even as late as Dante's *Divine Comedy*. The fact that the *Apocalypse of Peter,* despite its "apostolic" authorship, did not make it into the canon may be connected with the fact that it simply was written too late (ca. 135 C.E.).

The *Acts of Paul* appear as part of the canon only in the canonical list in Codex Claromontanus. Origen treasured them, and Eusebius places them among the disputed books. The reason for their rejection lies in their content. Tertullian wrote of them in about 200 C.E.: "But if the writings which wrongly go under Paul's name claim Thecla's example as a license for women's teaching and baptizing, let them know that, in Asia, the presbyter who composed that writing, as if he were augmenting Paul's fame from his own store, after being convicted, and confessing that he had done it from love of Paul, was removed from his office" (Tertullian, *Bapt.* 17). Here cultural power shoved a writing aside, because in the *Acts of Paul and Thecla* we find objection to the exclusion of women from offices of church leadership—in direct material opposition to the Pastorals.[49]

The *Shepherd of Hermas* was also very popular. In Codex Sinaiticus it follows the *Letter of Barnabas.* In the canonical list in Codex Claromontanus it appears in an appendix after the New Testament books. Eusebius knows of communities in which it is publicly read (Eusebius, *Hist. eccl.* 3.3.6). Athanasius recommends it as reading for catechumens. But despite its popularity it had no real chance of becoming part of the canon, since the Muratorian Fragment already says, "but Hermas wrote the Shepherd very recently, in our times, in the city of Rome, while bishop Pius, his brother, was occupying the [episcopal] chair of the church of the city of Rome. And therefore it ought indeed to be read; but it cannot be read publicly to the people in church either among the Prophets, whose number is complete, or among the Apostles, for it is after [their] time."

With regard to the apocryphal gospels (or those that became apocryphal) it is more difficult to say why they did not enter the canon, for they were long read in individual communities and groups. However, the four-gospel canon, with gospels from the first century, was such an early success that the gospels written later, in the second century, had no further chance of acceptance. In some apocryphal gospels there are clear motifs that account for their not being generally received, but for most we can only offer suppositions—not least because we often possess only fragments of these gospels.

Thus we hear that in a community in Rhossos near Antioch around 200 c.e. a gospel of Peter was read. It was at first accepted by Bishop Serapion of Antioch, but was then rejected because of its Docetic teachings (Eusebius, *Hist. eccl.* 6.12.3-6). The parts of the *Gospel of Peter* that remain to us are not Docetic, but in some places could be interpreted as Docetic if one were to read them with the presupposition that Jesus was not a real human being. The burden on the *Gospel of Peter* was, fundamentally, that Docetists appealed to it. That is how Serapion describes it: "For having obtained this gospel from others who had studied it diligently, namely, from the successors of those who first used it, whom we call Docetæ, we have been able to read it through, and we find many things in accordance with the true doctrine of the Saviour, but some things added to that doctrine" (Eusebius, *Hist. eccl.* 6.12.6).

The case of the *Gospel of the Egyptians* is similar. Radical ascetics who fundamentally rejected marriage appealed to this gospel. Clement of Alexandria wanted to protect the gospel against this ascetic interpretation, but the fragments he quotes seem to favor the idea that it did in fact represent a radical doctrine of salvation aimed at overcoming the difference of the sexes through ascesis. There is also an indirect indication in the name *Gospel of the Egyptians,* which was probably an outsider's designation. The gospel is regarded as belonging to a limited ethnic group; it remained tied to that group and was known only in the East. But that would not be an adequate reason for its "failure": the letter to the Hebrews, after all, did make its way into the canon even though it was seen as a letter to a particular ethnic group among Christians.

The Jewish-Christian gospels were also limited to particular groups, as indicated by their designation as the gospels of the Hebrews, the Nazarenes, and the Ebionites. Jerome became familiar with the *Gospel of the Nazarenes* among Jewish Christians from Berea in Syria. He regarded it as a variant of Matthew's Gospel (*Vir. ill.* 3). Further developments of this broadly disseminated and highly regarded gospel had little chance of being received alongside the acknowledged Gospel of Matthew. Tendencies that were not undisputed among Christians—such as the vegetarianism of the *Gospel of the Ebionites*—could have represented an additional obstacle for their dissemination. Once the ties to the marginal groups of Jewish Christians became irreversible, these writings shared the fate of their supporting groups: they remained marginal phenomena. Probably these Jewish-Christian gospels circulated primarily in the East. If it is true that the canon was based on a consensus between Rome and Asia Minor in the second century they had little chance of canonization from the start.

The same is true for the *Gospel of Thomas*. The Thomas tradition had a local focus in eastern Syria. Quite apart from this localization at the margins, it was a gospel of the "solitaries" (*Gos. Thom.* 18; 49; 75), not a book that was basic to a community. It advocated an individualistic mysticism and gave the traditional sayings of Jesus a mysterious aura in light of that mysticism. It could easily fall prey to the suspicion of being a Gnostic book—and in fact modern exegetes were probably not the first to interpret Gnostic systems into these fascinating words of Jesus. This gospel, too, remained the property of small groups in the East.

All these gospels appealed to the authority of Jesus and made partial claims to apostolic origins. Their theology fits within the spectrum of theological doctrines then in circulation. They do not offend against the basic consensus of faith in one God and the incarnation of the Redeemer. Most of them, it is true, were accused (rightly or wrongly) of being gospels especially for Docetics, ascetics, vegetarians, and mystics. The fact that they were associated with groups that were marginal, that is, Jewish Christians and Gnostics, restricted their chance of circulation. But this preference of marginal groups for particular gospels applied also to the canonical gospels. We should recall that, according to Irenaeus, the Ebionites preferred the Gospel of Matthew, the Marcionites the Gospel of Luke, the Docetists the Gospel of Mark, and the Valentinians the Gospel of John (*Haer.* 3.11.7). The claiming of a gospel by a deviant minority (or by "heretics") could thus not be in itself a definitive reason for rejecting such gospels.

There remain, then, two contingent factors: most of these gospels remained limited to localities in the East, mainly Syria and Egypt. But decisions about the content of the canon were made more often in the West, between Rome and Asia Minor. To these geographical factors was added a chronological one: the *Shepherd of Hermas* had no chance of being canonized because it was obviously created after the canon-building period of the apostles (and apostolic disciples). The same was true of the letters of Ignatius. They have an impressive theological profile, but they clearly come from Bishop Ignatius of Antioch, who suffered martyrdom in Rome between 107 and 110 C.E. It is true that the time of origin of the gospels that remained apocryphal is not precisely determinable, but *de facto* many of them were from the second century C.E. Early datings have for the most part not been sustainable and were all too often shaped by the desire to find ancient sources that would offer access to the historical Jesus independently of the canonical gospels. But the gospels that remained apocryphal are clearly documents of a clash over the image of Jesus in the second–third centuries C.E., and not sources for the history of Jesus in the first century C.E. The canonized writings had a temporal advantage over them and in many places successfully occupied the place reserved for gospels (for use in worship). What once becomes liturgically familiar is hard to change. This explains why unknown gospels had such a hard time finding a place for themselves—but also why they were used for a long time in some places.

If we consider the further destiny of all these "excluded" writings, that is, the scriptures that in some communities enjoyed a locally limited canonical status but did not enter the common canon, we cannot say that they were "suppressed." They continued to be read and were often very popular alongside the canonical scriptures, as in the case of the *Shepherd of Hermas,* which has come down to us in many manuscripts. Some of them would have been outstandingly suitable for establishing rank and order within the church. This is true especially of *1 Clement*, with its advocacy for the succession and non-removal of church officials, and of the letters of Ignatius, which advocated for the monarchical episcopate. If the exercise of power and censorship had been the decisive factors in establishing the canon, these writings would have had a foremost place in the canon. Instead, its center is the gospels, with their tendencies to critique authority. Our conclusion is that the construction of the canon was certainly associated with power and "suppression," but it was not so much the power of institutions and offices as it was the strength of deeply rooted basic cognitive structures in our minds, the so-called social-functional necessities, and the influence of contingent local and temporal circumstances.

20 Extra-Canonical Literature Provides Flexibility

Canonization furnishes stability. By building canons, minorities can preserve their identity and thus immunize their convictions against tendencies to dissolution and accommodation. The downside of such processes of canonization is a loss of creativity and vitality. Ongoing history produces challenges that can no longer be met with the convictions of the past. Every living tradition must thus add flexibility to stability. Early Christianity was affected by this profile in only limited ways. It lived with the existing canon of the Old Testament but had never bound itself unconditionally to its "sacred scriptures." There was an early consensus that the sacrificial laws were passé and that the Old Testament must be read anew in light of the revelation of Christ. Without Christ it remained under a veil (2 Cor 3:12-18). The early Christians placed their convictions above the Old Testament, but they found value in deriving them and legitimating them from it. They expressed their faith primarily in the production of an abundance of new writings that were set alongside the acknowledged Old Testament scriptures. Only toward the end of early Christianity can we discern the beginnings of a canon by means of which some writings were set apart as normative guidelines and the writing of newer normative and formational scriptures was regarded as impossible. The beginnings of this canonical structuring are attested primarily in the "West," especially Rome and Asia Minor, the home of Irenaeus. In the East, by the end of the second century C.E., people were still relatively generous toward the later gospels that remained apocryphal, as shown by the way Clement of Alexandria and Serapion of Antioch dealt with them. In any case, what was characteristic of early Christianity until about 180 C.E. was the origination of a new literature. This was the flexible element alongside the stability of the "Old Testament" Bible. With the canonization of a selection of those writings, the end of early Christianity was beginning.

The literary history of the New Testament is therefore only part of a history of early Christian literature, which comprised far more than the twenty-seven canonized writings in the New Testament. The production of writings continued beyond those twenty-seven. Our task is to summarize the non-canonical literature of early Christianity in groups and thus to understand all the writings that are dependent on the New Testament for their form and content and that draw on the same store of forms and motifs as do the writings in the New Testament. Only when a clear transition in forms and motifs is discernible can we speak of a patristic literature. But there is a further transitional field here. The question, then, is whether we can interpret the non-canonical early Christian writings as a continuation of the forms and tendencies we have encountered in the four phases of the history of the New Testament literature, and whether this literature retained the creative impulse of early Christianity. Within the framework of this programmatic proposal for a literary history of the New Testament, the answer to these questions can only be given in outline.

New Creations by New Charismatic Authors

Were there individual figures besides Jesus and Paul in early Christianity who, by the strength of a non-rational aura, shaped and exercised literary influence on the formal language of early Christianity? That is undoubtedly the case. We can distinguish two groups of authors known to us by name: bishops and teachers. To the extent that this literature was created by strong personalities it could dispense with pseudepigraphy. The authors wrote under their own names.

Church Officials

One of the best-delineated figures is Ignatius, the bishop of Antioch. Besides Jesus and Paul he is one of the outstanding figures in early Christianity who stand out as individuals. His seven letters give us an insight into a marginal situation in his life: the bishop of Antioch was being taken as a prisoner to Rome to be executed, and during this time he wrote to the communities in Asia Minor. He is clearly distinct from the two founding figures of early Christianity, Jesus and Paul. He did not craft any new forms, but continued existing ones: Paul, as letter writer and martyr, was his model. He presents new impulses not literarily, but theologically, through his insistence on the reality of the incarnation, his ideas about church unity, his advocacy for the three-level structure of office including bishops, presbyters, and deacons, and his theology of martyrdom. In literary terms, however, he imitates the *Corpus Paulinum* in that, alongside his community letters, he writes his "Pastoral" as a letter to Polycarp, with practical advice for community life!

The second such charismatic was Polycarp, the bishop of Smyrna, who reworks set pieces from Pauline literature in his letter. There is no truly new literary or theological impulse to be found in that letter, but his teaching, like his life, is impressive for its integrity. Like Ignatius, he died a martyr's death and thus obtained a charism beyond his "authority of office" that exercised influence beyond his death. By that very fact he indirectly initiated new literature: the story of his martyrdom was the beginning of the new genre of martyrdom accounts. Early Christian literature continued to live in these accounts through the use of motifs from the passion narrative. The martyrs are depicted as successors to Christ in his passion. The account of Polycarp's martyrdom is formally a letter of the community in Smyrna to that in the city of Philomelium in Asia Minor, and as such is an imitation of *1 Clement* (see below). But, unlike *1 Clement*, it is at the same time explicitly addressed to all Christian communities (*Mart. Pol.* 1).

We may perhaps add the author of *1 Clement* to the list of church officials with charismatic influence, even though the letter does not name him as its author. The earliest attribution to Clement is found in a letter from Dionysios of Corinth in about 170 C.E. (see Eusebius, *Hist. eccl.* 4.23.11). According to Irenaeus, Clement was the third successor to the apostles Peter and Paul in Rome (*Haer.* 3.3.3). He cannot have been the bishop there, since the Roman community maintained collegial leadership for a long time afterward. He may instead have been the one responsible for external correspondence, since a Clement with that office is mentioned in the Shepherd of Hermas (*Herm. Vis.* 2.4.3). His letter, like the martyrdom of Polycarp and the letter of the Christians in Lyons (Eusebius, *Hist. eccl.* 5.1-3), is a community letter in a twofold sense: it is addressed not only to the whole community in Corinth, in whose internal conflicts he grossly intervenes, but also is a letter of the whole community in Rome. He knows Paul's letter to the Romans and the first to the Corinthians and uses them as a formal inspiration. But something new appears here: a long, artistically structured and rhetorically fashioned document on church politics. While Paul's letters shaped letters of friendship into community letters by means of liturgical and rhetorical stylization, the community letter is made a matter of course in *1 Clement*. The liturgical and rhetorical styling are increased in comparison to the New Testament letters; consider only the long rhetorical series of paradigms, for example, on the deadly consequences of jealousy and envy at the beginning (*1 Clem.* 4–8) and the liturgical community prayer at the end (*1 Clem.* 59:3—61:3). One may point to the letters for community leadership in Judaism as formal predecessors to *1 Clement*.[1]

Christian Teachers

New literary beginnings in the second century are much more common among early Christian teachers—theological intellectuals who inhabited no (high) church leadership office but advocated for Christian faith by their teaching. These first "philosophers" of Christian faith also adapted genres common to general literature for their purposes. They developed the apology, the dialogue, and the commentary. Here we can distinguish two very different groups of teachers: the apologists and the Gnostics.

The apologetic teachers: To Aristides, the "philosopher of Athens" (Eusebius, *Hist. eccl.* 4.3.3) we owe the first completely preserved apology, in which the superiority of Christian belief in God, as that of a "new people" distinct from Jews and Gentiles, is presented with great confidence. Justin, who also regarded himself as a Christian philosopher, wrote two "apologies." He acknowledges a kernel of truth among Jews and Greeks: the *logos spermatikos*. He regards Abraham and Socrates as Christians before Christ. Unlike Aristides, he draws extensively on the Old Testament and the gospels. In his *Dialogue with Trypho* the demonstration from prophecy plays a significant role: he discusses the Old Testament with a Jew learned in the scriptures. The apologists sought to give their external world a rational depiction of Christianity. In their writings they attempted to present a "Christianity for its cultivated despisers," if you like: a reasonable Christianity for beginners.

The Gnostic teachers: Many of these teachers and philosophers were fascinated by *gnōsis*, the first attempt to think through Christianity in systematic theological terms. Here we find formulated a Christianity designed above all for the advanced, for people who were unsatisfied by mere faith and wanted to understand what they believed—and who therefore moved on to a bold mystical-speculative reinterpretation of Christian belief. For the first time since Paul, here the Christian message was consistently thought through from a single center. In these writings an "exploded" Platonism runs throughout the biblical tradition and leads to the first attempts at a Christian Platonist synthesis. The two great leaders of early Gnosticism, Valentinus and Basilides, were very productive writers, but only fragments of their writings have survived. Basilides wrote one of the first commentaries on a gospel. The Gnostics invented the new form of the dialogue gospel, the "conversation of the disciples with the Risen One." This was supremely useful for formulating further special revelations beyond the teachings of the earthly Jesus as a "second teaching" for the advanced.[2] But the Gnostics also spread their traditions in traditional forms. The *Gospel of Truth* is a discourse. Ptolemaeus wrote a letter to Flora on the validity of the Old Testament laws in which he distinguishes the pure law of God from the law of

Moses and that of the Jewish elders. Within the law of God he further distinguishes between the Decalogue, the law of talion (now abrogated), and the cultic laws, which since the coming of Christ are to be understood only symbolically. The *Letter to Rheginus* is a tract on the resurrection. Such tracts in letter form may be seen as the continuation of early Christian genres.

In both the apologists and the "Gnostics" we find attempts to give a rational depiction of Christianity within the framework of contemporary discourse—with the distinguishing factor that the apologists directed their attempts outward while the Gnostics did so much more inward, since they advocated a Christianity for the "advanced." In their content also they represented opposing tendencies: the apologists to an affirmation of a creation interpenetrated with the *Logos*, the Gnostics to a radical devaluation of this world. Both groups, however, by dint of their education, adapted common literary forms. There were models of apologies, dialogues, and commentaries in the ancient pagan world.

New Creations in the Form of Additional Pseudepigraphic Writings

Many authors of the later period of early Christianity did not write under their own names, but instead continued the second, pseudepigraphic phase of New Testament literature. Still, their emphases have shifted. The writing of pseudepigraphic letters diminished while the writing of gospels increased, and apocryphal stories of the apostles flourished only after the period of early Christianity. In addition, we can determine a "hierarchy of rank" among the pseudonymous authors. The name of Paul is less often adopted than in the first century C.E., while the name of Peter gained in pseudepigraphic attraction. There was a positive renaissance in Petrine literature. But the Pauline and Petrine literature was exceeded by the apocryphal Jesus literature, which is attributed to a number of different vehicles of tradition. Its crowning period was the second century; at the end of that century, with the flourishing of apocryphal apostolic literature, a new development again began: a kind of Christian novelistic literature for entertainment.

Apocryphal Pauline Literature

While the many pseudepigraphic Pauline letters in the second half of the first century made that period a springtime of Pauline literature—when within a short time the letters to the Colossians and Ephesians were created, along with 2 Thessalonians, the Pastorals, and Hebrews—in the second century the name of Paul lost its pseudepigraphic creative power:

only a few letters were falsified under his name after 100 C.E. The Muratorian Fragment mentions two letters of Paul forged by the Marcionites, to the Alexandrians and to the Laodiceans. In the latter case this may have been a misunderstanding. Probably Marcion identified Ephesians as the letter to the Laodiceans mentioned in Colossians 4:16. There remains only the letter to the Alexandrians, which has not survived. Of course, the "orthodox" also forged Pauline writings to combat those who in their eyes were "heretics." But only two of these can be dated with relative security to the second century C.E. Third Corinthians is a part of the *Acts of Paul,* created in the late second century; it contends against those who deny the resurrection and the incarnation (3.1-40). The *Acts of Paul* correct (in vain) the image of Paul in the Pastorals, a Paul who admitted no women to office in the church. As regards a brief letter to the Laodiceans that has survived in a Latin version, it is not certain whether it originated in the second century C.E. Datings extend into the fourth century. It is intended, like the Marcionite letter to the Laodiceans mentioned above, to fill the gap left by the reference to a no longer surviving letter of Paul to the Laodiceans mentioned in Colossians 4:16. In the West it made its way into a number of Latin biblical manuscripts, even though its content is without originality and is laced with Pauline phrases from Philippians. It warns broadly against some people's empty talk. Other Pauline literature was certainly created after the period of early Christianity: an *Apocalypse of Paul* was discovered in Tarsus in 388. It paints the assumption of Paul into Paradise according to 2 Corinthians 12, even though supposedly Paul heard only inexpressible words there. The discovery was probably staged. It was said that an angel had appeared in a dream and urged the dreamer to seek a writing in the foundations of Paul's house. Probably this apocalypse originated shortly before its discovery. Interesting from a literary-historical point of view is the exchange of letters between Paul and Seneca from the same century, whereby Paul is located, even in antiquity, within the literary history of his times—unmistakably in the awareness that his letters are not part of great literature. Seneca praises their content but criticizes their clumsy manner of expression. He even claims to have read them aloud to Nero (Letter 7). A letter from Paul's disciple Titus comes from the fifth century and combats "spiritual marriage," unmarried couples' living together while deliberately abstaining from sexual intercourse. Is the falling off in production of pseudepigraphic Pauline letters in the second century an accident? In the case of forged letters the intent to deceive is much greater than in the case of tracts and narratives, in which often a false name as *inscriptio* or *subscriptio* suffices. Letters, however, require an epistolary frame that may, of course, as in the letter of James or that of Barnabas, remain formal, but that only suggests genuineness if it causes the reader to perceive a concrete situation. For that purpose false names, places, and times and situations must be invented in order to lead readers astray. Was there, perhaps, a certain reluctance to produce such thorough forgeries in too great a number? Or was it more difficult to bring forged Pauline letters into circulation at a later date? One of the few cases of an uncovered forgery in the ancient church was the *Acts of Paul*: a presbyter in Asia Minor is supposed to have admitted having written them out of love for Paul (Tertullian, *Bapt.* 17).

Apocryphal Petrine Literature

The decline of Paul also signals a wavering "market value" in great names. His competitor, Peter, experienced a pseudepigraphic renaissance in a flourishing Petrine literature.[3] Of the writings then created in Peter's name, only 2 Peter achieved entry into the canon, but not the other writings that corresponded formally to other parts of the canon: the *Gospel of Peter,* the *Kerygma Petri*, the *Acts of Peter,* and the *Apocalypse of Peter.* The posthumous rise of Peter, the first among the apostles, is understandable: the farther one moves from the origins, the more desire there is to buttress the truth of the tradition through authoritative "eyewitnesses." Even the pseudo-Peter of 2 Peter affirms for his fellow Christians in unique fashion in the New Testament that "we did not follow cleverly devised myths (*mythoi*)," but were "eyewitnesses of his majesty" on the Mount of Transfiguration (2 Pet 1:16). The *Gospel of Peter* is written partly in the first person singular and thus suggests a false proximity to the historical events. The same is true of the *Apocalypse of Peter,* where Peter, speaking in the first person, is the crucial vehicle of revelation. Even the *Kerygma Petri*, only fragments of which have survived in the work of Clement of Alexandria, perhaps desired to be an "authentic" summary of Christian preaching with apologetic intent. Here the Christians appear as a "third race."

Apocryphal Gospel Literature

As the production of pseudepigraphic letters declined, the production of gospels rose. The second century is the apex of Jesus literature, far surpassing in number the examples of Pauline and Petrine literature. In this regard we have to consider that behind every papyrus fragment there could be an entire gospel, even though that is never certain. A number of papyrus fragments could belong to the same gospel, or some could be quotations from a gospel or interpretations of gospels. The following list of fourteen gospels is therefore burdened by uncertainties. Common to all is that they offer segments from the life and teaching of the earthly Jesus, not revelations of the Risen One after his death.[4]

1. Papyrus Egerton 2 (PEg 2) contains four pericopes from the life of Jesus, some of them Synoptic, others Johannine, still others of unknown origin and influence.
2. Oxyrhynchus Papyrus 840 (POxy 840) contains the story of a clash between Jesus and a high priest in the temple over questions of purity.
3. The Strasburg Coptic Papyrus consists of fragments of a farewell prayer of Jesus and a visionary experience by the disciples.
4. The *Gospel of Marcion* is a continuation of Luke's Gospel without the infancy narrative, purified of supposed Jewish falsifications.
5. The *Gospel of the Nazarenes* (*Gos. Naz.*) is a Jewish-Christian continuation of Matthew with a clearly social motive.
6. The *Gospel of the Ebionites* (*Gos. Eb.*) is probably also a Jewish-Christian continuation of Matthew, with traces of an early Christian vegetarianism.
7. The *Gospel of the Hebrews* (*Gos. Heb.*) is a Jewish-Christian continuation of the Synoptic Gospels with gnosticizing features.
8. The *Gospel of Peter* (*Gos. Pet.*) contains parts of the passion narrative with Synoptic and Johannine features, including an eyewitness description of the resurrection.
9. The Unknown Berlin Gospel (UBG = PBerol 22220) contains farewell discourses of Jesus and a heavenly journey by the disciples, perhaps a continuation of the *Gospel of Peter.*
10. The *Gospel of the Egyptians* (*Gos. Eg.*) is a gospel with ascetic tendencies.
11. Tatian's *Diatessaron* is a gospel harmony of the Synoptics, with John's Gospel as a frame.
12. The *Gospel of Thomas* (*Gos. Thom.*) consists of a gnosticizing account of Jesus' sayings—perhaps based on Tatian's *Diatessaron*?
13. The *Gospel of Philip* (*Gos. Phil.*) may be a *florilegium* of Gnostic Jesus traditions, probably written after the second century.
14. The *Gospel of Judas* (*Gos. Jud.*) contains parts of the passion narrative and a Gnostic reinterpretation of the event: Judas is the chosen Gnostic disciple who opens the way to salvation.[5]

In all these gospels the fictive self-interpretation of Jesus is carried further. Most of them clearly presume the gospels that were later canonized.

The precondition for this revival of gospel literature is the continuation of oral tradition alongside the gospels now fixed in writing. The first Christians were aware, well into the second century, that the written gospels did not contain everything Jesus had said. The conclusion of John's Gospel encouraged them to continue writing new gospels, or at least it legitimated such a practice, even though John's Gospel intends mainly to say that it in itself offers the decisive truth about Jesus, namely, the testimony of the Beloved Disciple. Since the living "word of the Lord" was more highly valued, well into the second century, than the written word, it was understandable that Jesus spoke again and again anew even outside the gospels already known. This multifaceted "apocryphal" Jesus always proclaimed what the group supporting this gospel, and to which it was addressed, held to be most vital. One gospel was written that spoke mainly to mystics (*Gos. Thom.*), another chiefly for ascetics (*Gos. Eg.*), a third for vegetarians (*Gos. Eb.*), a fourth especially for women (*Gospel of Mary*), another that could particularly address radical Gnostics (*Gos. Jud.*), even if these gospels may have had influence beyond such narrow reference groups. The names of the gospels often point to groups in which the particular gospel was read, and are thus probably outsiders' designations. The real author, independently of the various gospel names, is in principle always Jesus himself—as he appears in the light of different trajectories of belief that appealed for their image of Jesus to various disciples or Mary Magdalene as authorities.

The Gnostic authors were aware that in their writings they went beyond what had been circulated as Jesus' message. This led to a shift in literary form. The form in which Jesus was presented by Gnosis was the "dialogue gospel," in which secret revelations of the Risen One were disclosed to his disciples, going beyond what the earthly Jesus had taught all the disciples and that was therefore accessible to all Christians. These dialogue gospels were not intended to replace the known gospels, but to augment them with a deeper revelation. The *Sophia Jesu Christi* was probably the prototypical genre model for the dialogue gospel and was then followed by others: the *Book of Thomas,* the *Dialogue of the Savior,* the *Letter of James,* the *Letter of Peter to Philip,* the first and second *Apocalypse of James,* the *Gospel of Mary.* Altogether nearly twenty such dialogue gospels have survived. But in the middle of the second century an orthodox author also made use of the form of the dialogue gospel in the *Epistula Apostolorum*. All this wealth of Jesus literature has survived only in bits (either in the form of quotations by the church fathers or in papyrus fragments), or it was rediscovered accidentally in modern times. Most of the dialogue gospels we owe to the find at Nag Hammadi. Originally these books were indulged in the ancient church. Many were read, in addition to the gospels, in small circles of the Gnostic *illuminati*, but from the beginning they had no chance in the long run of establishing themselves in competition with the Synoptic Gospels and John.

However, one could augment the known gospels not only with revelations from the time after Jesus' resurrection but also with stories from the time before his public activity. The infancy gospels did not satisfy the desire for a more complete revelation, but instead provided pious entertainment. The *Protevangelium of James,* written between 150 and 200, is a Marian story. Jesus' miraculous birth is recounted. Although Mary has become pregnant while Joseph was away, a divine judgment confirms her fidelity. Even after the birth she remains a virgin. The birth of Jesus is enriched with legendary motifs. It takes place in a cave; all nature pauses. The *Infancy Gospel of Thomas*, by contrast, centers on the life of the growing boy Jesus. The story of the twelve-year-old Jesus in the temple inspired fable-rich imaginations to create a number of miracle novels in which Jesus succeeds through his wit, but also often with impudence and mischief against his father, his teacher, and his fellow scholars. Since Irenaeus knows one of the stories under the letter "A" (*Haer.* 1.20.1), this work may go back to the second century.

Apocryphal Acts of the Apostles

The flourishing of the (apocryphal) Jesus literature took place in the second century. Somewhat later, but still in the second century, began the springtime of apocryphal apostolic literature. The new acts of apostles were, form-critically speaking, not a continuation of the canonical Acts, even though they may have been inspired by that book. There are some obvious differences: the apocryphal apostolic acts end with the martyrdom of the apostles and to that extent take the gospels as their model. Acts, in contrast, ends with Paul preaching unhindered in Rome, despite his imprisonment. Also, the apocryphal acts each center on a single apostle, while the canonical Acts places two apostles as equals alongside one another: Peter dominates the first half and Paul the second. Additionally, the apocryphal acts of apostles contain motifs from ancient novels: the couple separated by misfortune keep celibate faith with one another despite temptations. The heroes and heroines of the apostolic acts therefore deny themselves all earthly partners in order to remain faithful to Jesus, the true bridegroom of the soul, with whom they are united at the end. The ethos (except in the *Clementines*) is very ascetic. Celibacy, virginity, and widowhood are the preferred ways of life. The apostolic acts have a Jewish predecessor in *Joseph and Aseneth,* the story of the Egyptian priest's daughter who falls in love with Joseph, converts to the Jewish faith, and accepts the break with her social world. Behind most of the apostolic acts is a subtle *gnōsis* that in these books, however, is not for the initiates; it is conveyed in popular and populist style for everyone. Miraculous events and rescues demonstrate the truth of the message.

The time and sequence of the origins of apostolic acts are disputed. Hans-Josef Klauck suggests the following chronology for the five major apostolic acts that have been salvaged for us by the Manicheans:[6]

1. *Acts of John* (ca. 150–160 C.E.)
2. *Acts of Paul* (ca. 170–180 C.E.)
3. *Acts of Peter* (ca. 190–200 C.E.)
4. *Acts of Andrew* (ca. 200–210 C.E.)
5. *Acts of Thomas* (ca. 220–240 C.E.)

In addition there are the Jewish-Christian *Clementines,* whose basic writing Klauck dates to 220–250 C.E.[7] Other apostolic acts were created still later, the *Acts of Philip* as late as 400.[8] According to Philipp Vielhauer, on the other hand, the *Acts of Peter,* written around 180/190, are the earliest apostolic acts.[9] He says that the *Acts of Paul* were created shortly before 200 C.E., and in the third century there followed the *Acts of Andrew, John, and Thomas.* Independently of such variation in dating, one may say that the springtime of the apocryphal acts of apostles was later than that of the apocryphal gospels. We may ask whether that was a consequence of the early closing of the gospel canon. When theology could no longer be successfully presented in new gospels, the theological imagination surrounding the apostolic figures became more powerful. In fact, in the apostolic acts they took the place of Jesus and were, like him, crucified and executed.

Add to this that the apocryphal acts of apostles are shaped, much more than are the apocryphal gospels, by a particular trajectory in piety. While there are some clear differences among the apostolic acts, we find an ascetic trend throughout almost all of them: true love for the bridegroom of the soul is played off against earthly love. Precisely for that reason everything is imbued with an erotic feeling. We find Gnostic ideas throughout. Women appear more independently than elsewhere. They have for the most part enjoyed advantages from the ascetic ideal propagated here.[10] The Manicheans loved, read, and handed down the five great apostolic acts. In them they found their dualistic-pessimistic view of the world confirmed. Probably they only transmitted the apostolic acts that fit with their theology, which may explain the unified theological mood in the apocryphal acts of apostles. But independently of that, the form also favored a particular theology: in their lives and deaths the apostles are images of Christ. Redemption takes place not through an objective event in salvation history but through discipleship and *imitatio Christi*. That corresponds to the Gnostic mentality. In contrast, a fundamental theological motive in the canonical Acts of the Apostles was to distinguish the apostles clearly from Christ: Christ alone is worthy of divine worship, not the apostles.

From a form-critical perspective the apocryphal apostolic acts are in any case Christian novels. This Christian entertainment literature adopted one of the great literary forms of antiquity, which arose only subsequent to the classic forms and therefore never found entry into the theories of higher literature. The fact that this pious entertainment literature bloomed within Christianity toward the end of the second century could be an indication that at the time Christianity was making inroads in classes with new literary requirements. Perhaps Eusebius is correct in writing that at the time of the emperor Commodus (180–192 C.E.) "now at Rome many who were highly distinguished for wealth and family turned with all their household and relatives unto their salvation" (*Hist. eccl.* 5.21.1). The *Life of Apollonius of Tyana* shows that in the upper classes at the beginning of the third century there was a taste for works with miracles and novelistic features in which an itinerant teacher presented his doctrine of salvation.

New Creations through Multiplication of Functional Genres

The largest part of the non-canonical early Christian scriptures continues a tendency that appears in the third, functional phase of the history of New Testament literature, in which sub-genres are made into independent genres. The following table shows that many of the early Christian writings can be understood (more or less) as continuations of the third phase of New Testament literary history. Writings we have already mentioned are found here, for the tendency to functional independence of literary forms and aims reveals itself both in the orthonymous and in the pseudonymous writings in the same way. It is perhaps the most striking characteristic of extra-canonical early Christian literature (Table 21).

For some of these new forms the connection to the New Testament models is tenuous—for example, in the acts of apostles, which are influenced by the ancient novel. Nevertheless, the shift of forms in the apocryphal early Christian literature was caused not only by borrowing from forms in the literary environment: partial texts and aspects of New Testament texts became differentiated as independent texts because of material necessity. More and more differentiated needs had to be met with specialized literary forms. The authority of the form gained increasing weight over the authority of persons. In the process, the orientation to genres and forms had

Table 21: Canonical and Apocryphal Literature

Sub-genre or Aspect in New Testament Literature	Independence in Later Earliest and Early Christian Literature
Community letter from an apostle	*Community letter from a congregation*
Paul's letters as expanded letters of friendship	*1 Clement*
Discourses	*Discourses*
1 Corinthians 1–4: the teaching of the cross	Letter to the Hebrews
	2 Clement
Five discourses of Jesus in Matthew's Gospel	*Gospel of Truth*
	Kerygma Petri (?)
Farewell discourses in John 14–16	Paschal Homily of Melito of Sardis
	Tatian, *Speech to the Greeks*
Community rules	*Community orders*
Matthew 18: community discourse	*Didache*
1–2 Timothy	Syrian *Didaskalia*
	Hippolytus's church order
Apocalyptic texts	*Apocalypses*
Synoptic apocalypse: Mark 13	Revelation (Apocalypse of John)
2 Thessalonians 2:1-12	*Shepherd of Hermas*
	Apocalypse of Peter
	Ascension of Isaiah
	Book of Elkasai
Jesus' teachings to his disciples about community	*Dialogues of the Savior*
	Sophia Jesu Christi
Secret teachings in Mark	*Apocryphon of John*
Farewell discourses in John	*Epistula Apostolorum*, Freer Logion
	Gospel of Mary
	Letter of Peter to Philip
	Dialogue of the Savior
	First Apocalypse of James
	Letter of James
	Book of Thomas
Infancy narratives	*Infancy Gospels*
Matthew 1–2	*Protevangelium of James*
Luke 1–3	*Infancy Gospel of Thomas*
Sayings compositions	*Collections of sayings*
Sayings Source	*Gospel of Thomas*
Sermon on the Mount	*Gospel of Philip*
	Sayings of Sextus

Sub-genre or Aspect in New Testament Literature	**Independence in Later Earliest and Early Christian Literature**
Passion narrative	*Accounts of the martyrs*
Jesus' passion in the gospels	*Martyrdom of Polycarp*
Passion of John the Baptizer (Mark 6:21-29)	*Martyrdom of Justin*
	Martyrdom of the Scilitan Martyrs
Martyrdom of Stephen (Acts 6:8–7:60)	
Hymns	*Hymn collection*
Philippians hymn (Phil 2:5-11)	Odes of Solomon
Colossians hymn (Col 1:15-20)	
Logos prologue (John 1:1-18)	
Exegesis of the Old Testament	*Exegeses*
Romans 4	*Letter of Barnabas*
Romans 9	Justin, *Dialogue with Trypho*
Historiographical texts	*Historical writing and other genres*
Galatians 1–2	Acts of the Apostles
Beginnings of historical writing in the gospels	*Hypomnemata* of Hegesippus
	Apocryphal Acts of the Apostles: Acts of Andrew, John, Paul, Peter, Thomas

of its very nature to lead to a new dependence on already existing forms in the non-Christian world—so that here (with Franz Overbeck) we can see the transition from early Christian to patristic literature, but within a broad and shifting transitional field. The end of early Christian literature begins when the Jesus tradition can no longer be implicitly interpreted through the writing of more and more new gospels, and the writings of the apostles cannot be interpreted through new pseudepigraphic apostolic writings, but instead normative existing New Testament scriptures are being explicitly interpreted.[11] Then texts are written that refer to existing normative texts: metacanonical texts such as exegeses and commentaries, introductions and hermeneutical reflections. The first of these appear in the second century. In them a fundamental shift makes its appearance, one that was hastened by the establishment of the canon. Theology will no longer be practiced by writing a new "Bible" but by interpreting the existing "Bible." The end of early Christianity begins with the exegesis of canonical texts.

New Creations as Metacanonical Texts

The first of these metacanonical texts can be located in the canonical phase of early Christian writing. These are all the writings in which already in early Christianity up to about 200 C.E. early Christian writing was not only continued but also reflected upon in order to preserve, evaluate, and sift it. Here we are talking of metatexts on New Testament texts that, however, in part did not yet presuppose the canon but potentially might influence its establishment. Essentially these are texts that were intended to secure traditions and were their first interpretations.[12] They constitute an important precondition for exegetical literature in which, after the establishment of the canon, theology would further develop as interpretation of the scriptures.

There are already writings in the New Testament meant to secure tradition; 2 Peter should be mentioned especially. As we have already seen, it probably presumes all the parts of the canon and gives us an insight into its prehistory. It points toward the "interpretation" of Paul's letters: in this writer's opinion they have been misunderstood when read as witness to an imminent expectation of the end.

The early Christian writings in which the Christian literature then coming into being is "secured" make use, as a rule, not of the letter form but of other genres. These include Hegesippus's *Hypomnemata*, of which only fragments remain in Eusebius and Philip of Sida. This writing contained narrative historical materials but was probably a work intended to secure the tradition.

The Muratorian Fragment should be mentioned again here. It is the earliest list of the canon—or, more precisely, the first sketch of a literary history of the New Testament. Here not only is the fourfold gospel a complete entity, but so is the collection of Paul's letters. According to the Muratorian Fragment, Paul wrote to seven communities (in Thessalonica, Galatia, Philippi, Corinth, Colossae, Ephesus, and Rome), just as the letters in Revelation are addressed to seven communities.

Above all, the first reflections on the New Testament writings belong to this metacanonical early Christian literature. Besides the "orthodox" exegeses of Papias (most certainly not exegeses in our sense of the word) we have, above all, the early Gnostic commentaries: the lost commentary of Basilides on a gospel that he may have put together himself, and the commentary of Heracleon on John, which has come to us only indirectly through quotations by Origen.[13] In addition, there are Marcion's "antitheses," with a "hermeneutics" of the entire Bible in which the contradictions between Old and New Testaments are systematically collated (Table 22).[14]

A response to these accumulating metacanonical texts in Gnostic circles and among the Marcionites comes from Irenaeus of Lyons, the church's first great theological writer. It is true that he wrote "nothing whose primary purpose was exegesis,"[15] but on the basis of a relatively precise group of citations and a considered canonical exegesis he made clear advances beyond his predecessors. "For the second century he is by far the most extensively preserved interpreter of the New Testament, both the gospels and the *Corpus*

Table 22: Marcion's Antitheses

The Old Testament God is a God of justice and vengeance.	The New Testament God is a God of love and mercy.
The Old Testament God is a subordinate God: the creator of this imperfect world and the God of Israel.	Jesus, in contrast, is the one sent by the supreme God, who has not previously been revealed in this world.
The Old Testament God teaches "eye for eye, tooth for tooth."	Jesus counters this with renunciation of retribution and love of enemies.
Elisha, in the name of the Old Testament God, causes children to be eaten by a bear.	Jesus, in contrast, says in the name of his God: "Let the little children come to me!"
Joshua in the Old Testament stops the sun in its course.	Paul, in contrast, admonishes in the New Testament: "Let not the sun go down on your anger."
The Old Testament God permits polygamy and divorce.	The New Testament God orders monogamy and forbids divorce.
The Old Testament God makes Sabbath and Law obligatory.	Jesus, in contrast, brings freedom from Sabbath and Law.

Johanneum."[16] He grounds all his theological positions by interpreting the scriptures in conversation with the challenges of his own time. In doing so he formulates a convincing answer to the challenges of Marcion's radical hermeneutics and those of the Gnostics: for him, creation and redemption are mutually related and not drastically separate. Redemption is not liberation from this world but a restoration of creation. God achieves this goal on the journey through a long history of salvation in which the Old Covenant also has its positive place. The first church father who had a theology of the canon is thus also the first to lay a foundation for interpreting it. He is therefore rightly placed at the end of the early Christian literature and the beginning of the patristic era, even though he, of course, had predecessors in the Apologists and early Christian literature was still being created after him. With the canon whose basic outlines have been drawn by him there arises a metacanonical literature for which the canon is increasingly the primary text. This metacanonical literature ensured continuing flexibility as a response to new challenges and did not leave it to bishops alone to seek again and again for new solutions.

Concluding Observation

It has generally been thought impossible to write a history of early Christian literature. The argument has been that the fragmentary character of the transmission permits no historical description of the New Testament within the frame of a literary history encompassing the whole corpus of early Christian writings. This skepticism is exaggerated. A literary history of the New Testament need not at all be content with describing its literary forms and setting them randomly alongside one another. It can give a historical description of its formal language, and in the process discern four phases of a literary history.[1] Early Christian literature developed in two basic forms: gospels and letters, with a comparable dynamic in these four phases. It may be characterized in summary as the literature of a religious movement that, in the brief history of its origins, programmatically crossed many boundaries—between oral and written literature, Jewish and non-Jewish culture, and upper and lower classes. In retrospect, therefore, we may once again state, in summary, our position on the three approaches to a literary-historical explanation of the unique features of the New Testament described at the outset.

The New Testament is "primeval literature" inasmuch as it looks back at the work of Jesus and Paul. The writings evoked and created by them are person-centered in a way that cannot be documented in Judaism. For that very reason *biography* and *letter* became the expressive forms of this charismatic movement. That means that the basic forms of this literature are not derivable from Judaism and its literature; rather, they borrow from common pagan forms even when they transform them in creative ways and shape them in terms of their own needs. They were generated by the impulse given by two great charismatics at the beginning of the early Christian movement. This is by no means acknowledged in the case of Jesus. In this proposal for a literary history we have advocated for the thesis that the formal language of his preaching is very clearly preserved for us, despite justified uncertainty about the authenticity of individual sayings. The historical Jesus is the first starting point for a history of early Christian literature. His formal language was handed on in the Sayings Source in continuity with his preaching, and then shaped in Mark's Gospel into a coherent narrative based on the narrative traditions about Jesus, which were highly heterogeneous in form. In the committing of the Jesus traditions to writing we can observe how the tempting idea of collecting Jesus' preaching into a prophetic book modeled on the Old Testament was already exploded by the Sayings Source, though it still influenced Mark's Gospel. Here the traditions were for the first time gathered in analogy to a *bios*, a biography. This *bios* was then fleshed out and rounded off in the other gospels by means of additions at the beginning and end.

The second charismatic impulse came from Paul. He further developed the letter of friendship, by fleshing it out liturgically and rhetorically, into a community letter, and increasingly endowed it with an authoritative "public" claim—perhaps inspired by Jewish letters for community leaders, but essentially through a creative transformation of the private letter of friendship, following models in the literary and diplomatic letters of pagan antiquity. The form of his letters is something unique and is his own creation. In the further development of his letters we can observe two formal tendencies: a systematic structuring of the letters in Galatians and Romans is augmented by a tendency to an additive structure in the interactively created letters 1 Corinthians, Philippians, and 2 Corinthians. The result is two basic forms of the early Christian letter. Crucial is that the charismatic impulse of the two starting points of early Christian literature, with Jesus and Paul, caused the early Christian groups to seek inspiration beyond the borders of their tradition. The biography and the letter collection were popular forms in the non-Jewish world but were almost totally absent from Jewish literature. This new literature did not arise on a territory free from all contacts with the world, as Franz Overbeck thought. We can discern the literature of a movement rooted in Judaism but very quickly finding a considerable echo outside Judaism. The developments in the spheres of gospels and letters thus ran parallel and were synchronous.

The New Testament is minor literature, that is, the literature of groups that were non-literate or marginally literate, but it cannot be explained simply as the expression of such classes. Characteristic of it is an exchange between literary upper class and non-literary lower class. Here people who were otherwise silenced found their voices. They were heard where they had never before been heard. For educated people with a classicist aesthetics the New Testament scriptures were written in the style of ordinary people; they were part of the *sermo humilis*.[2] The New Testament writings were, in their eyes, often uncultivated, simple, and crude. But apart from classicist aesthetics they could also seem heavy, confusing, and violent. Even in their time they brought not only a new tone to literature but also a new medium: it was with early Christian literature that the codex replaced the scroll. The codex was a type of book for practical, everyday use, not for high literature. All Christian manuscripts were intended from the outset to be codices. The few exceptions may be, at least in part, explained as writing exercises. Thus the Christians accomplished a small "media revolution": the everyday, useful form of the codex became the vehicle of the most valuable texts. Here again we see that early Christian literature is the scripture of a dynamic movement, rooted in the lower classes but very quickly attracting people from higher classes and giving them a space in which to exercise influence. In both of its basic forms this scripture reveals a clear intention to lead and guide communities. This is obvious in the letters; in the gospels it happens indirectly through a redactional shaping of the image of Jesus. In both forms people with a certain degree of literary education were at work, but they were not intent on creating a higher literature; they were deliberately fashioning a literature for ordinary people. This intermediate positioning between literarily competent authors and non-literate ordinary people also explains early Christian pseudepigraphy written in good conscience: its bases were the awareness of the authors that they were representatives, rooted in the oral messenger culture, and the initially perceptible link to the words of the Lord and the letters of the apostle in the work of people whose formal literary abilities were limited. At the beginning anything not characterized as the words of the Lord or a letter from an apostle was not accepted.

The New Testament is *koinē* literature following in the wake of the Septuagint. Originally, the aura of the Septuagint permeated Hellenistic Judaism, which through it had made *koinē* Greek a literary language and created a special Hellenistic Jewish literature within the literary corpus of antiquity. The New Testament was a special literature within this special literature. The Septuagint accompanied its origins inasmuch as some parts of the Christian scriptures were interpretations of texts from the Septuagint. The *Letter of Barnabas*, in fact, conveyed the Christian message only by interpreting the "Old Testament." The LXX also provided authors with stylistic narrative models. The episodic style and reticence toward authorial interference correspond to the LXX. In the last phase of early Christian literary history the LXX again served as a model when it was a matter of setting the new scriptural collection on the same footing as the Old Testament. But despite this significance of the LXX, early Christian literature was not simply part of Jewish-Hellenistic literature. It is an intercultural literature, that is, it crosses the boundaries between the peoples, for its basic forms, letter and gospel, were without models in the Septuagint.[3]

The first Christians, then, on the basis of a charismatic impulse from Jesus and Paul, produced a literature in two basic forms, expanded these as fictive self-interpretations of the two founding figures, then developed a functional, specialized formal language, and finally established the canon in partial imitation of the Septuagint.[4] The development of its formal language in four phases reflects the path from the charismatic beginnings of the early Christian movement to a pluralistic church: the two basic forms, gospel and letter, were entirely derived from the authority of the person; they owed their effectiveness to Jesus and Paul. Within a short time they produced an authoritative tradition. The pseudepigraphic writings are based on this traditional authority. These were intended to preserve traditions and bring the original authorities up to date by correcting them. The post-Pauline letters and the gospel redactions belong to this pseudepigraphic phase. Within the framework of such pseudepigraphic writings, then, functional forms developed, shaped by their material task and adapted more and more clearly from forms in their environment: Hebrews as a discourse, the Acts of the Apostles as a historical writing, John's Revelation as apocalypse.[5] The authority of the form—the persuasive power of a successful discourse, the attractive force of an apocalyptic revelation, or the material content of a historical depiction—were added to the authority of persons and traditions without making those sources of authority superfluous. Finally, the establishment of the canon was supported by the authority of the church, with a twofold effect: on the one hand, by means of the canon, ecclesial structures with an internal plurality of approaches and attitudes succeeded in the face of sectarian tendencies, and, on the other hand, marginal approaches were set apart and boundary lines were drawn against deviant movements. The canon thus originated not only as the expression of church-political power relationships but as a selection of writings corresponding to anthropologically anchored criteria of memorability: a "counterintuitive" message about the folly of the cross that awakened interest, combined with an intuitively obvious interpretation of life that lent it endurance. Added to this were, however, "church-political" tendencies in which nevertheless consensus building and compromise played an important role alongside "exercise of power." Marcion's canon served as a catalyst in that the consensus building within the church was made easier by a common distancing from him. The most important communities in the second century had a common "heretic," but as yet no common institutional power structures (no synods and no primacy of the bishop of Rome).

We can observe five social "church political" functions throughout, all of which can be shown to be at work in the shaping of early Christian literature. It served as literature for the use of a vital minority movement within the Roman Empire and had utility for the tasks of guiding and directing the community. Its intention is to express the consensus of the community and convey an image of the surrounding world in order to lead it through crises and conflicts with that world. It intends to define Christian identity in distinction from the mother religion of the first Christians, and to regulate conflicts within particular communities through proposals for integration. It is meant to secure a structure of authority within the community that is independent of persons and generations. Part of this is the formulation of criteria for legitimate authority that can be accepted by as many as possible. These five factors shaping the literature may be shown to exist from the earliest (written) literary witnesses of early Christianity, the letters of Paul, to the establishment of the canon. Not only the additions to the genuine Pauline letters by means of pseudepigraphic epistles serve this purpose, but so do the gospels, in which the words and deeds of Jesus are depicted in such a way that they can be a basis for community life. Writings that did not meet these requirements had less chance of being accepted. The many Gnostic writings excluded themselves from this development because their devaluation of normal community members as ignorant *simplices* excluded them from the start from a broader resonance.

In addition, we can observe the significance of the two basic forms in all phases throughout the history of the New Testament literature, for even the few individual genres borrow from them and were accepted into the canon only in the wake of the two basic forms of gospel and letters. They correspond to the relationship between the two wings that emerged very early in the history of early Christianity: Jewish and Gentile. The Synoptic tradition that was developed in the gospels goes back to Jesus traditions in Palestine, but in the gospel form it was shaped into writings that were also intended to address Gentile Christians. The greater dominance of Gentile Christianity appears here already in the development of literary forms. The epistolary literature, in contrast, was from the outset a product of the Gentile mission and without the conflicts surrounding this Gentile mission and its internal problems it would not have come to exist in this form. In its polemic writings (Galatians, Philippians, Romans) it documents how the Gentile mission triumphed over the Jewish-Christian counter-mission. It also shows, through the initial presence together of letters that originated interactively, with their additive structure (1 and 2 Corinthians, Philippians) and letters conceived as wholes, with their systematic structure (Galatians, Romans) the traces of a "utilitarian literature" by means of which communities were constructed and stabilized. The additive structure of the letters is, not accidentally, continued in the practically oriented Pastoral Letters. In the committing to writing of the Jesus tradition as well, the two oldest forms of that tradition, the Sayings Source and Mark's Gospel, reveal more sharply the characteristics of a literature for use than do the later gospels. In the Sayings Source the tradition of the itinerant charismatics was recorded; in Mark a Jesus tradition for local communities was deliberately shaped.

Both basic forms, gospel and letter, borrow from the outset in language, style, and quotation from the Septuagint. That in them a group stemming from Judaism is expressing itself is thus perceptible even in the formal language. The overall genre of a gospel and the collection of Paul's letters, however, go beyond Jewish models. The separation of the New Testament from the LXX as Old Testament reflects the process of separation from Judaism; the retention of the LXX against Marcion documents at the same time the enduring ties to Judaism.

The New Testament is only a section of a much more comprehensive early Christian literature. The non-canonical early Christian writings are the continuation of the three perceptible phases of the history of early Christian literature, especially the functional phase. In the so-called apocryphal literature sub-genres that previously had played a limited role within the framework of gospel and letter were repeatedly made independent: sermons, church orders, secret teachings, infancy and passion narratives, dialogues with the Exalted One, hymns, proverbs, etc. The two basic forms of the New Testament thus found a clearly distinct continuation in the second century: the production of pseudepigraphic letters declined somewhat, but in contrast there was a flowering of Jesus literature—in many gospels, often surviving only in fragments, which also include dialogue gospels with special revelations by the Risen One to his disciples. After a small and relatively early high point for the Petrine literature in the second century, the history of early Christian literature in the second half of the second century closed with a flowering of edifying and entertaining literature about the apostles in the form of the apocryphal acts of the apostles. With the assumption of forms from the breadth of ancient literature, Christian literature then was increasingly integrated into the general history of literature, beginning with the Apologists, especially the three great authors of the ancient church at the turn to the third century: Irenaeus of Lyons, Clement of Alexandria, and Tertullian in Carthage.

The history of their literary forms corresponds to the history of the early Christian groups. The three theses on the literary history of the New Testament with which we began have been affirmed in separate areas, but they must be augmented: the New Testament is underivable primal literature, non-literary minor literature, Jewish-Hellenistic *koinē* literature. But these three definitions each emphasize the limits of this literature: the delimitation of the primal literature from a literature that participates in common literary forms, the special character of minor literature in contrast to the literature of the upper-class culture, and the segregation of special Jewish literature from non-Jewish literature. The history of early Christian literature on all three "fronts," however, was characterized not only by drawing limits, but much more by crossing boundaries. It developed on the border between orality and writing, charism and institution, lower and upper classes, Jews and Gentiles.[6] It documents the path from charismatic beginnings to a church with responsible institutions. It reveals traces of a movement that spread within the lower classes but that very quickly gained for itself members from the upper classes. It is marked by the fact that here a Jewish renewal movement opened itself to all nations. The development of its formal language reflects the social dynamics of the religious movements that supported it. It began as primal literature, minor literature, and Jewish *koinē* literature, but it developed into a literature that crossed boundaries. It was the literature of a small subculture that hoped to be the beginning of a new humanity. That is why it traversed so many boundaries. Only because of that did it become part of the religious literature of the world.

Notes

Introduction

1. Klaus Berger and Christiane Nord, *Das Neue Testament und frühchristliche Schriften* (Frankfurt am Main: Insel Verlag, 1999), include ninety-two writings and fragments.

2. *New Testament Apocrypha*, 2 vols., ed. Edgar Hennecke and Wilhelm Schneemelcher, Engl. trans. ed. Robert McL. Wilson and others (Philadelphia: Westminster, 1963–66).

3. These writings were first collected under the name "Apostolic Fathers" in the seventeenth century and originally contained the letter of Barnabas, two letters of Clement, the letters of Ignatius, the letter of Polycarp of Smyrna and the account of his martyrdom, and the Shepherd of Hermas. Today we also include among them the *Didache*, the letter of Diognetus, the fragments of Papias, and the Quadratus. Cf. Andreas Lindemann, "Apostolische Väter," *RGG*[4] (1998) 1:652–53. For bilingual editions containing English, see *The Apostolic Fathers*, 2 vols., trans. Kirsopp Lake, LCL (London: Heinemann; New York: Macmillan, 1913); *The Apostolic Fathers; Greek Texts and English Translations*, ed. and trans. Michael W. Holmes (Grand Rapids: Baker Academic, 2007).

4. Tacitus *Ann.* 15.44.3: *exitiabilis superstitio*; cf. Suetonius *Nero* 16; Pliny *Ep.* 10.96.8. On this see Dieter Lührmann, "*Superstitio*—die Beurteilung des frühen Christentums durch die Römer," *TZ* 42 (1986): 193–213.

5. Albrecht Dihle, *Greek and Latin Literature of the Roman Empire*, trans. Manfred Malzahn (London and New York: Routledge, 1994), 312–13, gives a vivid description of the shift between the first and second halves of the second century.

6. In Eduard Mörike's poem on a lamp, the ending reads: "True beauty radiates from a light within." The beautiful is its own purpose and light. It is not: "*is* a light within," but "*radiates from* a light within"—which alludes to the purpose of the lamp, to give a bright light. That is its use value. But beyond that, it has an intrinsic value: beauty is light that makes life bright beyond all usefulness.

7. Reinhard Brandt, ed., Pseudo-Longinus, "*Vom Erhabenen*" (Berlin: Akademie-Verlag, 1966), 45. For English see http://evans-experientialism.freewebspace.com/longinus02.htm.

8. Rudolf Otto, quoted in Birgit Recki, "Erhabene, das," *RGG*[4] (1999) 2:1408–9.

9. If we regard all the apostolic letters as discourse by apostles, this special position of the letter to the Hebrews is unnecessary; it is "no longer in principle isolated within the letter corpus of the NT." So Klaus Berger, "Apostelbrief und apostolische Rede," *ZNW* 65 (1974): 190–231, at 231. It is true that the letters represent editions of apostolic speech, but they contain other sorts of texts as well: hymns, as in Phil 2:5-11 and Col 1:15-20; confessional formulae, such as 1 Cor 8:6-8 and 1 Cor 15:3ff.; exegeses, such as Romans 4; and paraeneses, such as Romans 12–13. All these can, naturally, be integrated into a discourse. But in any case this difference between speech and letter remains: a letter is sent to spatially separate addressees, so that writing and reading are not simultaneous—a circumstance that is sometimes further strengthened by the fact that a letter can be written down successively, but read out loud all at once.

10. The ancient church's view is developed by Irenaeus (*Haer.* 3.1.1 = Eusebius, *Hist. eccl.* 5.8.2-4). "Matthew composed a written gospel for the Hebrews in their own language, while Peter and Paul were preaching the gospel in Rome and founding the church there. After their deaths, Mark too, the disciple and interpreter of Peter, handed on to us in writing the things proclaimed by Peter. Luke, the follower of Paul, wrote down in a book the gospel preached by him. Then John, the disciple of the Lord who had rested on his breast, produced a gospel while living at Ephesus in Asia."

11. However, this principle of order was not consistently maintained. Among the catholic letters, 2 and 3 John each had a concrete addressee, but they were connected to 1 John, which has a general audience. The first letter of Peter names concrete regions as addressees (1 Pet 1:1). Only its combination with 2 Peter made it a general letter "to all who, together with us, have received the same precious gospel" (2 Pet 1:1).

12. According to David Trobisch, *Die Paulusbriefe und die Anfänge der christlichen Publizistik* (Gütersloh: Kaiser, 1994), 80.

13. In the manuscript tradition, Hebrews is regarded as a letter of Paul. The superscription "to the Hebrews" corresponds to the superscriptions of all the Pauline letters, according to addressee ("to the Romans," "to the Corinthians"), while the catholic letters are distinguished by their authors, such as "James," "Peter," "John," "Jude." The *inscriptio* "to the Hebrews" is striking because the word "Hebrews" does not appear in the letter. In the manuscript tradition the letter to the Hebrews is found in different places within the Pauline letters (cf. the table below): In Papyrus 46 it follows the letter to the Romans (being the second-longest letter); in the majuscules Sinaiticus, Alexandrinus, Vaticanus, Ephraimi Rescriptus, and in Minuscule 5 it is placed before the Pastorals; in the *textus receptus* of the Byzantine recension and in Codex Claromontanus it concludes the Pauline letters. In Minuscule 794 it even appears in two places: before the Pastorals and after all the Pauline letters—a secondary combination of two different traditions. In one model text for Vaticanus it followed the letter to the Galatians because it continues that letter's numbering of chapters, although it is now placed after 2 Thessalonians. It is always a mirror to Romans. Either the two follow one another immediately (Papyrus 46) or they

constitute the first and last community letters in contrast to the letters to individuals (Sinaiticus, Vaticanus, etc.), or they form a frame as the first and last Pauline letters. It is possible that the editors understood the "Romans" not only as inhabitants of Rome, but as the race ruling the world, and contrasted the "Hebrews" to them as a separate nation.

14. Thus Adolf Jülicher regretted that "the ideal literary-critical view is unfortunately unattainable for the New Testament" (*Einleitung in das Neue Testament* [Freiburg: Mohr/Siebeck, 1894], 4). Rudolf Bultmann repeatedly declared that literary-critical work "in the true sense" was not possible for the New Testament ("Neues Testament. Einleitung II," *TRu* 17 [1914]: 79–90, at 79; idem, review of Martin Dibelius, *Geschichte der urchristlichen Literatur*, *TLZ* 52 [1927]: 80–83; idem, "Literaturgeschichte, Biblische," *RGG*[2] [1927] 3:1675–82). This had its effect. Bultmann's students have done little to advance the work of literary-historical criticism.

15. Johann Wolfgang von Goethe, *Wilhelm Meisters Wanderjahre* [1821], in Dieter Borchmeyer, ed., *Johann Wolfgang von Goethe. Werke* ([4]Munich: Artemis & Winkler, 1992) 4:547–980, at 809.

16. Johann Gottfried Herder is described by Martin Dibelius, *From Tradition to Gospel* [1919], trans. Bertram Lee Woolf (Cambridge: James Clarke, 1971), 5, in these words: "His understanding of the popular mind revealed to him the special character of religious popular literature, and his understanding of human nature what was the typical character of such writings. His understanding of folk poetry enabled him to recognize the naïve and creative element in the biblical writings."

17. Johann Gottfried Herder, *Vom Erlöser der Menschen* (1796), in Bernhard Suphan, ed., *Herders Sämmtliche Werke*, 33 vols. (Berlin: Weidmann, 1877–1913), 19 [1880]: 135–252, at 211.

18. Herder, *Von Gottes Sohn, der Welt Heiland* (1797), in Suphan, ed., *Herders Sämmtliche Werke*, 19:253–424, at 418.

19. Ibid.

20. Herder, *Vom Erlöser der Menschen*, 149, 195, 196.

21. Klaus Scholder, "Herder und die Anfänge der historischen Theologie," *EvT* 22 (1962): 425–40, on p. 433 attributes to Herder a "historical-aesthetic method."

22. Franz Overbeck, "Über die Anfänge der patristischen Literatur," *HZ* 48 (1882) 417–72 (= *Libelli* 15, 1984). Cf. Philipp Vielhauer, "Franz Overbeck und die neutestamentliche Wissenschaft," *EvT* 19 (1950/51): 193–207 (= *Aufsätze zum Neuen Testament* [Munich: Kaiser, 1965], 235–52).

23. Overbeck, "Anfänge," 423: "A literature has its history in its forms, thus every genuine literary criticism is form criticism" (= *Libelli*, 12).

24. Ibid., 443: "This is a literature created by Christianity, so to speak, out of its own materials, to the extent that it grew exclusively from the soil and the particular internal interests of the Christian community, before its integration with the surrounding world. It was not that the forms of this literature . . . were entirely new. This is true only of the gospel form, which in fact is the sole original form with which Christianity has enriched literature. . . . But in reality it kept itself apart from the forms of the existing secular world literature, so that to that extent it can

be called, if not purely Christian, certainly something purely religious. But this is precisely the most important phenomenon in the history of Christian literature in its initial period . . . that the trunk of Christian literature came to an early end and that the Christian literature that lived on in and with the church, and in early times was customarily called patristic literature, did not grow from it" (= *Libelli*, 36–37).

25. Rudolf Bultmann, *The History of the Synoptic Tradition* [1921], trans. John Marsh (New York: Harper & Row, 1963); Martin Dibelius, *Geschichte der urchristlichen Literatur* (Munich: Kaiser, 1926); Karl Ludwig Schmidt, "Die Stellung der Evangelien in der allgemeinen Literaturgeschichte," in idem, ***ΕΥΧΑΡΙΣΤΗΡΙΟΝ***, Part 2 (1923), 50–134 (= *Neues Testament, Judentum, Kirche: Kleine Schriften* [Munich: Kaiser, 1981], 37–130); Philipp Vielhauer, *Geschichte der urchristlichen Literatur* (Berlin and New York: de Gruyter, 1975).

26. Adolf Deissmann, *Light from the Ancient East: The New Testament Illustrated by Recently Fiscovered Texts of the Graeco-Roman World* [[4]1923], trans. Lionel R. M. Strachan (Grand Rapids: Baker, 1965), was in this regard the inspiration for the form critics.

27. Cf. Dibelius, *From Tradition to Gospel*, 2: The gospels "without a doubt . . . are unliterary writings. They should not and cannot be compared with 'literary' works. Nevertheless they are certainly not private notes but are designed for a definite publicity even if it be only humble."

28. Martin Dibelius in particular, in *Formgeschichte*, 8–34, found an answer for the oral tradition: behind it was an interest in preaching and mission, the proclamation of the approaching end of the world and the *parousia*. Unlike Franz Overbeck, Martin Dibelius discovered even in the history of the minor forms a tendency to adopt secular genres: paradigms and the passion story were, for him, an original expression of early Christian preaching, while novellas and legends were accommodations to secular forms.

29. Marius Reiser, *Sprache und literarische Formen des Neuen Testaments: eine Einführung* (Paderborn: Schöningh, 2001); idem, "Literaturgeschichte/Literaturgeschichtsschreibung III. Neues Testament," *RGG*[4] 5 (2002), 408–9.

30. These influences were demonstrated especially by Klaus Berger, "Hellenistische Gattungen im Neuen Testament," *ANRW* II/25.2 (Berlin and New York: de Gruyter, 1984), 1031–1432, 1831–85, in an essay replete with material on both the major genres and the lesser forms of the New Testament and giving new definition to a number of minor forms. Cf. more recently his summary work: Klaus Berger, *Formen und Gattungen im Neuen Testament* (Tübingen: Francke, 2005). David E. Aune, *The New Testament in its Literary Environment* (Philadelphia: Westminster, 1987), gives a briefer overview especially of the major genres of the New Testament.

31. There is an example in modern church history of the way in which imminent expectation of the end can intensify the literary activity of a group. William Miller (1782–1849), founder of the Seventh-Day Adventists, expected the end of the world in the Jewish year 1843/44. The year of the Second Coming ended on 21 March 1844 without the *parousia* having happened. New prophecies dated the

end of the world now to the fall of 1844; it was to arrive by 22 October of that year. Miller's adherents produced newspapers and tracts in great numbers. In May 1844 there were fifteen regularly appearing periodicals based on this end-time expectation, with a circulation of about five million copies. After Miller's death, the prophet Ellen Gould Harmon-White (1827–1915) became the most important figure in Adventism. She wrote more than fifty books and articles that until today enjoy a nearly deuterocanonical reputation among Adventists. Cf. Horst Reller et al., eds., *Handbuch Religiöse Gemeinschaften und Weltanschauungen* (Gütersloh: Gütersloher Verlagshaus, ^{4}1993), 226–42, esp. 226–30.

32. For the problem of a religious aesthetics between a *theologia gloriae* and a *theologia crucis* cf. Gerd Theissen, "Moderne religiöse Kunst. Theologische Ästhetik zwischen *theologia gloriae* und *theologia crucis*," *EvT* 67 (2007): 5–22.

33. Since until now the literary-historical criticism of the New Testament has only used the categories of genres and lines of development, the demonstration of phases in early Christian literature would be an advance. Paul Wendland, *Die urchristlichen Literaturformen* (Tübingen: Mohr/Siebeck, 1912), distinguished by genres: (1) gospels, (2) stories of the apostles, (3) letters, (4) apocalypses, (5) Christian apologetics. Martin Dibelius, *Geschichte der urchristlichen Literatur*, distinguished (1) gospels, (2) apocalypses, (3) letters, (4) discussions, sermons, tracts in the form of letters, (6) admonitions in ethical and canonical style, (7) cultic matters, (8) stories of the apostles; Georg Strecker, *History of New Testament Literature* [1992], trans. Calvin Katter with the assistance of Hans-Joachim Mollenhauer (Harrisburg, PA: Trinity Press International, 1997), traces four genres in the New Testament. The only new direction has been the proposal for lines of development through early Christianity: Helmut Koester, *Introduction to the New Testament*, vol. 1, *History, Culture, and Religion of the Hellenistic Age*; vol. 2, *History and Literature of Early Christianity* (Berlin and New York: de Gruyter, 1982).

34. William Harris, *Ancient Literacy* (Cambridge, MA: Harvard University Press, 1989), estimates the literacy of the population at about ten percent, but not more than fifteen or twenty percent, even though in some individual Hellenistic cities with favorable educational conditions the level may have been higher. Here we have to distinguish: the ability to read and write was more common in the cities and towns than in the countryside. On the basis of archaeological findings we must reckon with a clearly higher percentage of literate people in the cities. (Oral communication from Géza Alföldy.) Christian groups were more common in cities. What is not so clear is that the ability to read and write was more common among Jews than among Gentiles, even though the sacred book played a special role in their life. According to Catherine Hezser, *Jewish Literacy in Roman Palestine* (Tübingen: Mohr Siebeck, 2001), Jews in Palestine were not better off in this regard than the rest of the population.

35. Philip S. Alexander, "Rabbinic Biography and the Biography of Jesus," in Christopher M. Tuckett, ed., *Synoptic Studies* (Sheffield: JSOT Press, 1984), 19–50.

36. Berger, "Hellenistische Gattungen"; Aune, *The New Testament in its Literary Environment*.

1. *The Oral Prehistory of Early Christian Literature with the Historical Jesus*

1. The classic descriptions of the formal language of the Jesus tradition are still those by Martin Dibelius, *From Tradition to Gospel* [1919], trans. Bertram Lee Woolf (Cambridge: James Clarke, 1971), and Rudolf Bultmann, *The History of the Synoptic Tradition* [1921], trans. John Marsh (Oxford: Blackwell; New York: Harper & Row, 1963). Cf. Gerd Theissen, "Die Erforschung der synoptischen Tradition seit R. Bultmann," in Bultmann, *Geschichte der synoptischen Tradition* ([10]1995), 409–52.

2. The restriction to Israel is stated in Matt 10:5-6: "Go nowhere among the Gentiles, and enter no town of the Samaritans, but go rather to the lost sheep of the house of Israel." There is a reflection of this also in Matt 10:23 and Matt 15:24.

3. Walter Schmithals, "Vom Ursprung der synoptischen Tradition," *ZTK* 94 (1997): 288–316, disputes the existence of an oral tradition.

4. Helmut Koester, *Synoptische Überlieferung bei den Apostolischen Vätern* (Berlin: Akademie-Verlag, 1957).

5. For the Montanists cf. Gerd Theissen and Dagmar Winter, *The Quest for the Plausible Jesus: The Question of Criteria* [1997], trans. M. Eugene Boring (Louisville: Westminster John Knox, 2002), 213–21.

6. Samuel Byrskog, *Story as History—History as Story. The Gospel Tradition in the Context of Ancient Oral History* (Tübingen: Mohr Siebeck, 2000).

7. James D. G. Dunn, *Jesus Remembered* (Grand Rapids: Eerdmans, 2003), 192–210. Erhardt Güttgemanns, *Candid Questions Concerning Gospel Form Criticism: A Methodological Sketch of the Fundamental Problematics of Form and Redaction Criticism* [1970], trans. William G. Doty (Pittsburgh: Pickwick Press, 1979), was the first to suggest the analogy with the oral epics of ancient Greece and Serbo-Croatia in the sense of a relativization of a primal text.

8. Albert B. Lord, *The Singer of Tales* (Cambridge, MA: Harvard University Press, 1960).

9. Kenneth E. Bailey, "Informal Controlled Oral Tradition and the Synoptic Gospels," *AJT* 5 (1991): 34–53; idem, "Middle Eastern Oral Tradition and the Synoptic Gospels," *ExpTim* 106 (1995): 363–67.

10. As early as the 1970s I interpreted the tradition of miracle stories as individual new creations based on a repertoire of motifs (Gerd Theissen, *The Miracle Stories of the Early Christian Tradition* [1974], trans. Francis McDonagh; ed. John Riches [Philadelphia: Fortress Press, 1983]). Following folklore research, I called the indirect social control exercised "preventive censorship by the community" (Gerd Theissen, "Wanderradikalismus," *ZTK* 70 [1973]: 245–71; idem, *Social Reality and the Early Christians* [1973], trans. Margaret Kohl [Minneapolis: Fortress Press, 1992]).

11. Heinz Schürmann, "Die vorösterlichen Anfänge der Logientradition," in Helmut Ristow and Karl Matthiae, *Der historische Jesus und der kerygmatische Christus* (Berlin: Evangelische Verlagsanstalt, 1962), 342–70.

12. Paul Hoffmann, *Studien zur Theologie der Logienquelle* (Münster: Aschendorff, 1972; 3d ed. 1982), 296–302, 310–11.

13. Cf. Gerd Theissen, "Jesus as an Itinerant Teacher, Reflections from Social History on Jesus' Roles," in J. H. Charlesworth and P. Pokorný, *Jesus Research: An International Perspective*, The First Princeton-Prague Symposium on Jesus Research (Grand Rapids/Cambridge, U.K.: Eerdmans, 2009), 98–122. For Judas Galilaios cf. Martin Hengel, *The Zealots*, trans. David Smith (Edinburgh: T & T Clark, 1989), 90–106.

14. The translation by Otto Michel and Otto Bauernfeind (*De bello Judaico* [Munich: Kösel, 1962–69]) renders this "itinerant speaker" (Wanderredner). Henry St. John Thackeray uses "sophist" in the Loeb edition.

15. This is what he is almost always called: Josephus, *Ant.* 18.23; 20.102; *B.J.* 2.433; one exception is *B.J.* 7.253; see also Acts 5:37.

16. Cf. his remarks on the Epicureans in *Ant.* 10.277; 19.32; cf. *C. Ap.* 2.180.

17. This is also suggested by Hengel, *Zealots*, 80 n. 22.

18. Judas Galilaios appeared to recall the Cynics in that he is said to have "upbraided" (*B.J.* 2.118, 433) and "exhorted" (*Ant.* 18.4) the Jews. Cynic philosophers "insulted" their audiences in order to move them to live a good life. Judas Galilaios also taught that God alone should be acknowledged as Lord and no human lords beside him (*B.J.* 2.118; cf. 2.433; *Ant.* 18.23). The sharp contrast between God and the human recalls the Cynics' contrast between nature and convention.

19. The Cynic and satirist Menippus of Gadara lived in the third century B.C.E. The epigrammatist Meleagros of Gadara (ca. 130–70 B.C.E.) regarded himself as Menippus's successor. In the time of Hadrian in the second century C.E. the Cynic tradition was revived by Oinomaos of Gadara.

20. The fruitful thesis that Jesus and his disciples were Jewish Cynics was developed by F. Gerald Downing, "Cynics and Christians," *NTS* 30 (1984): 584–93, and independently by Burton L. Mack, *A Myth of Innocence: Mark and Christian Origins* (Philadelphia: Fortress Press, 1988); idem, *The Lost Gospel: The Book of Q and Christian Origins* (San Francisco: HarperSanFrancisco, 1994).

21. Cf. the fable of the thorn bush (Judg 9:7-15), Nathan's parable (2 Sam 12:1-4), the song of the vineyard (Isa 5:1-7).

22. Petra von Gemünden, *Vegetationsmetaphorik im Neuen Testament und seiner Umwelt: eine Bildfelduntersuchung* (Fribourg: Universitätsverlag; Göttingen: Vandenhoeck & Ruprecht, 1993), 130–38.

23. David Flusser, *Die rabbinischen Gleichnisse und der Gleichniserzähler Jesus* (Bern, Frankfurt, and Las Vegas: Peter Lang, 1981); cf. also Bernd Kollmann, "Jesus als jüdischer Gleichnisdichter," *NTS* 50 (2004): 457–75.

24. Later we also find apophthegms in rabbinic literature. Catherine Hezser, "Die Verwendung der hellenistischen Gattung Chrie im frühen Christentum und Judentum," *JSJ* 27 (1996): 371–439.

2. The Sayings Source Q

1. However, the existence of a Sayings Source is again and again disputed, for example by Martin Hengel, *The Four Gospels and the One Gospel of Jesus Christ*,

trans. John Bowden (Harrisburg, PA: Trinity Press International, 2000), 169–207, who tries to explain the kinship between Matthew and Luke by Matthew's use of Luke. Independently of this, however, he assumes that Papias attests to a collection of Jesus' sayings.

2. Translation by Paul L. Maier, *Eusebius, The Church History. A New Translation with Commentary* (Grand Rapids: Kregel, 1999), 129–30.

3. I developed this interpretation in my *The Gospels in Context: Social and Political History in the Synoptic Tradition*, trans. Linda M. Maloney (Minneapolis: Fortress Press, 1991), 215–21.

4. Maier's translation (see n. 2 above), 127.

5. Hanna Roose, *Eschatologische Mitherrschaft: Entwicklungslinien einer urchristlichen Erwartung* (Göttingen: Vandenhoeck & Ruprecht, 2004).

6. James M. Robinson, "LOGOI SOPHON: On the Gattung of Q," in James M. Robinson, ed., *The Future of Our Religious Past: Essays in Honour of Rudolf Bultmann* (New York: Harper & Row, 1971), 84–130; Migaku Sato, *Q und Prophetie: Studien zur Gattungs- und Traditionsgeschichte der Quelle Q* (Tübingen: Mohr, 1988). According to Marco Frenschkowski, Q is a "genre-critical patchwork made up of wisdom, didactic, pneumatic, and apocalyptic elements, without being susceptible to complete explanation in terms of continuity with the existing genres" (quoted from Paul Hoffmann and Christoph Heil, *Die Spruchquelle Q* [Darmstadt: Wissenschaftliche Buchgesellschaft, 2002], 19). We may include the didactic elements within the wisdom category, and summarize the pneumatic and apocalyptic elements as prophetic features, since the "Spirit" is associated with the prophets. In my opinion it is not necessary to give up on a determination of the genre!

7. Thus John S. Kloppenborg, *The Formation of Q: Trajectories in Ancient Wisdom Collections* (Philadelphia: Fortress Press, 1987), in an acute study.

8. The Sayings Source as a genre had its successors. The *Gospel of Thomas* is also a collection of Jesus' sayings without a passion narrative. Here Jesus appears as a revealer who brings a saving knowledge (*gnōsis*) from heaven. It thus represents a developed form of such sayings collections whose purpose is not only the handing on of Jesus' words but also their interpretation. This is stated programmatically by the first logion: "Whoever finds the meaning of these words will not taste death" (*Gos. Thom.* 1). Before the discovery of the *Gospel of Thomas* in 1945 it was possible to doubt the existence of a Sayings Source because there was no example to show that such a genre had existed in early Christianity. That argument has now been refuted. However, we should note that the *Gospel of Thomas* is purely a collection of sayings, whereas Q contains some narratives.

3. *The Gospel of Mark*

1. Thus Mark 15:38: the curtain of the temple (of the *naos*) is torn in two (cf. Matt 23:35; Luke 1:9, 21, 22; differently Rev 11:2, contrast 11:19). On the other hand, "sanctuary" (*hieron*) often refers to the whole temple complex (cf. Mark

11:15; 16:27; 13:1, 3; 14:49). Since all the instances in Mark can be clearly categorized in one or the other meaning, we can posit a semantic distinction in his work (*naos* = inner temple; *hieron* = the whole temple complex).

2. Thus, against critical consensus, Martin Hengel. Cf. his *Der unterschätzte Petrus: zwei Studien* (Tübingen: Mohr Siebeck, 2006), 58–78.

3. William Wrede, *Das Messiasgeheimnis in den Evangelien* (Göttingen: Vandenhoeck & Ruprecht, 1901, 4th ed. 1969). But Jesus did not for that reason live an "unmessianic life." He was a charismatic who attributed to himself the crucial role in history between God and humanity. But the Christians after Easter said more about him than he said of himself before Easter. A further enormous expansion of his majesty was associated with Easter.

4. Heikki Räisänen, *The "Messianic Secret" in Mark's Gospel*, trans. Christopher Tuckett (Edinburgh: T & T Clark, 1990), 220–22.

5. Cf. Albrecht Dihle, "Die Evangelien und die biographischen Traditionen der Antike," *ZTK* 80 (1983): 33–49; Hubert Cancik, "Die Gattung Evangelium," in idem, ed., *Markus–Philologie: historische, literargeschichtliche und stilistische Untersuchungen zum zweiten Evangelium* (Tübingen: Mohr, 1984), 85–113; idem, "Bios und Logos," in ibid., 115–30.

6. Eve-Marie Becker, *Das Markus-Evangelium im Rahmen antiker Historiographie* (Tübingen: Mohr, 2006) has opened a new direction with her assertion that the Gospel of Mark is part of ancient historiography, that the author worked in many respects as a writer of history when editing sources, interpreting current events such as the destruction of the temple, and relating the "beginning" of a historical phenomenon. But biography and history are related. Mark writes in historiographical fashion, and yet his book is a biography: everything is focused on Jesus. The sources are evaluated in relation to him; the destruction of the temple is not narrated, but is prophesied by Jesus; the Christian proclamation begins with Jesus, even though the Gospel of Mark itself begins with the Baptizer, for only his messianic preaching is reported—that is, only what points to Jesus.

7. In addition, it is part of a more comprehensive work that retells the Pentateuch. For Philo the life of Moses remains embedded in the history of his people.

8. In Mark 5:19-20 the proclamation in the Decapolis is the beginning of preaching in Gentile lands.

9. The commandments of Jesus collected in the Gospel of Matthew are to be taught to all nations (Matt 28:18-20).

10. "Now fame carried this news abroad more suddenly than one could have thought, that he was emperor over the east, upon which every city kept festivals, and celebrated sacrifices and oblations for such good news (*euangelia*)" (Josephus, *B.J.* 4.618). "And now, as Vespasian was come to Alexandria, this good news (*euangelia*) came from Rome" (*B.J.* 4.656). Josephus even names the east as well as Rome as the place where the *euangelia* were made known—that is, both places that are discussed in New Testament scholarship as places of origin for the Gospel of Mark: Syria in the East and Rome in the West.

11. I have elaborated this thesis in *The Gospels in Context* (1991), 262–81.

12. Thus for Paul also the concept of *euangelion* has political associations. The

pre-Pauline summary of the *euangelion* in Rom 1:3-4 proclaims a descendant of David who rises to rule the world. The pre-Pauline summary of the *euangelion* in 1 Cor 15:3-8 speaks of the death and resurrection of Christ—a few verses farther on his *parousia* (return) is announced as the advent of a ruler who will reign over all his enemies (1 Cor 15:23-28). The Gospel of Mark also associates the "gospel" with the coming of God's reign (Mark 1:14-15).

13. Mark 1:1; 1:14-15; 8:35; 10:29; 13:10; 14:9.

14. The concept of *euangelion* has an Old Testament root in the "messenger of good news" in Deutero-Isaiah (Isa 52:7; 61:1-11; cf. Rom 10:15-16 with Isa 52:7). But it cannot simply be derived from the Old Testament. In the Septuagint we encounter primarily the verb *euangelizesthai*. Nouns from this stem describe "the messenger's wages." It is, of course, an obstacle to the derivation of this term from the imperial cult that the first Christians spoke of *euangelion* in the singular, not in the plural as does the inscription at Priene (OGIS 456, 20ff.). Even in Mark, an author within the field of biblical tradition, one must reckon with an influence of the prior Old Testament history of the "concept of gospel," especially since he uses this concept to describe Jesus' prophetic message about the reign of God (Mark 1:14-15). The Old Testament and secular traditions converge, as William Horbury, "'Gospel' in Herodian Judaea," in idem, *Herodian Judaism and New Testament Study* (Tübingen: Mohr Siebeck, 2006), 80–103, has shown.

15. Gerd Theissen, "Auferstehungsgeschichte und Zeitgeschichte," in Sabine Bieberstein and Daniel Kosch, eds., *Auferstehung hat einen Namen* (Luzerne: Exodus, 1998), 58–67.

16. With Marius Reiser, *Sprache und literarische Formen des Neuen Testaments: eine Einführung* (Paderborn: Schöningh, 2001).

17. Cf. also the additions to Daniel, *Greek Enoch,* the Wisdom of Solomon, and the *Testaments of the Twelve Patriarchs.*

18. Cf. also the Jewish *Sibyllines* and 2, 3, and 4 Maccabees.

19. That the preaching of cross and resurrection was an offer of identification to those socially inferior is evident from 1 Cor 1:18-31: the foolishness of the saving preaching of the cross corresponds to the social composition of the Corinthian community, which does not include many who are wise, powerful, and respected (1:26). Paul, in prison, sings the "Philippians hymn" about the preexistent Christ who humbled himself even to the cross in order thus to be exalted above all names—a defiant countermelody to the situation of a prisoner awaiting a possible sentence of death. He knows that even his judges will at some point acknowledge his Lord as lord of lords (Phil 2:5-11). The first letter of Peter presents slaves as the disciples of the suffering Christ (1 Pet 2:18-25). They are the model for the whole community (1 Pet 3:8-22).

20. For the downward transfer of upper-class values cf. Gerd Theissen, *Die Religion der ersten Christen: eine Theorie des Urchristentums* (Gütersloh: Kaiser, 2000), 123–46 (= Gerd Theissen, *A Theory of Primitive Christian Religion,* trans. John Bowden [London: SCM], 81–117). For the beatitude of the peacemaker (Matt 5:9)

as adoption of a ruler's ideal cf. Hans Windisch, "Friedensbringer—Gottessöhne," *ZNW* 24 (1925): 240–60.

B. *The Charismatic Phase of Paul's Epistolary Literature*

1. Phillipp Vielhauer, *Geschichte der urchristlichen Literatur* (Berlin and New York: de Gruyter, 1975); Udo Schnelle, *The History and Theology of the New Testament Writings*, trans. M. Eugene Boring (Minneapolis: Fortress Press, 1998).

4. *The Historical Conditions for Paul's Letters*

1. Cf. Hans-Josef Klauck, *Die antike Briefliteratur und das Neue Testament*, UT 2022 (Paderborn: Schöningh, 1998).

2. All the letters in the Old Testament are embedded in narratives. The independent Letter of Jeremiah, found only in the Septuagint, is the exception that proves the rule, because it is a freely-composed re-creation of the famous letter of Jeremiah to the exiles (Jeremiah 29). It is true that there were official letters from Jerusalem to the Diaspora; cf. Irene Taatz, *Frühjüdische Briefe: die paulinischen Briefe im Rahmen der offiziellen religiösen Briefe des Frühjudentums* (Fribourg: Universitätsverlag, 1991). But these letters were not published as a collection. In early Christianity the item most similar to such letters of community guidance is *1 Clement*.

5. *The Pre-Pauline Oral Tradition*

1. Björn Fjärstedt, *Synoptic Traditions in 1 Corinthians. Themes and Clusters of Theme Words in 1 Corinthians 1–4 and 9* (Uppsala: Teologiska Institutionen, 1974), 65–77.

2. Eric K. C. Wong, "The Deradicalization of Jesus' Ethical Sayings in 1 Corinthians," *NTS* 48 (2002): 181–94.

3. Cf. the overview in Vielhauer, *Geschichte der urchristlichen Literatur*, 9–57.

6. *The Pauline Letter as Literary Form*

1. Klauck, *Briefliteratur*, 152–53.

2. Régis Burnet, *Épîtres et lettres Ier-IIe siècle. De Paul de Tarse à Polycarpe de Smyrne* (Paris: Cerf, 2003).

3. Adolf Deissmann, *Light from the Ancient East: The New Testament Illustrated by Recently Discovered Texts of the Graeco-Roman World* [1909], trans. Lionel R. M. Strachan (London: Hodder & Stoughton, 1910; repr. Grand Rapids: Baker Book House, 1978), esp. 220–41, wanted to distinguish literary epistles like

Hebrews and James from genuine correspondence. That is correct in principle, but even in the genuine Pauline letters there is a visible tendency toward the "literary letter" (epistle).

4. The *Letter of Aristeas* describes the origins of the LXX and, in a discussion with the Ptolemaic king of Philadelphia, proposes an ideal for kingship. It contains the superscription "Aristeas for Philocrates," but it is not a letter; rather, it is an account of the origin of the LXX in the work of seventy Jewish translators, written for Philocrates. The JSHRZ rightly locates the *Letter of Aristeas* within the genre of "instruction in narrative form."

5. The *Epistula Jeremiae* is attested in the first century B.C.E. by the discovery of a Greek fragment in 7Q2. The JSHRZ also locates the Letter of Jeremiah under "Instructions in Didactic Form."

6. The pseudepigrapha contain the *Epistula Henochi* (= *1 Enoch* 91–106), which does not have epistolary character, but is also called a paraenetic book. It is a collection of woes against the rich and powerful and could at one time have existed independently.

7. Irene Taatz, *Frühjüdische Briefe*.

8. Albrecht Dihle, *Greek and Latin Literature of the Roman Empire: from Augustus to Justinian* [1989], trans. Manfred Malzahn (London and New York: Routledge, 1994), cf. 208, 302–3, names two possible models for the community letter created by Paul: political messages and philosophical letters (included above among literary letters). Since the early Hellenistic period there had been "messages from rulers and officials directed to the whole community and communicating important political or cultic measures and prescriptions to the public in question. We know them primarily from the inscriptions by means of which they were published. There were also genuine and attributed philosophical letters in which the author explained details of his teaching not only to an addressee, but also to whole groups of followers, or entered into conflict with his opponents and competitors." The Pauline community letter is, indeed, different from these, but when in 2 Cor 3:1-3 Paul contends with competitors and their letters of recommendation and thus regards the community as his letter of Christ, written not on stone but on living hearts, he makes an association not only with the tablets of Sinai but also with the inscriptions by which official letters were chiseled in stone.

9. Klauck, *Briefliteratur*, 54.

10. Franz Schnider and Werner Stenger, *Studien zum neutestamentlichen Briefformular* (Leiden and New York: Brill, 1987).

11. There is a related formula in the eucharistic liturgy in *Didache* 10:6: "If anyone is holy, let that one come; if one is not so, let that one do penance! Our Lord come. Amen." Does Paul expect that after a letter to the Corinthians is read, the Lord's Supper will be celebrated, so that he therefore places "Maranatha" at the end of 1 Corinthians?

12. Hans Conzelmann, "Paulus und die Weisheit," in idem, *Theologie als Schriftauslegung: Aufsätze zum Neuen Testament* (Munich: Kaiser, 1974), 177–90.

13. Ernst Lohmeyer, "Probleme paulinischer Theologie," *ZNW* 26 (1927): 158–73.

14. For the state of rhetorical analysis cf. Peter Lampe, "Rhetorische Analyse paulinischer Texte—Quo vadis?" in Dieter Sänger and Matthias Konradt, eds., *Das Gesetz im frühen Judentum und im Neuen Testament: FS Christoph Burchard* (Göttingen: Vandenhoeck & Ruprecht; Fribourg: Universitätsverlag, 2006), 170–90.

15. Klauck, *Briefliteratur*, 149–52.

16. "Rhetoric by its nature had oral public speaking as its object. Letters, on the contrary, were conceived as written and in their ideal type, the letter of friendship, programmatically excluded a broad audience" (Klauck, *Briefliteratur*, 167).

17. Hans-Dieter Betz, *Galatians*, Hermeneia (Philadelphia: Fortress Press, 1979), conducted a rhetorical analysis of this one letter, Galatians, and thus founded rhetorical criticism, which investigates not only individual rhetorical figures and tropes in the texts, but also the structure and divisions of entire texts. Klaus Berger, "Hellenistische Gattungen im Neuen Testament," *ANRW* II, 25.2 (Berlin: de Gruyter, 1994), 1031–1432, has offered a thorough classification of the formal language of the New Testament, using rhetorical categories.

18. Johannes Schoon-Janssen, *Umstrittene "Apologien" in den Paulusbriefen: Studien zur rhetorischen Situation des 1. Thessalonicherbriefes, des Galaterbriefes und des Philipperbriefes*, GTA 45 (Göttingen: Vandenhoeck & Ruprecht, 1991).

19. The paraenesis in Galatians is regularly regarded as a decisive objection to the idea that this is an apologetic speech to the court in the form of a letter. In court the accused would not formulate any admonitions. The most engaging interpretation is that of Dieter Kremendahl, *Die Botschaft der Form. Zum Verhältnis von antiker Epistolographie und Rhetorik im Galaterbrief*, NTOA 46 (Fribourg: Universitätsverlag; Göttingen: Vandenhoeck & Ruprecht, 2000): the speech to the court ends at Gal 5:6, and 5:7–6:18 are a postscript, part of the letter frame. In that way the shift in genre from rhetorical apology to epistolary paraenesis is made possible.

20. Margaret M. Mitchell, *Paul and the Rhetoric of Reconciliation*, HUT 28 (Tübingen: Mohr, 1991).

21. Robert Jewett, "Romans as an Ambassadorial Letter," *Int* 36 (1982): 5–20.

7. The Sequence and Development of the Pauline Letters

1. But who can say that the tensions had not already been overcome? Paul may have given instructions about the collection to the messengers who delivered the letter to the Galatians! Apart from that it is a fact that if Paul had problems with the Corinthians, he would not have written to Corinth that he had problems with the Galatians.

2. Cf. Kremendahl, *Botschaft der Form*, 38–73, who sees the autographic conclusion as a mark of juridical form and on pp. 75–95 cites other characteristics of that form: the oath formula (Gal 1:20), the reference to his stigmata as identifying marks (Gal 6:17b), the threat of punishment with an anathema (Gal 1:8-9), and the quotation of a document from the apostolic council (Gal 2:7-8).

3. Cf. Hans-Dieter Betz, "Geist, Freiheit und Gesetz," *ZTK* 71 (1974): 78–93: favoring a beginning phase is that the Galatians are overtasked by the freedom of

the Spirit. Paul speaks to them as if he had not yet had experience with Corinthian enthusiasm. —A late dating of Galatians would be interesting for the development of Paul's thought. In that case it would be easier to support the thesis that Paul developed his doctrine of justification only later, in reaction to the counter-mission. It is missing in three previous letters (1 Thessalonians, 1 and 2 Corinthians)! But if Galatians is dated before 1 Corinthians, we cannot conclude from silence about the doctrine of justification in 1 Corinthians that it did not yet exist. The same would be true, *mutatis mutandis*, for 1 Thessalonians. The doctrine of justification could always have been an element of Pauline theology.

4. David Trobisch, *Die Entstehung der Paulusbriefsammlung. Studien zu den Anfängen christlicher Publizistik*, NTOA 10 (Fribourg: Universitätsverlag; Göttingen: Vandenhoeck & Ruprecht, (1989), 123–28. Eve-Marie Becker, *Schreiben und Verstehen. Paulinische Briefhermeneutik im Zweiten Korintherbrief*, NET 4 (Tübingen: Francke, 2002), also assumes a successive origin of the letter as new pieces of news accumulated. Cf. eadem, "2. Korintherbrief," in Oda Wischmeyer, ed., *Paulus. Leben, Umwelt, Werk, Briefe*, UTB 2767 (Tübingen and Basel: Francke, 2006), 164–90.

5. Berthold Mengel, *Studien zum Philipperbrief*, WUNT 2d ser. 8 (Tübingen: Mohr, 1982).

6. Charlotte Hartwig and Gerd Theissen, "Die korinthische Gemeinde als Nebenadressat des Römerbriefs," *NT* 46 (2004): 229–52.

7. Günther Bornkamm, "Der Römerbrief als Testament des Paulus," in idem, ed., *Geschichte und Glaube, 2. Gesammelte Aufsätze*, vol. 4 (Munich: Kaiser, 1971), 120–39.

8. David Trobisch, *Die Entstehung der Paulusbriefsammlung* (1989); idem, *Die Paulusbriefe und die Anfänge der christlichen Publizistik*, KT 135 (Gütersloh: Kaiser, 1994) gives arguments for an authorial edition collected by Paul himself. That is not impossible for an ancient Pauline letter collection (Romans, 1 and 2 Corinthians, Galatians). But in making an authorial edition, would Paul not have "meshed" the letters much more closely through redactional connections?

9. This is not contradicted by the fact that *de facto* they created a literature for small groups. Their "literature" had a larger claim. As they understood themselves, Christians were not a "small group," but the beginning of a new humanity.

8. The Collection of Paul's Letters

1. Trobisch, *Anfänge der christlichen Publizistik*, 80.

2. According to Outi Leppä, *The Making of Colossians. A Study on the Formation and Purpose of a Deutero-Pauline Letter*, SESJ 86 (Göttingen: Vandenhoeck & Ruprecht, 2003), Colossians presupposes all the genuine Pauline letters.

3. Andreas Lindemann, "Die Sammlung der Paulusbriefe im 1. und 2. Jahrhundert," in Jean-Marie Auwers and Henk Jan de Jonge, eds., *The Biblical Canons*, BETL 163 (Leuven: Leuven University Press, 2003), 321–51, at 337: "Speaking against the supposition of such an early collection [i.e., at the time of Colossians] is

precisely the creation of the pseudopauline letters themselves; their reception in the communities would probably have been a rather difficult matter if those communities already had at their disposal something like a *Corpus Paulinum*."

4. Andreas Lindemann, *Paulus im Ältesten Christentum. Das Bild des Apostels und die Rezeption der paulinischen Theologie in der frühchristlichen Literatur bis Marcion* (Tübingen: Mohr, 1979), 171.

5. Ibid., 177–99; idem, "Sammlung der Paulusbriefe," 338–39.

6. Lindemann, *Paulus im Ältesten Christentum*, 191.

7. *1 Clement* 32:1-2 recalls Rom 9:5; *1 Clem.* 30:6 echoes Rom 2:29b; *1 Clem.* 61:1-2 is reminiscent of Rom 13:1-7.

8. Annette Merz, *Die fiktive Selbstauslegung des Paulus. Intertextuelle Studien zur Intention und Rezeption der Pastoralbriefe*, NTOA 52 (Fribourg: Universitätsverlag; Göttingen: Vandenhoeck & Ruprecht, 2004), 140–94.

9. Cf. Trobisch, *Paulusbriefsammlung*, 123–28.

Part Two: The Fictive Self-Interpretation of Paul and Jesus

1. This is my thesis in Gerd Theissen, *Gospel Writing and Church Politics: A Socio-rhetorical Approach*, Chuen King Lecture Series 3 (Hong Kong: Theology Division, 2001).

9. Pseudepigraphy as a Literary-Historical Phase in Early Christianity

1. Annette Merz, *Die fiktive Selbstauslegung des Paulus. Intertextuelle Studien zur Intention und Rezeption der Pastoralbriefe*, NTOA 52 (Göttingen: Vandenhoeck & Ruprecht; Fribourg: Universitätsverlag, 2004), developed the concept of "fictive self-interpretation" in terms of the Pastorals. In this proposal for a literary history of the New Testament we will expand the concept, seeing it as a characteristic feature of a whole phase in early Christian literature.

2. Contra Franz Overbeck, who did not see the letter as literature and undervalued the originality of the community letter.

3. Michael Wolter, "Die anonymen Schriften des Neuen Testaments," *ZNW* 79 (1988): 1–16.

4. Martin Hengel, *Die Evangelienüberschriften*, SAHW.PH, no. 3 (Heidelberg: C. Winter, 1984).

5. *1 Clement* was handed down without an author called "Clement." Nevertheless, there is a probably reliable historical tradition attributing it to a Clement. The attribution of the gospels to particular authors was certainly not arbitrary, but was based on traditions and astute deductions.

6. For this appealing theory see Martin Hengel, *Die johanneische Frage. Ein Lösungsversuch*, WUNT 67 (Tübingen: Mohr, 1993).

7. We must differentiate still further: primary pseudepigraphy can (1) be deliberately deceptive pseudepigraphy, but it can (2) be confined to naming (= onomas-

tic pseudepigraphy), and it can (3) be open pseudepigraphy meant to be perceived by the reader. Secondary pseudepigraphy can (4) appeal to passages in the text that deliberately suggest a particular (false) authorial name, or (5) to indications that only the reader can evaluate on the basis of knowledge of accessible sources.

8. Cf. Armin D. Baum, *Pseudepigraphie und literarische Fälschung im frühen Christentum. Mit ausgewählten Quellentexten samt deutscher Übersetzung*, WUNT 2d ser. 138 (Tübingen: Mohr, 2001).

9. In Jewish-Hellenistic literature pseudepigraphic writings were the rule, writings under the name of the genuine author the exception. Thus Martin Hengel, "Anonymität. Pseudepigraphie und 'literarische Fälschung' in der jüdisch-hellenistischen Literatur," in Roland Deines and Martin Hengel, eds., *Judaica et Hellenistica. Kleine Schriften I*, WUNT 90 (Tübingen: Mohr, 1996), 196–251.

10. We find the derivation of pseudepigraphy from the knowledge of messengers in Harald Hegermann, "Der geschichtliche Ort der Pastoralbriefe," *Theologische Versuche* 2 (1970): 47–64. Their good conscience is also explained by the fact that at that time oral Jesus traditions were still circulating in many variations. Hence a further transformation of Jesus traditions was not a big step.

11. Marco Frenschkowski, "Pseudepigraphie und Paulusschule," in Friedrich Wilhelm Horn, ed., *Das Ende des Paulus*, BZNW 106 (Berlin: de Gruyter, 2001), 239–72.

12. Klauck, *Briefliteratur*, 304.

13. Ibid., 144.

14. We can make a counter-test in the early Christian writings that appeared under the names of their authors. All these writings have their own source of authority: the Revelation of John and the Shepherd of Hermas derived it directly from heaven. In the case of letters, this form of foundation for authority was lacking. The bishop of Antioch wrote his letters on the road to his martyrdom, drawing his entire authority from this "heavenly journey" before him. The letter of Polycarp owes its authority to Polycarp's martyrdom. Behind *1 Clement* was a powerful community that did not need to conceal itself under a false name.

15. Pseudepigraphy was occasionally justified even in antiquity by such social motives. Thus the Neoplatonic David writes in the sixth century: "If someone was obscure and of little account but wanted to have his writing read, he wrote in the name of an old and respected man so that the latter's esteem would cause his work to be well received" (*In Porphyrii isagogen commentarium* 1, quoted from the source collection in Armin D. Baum, *Pseudepigraphie*, 215).

16. Klauck, *Briefliteratur*, 304.

10. Paul's Fictive Self-Interpretation in the Deutero-Pauline Writings

1. Taeseong Roh, *Der zweite Thessalonicherbrief als Erneuerung apokalyptischer Zeitdeutung*, NTOA 62 (Fribourg: Universitätsverlag; Göttingen: Vandenhoeck & Ruprecht, 2007), suggests a new interpretation: that 2 Thessalonians was

intended to renew imminent expectation of the end. He shows that the preconditions for the imminence of the end and the coming of the Antichrist had already been fulfilled in Vespasian's reign. Second Thessalonians corrects a mistaken expectation of the coming end in 1 Thessalonians, but only to advocate for it on better grounds in a new situation.

2. Frenschkowski, "Pseudepigraphie und Paulusschule" (2001), 239–72.

3. Annette Merz, *Selbstauslegung*, 268–372.

4. One should not imagine that the later (pseudepigraphic) New Testament writings were intended to be read by themselves. They were from the beginning expansions, commentary, and introductions to reading the other Pauline letters and the Synoptic Jesus tradition. Their intent was to let the older literature be read in their light. The Gospel of John is aware either of the Synoptic Gospels or of the Synoptic tradition behind the gospels. The non-genuine Pauline letters know the genuine ones. Even in the oldest of the non-genuine Pauline letters, Colossians, we may be able to find echoes of all the genuine letters of Paul.

5. Merz, *Selbstauslegung*, 247–67.

6. Annette Merz, "Why Did the Pure Bride of Christ Become a Wedded Wife (Eph. 5.22-33)?" *JSNT* 79 (2000): 131–47.

7. Merz, *Selbstauslegung*, 268–372.

8. Certainly one cannot reduce the motivation for the origins of the pseudepigraphic Pauline letters to such corrections of Paul, but that letters were circulating under his name becomes a necessity, at the latest, when such corrections were made.

9. Tertullian, *Bapt.* 17.4-5.

10. Matthias Konradt, *Christliche Existenz nach dem Jakobusbrief. Eine Studie zu seiner soteriologischen und ethischen Konzeption*, SNT 22 (Göttingen: Vandenhoeck & Ruprecht, 1998), 241–26, has disputed that this is anti-Pauline polemic. It is true that the letter of James revives an Abrahamic tradition independent of Paul; nevertheless, there is a reference to Paul. Cf. Gerd Theissen, "Die pseudepigraphe Intention des Jakobusbriefs," in Petra von Gemünden, Matthias Konradt, and Gerd Theissen, eds., *Der Jakobusbrief. Beiträge zur Rehabilitierung der "strohernen Epistel,"* BVB 3 (Münster: Lit Verlag, 2003), 54–82, esp. 71–77.

11. Karl-Wilhelm Niebuhr, "'A New Perspective on James,' Neuere Forschungen zum Jakobusbrief," *TLZ* 129 (2004): 1019–44, objects to my interpretation of James as an apology for Jewish Christianity against Pauline distortions by saying that there is no evidence for a negative view of Jewish Christianity at the end of the first century C.E. Such objections are easily dismissed: the Pauline letters to the Galatians, Philippians, Romans, and 2 Corinthians were circulating at the end of the first century, and were collected and read.

12. Martin Hengel, "Der Jakobusbrief als antipaulinische Polemik," in idem, *Paulus und Jakobus. Gesammelte Aufsätze 3*, WUNT 141 (Tübingen: Mohr, 2002), 511–48, interpreted the letter of James as polemic by the historical James against the historical Paul. Taking this interpretation farther, I would instead interpret it as the apologetic of a later Jewish Christian against Pauline Christianity (cf. my essay cited in the previous note).

13. The following six motifs are drawn from Hans-Martin Schenke and Karl Martin Fischer, *Einleitung in die Schriften des Neuen Testaments 1: Die Briefe des Paulus und Schriften des Paulinismus* (Berlin: Evangelische Verlagsanstalt, 1978), 208–11.

14. Of course, the motives for the origin of the post-Pauline letters were manifold; each of them opens up its own little theological world.

15. Dieter Lührmann, "Gal 2,9 und die katholischen Briefe," *ZNW* 72 (1981): 65–87.

11. Jesus' Fictive Self-Interpretation through the Redaction of the Jesus Traditions in the Synoptic Gospels

1. This view of the origin of the gospels as writings shaped by the problems of concrete communities, common among redaction critics, has been challenged by Richard Bauckham, *The Gospels for All Christians. Rethinking the Gospel Audiences* (Grand Rapids: Eerdmans, 1998), with the idea that the gospels were written for all Christians and do not think of concrete communities as their addressees. Here we find a twofold misunderstanding: the intended readers and hearers of the gospels were on the one hand not only all Christians, but all people; the gospel is to be preached to all nations. The actual hearers and readers, on the other hand, were always only a limited circle; the writer is always an author shaped by a concrete milieu. Even scientific works are intentionally addressed to all, but are in fact the expression of particular, often clearly localizable problem traditions and speak to specific scientific groups.

2. Cf. Theissen, *Gospel Writing*, 8–39, 161.

3. Heike Räisänen, *The "Messianic Secret,"* 220–22.

4. Eric Kun Chun Wong, *Interkulturelle Theologie und multikulturelle Gemeinde im Matthäusevangelium*, NTOA 22 (Fribourg: Universitätsverlag; Göttingen: Vandenhoeck & Ruprecht, 1992).

5. Cf. Gerd Theissen, "Vom Davidssohn zum Weltherrscher," in Michael Becker and Wolfgang Fenske, eds., *Das Ende der Tage und die Gegenwart des Heils. Begegnungen mit dem Neuen Testament und seiner Umwelt, FS H. W. Kuhn*, AGAJU 44 (Leiden: Brill, 1999), 145–64.

6. Quoted from William David Davies et al., *The Cambridge History of Judaism. 3. The Early Roman Period* (Cambridge: Cambridge University Press, 1999), 316.

7. For the distancing of rabbinic Judaism from the Pharisees cf. Peter Schäfer, "Der vorrabinische Pharisäismus," in Martin Hengel and Ulrich Heckel, eds., *Paulus und das antike Judentum*, WUNT 58 (Tübingen: Mohr, 1991), 125–75.

8. Theissen, *Gospel Writing*, 45–78.

9. Wong, *Interkulturelle Theologie und multikulturelle Gemeinde* (1992).

10. Cf. Ilze Kezbere, *Umstrittener Monotheismus. Wahre und falsche Apotheose im lukanischen Doppelwerk*, NTOA 60 (Fribourg: Universitätsverlag; Göttingen: Vandenhoeck & Ruprecht, 2007).

11. Hans Conzelmann, *The Theology of St. Luke* (1954), trans. Geoffrey Buswell (Philadelphia: Fortress Press, 1961).

12. What is primarily criticized in Luke's two-volume work is a certain "worldliness." Luke is accused of relying on confirmed historical data and representing (in the prologue) a *fides historica*; further, he is said to build on a worldly experience transparent to God and to offer (in the Areopagus discourse) a natural theology. Likewise, he is said to present an early Catholic idea of the church, with succession, and on the whole, through his political apologetics, to prepare Christianity to accommodate itself to the world. Lukan exegesis therefore for a long time was subject to the maxim: "beat up on Luke." Cf. Werner G. Kümmel, "Lukas in der Anklage der heutigen Theologie" (1970) in idem, *Heilsgeschehen und Geschichte*, vol. 2 (Marburg: Elwert, 1978), 87–100.

13. Two further examples: (1) In Luke 12:45-46 the wicked slave says in his heart: "My master is delayed in coming" and therefore mistreats his fellow slaves. Here again it is not that imminent expectation of the end is defended, but rather that ethics are given a basis independent of it. Those who use the delay of the *parousia* as an excuse for acting immorally will be harshly punished in the final judgment. (2) In Luke 21:32 the evangelist takes from Mark the words: "Truly I tell you, this generation will not pass away until all things have taken place. Heaven and earth will pass away, but my words will not pass away." What is crucial here is: what is Luke's application of "this generation"? If he sees it as encompassing the whole human race, the logion says nothing about his imminent expectation.

14. Cf. Jacques Dupont, "Die individuelle Eschatologie im Lukas-Evangelium und in der Apostelgeschichte," in Paul Hoffmann, ed., *Orientierung an Jesus. Zur Theologie der Synoptiker* (Freiburg et al.: Herder, 1973), 37–47. Alongside this individual expectation of the imminent end there are passages that hold fast to an imminent cosmic expectation. Are they really only traditional material that was incorporated? After Jesus' death there is supposed to be still a "time of the Gentiles" (Luke 21:24). This time is presented in Acts as an independent phase. Perhaps in the meantime Luke has become convinced that this phase is now nearing its end. Acts 1:8 has been fulfilled: the gospel has been preached from Jerusalem to Samaria and to the ends of the earth (as far as Rome). Now all that remains is for the end to come. Cf. Christoph Burchard, *Der dreizehnte Zeuge*, FRLANT 103 (Gottingen: Vandenhoeck & Ruprecht, 1970), 177–83.

15. Theissen, *Gospel Writing*, 84–120.

16. In the Pentecost miracle the Spirit appears to be independent of baptism (Acts 2:1-4). In the baptism of the Ethiopian court official the Spirit participates only by bringing Philip and the official together (Acts 8:29) and separating them again (Acts 8:39). In principle, of course, the Spirit is promised in baptism (Acts 2:38). But the Spirit can also precede baptism—in the cases of Paul (Acts 9:17) and Cornelius (Acts 10:44-48)—or can follow it, as with the Samaritans (Acts 8:4-8, 14-17) and the disciples of John in Ephesus (Acts 19:1-7). The ritualization of the bestowal of the Spirit, that is, its uniting to baptism and the imposition of hands, is clearly discernible, but it is not an indissoluble tie.

17. In codices Vaticanus and Alexandrinus the gospels are followed by Acts and the catholic letters, and then the letters of Paul. 𝔓45, from the third century C.E., contains the four gospels in the canonical order, followed by Acts.

12. Jesus' Fictive Self-Interpretation through the Transformation of the Jesus Traditions in the Gospels Associated with Gnosis

1. For John's Gospel as *relecture* cf. Andreas Dettwiler, *Die Gegenwart des Erhöhten. Eine exegetische Studie zu den johanneischen Abschiedsreden (Joh 13,31–16,33) unter besonderer Berücksichtigung ihres Relecture-Charakters*, FRLANT 169 (Göttingen: Vandenhoeck & Ruprecht, 1995). I introduced the idea of a hermeneutic in stages in some 1987 lectures in Montpellier; it was taken up and used positively by Jean Zumstein, "L'évangile johannique: une strategie de croire," *RSC* 77 (1989): 217–32 = "Das Johannesevangelium: Eine Strategie des Glaubens," in idem, *Kreative Erinnerung. Relecture und Auslegung im Johannesevangelium* (Zürich: Pano, 1999), 15–45. In *Die Religion der ersten Christen*, 257–80, I have described the hermeneutic in stages in John's Gospel at greater length.

2. Cf. the review of research in Stefan Schreiber, "Kannte Johannes die Synoptiker? Zur aktuellen Diskussion," *VF* 51 (2006): 7–24.

3. Klaus Berger, *Im Anfang war Johannes. Datierung und Theologie des vierten Evangeliums* (3d ed. Gütersloh: Kaiser, 2004); Peter L. Hofrichter, ed., *Für und wider die Priorität des Johannesevangeliums* (Hildesheim: Olms, 2002).

4. Michael Theobald, *Herrenworte im Johannesevangelium* (Freiburg: Herder, 2002).

5. Cf. W. H. C. Frend, "Montanismus," *TRE* 23 (1994): 271–79, at 274. Montanus (no. 2): "Neither an angel nor a messenger, but I, the Lord, God, the Father, have come"; Maximilla (no. 1): "Do not listen to me, but listen to Christ," etc.

6. Theissen, *Gospel Writing*, 125–57.

7. Translation by Marvin W. Meyer in Robert J. Miller, ed., *The Complete Gospels* (Sonoma, CA: Polebridge Press, 1992).

8. Examples in the Matthean special material include Matt 5:10 = *Gos. Thom.* 69a; Matt 5:14 = *Gos. Thom.* 32; Matt 6:2-4 = *Gos. Thom.* 6 and 14. In the Lukan special material cf. Luke 11:27-28 = *Gos. Thom.* 79; Luke 17:20-21 = *Gos. Thom.* 3, etc.

9. Cf. Nicholas Perrin, *Thomas and Tatian. The Relationship between the Gospel of Thomas and the Diatessaron* (Atlanta: Society of Biblical Literature, 2002).

13. Jesus' Fictive Self-Interpretation through the Continuation of the Synoptic Jesus Tradition in the Jewish-Christian Gospels

1. Cf. Hans-Josef Klauck, *Apokryphe Evangelien. Eine Einführung* (2d ed. Stuttgart: Katholisches Bibelwerk, 2005), 53–76; Philipp Vielhauer, *Geschichte der*

urchristlichen Literatur, 648–61; Dieter Lührmann, *Fragmente apokryph gewordener Evangelien in griechischer und lateinischer Sprache* (Marburg: Elwert, 2000), 32–55. For English texts see Wilhelm Schneemelcher, ed., *New Testament Apocrypha*, Vol. 1: *Gospels and Related Writings*, trans. Robert McLachlan Wilson (rev. ed. Louisville: Westminster John Knox, 2003).

14. Jesus' Fictive Self-Interpretation through the Harmonizing of the Jesus Tradition in Other Apocryphal Gospels

1. Thus especially Helmut Koester, *Ancient Christian Gospels* (Berlin and New York: de Gruyter, 1990). In his literary history he treats the *Gospel of Thomas* before the Sayings Source, the dialogical gospels before John, the infancy gospels before Matthew and Luke. This turns the chronological relationship of the writings on its head. In the apocryphal gospels and gospel fragments we do not find the prehistory of our canonical gospels; rather, for the most part they belong to the history of their influence.

2. There is an English translation edited by Charles W. Hedrick and Paul Allan Mirecki, *The Gospel of the Savior: A New Ancient Gospel* (Santa Rosa, CA: Polebridge Press, 1999).

3. Ibid., 33. For a long time the Secret Gospel of Mark, discovered and edited by the famous scholar Morton Smith, was a puzzle. Is it a fake produced by this scholar? Stephen C. Carlson, *The Gospel Hoax: Morton Smith's Invention of Secret Mark* (Waco: Baylor University Press, 2005).

4. Cf. 𝔓Eg 2, 𝔓Oxy 840, the Strasbourg Coptic papyrus, the *Gospel of Marcion,* the *Gospel of the Nazareans,* the *Gospel of the Ebionites,* the *Gospel of the Hebrews,* the *Gospel of Peter,* the unknown Berlin Gospel, the *Gospel of the Egyptians,* Tatian's *Diatessaron*, the *Gospel of Thomas*, the *Gospel of Philip,* the *Gospel of Judas.* This phenomenon will be treated in detail in the last chapter.

5. Col 1:24-26; Eph 3:3-19; Rom 16:25-26 (in the secondary doxology); 1 Tim 3:16; 2 Tim 1:9; Titus 1:2-3; 1 Pet 1:20. On this see Nils A. Dahl, "Formgeschichtliche Beobachtungen zur Christusverkündigung in der Gemeindepredigt," in Walter Eltester, ed., *Neutestamentliche Studien für Rudolf Bultmann*, BZNW 21 (Berlin: Töpelmann, 1954), 3-9. In Mark we already find approaches to such a consciousness of revelation in the messianic secret: Jesus is surrounded by mystery that can only be dissolved by God through direct revelation from heaven—his voice at the baptism and transfiguration. But Mark lacks the preexistence of the Redeemer.

6. We cannot generalize here. Christian apocalypses also appeared under an Old Testament name in the *Ascension of Isaiah* and under a New Testament name in the *Apocalypse of Peter.*

Part Three: The Authority of the Independent Forms

1. This morphological change was associated in part with pseudepigraphy. Pseudepigraphic letters are not genuine letters with a correspondence character and

reference to situations. They are thus more oriented to substantive statements and the forms appropriate to them. They develop a tendency to allow the letter form to wither away into an external shell into which quite different kinds of texts were transported.

15. The Independent Differentiation of Partial Texts and Tendencies

1. In Mark we find two secret teachings to the disciples in the open: in the parables discourse (Mark 4:10-25) and in the Synoptic apocalypse (13:3-37), and four brief secret teachings in the house (Mark 7:17-23; 9:28-29, 33-37; 10:10-16). Since in the case of the longer discourses in the open the later conditions in the congregation are clearly addressed, the same must be true of the short secret teachings. That they take place in the house indicates that they reflect on the problems of the house and the house churches: food questions (Mark 7:17-23), healings (9:28-29), disputes over rank (9:33-37), and marriage and children (10:10-12, 13-16).

2. Judith Hartenstein, *Die zweite Lehre. Erscheinungen des Auferstandenen als Rahmenerzählungen frühchristlicher Dialoge*, TU 146 (Berlin: Akademie-Verlag, 2000), has shown that the *Sophia Jesu Christi* was the work that shaped the genre.

3. That the farewell discourses are fundamentally dialogues with the Risen One is evident when the Johannine Jesus says: "I am no longer in the world, but they are in the world, and I am coming to you" (John 17:11).

4. Michael Wolter, "Apokalyptik als Redeform im Neuen Testament," *NTS* 51 (2005): 171–91: apocalyptic texts in the strict sense presuppose an epistemological transcendence and crossing of cognitive boundaries.

5. These are very different in content, but in their form all borrow from apocalypses. Dependence on the traditional apocalypses is evident from the very fact that yet another early Christian apocalypse was published as the *Ascension of Isaiah*.

6. In this third phase also we can see differences between the development in the field of gospel literature and that of the letters. The development to pure collections of sayings and secret teachings was pursued especially in Gnostic literature. It is true that that corpus does not lack letters (cf. the Letter of Eugnostos, the Letter of Rheginus, the Letter of Ptolemaeus to Flora), but the letter form belongs more to "orthodox" Christianity, as *1 Clement*, the letters of Ignatius, the Letter of Polycarp, and the Letter of Barnabas show.

16. The Acts of the Apostles

1. Loveday C. A. Alexander, *The Preface to Luke's Gospel: Literary Convention and Social Context in Luke 1:1-4 and Acts 1:1*, SNTSMS 78 (Cambridge: Cambridge University Press, 1993).

2. Michael Labahn, "'Boldly and Without Hindrance He Preached the Kingdom of God and Taught about the Lord Jesus Christ' (Acts 28:31). Paul's Public Proclamation in Rome as the Finale of a Shipwreck," in Jürgen Zangenberg and

Michael Labahn, eds., *Christians as a Religious Minority in a Multicultural City. Modes of Interaction and Identity Formation in Early Imperial Rome*, JSNTSup 268 (London and New York: T & T Clark, 2004), 56–76, points to the connection between rescue from the storm at sea and public proclamation in the name of the saving God.

3. Alexander J. M. Wedderburn, "Zur Frage der Gattung der Apostelgeschichte," in Hubert Cancik et al., eds., *Geschichte—Tradition—Reflexion III: Frühes Christentum* (Tübingen: Mohr, 1996), 303–22.

4. Franz Overbeck, *Christentum und Kultur. Gedanken und Anmerkungen zur modernen Theologie*, ed. Carl Albrecht Bernoulli (Basel: Schwabe, 1919; 2d ed. Darmstadt: Wissenschaftliche Buchgesellschaft, 1963), 78.

5. Ibid., 79.

6. More precisely: it belongs within tragico-pathetic historiography. Cf. Eckhard Plümacher, "Apostelgeschichte," *TRE* 3 (1978): 483–528, at 509–13.

7. Dietrich-Alex Koch, "Kollektenbericht, 'Wir'-Bericht und Itinerar," *NTS* 45 (1999): 367–90.

17. The Revelation to John

1. Cf. Ferdinand Hahn, "Die Sendschreiben der Johannesapokalypse. Ein Beitrag zur Bestimmung prophetischer Redeformen," in Gerd Jeremias, ed., *Tradition und Glaube. FS Karl Georg Kuhn* (Göttingen: Vandenhoeck & Ruprecht, 1971), 357–94.

2. Georg Strecker, *Literaturgeschichte*, 274–75, assumes pseudepigraphy for Revelation also—above all because it is a characteristic of the apocalyptic genre. But the seer certainly does not identify himself as the apostle John, since for him the apostles are a phenomenon of the past (Rev 18:20; 21:14). The concrete statements about his stay in Patmos and the concrete addressees of the seven letters (Rev 1:9-11) point to a concrete person familiar to the communities in Asia Minor.

3. Günther Bornkamm, "Die Komposition der apokalyptischen Visionen in der Offenbarung Johannis," in idem, ed., *Studien zu Antike und Urchristentum. Gesammelte Aufsätze*, vol. 2 (3d ed. Munich: Kaiser, 1970), 204–22, interpreted these as preliminary (8:2–14:20) and final (15:1–22:5) depictions of the last events.

4. J.-W. Taeger, "Offenbarung 1,1-3," *NTS* 49 (2003): 176–92, assumes a deliberate identification by a later editor of the author of Revelation with the author of the Johannine writings.

5. The author of the Gospel of John received his message from the Paraclete, who recalls for him the words of Jesus (John 14:26). The Paraclete is Jesus' representative, sent by God and Jesus, in whose bosom the Beloved Disciple lay (John 13:23; 21:20), but Christ came directly from the bosom of God (John 1:18).

6. Rev 7:16-17; 21:6; 22:1, 17; cf. John 4:10-15; 7:37-39.

7. Rev 19:13; John 1:1.

8. Twenty-nine times in Revelation; John 1:29, 36.

18. The Letter to the Hebrews

1. Cf. Gerd Theissen, *Untersuchungen zum Hebräerbrief*, SNT 2 (Gütersloh: Mohn, 1969), 34–37.

2. In addition, there are two other Psalms citations: Pss 44:7-8 LXX; 101:26-28 LXX.

3. Thus Hartwig Thyen, *Der Stil der jüdisch-hellenistischen Homilie*, FRLANT 47 (Göttingen: Vandenhoeck & Ruprecht, 1955).

4. Folker Siegert, ed., *Drei hellenistisch-jüdische Predigten. Ps.-Philon, "Über Jona," "Über Simon" und "Über die Gottesbezeichnung 'wohltätig verzehrendes Feuer,'"* WUNT 20 (Tübingen: Mohr, 1980).

5. Folker Siegert, *Drei hellenistisch-jüdische Predigten, II*, Diss. habil. Heidelberg (1989), 36–42, at 42: "After all that has been said, we leave them in the first pre-Christian to the second post-Christian century, with weight placed on the middle of that period."

6. It is different in the puzzling "we passages" in Acts, which begin with the movement from Asia Minor (Troas) to Europe (Acts 16:11) and recur in Acts from then until the end. Here the author suggests eyewitness testimony to the last phase of Paul's mission—and it is disputed even today whether he could really claim it for himself or whether it belongs to a source behind Acts (an account of the delivery of the collection could have contained a "we"), or whether it is an authorial method that should be primarily interpreted within the text.

Part Four: The New Testament on Its Way to Becoming a Religious World Literature

1. Cf. the two groundbreaking works of Bernhard Mutschler, *Irenäus als johanneischer Theologe. Studien zur Schriftauslegung bei Irenäus von Lyon*, SANT 21 (Tübingen: Mohr, 2004); idem, *Das Corpus Johanneum bei Irenäus von Lyon. Studien und Kommentar zum dritten Buch von Adversus Haereses*, WUNT 189 (Tübingen: Mohr, 2006). Biblical theology and "canonical approach" had a predecessor in Irenaeus.

19. Canon as a Means to Stability Based on Compromise and Demarcation

1. Cf. the review of research in Katharina Greschat, "Die Entstehung des neutestamentlichen Kanons. Fragestellungen und Themen der neueren Forschung," *VF* 51 (2006): 56–63.

2. Theo K. Heckel, *Vom Evangelium des Markus zum viergestaltigen Evangelium*, WUNT 120 (Tübingen: Mohr, 1999), 337–39.

3. Erkki Koskenniemi, *Apollonios von Tyana in der neutestamentlichen Exegese. Forschungsbericht und Weiterführung der Diskussion*, WUNT 2d ser. 61 (Tübingen: Mohr, 1994). Hans-Josef Klauck, *Die religiöse Umwelt des Urchristentums*, vol. 1, *Stadt- und Hausreligion, Mysterienkulte, Volksglaube* (Stuttgart: Kohlhammer, 1995), 140–44.

4. Guy G. Stroumsa, "The Body of Truth and Its Measures. New Testament Canonization in Context," in Holger Preissler et al., eds., *Gnosisforschung und Religionsgeschichte, FS Kurt Rudolph* (Marburg: Diagonal, 1994), 307–16.

5. Albrecht Dihle, *Die griechische und lateinische Literatur der Kaiserzeit. Von Augustus bis Iustinian* (Munich: Beck, 1989), 13–74.

6. Cf. Marius Reiser, *Sprache und literarische Formen des Neuen Testaments*, 29–33.

7. Mutschler, *Corpus Johanneum*, 504–5; Irenaeus does not cite Ruth, Esther, Nahum, Zephaniah, or Haggai.

8. Cf. the text of the Muratorian Fragment in Schneemelcher, *New Testament Apocrypha*, vol. 1, 27–29. The late dating given it by Geoffrey M. Hahneman, *The Muratorian Fragment and the Development of the Canon* (Oxford and New York: Oxford University Press, 1992), in the fourth or fifth century, is in my opinion improbable. The *Shepherd of Hermas,* according to it, had originated in Rome "shortly before." If that is not a subtle pseudepigraphic leading astray, the Muratorian Fragment probably originated in the second century.

9. But 1 Peter is missing from the Muratorian Fragment, while letters of John are mentioned. For Origen in the third century the canon contained, for example, the four gospels, fourteen Pauline letters, Acts, 1 Peter, 1 John, Jude, and Revelation. He is skeptical about James, 2 Peter, 2 and 3 John. Cf. Bruce M. Metzger, *The Canon of the New Testament: Its Origin, Development, and Significance* (Oxford and New York: Oxford University Press, 1987), 135–41.

10. I am adapting the schema found in Metzger, *Canon*, 205; between the extra-canonical orthodox c.) and the heretical writings (B) Eusebius distinguishes so emphatically that, unlike Metzger, one should not summarize them in a single group. The distinction between "orthodox" and "heretical" was more important for Eusebius than that between "canonical" and "extra-canonical."

11. Cf. Adolf M. Ritter, "Die Entstehung des neutestamentlichen Kanons: Selbstdurchsetzung oder autoritative Entscheidung?" in Aleida and Jan Assmann, eds., *Kanon und Zensur. Beiträge zur Archäologie der literarischen Kommunikation*, vol. 2 (Munich: Fink, 1987), 93–99.

12. The catholic letters were attributed to the brothers of the Lord, James and Jude, as well as to the apostles Peter and John. Jude is introduced in his letter as the brother of James and subordinated to him (Jude 1). The authority of the catholic letters thus rests on the three "pillars" of the Jerusalem community with whom Paul made an agreement at the Apostolic Council recognizing his mission to the Gentiles (Gal 2:1-10). The usual sequence of the letters as early as 𝔓74 (James, 1/2 Peter, 1–3 John, Jude) in fact corresponds to their sequence in Galatians 2:9: James, Peter, John. Cf. Dieter Lührmann, "Gal 2,9 und die katholischen Briefe," *ZNW* 72 (1981): 65–87. The expansion of the *Corpus Paulinum* by the catholic letters of the apostles

named in them was intended to underscore the consensus of all the apostles. James, the brother of the Lord, was not really one of the twelve apostles, but the apostolic title was appropriated to him on the basis of Galatians 1:19. The indirect reference to the Apostolic Council shows how crucial Paul was for the existence of the whole of early Christian epistolary literature—even for the letters not attributed to him.

13. In particular Hans von Campenhausen, *Die Entstehung der christlichen Bibel*, BHT 39 (Tübingen: Mohr, 1968), saw Marcion as the principal factor in the establishment of the canon: he rejected as a forgery the traditions about Christ that were so vivid in his own time and made it necessary for the church to present a broad collection of canonical writings in opposition to his canon. The influence of Marcion was probably more modest: his rejection speeded a consensus that was in the process of formation independently of him.

14. Fundamental on this question is Martin Hengel, *The Four Gospels and the One Gospel of Jesus Christ. An Investigation of the Collection and Origin of the Canonical Gospels* (London: SCM, 2000); Theo K. Heckel, *Vom Evangelium des Markus zum viergestaltigen Evangelium*, WUNT 120 (Tübingen: Mohr, 1999).

15. That Justin already presumes the four-gospel canon is shown by Graham N. Stanton, "The Fourfold Gospel," *NTS* 43 (1997): 317–46. For the passage cited above see pp. 330–31.

16. Theodore C. Skeat, "The Oldest Manuscript of the Four Gospels?" *NTS* 43 (1997): 1–34.

17. This is the opinion of Philipp Vielhauer, *Geschichte der urchristlichen Literatur*, 783.

18. Cf. David Trobisch, *Die Endredaktion des Neuen Testaments. Eine Untersuchung zur Entstehung der christlichen Bibel*, NTOA 31 (Fribourg: Universitätsverlag; Göttingen: Vandenhoeck & Ruprecht, 1996), 158–59.

19. Rightly skeptical about Papias's knowledge of the four gospels is Ulrich H. Körtner, *Papias von Hierapolis. Ein Beitrag zur Geschichte des frühen Christentums*, FRLANT 133 (Göttingen: Vandenhoeck & Ruprecht, 1983), 163–68, 173–78.

20. According to Theo K. Heckel, *Vom Evangelium des Markus zum viergestaltigen Evangelium*, 261–65, Papias had read the proemium of Luke's Gospel and echoed it in his own proemium.

21. Above all Theo K. Heckel, ibid., argues for an early origin of the four-gospel collection at the beginning of the second century C.E.

22. On this see Silke Petersen, "Die Evangelienüberschriften und die Entstehung des neutestamentlichen Kanons," *ZNW* 97 (2006): 250–74. She argues for a collection of a number of gospels even before the middle of the second century.

23. The Marcionites were later able to adopt the Pastorals. They did not apply the polemic against the "antitheses" to themselves, but probably to the "Gnosis" attacked there, from which they did in fact distance themselves.

24. Gerd Theissen, "Kirche oder Sekte?" *TGl* 48 (2005): 162–75.

25. Somewhat differently Ernst Käsemann, "Begründet der neutestamentliche Kanon die Einheit der Kirche?" (1951–52) in idem, ed., *Exegetische Versuche und Besinnungen*, vol. 1 (6th ed. Göttingen: Vandenhoeck & Ruprecht, 1970), 214–23. According to Käsemann the canon is the basis for the plurality of confessions.

26. In a second step the New Testament writings were equated with those of the Old Testament. Such a collection of writings then advanced the same claim as the Old Testament. When the canon was regarded as a closed corpus (though some writings may have remained in dispute) the final step had been taken.

27. I owe this idea to Hee-Seong Kim, *Die Geisttaufe des Messias. Eine kompositionsgeschichtliche Untersuchung zu einem Leitmotiv des lukanischen Doppelwerks* (Frankfurt: Peter Lang, 1991).

28. Gunnar Garleff, *Urchristliche Identität im Matthäusevangelium, Didachē und Jakobusbrief*, BVB 9 (Münster: LIT, 2004).

29. This opened space for other apostles besides Paul that could then be filled by the catholic letters.

30. Annette Merz, *Die fiktive Selbstauslegung des Paulus*, 172–87.

31. Oral communication from Annette Merz. With Jesus and Paul, Ignatius represents a third charismatic beginning in early Christian writings. These are the only three individuals of whom we have a clear profile.

32. Silke Petersen, *Evangelienüberschriften*, 273, thinks that the encounter of different gospels, not necessarily a collection, was enough to explain the origin of the gospel superscriptions.

33. Wolfram Kinzig, "Καινὴ διαθήκη," *JTS* 45 (1994): 519–44.

34. For what follows cf. the intriguing theory by David Trobisch, *Endredaktion* (1996), who supposes a unified edition of the New Testament by a single figure in the first half of the second century, with four characteristics: (1) unified superscriptions, (2) the same sequence of writings, (3) the same abbreviations of the *nomina sacra*, (4) codex form instead of scrolls.

35. There are papyri that contain fragments of several gospels (𝔓 44, 45, 75, 84) or a gospel and Acts (𝔓 53, Matthew/Acts), but not a single papyrus that combined a gospel with letters. On the other hand, there are a number of papyri containing a number of Paul's letters (𝔓 30, 34, 82, 99) or even most of them (𝔓 46, 61). But there is no papyrus that hands on Paul's letters together with a gospel, nor is there any papyrus that combined Pauline and catholic letters (𝔓 contains 1 Peter, 2 Peter, Jude; 𝔓 74 contains Acts, 1 and 2 Peter, 1–3 John, and Jude). This manuscript finding also points to partial collections.

36. Cf. the tables in Silke Petersen, *Evangelienüberschriften*, 255–56. Minor deviations from these numbers are found in the summary by Mutschler, *Irenäus*, 237: Matthew 12, Mark 1, Luke 6, John 15.

37. The majuscules E, F, G, V, Y, P, 047, 0233, 0250, and the minuscules 4, 13, 21, 22, 174, etc.

38. The divine voice at the transfiguration is given, with deviations, according to Matthew 17:5: "This is my beloved Son, *in whom I am well pleased*." There are other echoes of Matthew: "Sodom and Gomorrah" (2 Pet 2:6) recalls Matthew 10:15; the "way of righteousness" (2 Pet 2:21) Matthew 21:32; "dogs and swine" (2 Pet 2:22) Matthew 7:6. If 2 Peter 1:17 refers to the transfiguration as an appearance of Jesus' *doxa* (glory), it may be following the Lukan redaction of the transfiguration story (Luke 9:31, 32). The understanding of the apostles as eyewitnesses is

also close to the Lukan work. Cf. *epoptai* (2 Pet 1:16) and *autoptai* (Luke 1:2)—with different words for the "eyewitnesses"—and also the characterization of the apostles in Acts 1:21-22 and Acts 4:20. He may be thinking of Mark (and not the letters of Peter) when Peter wants to make sure that after his death his addressees will be able to remember his preaching (2 Pet 1:15).

39. References to the two individual genres in the New Testament in 2 Peter are uncertain: Revelation may be presumed by the hope for a new heaven and a new earth (2 Pet 3:13), Acts by the understanding of the apostles as eyewitnesses (2 Pet 1:16).

40. If Marcion were *also* discernible behind the heretics, the relationship of 2 Peter to the construction of the canon would be clear. It is true that 2 Peter advocates for the Old Testament when it speaks of the inspired words of the prophets (2 Pet 1:19-21). He adopts from the letter of Jude only examples from Old Testament history that are in the canon. The letters of Paul were distorted in the second century (in the eyes of orthodox communities) primarily by Marcionites (cf. 2 Pet 3:16). But that is not sufficient to establish a reference to Marcion. The delay of the *parousia* must have played a role in the heretics' arguments against the simple faith of the communities, but above all, 2 Peter lacks any polemic against two divinities.

41. David Trobisch, *Endredaktion*, 125–54, would like to see an editorial comment on the New Testament in John 21, Acts, 2 Timothy, and 2 Peter. But his observations would also apply if we see in John 21 only references to the *Corpus Iohanneum* (with broader references to other gospels), in 2 Timothy only references to the collection of Paul's letters, and in Acts only the continuation of Luke's Gospel. Only 2 Peter has clear references to a number of parts of the canon and assumes a complete collection of Paul's letters when it speaks of all the letters of Paul (2 Pet 3:16). If the writings and pieces of text referred to above were all part of the same canonical final redaction, one would expect a greater stylistic and content relationship among these redactional texts.

42. Or was it precisely the disputed books (James, 2 and 3 John, Jude, 2 Peter, Hebrews, Revelation) that belonged to an original canon that only in the final edition was included in the canon in addition to the previously-achieved consensus—and that for that very reason remained in dispute in many communities? Would they have had any chance at all of getting into the canon if they had not enjoyed great respect as parts of an early unified final redaction of the canon? For in terms of the weight of their material they often had little chance of creating spontaneous enthusiasm.

43. There is an overview in Armin W. Geertz, "Cognitive Approaches to the Study of Religion," in Peter Antes et al., eds., *New Approaches to the Study of Religion*, vol. 2, *Textual, Comparative, Sociological, and Cognitive Approaches* (Berlin and New York: de Gruyter, 2004), 247–418. An application to the New Testament is found in István Czachesz, "The Transmission of Early Christian Thought: Toward a Cognitive Psychological Model," *SR* 35 (2007): 65–83; idem, "The Gospels and Cognitive Science," in Alasdair A. MacDonald et al., eds., *Learned Antiquity: Scholarship and Society in the Near East, the Greco-Roman World, and the Early Medieval*

West (Leuven: Peeters, 2003), 25–36. We may mention the fundamental work of Pascal Boyer, *Religion Explained. The Evolutionary Origins of Religious Thought* (New York: Basic Books, 2001).

44. István Czachesz, "Kontraintuitive Ideen im Urchristentum," in Gerd Theissen et al., eds., *Erkennen und Erleben. Beiträge zur psychologischen Erforschung des frühen Christentums* (Gütersloh: Gütersloher Verlagshaus, 2007), 197–208.

45. Cf. Mutscher, *Corpus Johanneum*, 249–54.

46. It is interesting that the establishment of the Old Testament canon (especially the Pentateuch as its core) is often interpreted today as the result of a compromise. Cf. Erich Zenger et al., *Einleitung in das Alte Testament* (5th ed. Stuttgart: Kohlhammer, 2004), 131–33.

47. Cf. Schneemelcher, *New Testament Apocrypha*, vol. 1, 15, 18, 31–32.

48. Cf. Horacio E. Lona, *Der erste Clemensbrief*, KAV 2 (Göttingen: Vandenhoeck & Ruprecht, 1998), esp. 13–110. For the canonical question see the summary there on pp. 109–10.

49. Let me refer here to a work in progress by Annette Merz in which the intertextual references in the *Acts of Thecla* to the letters of Paul are compared, showing them to be a contradiction of the Pastorals.

20. Extra-Canonical Literature Provides Flexibility

1. *First Clement* may also be understood as a symbouleutic discourse or petition (*1 Clem.* 63:2) with which the Corinthian community is to engage on its own behalf; thus Andreas Lindemann, *Die Clemensbriefe*, HNT 7 (Tübingen: Mohr, 1992), 13.

2. Judith Hartenstein, *Die zweite Lehre. Erscheinungen des Auferstandenen als Rahmenerzählungen frühchristlicher Dialoge*, TU 146 (Berlin: Akademie-Verlag, 2000).

3. Thus Martin Hengel, *Four Gospels*, 133–34.

4. For all the gospels see Dieter Lührmann, *Fragmente apokryph gewordener Evangelien in griechischer und lateinischer Sprache*, MTSt 59 (Marburg: Elwert, 2000).

5. Cf. Rodolphe Kasser, Marvin Meyer, and Gregor Wurst, eds., *The Gospel of Judas: from Codex Tchacos* (Washington, DC: National Geographic, 2008). Since Irenaeus (*Haer.* 1.30) attests to a Gnostic gospel of Judas, it belongs to the second century C.E.

6. Hans-Josef Klauck, *The Apocryphal Acts of the Apostles: An Introduction* (2005), trans. Brian McNeil (Waco, TX: Baylor University Press, 2008), Introduction.

7. Ibid.

8. Ibid., 242.

9. Vielhauer, *Geschichte der urchristlichen Literatur*, 696–718.

10. The *Acts of Paul* are an exception: *3 Corinthians,* which is part of these

acts, combats *gnōsis*. The *Clementines,* too, in the figure of Simon oppose Gnostic heretical ideas, but they adopt a good many motifs from their opponents.

11. Cf. Winrich A. Löhr, "Fixierte Wahrheit?—Der neutestamentliche Kanon als 'Heilige Schrift,'" *Freiburger Universitätsblätter* 32, 121 (1993): 65–79, at 71: "The Christian teacher Basilides in Alexandria and Bishop Papias at Hierapolis in Asia Minor both mark an important transition in the history of the canon: both of them put together a gospel or sayings of the Lord and thus still have one foot in the canon-critical epoch in which the tradition was continued by the writing of new gospels. With the other foot, however, they stand already in a new epoch, namely that of explicit commentary that presupposes the scripture. One could say that both Basilides and Papias announce the transition from implicit to explicit interpretation of the gospel material."

12. For this literature cf. Philipp Vielhauer, *Geschichte der urchristlichen Literatur*, 757–74: he treats these writings as "The Final Phase of Early Christian Literature."

13. Ansgar Wucherpfennig, *Heracleon Philologus. Gnostische Johannesexegese im zweiten Jahrhundert*, WUNT 142 (Tübingen: Mohr, 2002).

14. Cf. Adolf von Harnack, *Marcion. The Gospel of the Alein God* (1924), trans. John E. Steely and Lyle D. Bierma (Durham, NC: Labyrinth Press, 1990).

15. Mutschler, *Corpus Johanneum*, 496.

16. Ibid.

Concluding Observation

1. Philipp Vielhauer, *Geschichte der urchristlichen Literatur*, 6–8, had already freed himself from the limitations of genre in order to treat historically related texts of different genres (e.g., Luke and Acts; John's Gospel and the Johannine letters) together. We can discern three phases in his treatment: (1) the older genres (*Corpus Paulinum*; Synoptic Gospels and Acts; the Johannine circle; Revelation); (2) the newer genres, continuing the older ones (pseudepigraphic and late letters, apocryphal gospels and acts of apostles, community orders and cultic materials); and (3) a final layer reflecting on Christian tradition (Papias, Hegesippus) that is treated in parallel to the establishment of the canon. My proposal for a literary history in four phases continues his thought.

2. Marius Reiser, *Sprache und literarische Formen*, 29–33, has clarified the misunderstanding that the stylistic classification of the New Testament writings as *sermo humilis* meant that they had no place in the three *genera* of discourse. Rather, it characterizes these writings as the language and style of simple, non-literary people.

3. The LXX was quoted only once in a pagan writing independently of early Christian literature (in Pseudo-Longinus, *On the Sublime*). Only through the Christians did it become known outside Judaism and Christianity to any degree worth

mentioning, and only Christians retained the entirety of Jewish-Hellenistic literature as part of their tradition.

4. It is correct that the individual functional forms in their further development reveal an approach to the genres in use in the surrounding environment. Here begins the patristic literature, as is especially evident when new needs created entirely new genres borrowing from forms found in literature in general, e.g., apologies for the defense of Christians toward the world outside, heresiology for combating heretics within, and exegetical commentaries for interpreting the Bible.

5. In the three phases of canonization of these writings we can observe the succession of *charismatic* authority of the two founder figures of early Christianity, *traditional* authority of the traditions produced by them, and an analogy to *legal* authority in the individual genres as they made themselves independent. We may associate this development with the three forms of legitimation in Max Weber's sociology of governance.

6. Eduard Norden, *Die antike Kunstprosa. Vom VI. Jahrhundert v. Chr. bis in die Zeit der Renaissance*, vol. 2 (Leipzig: Teubner, 1898; 5th ed. Darmstadt: Wissenschaftliche Buchgesellschaft, 1958), 452–60, characterizes Christian literature in negative contrast to Hellenistic literature through four "eliminations": (1) the "elimination of ancient individualism" (p. 453); (2) the "elimination of ancient humor" (p. 455); (3) the "elimination of national exclusivity" and "of the social exclusivity of antiquity" (p. 456); and finally (4) the "elimination of the formal beauty of antiquity" (p. 457). Under point (3) he emphasizes, with regard to international character: "Hellenistic literature in its flowering was exclusively national: that the barbarian soul was of a servile nature was the proud maxim according to which one acted in practice. In contrast, Christian literature was international from the beginning and accomplished its highest cultural mission precisely in the joining of nations and leveling of differences" (p. 456). Regarding the elimination of social exclusivity, he says: "In contrast, Christianity brought forth a popular literature that worked directly on the humors even of the poor in spirit through its purely human content, not tied to any particular time and condition" (p. 457).

Bibliography

Alexander, Loveday C. A. *The Preface to Luke's Gospel: Literary Convention and Social Context in Luke 1:1-4 and Acts 1:1*. SNTSMS 78. Cambridge: Cambridge University Press, 1993.

Alexander, Philip S. "Rabbinic Biography and the Biography of Jesus: A Survey of the Evidence," in Christopher M. Tuckett, ed., *Synoptic Studies. The Ampleforth Conferences of 1982 and 1983*. Sheffield: JSOT Press, 1984, 19–50.

Aune, David. *The New Testament in Its Literary Environment*. Philadelphia: Westminster, 1987.

Bailey, Kenneth E. "Informal Controlled Oral Tradition and the Synoptic Gospels," *Asia Journal of Theology* 5 (1991): 34–53.

———. "Middle Eastern Oral Tradition and the Synoptic Gospels," *Expository Times* 106 (1995): 363–67.

Bauckham, Richard. *The Gospels for All Christians. Rethinking the Gospel Audiences*. Grand Rapids: Eerdmans, 1998.

Baum, Armin Daniel. *Pseudepigraphie und literarische Fälschung im frühen Christentum. Mit ausgewählten Quellentexten samt deutscher Übersetzung*. WUNT 2d. ser. 138. Tübingen: Mohr, 2001.

Becker, Eve-Marie. *Schreiben und Verstehen. Paulinische Briefhermeneutik im Zweiten Korintherbrief*. NET 4. Tübingen: Francke, 2002.

———. "2. Korintherbrief," in Oda Wischmeyer, ed., *Paulus. Leben, Umwelt, Werk, Briefe*. UTB 2767. Tübingen and Basel: Francke, 2006, 164–90.

———. *Das Markus-Evangelium im Rahmen antiker Historiographie*. WUNT 194. Tübingen: Mohr, 2006.

Berger, Klaus. "Apostelbrief und apostolische Rede," *Zeitschrift für die neutestamentliche Wissenschaft* 65 (1974): 190–231.

———. "Hellenistische Gattungen im Neuen Testament." ANRW II/25,2. Berlin: de Gruyter, 1984.

———. *Im Anfang war Johannes. Datierung und Theologie des vierten Evangeliums*. Stuttgart: Quell, 1997 = Gütersloh: Kaiser, 2000, [3]2004.

———, and Christiane Nord. *Das Neue Testament und frühchristliche Schriften*. Frankfurt: Insel, 1999.

———. *Formen und Gattungen im Neuen Testament*. UTB 2532. Tübingen and Basel: Francke, 2005.

Betz, Hans Dieter. "Geist, Freiheit und Gesetz. Die Botschaft des Paulus an die Gemeinden in Galatien," *Zeitschrift für Theologie und Kirche* 71 (1974): 78–93.

———. *Galatians: A Commentary on Paul's Letter to the Churches in Galatia*. Philadelphia: Fortress Press, 1979.

Billerbeck, Paul, and Hermann Strack. *Das Evangelium nach Matthäus erläutert aus Talmud und Midrasch*. Munich: Beck, 1926.

Bornkamm, Günther. "Die Komposition der apokalyptischen Visionen in der Offenbarung Johannis," in idem, ed., *Studien zu Antike und Urchristentum, Gesammelte Aufsätze*. Vol. 2. BET 28. Munich: Kaiser, [3]1970, 204–22.

———. "Der Römerbrief als Testament des Paulus," in idem, ed., *Geschichte und Glaube. Zweiter Teil, Gesammelte Aufsätze*. Vol. 4. Munich: Kaiser, 1971, 120–39.

Boyer, Pascal. *Religion Explained. The Evolutionary Origins of Religious Thought*. New York: Basic Books, 2001.

Brandt, Reinhard, ed. *Pseudo-Longinus, Vom Erhabenen. Griechisch und Deutsch*. Darmstadt: Wissenschaftliche Buchgesellschaft, 1966.

Bultmann, Rudolf. "Literaturgeschichte, Biblische." *RGG*[2] 3 (1927), 1675–82.

———. *The History of the Synoptic Tradition*. Translated by John Marsh. Oxford: Blackwell; New York: Harper & Row, 1963.

———, and Martin Dibelius. "Geschichte der urchristlichen Literatur," *Theologische Literaturzeitung* 52 (1927): 80–83.

Burchard, Christoph. *Der dreizehnte Zeuge*. FRLANT 103. Göttingen: Vandenhoeck & Ruprecht, 1970.

Burnet, Régis. *Épîtres et lettres Ier–II[er] siècle. De Paul de Tarse à Polycarpe de Smyrne*. LD. Paris: Cerf, 2003.

Byrskog, Samuel. *Story as History—History as Story. The Gospel Tradition in the Context of Ancient Oral History*. WUNT 123. Tübingen: Mohr, 2000.

Campenhausen, Hans von. *Die Entstehung der christlichen Bibel*. BHT 39. Tübingen: Mohr, 1968.

Cancik, Hubert. "Bios und Logos. Formgeschichtliche Untersuchungen zu Lukians 'Demonax,'" in idem, ed., *Markus Philologie. Historische, literaturgeschichtliche und stilistische Untersuchungen zum zweiten Evangelium*. WUNT 33. Tübingen: Mohr, 1984, 115–30.

———. "Die Gattung Evangelium. Das Evangelium des Markus im Rahmen der antiken Historiographie," in idem, ed., *Markus-Philologie* (1984), 85–113.

Carlson, Stephen C. *The Gospel Hoax. Morton Smith's Invention of Secret Mark*. Waco: Baylor University Press, 2005.

Conzelmann, Hans. *Die Mitte der Zeit. Studien zur Theologie des Lukas*. BHT 17. Tübingen: Mohr, 1954.

———. "Paulus und die Weisheit," in idem, *Theologie als Schriftauslegung*. BET 65. Munich: Kaiser, 1974, 177–90.

Czachesz, István. "The Gospels and Cognitive Science," in Alasdair A. MacDonald, Michael W. Twomey, and Gerrit J. Reinink, eds., *Learned Antiquity: Scholarship and Society in the Near East, the Greco-Roman World, and the Early Medieval West*. Leuven: Peeters, 2003, 25–36.

———. "Kontraintuitive Ideen im Urchristentum," in Gerd Theissen and Petra von Gemünden, eds., *Erkennen und Erleben. Beiträge zur psychologischen Erforschung des frühen Christentums*. Gütersloh: Gütersloher Verlagshaus, 2007, 197–208.

———. "The Transmission of Early Christian Thought. Toward a Cognitive Psychological Model," *Studies in Religion* 36 (2007): 65–83.

Dahl, Nils Alstrup. "Formgeschichtliche Beobachtungen zur Christusverkündigung in der Gemeindepredigt," in Walther Eltester, ed., *Neutestamentliche Studien für Rudolf Bultmann*. BZNW 21. Berlin: Töpelmann, 1954, 3–9.

Deissmann, Gustav Adolf. *Light From the Ancient East: The New Testament Illustrated by Recently Discovered Texts of the Graeco-Roman World*. Translated by Lionel R. M. Strachan. Edinburgh: T & T Clark, 1908. Repr. Grand Rapids: Baker Book House, 1978.

Dettwiler, Andreas. *Die Gegenwart des Erhöhten. Eine exegetische Studie zu den johanneischen Abschiedsreden (Joh 13,31–16,33) unter besonderer Berücksichtigung ihres Relecture-Charakters*. FRLANT 169. Göttingen: Vandenhoeck & Ruprecht, 1995.

Dibelius, Martin. *Geschichte der urchristlichen Literatur*. Munich: Kaiser, 1926.

———. *From Tradition to Gospel*. Translated by Bertram Lee Woolf. London: Ivor Nicholson and Watson, 1934.

Dihle, Albrecht. "Die Evangelien und die biographischen Traditionen der Antike," *Zeitschrift für Theologie und Kirche* 80 (1983): 33–49.

———. *Greek and Latin Literature of the Roman Empire: from Augustus to Justinian*. Translated by Manfred Malzahn. London and New York: Routledge, 1994.

Dunn, James D. G. *Jesus Remembered. Christianity in the Making*. Vol. 2. Grand Rapids: Eerdmans, 2003.

Dupont, Jacques. "Die individuelle Eschatologie im Lukas-Evangelium und in der Apostelgeschichte," in Paul Hoffmann, ed., *Orientierung an Jesus. Zur Theologie der Synoptiker, FS J. Schmidt*. Freiburg et al.: Herder, 1973, 37–47.

Fischer, Joseph A., ed. *Schriften des Urchristentums*. Vol. 1. *Die Apostolischen Väter*. Darmstadt: Wissenschaftliche Buchgesellschaft, 2d ed. 1958.

Fjärstedt, Björn. *Synoptic Traditions in 1 Corinthians. Themes and Clusters of Theme Words in 1 Corinthians 1–4 and 9*. Uppsala: Teologiska Institutionen, 1974.

Flusser, David. *Die rabbinischen Gleichnisse und der Gleichniserzähler Jesus*. Judaica et Christiana 4. Bern: Peter Lang, 1981.

Frend, William H. C. "Montanismus." *TRE* 23 (1994), 271–79.

Frenschkowski, Marco. "Pseudepigraphie und Paulusschule. Gedanken zur Verfasserschaft der Deuteropaulinen, insbesondere der Pastoralbriefe," in Friedrich Wilhelm Horn, ed., *Das Ende des Paulus. Historische, theologische und literaturgeschichtliche Aspekte*. BZNW 106. Berlin: de Gruyter, 2001, 239–72.

Garleff, Gunnar. *Urchristliche Identität in Matthäusevangelium, Didache und Jakobusbrief*. BVB 9. Münster: LIT, 2004.

Geertz, Armin W. "Cognitive Approaches to the Study of Religion," in Peter Antes, Armin W. Geertz, und Randi R. Warne, eds., *New Approaches to the Study of Religion*. Vol. 2. *Textual, Comparative, Sociological, and Cognitive Approaches*. Religion and Reason 43. Berlin and New York: de Gruyter, 2004, 247–418.

Gemünden, Petra von. *Vegetationsmetaphorik im Neuen Testament und seiner Umwelt. Eine Bildfelduntersuchung*. NTOA 18. Fribourg: Universitätsverlag; Göttingen: Vandenhoeck & Ruprecht, 1993.

Goethe, Johann Wolfgang von. *Wilhelm Meisters Wanderjahre* (1821), in Dieter Borchmeyer, ed., *Johann Wolfgang von Goethe. Werke*. Vol. 4. Munich: Artemis & Winkler, 4th ed. 1992, 547–980.

Greschat, Katharina. "Die Entstehung des neutestamentlichen Kanons. Fragestellungen und Themen der neueren Forschung," *Verkündigung und Forschung* 51 (2006): 56–63.

Hahn, Ferdinand. "Die Sendschreiben der Johannesapokalypse. Ein Beitrag zur Bestimmung prophetischer Redeformen," in Gert Jeremias, ed., *Tradition und Glaube. FS Karl Georg Kuhn*. Göttingen: Vandenhoeck & Ruprecht, 1971, 357–94.

Harnack, Adolf von. *Marcion: The Gospel of the Alien God*. Translated by John E. Steely and Lyle D. Bierma. Durham, NC: Labyrinth Press, 1990.

Harris, William. *Ancient Literacy*. Cambridge, MA: Harvard University Press, 1989.

Hartenstein, Judith. *Die zweite Lehre. Erscheinungen des Auferstandenen als Rahmenerzählungen frühchristlicher Dialoge*. TU 146. Berlin: Akademie-Verlag, 2000.

Hartwig, Charlotte, and Gerd Theissen. "Die korinthische Gemeinde als Nebenadressat des Römerbriefs. Eigentextreferenzen des Paulus und kommunikativer Kontext des längsten Paulusbriefes," *Novum Testamentum* 46 (2004): 229–52.

Heckel, Theo K. *Vom Evangelium des Markus zum viergestaltigen Evangelium*. WUNT 120. Tübingen: Mohr, 1999.

Hegermann, Harald. "Der geschichtliche Ort der Pastoralbriefe," *Theologische Versuche* 2 (1970): 47–64.

Hengel, Martin. *Die Evangelienüberschriften*. SAHW.PH. No. 3. Heidelberg: C. Winter, 1984.

———. *The Johannine Question*. London: SCM; Philadelphia: Trinity Press International, 1989.

———. *The Zealots: Investigations into the Jewish Freedom Movement in the Period from Herod I until 70 A.D.* Translated by David Smith. Edinburgh: T & T Clark, 1989.

———. "Anonymität, Pseudepigraphie und 'literarische Fälschung' in der jüdisch-hellenistischen Literatur," in Roland Deines and Martin Hengel, eds., *Judaica et Hellenistica. Kleine Schriften I*. WUNT 90. Tübingen: Mohr, 1996, 196–251.

———. *The Four Gospels and the One Gospel of Jesus Christ. An Investigation of the Collection and Origin of the Canonical Gospels*. London: SCM, 2000.

———. "Der Jakobusbrief als antipaulinische Polemik," in Gerald F. Hawthorne and Otto Betz, eds., *Tradition and Interpretation in the New Testament, FS E. E. Ellis*. Grand Rapids: Eerdmans; Tübingen: Mohr, 1987, 248–78. Expanded in Martin Hengel, *Paulus und Jakobus, Gesammelte Aufsätze*. Vol. 3. WUNT 141. Tübingen: Mohr, 2002, 511–48.

———. *Der unterschätzte Petrus. Zwei Studien.* Tübingen: Mohr, 2006.

Herder, Johann Gottfried. *Vom Erlöser der Menschen* (1796), in Bernhard Suphan, ed., *Herders Sämmtliche Werke.* Vol. 19. Berlin: Weidmannsche Buchhandlung, 1880, 135–252.

———. *Von Gottes Sohn, der Welt Heiland* (1797), in Bernhard Suphan, ed., *Herders Sämmtliche Werke.* Vol. 19. Berlin: Weidmannsche Buchhandlung, 1880, 253–424.

Hezser, Catherine. "Die Verwendung der hellenistischen Gattung *Chrie* im frühen Christentum und Judentum," *Journal for the Study of Judaism in the Persian, Hellenistic, and Roman Period* 27 (1996): 371–439.

Hoffmann, Paul. *Studien zur Theologie der Logienquelle.* NTA n.s. 8. Münster: Aschendorf, 1972.

———, and Christoph Heil. *Die Spruchquelle Q.* Darmstadt: Wissenschaftliche Buchgesellschaft, 2002. See also James M. Robinson, Paul Hoffmann, and John S. Kloppenborg, eds., *The Critical Edition of Q: A Synopsis Including the Gospels of Matthew and Luke and Thomas with English, German, and French translations of Q and Thomas.* Hermeneia. Minneapolis: Fortress Press, 2000.

Hofrichter, Peter L., ed. *Für und wider die Priorität des Johannesevangeliums* TTS 9. Hildesheim: Olms, 2002.

Horbury, William. "'Gospel' in Herodian Judaea," in idem, *Herodian Judaism and New Testament Study.* WUNT 193. Tübingen: Mohr, 2006, 80–103.

Jewett, Robert. "Romans as an Ambassadorial Letter," *Interpretation* 36 (1982): 5–20.

Josephus, Flavius. *The Jewish War.* Translated by G. A. Williamson. Harmondsworth: Penguin, 1959.

Jülicher, Adolf. *An Introduction to the New Testament.* Translated by Janet Penrose Ward. New York: G. P. Putnam's Sons, 1904.

Käsemann, Ernst. "Begründet der neutestamentliche Kanon die Einheit der Kirche? (1951/52)," in idem, ed., *Exegetische Versuche und Besinnungen.* Vol. 1. Göttingen: Vandenhoeck & Ruprecht, 6th ed. 1970, 214–23.

Kasser, Rodolphe, Marvin Meyer, and Gregor Wurst, eds., *The Gospel of Judas: from Codex Tchacos.* Washington, DC: National Geographic, 2008.

Kezbere, Ilze. *Umstrittener Monotheismus. Wahre und falsche Apotheose im lukanischen Doppelwerk.* NTOA 60. Fribourg: Universitätsverlag; Göttingen: Vandenhoeck & Ruprecht, 2007.

Kim, Hee-Seong. *Die Geisttaufe des Messias. Eine kompositionsgeschichtliche Untersuchung zu einem Leitmotiv des lukanischen Doppelwerks.* Studien zur klassischen Philologie 81. Frankfurt: Peter Lang, 1993.

Kinzig, Wolfram. "*Kainē diathēkē.* The Title of the New Testament in the Second and Third Centuries," *Journal of Theological Studies* n.s. 45 (1994): 519–44.

Klauck, Hans-Josef. *Die antike Briefliteratur und das Neue Testament.* UTB 2022. Paderborn: Schöningh, 1998.

———. *Apocryphal Gospels: An Introduction.* Translated by Brian McNeil. London and New York: T & T Clark, 2003.

———. *The Religious Context of Early Christianity: A Guide to Graeco-Roman Religions*. Translated by Brian McNeil. Minneapolis: Fortress Press, 2003.

———. *The Apocryphal Acts of the Apostles: An Introduction*. Translated by Brian McNeil. Waco, TX: Baylor University Press, 2008.

Koch, Dietrich-Alex. "Kollektenbericht, 'Wir'-Bericht und Itinerar. Neue (?) Überlegungen zu einem alten Problem," *New Testament Studies* 45 (1999): 367–90.

Koester, Helmut. *Synoptische Überlieferung bei den Apostolischen Vätern*. TU 65. Berlin: Akademie-Verlag, 1957.

———. *Introduction to the New Testament*. 2 vols. Foundations and Facets. Philadelphia: Fortress Press; Berlin and New York: de Gruyter, 1982.

———. *Ancient Christian Gospels. Their History and Development*. London: SCM; Philadelphia: Trinity Press, 1990.

Kollmann, Bernd. "Jesus als jüdischer Gleichnisdichter," *New Testament Studies* 50 (2004): 457–75.

Konradt, Matthias. *Christliche Existenz nach dem Jakobusbrief. Eine Studie zu seiner soteriologischen und ethischen Konzeption*. SNT 22. Göttingen: Vandenhoeck & Ruprecht, 1998.

Körtner, Ulrich H. *Papias von Hierapolis. Ein Beitrag zur Geschichte des frühen Christentums*. FRLANT 133. Göttingen: Vandenhoeck & Ruprecht, 1983.

———, and Martin Leutzsch, eds., *Schriften des Urchristentums*. Vol. 3. *Papiasfragmente*. Darmstadt: Wissenschaftliche Buchgesellschaft, 1998.

Koskenniemi, Erkki. *Apollonios von Tyana in der neutestamentlichen Exegese. Forschungsbericht und Weiterführung der Diskussion*. WUNT 2d ser. 61. Tübingen: Mohr, 1994.

Kremendahl, Dieter, *Die Botschaft der Form. Zum Verhältnis von antiker Epistolographie und Rhetorik im Galaterbrief*. NTOA 46. Fribourg: Universitätsverlag; Göttingen: Vandenhoeck & Ruprecht, 2000.

Kümmel, Werner Georg. "Lukas in der Anklage der heutigen Theologie" (1970), in idem, *Heilsgeschehen und Geschichte*. Vol. 2. MTS 16. Marburg: Elwert, 1978, 87–100. Also in Georg Braumann, ed., *Das Lukas-Evangelium*. WdF 280. Darmstadt: Wissenschaftliche Buchgesellschaft, 1974, 416–36.

Labahn, Michael. "'Boldly and Without Hindrance He Preached the Kingdom of God and Taught about the Lord Jesus Christ' (Acts 28,31). Paul's Public Proclamation in Rome as the Finale of a Shipwreck," in Jürgen Zangenberg and Michael Labahn, eds., *Christians as a Religious Minority in a Multicultural City. Modes of Interaction and Identity Formation in Early Imperial Rome*. JSNTSup 243. London and New York: T & T Clark, 2004, 56–76.

Lampe, Peter. "Rhetorische Analyse paulinischer Texte—Quo vadit? Methodologische Überlegungen," in Dieter Sänger and Matthias Konradt, eds., *Das Gesetz im frühen Judentum und im Neuen Testament, FS Ch. Burchard*. NTOA 57. Göttingen: Vandenhoeck & Ruprecht; Fribourg: Universitätsverlag, 2006, 170–90.

Leppä, Outi. *The Making of Colossians. A Study on the Formation and Purpose of a Deutero-Pauline Letter*. SESJ 86. Göttingen: Vandenhoeck & Ruprecht, 2003.

Lindemann, Andreas. *Paulus im ältesten Christentum. Das Bild des Apostels und die Rezeption der paulinischen Theologie in der frühchristlichen Literatur bis Marcion*. Tübingen: Mohr, 1979.

———. *Die Clemensbriefe*. HNT 17. Tübingen: Mohr, 1992.

———. "Apostolische Väter." *RGG*[4] 1 (1998), 652–53.

———. "Die Sammlung der Paulusbriefe im 1. und 2. Jahrhundert," in Jean-Marie Auwers and Henk Jan de Jonge, eds., *The Biblical Canons*. BETL 163. Leuven: University Press, 2003, 321–51.

Lohmeyer, Ernst. "Probleme paulinischer Theologie," *Zeitschrift für die neutestamentliche Wissenschaft* 26 (1927): 158–73.

Löhr, Winrich A. "Fixierte Wahrheit?—Der neutestamentliche Kanon als 'Heilige Schrift,'" *Freiburger Universitätsblätter* 32, No. 121 (1993): 65–79.

Lona, Horacio E. *Der erste Clemensbrief*. KAV 2. Göttingen: Vandenhoeck & Ruprecht, 1998.

Lord, Albert B. *The Singer of Tales*. Cambridge, MA: Harvard University Press, 1960.

Lührmann, Dieter. "Gal 2,9 und die katholischen Briefe. Bemerkungen zum Kanon und zur regula fidei," *Zeitschrift für die neutestamentliche Wissenschaft* 72 (1981): 65–87.

———. "SUPERSTITIO—die Beurteilung des frühen Christentums durch die Römer," *Theologische Zeitschrift* 42 (1986): 193–213.

———. *Fragmente apokryph gewordener Evangelien in griechischer und lateinischer Sprache*. MTS 59. Marburg: Elwert, 2000.

Mengel, Berthold. *Studien zum Philipperbrief*. WUNT 2d ser. 8. Tübingen: Mohr, 1982.

Merz, Annette. "Why Did the Pure Bride of Christ Become a Wedded Wife (Eph. 5.22–33)? Theses about the Intertextual Transformation of an Ecclesiological Metaphor," *Journal for the Study of the New Testament* 79 (2000): 131–47.

———. *Die fiktive Selbstauslegung des Paulus. Intertextuelle Studien zur Intention und Rezeption der Pastoralbriefe*. NTOA 52. Göttingen: Vandenhoeck & Ruprecht; Fribourg: Universitätsverlag, 2004.

Metzger, Bruce M. *The Canon of the New Testament: Its Origin, Development, and Significance*. Oxford: Clarendon Press; New York: Oxford University Press, 1987.

Mitchell, Margaret M. *Paul and the Rhetoric of Reconciliation*. HUT 28. Tübingen: Mohr, 1991.

Moreschini, Claudio, and Enrico Norelli. *Histoire de la littérature chrétienne ancienne grecque et latine. 1. De Paul à l'ère de Constantin*. Geneva: Labor et Fides, 1995.

Mutschler, Bernhard. *Irenäus als johanneischer Theologe. Studien zur Schriftauslegung bei Irenäus von Lyon*. Studien und Texte zu Antike und Christentum 21. Tübingen: Mohr, 2004.

———. *Das Corpus Johanneum bei Irenäus von Lyon. Studien und Kommentar zum dritten Buch von Adversus Haereses*. WUNT 189. Tübingen: Mohr, 2006.

Niebuhr, Karl Wilhelm. "'A New Perspective on James.' Neuere Forschungen zum Jakobusbrief," *Theologische Literaturzeitung* 129 (2004): 1019–44.

Norden, Eduard. *Die antike Kunstprosa. Vom VI. Jahrhundert v. Chr. bis in die Zeit der Renaissance*. Vol. 2. Darmstadt: Wissenschaftliche Buchgesellschaft, 5th ed. 1958.

Overbeck, Franz. "Über die Anfänge der patristischen Literatur," *Historische Zeitschrift* 48 (1882): 417–72 = *Libelli* 15. Darmstadt: Wissenschaftliche Buchgesellschaft, 1984.

———. *Christentum und Kultur. Gedanken und Anmerkungen zur modernen Theologie*, ed. Carl Albrecht Bernoulli. Basel: Schwabe, 1919; repr. Darmstadt: Wissenschaftliche Buchgesellschaft, 2d ed. 1963.

Perrin, Nicholas. *Thomas and Tatian: The Relationship between the Gospel of Thomas and the Diatessaron*. Academia Biblica 5. Atlanta: Society of Biblical Literature, 2002.

Petersen, Silke. "Die Evangelienüberschriften und die Entstehung des neutestamentlichen Kanons," *Zeitschrift für die neutestamentliche Wissenschaft* 97 (2006): 250–74.

Plisch, Uwe-Karsten. *Verborgene Worte Jesu—verworfene Evangelien. Apokryphe Schriften des frühen Christentums*. Brennpunkt: Die Bibel 5. Berlin: Evangelische Haupt-Bibelgesellschaft und von Cannsteinsche Bibelanstalt, 2000.

Plümacher, Eckhard. "Apostelgeschichte." *TRE* 3 (1978), 483–528.

Räisänen, Heikki. *The 'Messianic Secret' in Mark's Gospel*. Edinburgh: T & T Clark, 1990, 220–22.

Recki, Birgit. "Erhabene, das." *RGG*[4] 2 (1999), 1408–9.

Reiser, Marius. "Die Stellung der Evangelien in der antiken Literaturgeschichte," *Zeitschrift für die neutestamentlichen Wissenschaft* 90 (1999): 1–27.

———. *Sprache und literarische Formen des Neuen Testaments*. UTB 2197. Paderborn: Schöningh, 2001.

———. "Literaturgeschichte/Literaturgeschichtsschreibung III. Neues Testament." *RGG*[4] 5 (2002), 408–9.

Reller, Horst, et al., eds. *Handbuch Religiöse Gemeinschaften und Weltanschauungen*. Gütersloh: Gütersloher Verlagshaus, 4th ed. 1993.

Ritter, Adolf Martin. "Die Entstehung des neutestamentlichen Kanons: Selbstdurchsetzung oder autoritative Entscheidung?" in Aleida and Jan Assmann, eds., *Kanon und Zensur. Beiträge zur Archäologie der literarischen Kommunikation*. Vol. 2. Munich: Fink, 1987, 93–99.

Robinson, James M. "LOGOI SOPHŌN: On the Gattung of Q," in idem and Helmut Koester, *Trajectories Through Early Christianity*. Philadelphia: Fortress Press, 1971, 71–113.

Roh, Taeseong. *Der zweite Thessalonicherbrief als Erneuerung apokalyptischer Zeitdeutung*. NTOA 62. Fribourg: Universitätsverlag; Göttingen: Vandenhoeck & Ruprecht, 2007.

Sato, Migaku. *Q und Prophetie. Studien zur Gattungs- und Traditionsgeschichte der Quelle Q*. WUNT 2d ser. 29. Tübingen: Mohr, 1988.

Schäfer, Peter. "Der vorrabbinische Pharisäismus," in Martin Hengel and Ulrich Heckel, eds., *Paulus und das antike Judentum. Tübingen-Durham-Symposium im Gedenken an den 50. Todestag Adolf Schlatters*. WUNT 58. Tübingen: Mohr, 1991, 125–75.

Schenke, Hans-Martin, and Karl Martin Fischer. *Einleitung in die Schriften des Neuen Testaments I: Die Briefe des Paulus und Schriften des Paulinismus*. Berlin: Evangelische Verlagsanstalt, 1978.

Schmidt, Karl Ludwig. "Die Stellung der Evangelien in der allgemeinen Literaturgeschichte," in Hans Schmidt, ed., *Studien zur Religion und Literatur des Alten und Neuen Testaments, FS Hermann Gunkel*. Part 2. Göttingen: Vandenhoeck & Ruprecht, 1923, 50–134. Repr. in *Neues Testament, Judentum, Kirche. Kleine Schriften*. TB 69. Munich: Kaiser, 1981, 37–130.

Schmithals, Walter. "Vom Ursprung der synoptischen Tradition," *Zeitschrift für Theologie und Kirche* 94 (1997): 288–316.

Schneemelcher, Wilhelm, ed. *New Testament Apocrypha*. English translation edited by Robert McLachlan Wilson. 2 vols. Louisville: Westminster John Knox, 2003.

Schnelle, Udo. *Einleitung in das Neue Testament*. UTB 1830. Göttingen: Vandenhoeck & Ruprecht, 1994.

Schnider, Franz, and Werner Stenger. *Studien zum neutestamentlichen Briefformular*. NTTS 11. Leiden: Brill, 1987.

Scholder, Klaus. "Herder und die Anfänge der historischen Theologie," *Evangelische Theologie* 22 (1962): 425–40.

Schoon-Janssen, Johannes. *Umstrittene "Apologien" in den Paulusbriefen: Studien zur rhetorischen Situation des 1. Thessalonicherbriefes, des Galaterbriefes und des Philipperbriefes*. GTA 45. Göttingen: Vandenhoeck & Ruprecht, 1991.

Schreiber, Stefan. "Kannte Johannes die Synoptiker? Zur aktuellen Diskussion," *Verkündigung und Forschung* 51 (2006): 7–24.

Schürmann, Heinz. "Die vorösterlichen Anfänge der Logientradition. Versuch eines formgeschichtlichen Zugangs zum Leben Jesu," in Helmut Ristow and Karl Matthiae, eds., *Der historische Jesus und der kerygmatische Christus*. Berlin: Evangelische Verlagsanstalt, 1961, 342–70.

Siegert, Folker, ed. *Drei hellenistisch-jüdische Predigten. Ps.-Philon, "Über Jona," "Über Simon" und "Über die Gottesbezeichnung 'wohltätig verzehrendes Feuer.'"* WUNT 20. Tübingen: Mohr, 1980.

———. *Drei hellenstisch-jüdische Predigten. II. Kommentar zu* De Jona *mit Einleitung zu den drei Texten und weiteren Beigaben*. Diss. habil. Heidelberg, 1989.

Skeat, Theodore C. "The Oldest Manuscript of the Four Gospels?" *New Testament Studies* 43 (1997): 1–34.

Stanton, Graham N. "The Fourfold Gospel," *New Testament Studies* 43 (1997): 317–46.

Strecker, Georg. *Literaturgeschichte des Neuen Testaments*. UTB 1682. Göttingen: Vandenhoeck & Ruprecht, 1992.

Stroumsa, Guy G. "The Body of Truth and its Measures. New Testament Canonization in Context," in Holger Preissler and Hubert Seiwert, eds., with Heinz Mürmel, *Gnosisforschung und Religionsgeschichte, FS Kurt Rudolph*. Marburg: Diagonal, 1994, 307–16.

Taatz, Irene. *Frühjüdische Briefe. Die paulinischen Briefe im Rahmen der offiziellen religiösen Briefe des Frühjudentums*. NTOA 16. Fribourg: Universitätsverlag; Göttingen: Vandenhoeck & Ruprecht, 1991.

Taeger, Jens-W. "Offenbarung 1,1–3: Johanneische Autorisierung einer Aufklärungsschrift," *New Testament Studies* 49 (2003): 176–92.

Theissen, Gerd. *Untersuchungen zum Hebräerbrief.* SNT 2. Gütersloh: Mohn, 1969.

———. *The Miracle Stories of the Early Christian Tradition.* Translated by Francis McDonagh; edited by John Riches. Philadelphia: Fortress Press, 1983.

———. *The Gospels in Context: Social and Political History in the Synoptic Tradition.* Translated by Linda M. Maloney. Minneapolis: Fortress Press, 1991.

———. "Wandering Radicals: Light Shed by the Sociology of Literature on the Early Transmission of Jesus Sayings," in *Social Reality and the Early Christians: Theology, Ethics, and the World of the New Testament.* Translated by Margaret Kohl. Minneapolis: Fortress Press, 1992, 33–59.

———. "Die Erforschung der synoptischen Tradition seit R. Bultmann. Ein Überblick über die formgeschichtliche Arbeit im 20. Jahrhundert," in Rudolf Bultmann, *Geschichte der synoptischen Tradition.* FRLANT 12. Göttingen: Vandenhoeck & Ruprecht, 10th ed. 1995, 409–52.

———. "Auferstehungsgeschichte und Zeitgeschichte. Über einige politische Anspielungen im ersten Kapitel des Römerbriefs," in Sabine Bieberstein, ed., *Auferstehung hat einen Namen, FS H. J. Venetz.* Luzern: Exodus, 1998, 58–67.

———. "Vom Davidssohn zum Weltherrscher. Pagane und jüdische Endzeiterwartungen im Spiegel des Matthäusevangeliums," in Michael Becker and Wolfgang Fenske, eds., *Das Ende der Tage und die Gegenwart des Heils. Begegnungen mit dem Neuen Testament und seiner Umwelt, FS Heinz-Wolfgang Kuhn.* AGAJU 44. Leiden: Brill, 1999, 145–64.

———. *Die Religion der ersten Christen. Eine Theorie des Urchristentums.* Gütersloh: Kaiser, 2000.

———. *Gospel Writing and Church Politics. A Socio-rhetorical Approach.* Chuen King Lecture Series 3. Hong Kong: Theology Division, 2001.

———. "Die pseudepigraphe Intention des Jakobusbriefs. Ein Beitrag zu seinen Einleitungsfragen," in Petra von Gemünden, Matthias Konradt, and Gerd Theissen, eds., *Der Jakobusbrief. Beiträge zur Rehabilitierung der "strohernen Epistel."* BVB 3. Münster: LIT, 2003, 54–82.

———. "Kirche oder Sekte? Über Einheit und Konflikt im frühen Urchristentum," *Theologie und Glaube* 48 (2005): 162–75.

———. "Jesus as an Itinerant Teacher, Reflections from Social History on Jesus' Roles," in J. H. Charlesworth and P. Pokorný, *Jesus Research: An International Perspective,* The First Princeton-Prague Symposium on Jesus Research (Grand Rapids/Cambridge U.K.: Eerdmans, 2009), 98–122.

———, and Dagmar Winter. *The Quest for the Plausible Jesus: The Question of Criteria.* Translated by M. Eugene Boring. Louisville: Westminster John Knox. 2002.

Theobald, Michael. *Herrenworte im Johannesevangelium.* HBS 34. Freiburg: Herder, 2002.

Thyen, Hartwig. *Der Stil der jüdisch-hellenistischen Homilie.* FRLANT 47. Göttingen: Vandenhoeck & Ruprecht, 1955.

Trobisch, David. *Die Entstehung der Paulusbriefsammlung. Studien zu den Anfängen christlicher Publizistik*. NTOA 10. Fribourg: Universitätsverlag; Göttingen: Vandenhoeck & Ruprecht, 1989.

———. *Die Paulusbriefe und die Anfänge der christlichen Publizistik*. KT 135. Gütersloh: Kaiser, 1994.

———. *Die Endredaktion des Neuen Testaments. Eine Untersuchung zur Entstehung der christlichen Bibel*. NTOA 31. Fribourg: Universitätsverlag; Göttingen: Vandenhoeck & Ruprecht, 1996.

Vielhauer, Philipp. "Franz Overbeck und die neutestamentliche Wissenschaft," *Evangelische Theologie* 19 (1950–51): 193–207. Repr. in idem, *Aufsätze zum Neuen Testament*. TB 31. Munich: Kaiser, 1965, 235–52.

———. *Geschichte der urchristlichen Literatur*. Berlin: de Gruyter, 1975.

Wedderburn, Alexander J. M. "Zur Frage der Gattung der Apostelgeschichte," in Hubert Cancik, Hermann Lichtenberger, and Peter Schäfer, eds., *Geschichte—Tradition—Reflexion III: Frühes Christentum*. Tübingen: Mohr, 1996, 303–22.

Wendland, Paul. *Die urchristlichen Literaturformen*. HNT I, 3. Tübingen: Mohr, 1912.

Wengst, Klaus, ed. *Schriften des Urchristentums*. Vol. 2. *Didachē*. Darmstadt: Wissenschaftliche Buchgesellschaft, 1984.

Windisch, Hans. "Friedensbringer—Gottessöhne. Eine religionsgeschichtliche Interpretation der 7. Seligpreisung," *Zeitschrift für die neutestamentliche Wissenschaft* 24 (1925): 240–60.

Wolter, Michael. "Die anonymen Schriften des Neuen Testaments," *Zeitschrift für die neutestamentliche Wissenschaft* 79 (1988): 1–16.

———. "Apokalyptik als Redeform im Neuen Testament," *New Testament Studies* 51 (2005): 171–91.

Wong, Eric Kun Chun. *Interkulturelle Theologie und multikulturelle Gemeinde im Matthäusevangelium*. NTOA 22. Fribourg: Universitätsverlag; Göttingen: Vandenhoeck & Ruprecht, 1992.

———. "The Deradicalization of Jesus' Ethical Sayings in 1 Corinthians," *New Testament Studies* 48 (2002): 181–94.

Wrede, William. *Das Messiasgeheimnis in den Evangelien. Zugleich ein Beitrag zum Verständnis des Markusevangeliums*. Göttingen: Vandenhoeck & Ruprecht, 1901.

Wucherpfennig, Ansgar. *Heracleon Philologus. Gnostische Johannesexegese im zweiten Jahrhundert*. WUNT 142. Tübingen: Mohr, 2002.

Wünsche, Dietrich. "Evangelienharmonie." *TRE* 10 (1982), 626–36.

Zenger, Erich, et al. *Einleitung in das Alte Testament*. Studienbücher Theologie I, 1. Stuttgart: Kohlhammer, 5th ed. 2004.

Zumstein, Jean. "L'évangile johannique: une strategie de croire," *Recherches de science religieuse* 77 (1989): 217–32. Reprinted as "Das Johannesevangelium: Eine Strategie des Glaubens," in idem, *Kreative Erinnerung. Relecture und Auslegung im Johannesevangelium*. Zürich: Pano, 1999, 15–45.

Index